Professional Learning and Development in Schools and Higher Education

Volume 10

Series Editors
Christopher Day
Judyth Sachs

For further volumes:
http://www.springer.com/series/7908

Professional Learning and Development in Schools and Higher Education dissemi-nates original, research informed writing on the connections between teacher learning and professionalism in schools and higher education. Global in their coverage, the texts deal with the problems and practices of the field in different national and international cultural, policy and practice contexts. The methodology employed en-compasses a broad spectrum of conceptual, theoretical, philosophical and empirical research activities. The series explicitly encompasses both the fields of schools and higher education.

The subject areas covered by the series are: professional learning in schools; con-texts for professional learning; professional learning in higher education; change; the (new) meanings of professionalism in schools and higher education; training and development in schools and higher education; the 'well-being' agenda in schools and higher education; autonomy, compliance and effectiveness in schools and higher edu-cation; principal leadership in schools and higher education; middle-level leadership in schools and higher education.

Olwen McNamara • Jean Murray • Marion Jones
Editors

Workplace Learning in Teacher Education

International Practice and Policy

 Springer

Editors
Olwen McNamara
School of Education
The University of Manchester
Manchester
United Kingdom

Marion Jones
Faculty of Education, Health and Community
Liverpool John Moores University
Liverpool
United Kingdom

Jean Murray
Cass School of Education and Communities
University of East London
London
United Kingdom

ISBN 978-94-007-7825-2   ISBN 978-94-007-7826-9 (eBook)
DOI 10.1007/978-94-007-7826-9
Springer New York Heidelberg Dordrecht London

Library of Congress Control Number: 2013951779

Printed on acid-free paper

Springer is part of Springer Science+Business Media (www.springer.com)

Contents

Contributors

Yvonne Barnes Faculty of Education, Manchester Metropolitan University, Manchester, UK

Natalia Buckler Centre for the Use of Research and Evidence in Education, Coventry, UK

Bob Burstow King's College London, London, UK

Anne Campbell Edinburgh, Scotland

Ann Childs Department of Education, University of Oxford, Oxford, UK

James Conroy University of Glasgow, Glasgow, UK

Paul F. Conway School of Education, University College Cork, Cork, Ireland

Philippa Cordingley Centre for the Use of Research and Evidence in Education, Coventry, UK

Graham Donaldson University of Glasgow, Glasgow, UK

Tim Dornan Maastricht University, Maastricht, Netherlands
The University of Manchester, Manchester, UK

Anne Edwards Department of Education, University of Oxford, Oxford, UK

Michael Eraut University of Sussex, East Susex, UK

Maria Assunção Flores Institute of Education, University of Minho, Braga, Portugal

Marion Jones Liverpool John Moores University, Liverpool, UK

Pertti Kansanen University of Helsinki, Helsinki, Finland

Meg Maguire King's College London, London, UK

Olwen McNamara School of Education, The University of Manchester, Manchester, UK

Jane McNicholl Department of Education, University of Oxford, Oxford, UK

Ian Menter Department of Education, University of Oxford, Oxford, UK

Siân Morgan School of Education, The University of Manchester, Manchester, UK

Jean Murray University of East London, London, UK

Rosaleen Murphy School of Education, University College Cork, Cork, Ireland

Anne-Mette Mørcke Centre for Medical Education, Aarhus University, Aarhus, Denmark

Vanessa Rutherford School of Education, University College Cork, Cork, Ireland

Julie Ryan Faculty of Education, Manchester Metropolitan University, Manchester, UK

Kari Smith Department of Education, University of Bergen, Bergen, Norway

Yvette Solomon Education and Social Research Institute, Manchester Metropolitan University, Manchester, UK

Julian Williams School of Education, The University of Manchester, Manchester, UK

Kevin Woods School of Education, The University of Manchester, Manchester, UK

Marit Ulvik Department of Education, University of Bergen, Bergen, Norway

About the Authors

Yvonne Barnes is a Senior Lecturer in Primary Mathematics Education at Manchester Metropolitan University, teaching on both undergraduate and postgraduate primary courses. Her doctoral research focused on the evolving pedagogical practices of Primary Mathematics Specialist teachers and their developing identities as learners, researchers and classroom practitioners.

Natalia Buckler is Principal Research Manager and leads for CUREE (Centre for the Use of Research and Evidence in Education) on research and evaluation specification, design and delivery. Since joining CUREE in 2008, Natalia has worked on a number of research, evaluation, consultation and bespoke training development projects including Master's in Teaching and Learning and the Evaluation of the Postgraduate Professional Development programme for the Training and Development Agency. Natalia holds a PhD in Education from Hertzen Pedagogical University (Russia).

Bob Burstow is a Senior Lecturer at Kings College London. His interests lie in effective continuing professional development, education management and school effectiveness and improvement. He comes to this role after over 30 years teaching and leading in secondary schools in and around London.

Anne Campbell recently retired from the post of Professor of Professional Learning at Leeds Metropolitan University. Her research interests focus around professional learning through action research and inquiry. Recent books are, *An Ethical Approach to Practitioner Research* (2007); *Connecting Inquiry and Professional Learning* (2009); a three volume series *Action Research in Education* for the Sage Fundamentals of Applied Research series, (2010); and *Working with Children and Young People: Ethical Debates and Practices across Disciplines and Continents.* (2011). She directed and worked on various governmental research projects relating to professional practice.

Ann Childs is a University Lecturer in Science Education at the Oxford University Department of Education and a Fellow of Lady Magaret Hall. She has written extensively on the professional learning associated with science teaching, both in the UK and internationally and on the implications of government education policies for teacher education.

Paul Conway is a Senior Lecturer, Director of the Cohort PhD in Education programme in the School of Education University College Cork and Associate Director of UCC's Centre for Global Development (CGD). He has a PhD in Educational Psychology from Michigan State University and his research interests are in teacher learning, teacher education policy and digital technologies in education. He is on the editorial boards of a number of international journals and is currently joint General Editor of *Irish Educational Studies* (Routledge). A former President of the Educational Studies Association of Ireland, he is the association's current representative on the Council of the World Education Research Association (WERA).

James C. Conroy is Professor of Religious and Philosophical Education and Dean for European engagement at the University of Glasgow. Previously he has held positions as Dean of the Faculty of Education, Department Chair and inaugural Head of the Graduate School at the University. He has taught in schools and universities in England and Scotland for 30 years. Previously he has been President of the Association for Moral Education and is Chair-Elect of the Philosophy of Education Society. His latest monograph, published by Bloomsbury, is entitled 'Does Religious Education Work?' and is based on a three-year ethnographic study funded by the AHRC/ESRC.

Philippa Cordingley is Chief Executive of CUREE (Centre for the Use of Research and Evidence in Education) and an internationally acknowledged expert in effective Continuing Professional Development and Learning. She has led CUREE projects in a range of research, evaluation and development projects including the creation of the evidence based National Framework for Mentoring and Coaching; the Research Informed Practice web site and the creation of banks of coaching and micro enquiry tools. She is the founder and professional adviser to the National Teacher Research Panel and Chair of the EPPI Centre Impact of Continuing Professional Development Review Group. CUREE's long standing and continuous stream of continuing professional development research and development includes a three-year evaluation of the implementation of the National Curriculum. Philippa is Chair of Governors of the RSA Academy, an Honorary Fellow of the College for Teachers and a member of the Steering Group of the Sheffield University Education Research Centre.

Tim Dornan is a doctor, who worked as a specialist in internal medicine and endocrinology until recently. He developed an interest in education mid-career and completed a master's degree and subsequently a PhD in Maastricht University, Netherlands. He was Professor of Medical Education in Manchester, UK until he joined the Maastricht Group in 2010. He teaches qualitative methodology and social learning theories. His main research interest is clinical workplace learning.

Graham Donaldson is currently an Honorary Professor at the University of Glasgow and professional advisor on teacher education to the Scottish Government. He completed a major review of teacher education in Scotland in 2010, Teaching Scotland's Future, which has given rise to a radical programme of implementation. He has worked extensively internationally, including as an international expert for the

OECD, and was President of the Standing International Conference of Inspectorates. He was head of H M Inspectorate of Education in Scotland from 2002 to 2010.

Anne Edwards is a Professor in the Oxford University Department of Education where she co-convenes the Oxford Centre for Socio-cultural and Activity Research. She has written extensively on teachers' professional learning, inter-professional collaborations, cultural historical theory and children's learning in educational settings. She is one of the founding editors of Learning, Culture and Social Interaction.

Michael Eraut is Emeritus Professor of Education at the University of Sussex. He is a world expert and the UK's leading researcher into how professionals learn in workplace settings. His pioneering research has found that most learning occurs informally during normal working processes. His books include the highly acclaimed Developing Professional Knowledge and Competence. His research interests include the nature of professional knowledge, the epistemology of practical knowledge; enhancement of informal learning, initial and continuing education of managers, professionals and technicians; the relationship between theory and practice; learning organisations; and learning trajectories in a wide range of contexts.

Maria Assunção Flores PhD is an Associate Professor with qualification at the University of Minho, Portugal. She received her PhD at the University of Nottingham, UK, in 2002. Her research interests include teacher professionalism and leadership, teacher education and professional development, induction and change. She has published books, chapters, articles in national and international journals. She is a member of various international associations. She is currently the Chair-elect of the Board of Directors of the International Council on Education for Teaching (ICET).

Marion Jones is Professor of Teacher Education at Liverpool John Moores University. In her research, which is concerned with the professional training and continuous development of the educational workforce, she draws on her extensive experience as a secondary school teacher and teacher educator. She has developed mentor training programmes for induction tutors and provided consultancy on mentoring to local authority groups and schools. A key area of her research is mentoring in pre-service teacher training and induction. She has disseminated her work at national and international conferences and published widely in academic journals.

Pertti Kansanen is Professor Emeritus in Education, Department of Teacher Education, University of Helsinki, Finland. His main research areas are ethics of education, teachers' pedagogical thinking and research on teaching and teacher education. More information can be found on the website: www.helsinki.fi/~pkansane/.

Meg Maguire is Professor of Sociology of Education, King's College London UK. She has an interest in teacher education, social policy and social justice issues. She is lead editor for the *Journal of Education Policy*.

Jane McNicholl is a University Lecturer in Science Education at the Oxford University Department of Education and a Fellow of St Cross College. Her work has focused on the professional development associated with science teaching and, with Viv

Ellis, she is author of 'Transforming Teacher Education: Reconfiguring the Academic Work' (Bloomsbury, 2014).

Olwen McNamara is a Professor of Teacher Education at the University of Manchester where she is currently Head of the School of Education and Director of Initial Teacher Education. Her research interests are in the area of teacher professional learning and she has a special interest in mathematics education. She has served on the executive council of a number of national committees including the British Educational Research Association and the Universities' Council for the Education of Teachers, where she is currently Chair of the Research and International Committee.

Rosaleen Murphy is an Irish Research Council funded Research Fellow at the School of Education, University College Cork. She has previously been involved with several other major externally funded research projects on pre-service teacher education in Ireland. She also has a particular interest in early childhood education and care. She was part of the National Council for Curriculum and Assessment team that developed Aistear, the Early Childhood Curriculum Framework, and she also edits An Leanbh Óg, the OMEP Ireland of Early Childhood Studies, a peer-reviewed journal, published annually.

Jean Murray is a Professor of Education and the Research and Knowledge Exchange Leader in the Cass School of Education at the University of East London in England. Her research focuses on the sociological analysis of teacher education policies and practices internationally. She has a particular interest in the identities and career trajectories of teacher educators as key agents in teacher education. Jean has written well over 100 books, chapters, journal articles and official reports on these issues and has also run a large number of educational research projects. She has taught at all levels of higher education and acted as an educational consultant on professional learning for governments, NGOs and many universities across the world. She has been an active member of the academic community in the UK and internationally for more than twenty years.

Ian Menter is Professor of Teacher Education and Director of Professional Programmes in the Department of Education at the University of Oxford, UK. Previously he worked at the University of Glasgow and at a number of other UK institutions, having been a primary school teacher in Bristol at the outset of his professional career. He is a past President of the Scottish Educational Research Association and will hold the Presidency of the British Educational Research Association from 2013 to 2015.

Anne-Mette Morcke is a doctor, who early in her career developed an interest in medical education and completed a PhD at Aarhus University, Denmark. She is currently also the director of undergraduate medical education at her university and leads the implementation of a major curriculum reform that aim to reinstate patient-centered teaching and clinical workplace learning as a core value and method. Her main research interest is curriculum development.

Siân Morgan is lecturer and tutor in secondary mathematics education at The University of Manchester and mathematics teacher and subject mentor at Altrincham Grammar School for Girls. In her previous role as a mathematics consultant for a local authority she supported teachers in developing mathematics pedagogy and subject knowledge. Her research interests lie in dialogue and questioning in the mathematics classroom and lesson study. She is currently completing a Master's in Educational Research.

Vanessa Rutherford is an Irish Research Council Post Doctoral Researcher in the School of Education, University College Cork, Ireland. Her research interests include the history of education; the social, cultural and historical construction of childhood and socio-cultural aspects of learning and pedagogy. She is a member of the Educational Studies Association of Ireland; the Royal Academy of Medicine in Ireland; the international Platform for a Cultural History of Children's Media and the Society for the History of Children and Youth.

Julie Ryan is a teacher and researcher in mathematics education at Manchester Metropolitan University. She has taught in schools and universities in Australia and England. Her recent research work has been drawn across the primary and secondary school stages and has promoted the positive use of children's errors and misconceptions for learning through mathematical peer discussion in classrooms. She is currently working on a long-term project to develop a dialogic pedagogy for mathematics.

Yvette Solomon is Professor of Education in the Education and Social Research Institute, Manchester Metropolitan University, and Professor II in Mathematics Education in the Faculty of Education and International Studies, Oslo and Akershus University College. Her main interest is in the development of mathematical identities in secondary and undergraduate mathematics students, and of professional identities in pre-service teachers.

Kari Smith is a Professor at the Department for Education at the University of Bergen in Norway. She is currently the Co-coordinator of the EARLI SIG 11, Research on Teaching and Teacher Education. Her main research interests are evaluation and assessment for and of learning, teacher education, and professional development. She has published widely in national and international journals and books.

Marit Ulvik is an Associate Professor at the Department for Education at the University of Bergen in Norway. Her main research interests are teacher education, mentoring and professional development. She has published in national and international journals and books.

Julian Williams is Professor of Mathematics Education at The University of Manchester, England. His research interests are in Social Theory, particularly Cultural-historical Activity Theory and Bourdieusian sociology, and broadly in learning, teaching and assessment in Mathematics Education. Recent topics of research include post-compulsory mathematics education, and professional development.

Kevin Woods is employed as Professor of Educational and Child Psychology at the University of Manchester, where he works as the director of initial professional training in educational psychology. He has been a practitioner educational psychologist for over 20 years and his research interests include the role and training of educational psychologists, student assessment needs, and child protection/safeguarding.

Chapter 1
Framing Workplace Learning

Olwen McNamara, Marion Jones and Jean Murray

Introduction

A historical analysis of the professional learning of teachers, and especially their pre-service education, shows that the locus of learning and the pedagogy of instruction has been subject to many conceptual and structural changes. In pre-service education, characteristically, this has been defined by the organisational culture of the teacher education providers and their relationship with validating bodies and ultimately the state. In the nineteenth century, in England, a classroom-based apprenticeship model of teacher preparation was favoured. However, as the next century progressed, there was movement towards the theory-laden academic programme, which was delivered by higher education for a significant part of the twentieth century. In England—in contrast to many, if not most, other European countries—this tide, which has been ebbing since the 1990s, could be said to have well and truly turned again. Recent governments of all political persuasions have, with increasingly radical ideological fervour, once again pursued a more extensively workplace-based model of teacher pre-service and continuing professional learning.

Demonstrating an unquestioning belief that gaining more experience in schools will automatically and inevitably lead to a better quality learning for pre-service teachers, the Secretary of State for Education in England, Michael Gove (2010), announced in June 2010 his intention to move pre-service teacher education out of higher education and back into schools, because of his belief that 'Teaching is a

O. McNamara (✉)
School of Education, The University of Manchester,
Manchester, UK
e-mail: olwen.mcnamara@manchester.ac.uk

M. Jones
Liverpool John Moores University, Liverpool, UK
e-mail: M.Jones@ljmu.ac.uk

J. Murray
University of East London, London, UK
e-mail: j.m.f.murray@uel.ac.uk

O. McNamara et al. (eds.), *Workplace Learning in Teacher Education,*   1
Professional Learning and Development in Schools and Higher Education 10,
DOI 10.1007/978-94-007-7826-9_1, © Springer Science+Business Media Dordrecht 2014

craft and it is best learnt as an apprentice, observing a master craftsman or woman'. The continuing professional leaning of new and experienced teachers and leaders he also considered to be better served within the school community, led by the newly established raft of Teaching Schools. Gove envisages that the Teaching Schools, projected to number 500 by 2014/15, will 'turn around' the school system and the wider community.

> Teaching Schools are part of the government's drive to give schools more freedom and to enable schools to take increasing responsibility for managing the education system. They will provide coherent training and development for new and experienced teachers and leaders, which in turn supports school improvement and meets the needs and context of the local area. Teaching schools are among the best schools in the country. They are outstanding in their own performance and have a track record of working with others to raise standards for children and young people beyond their own school. (National College 2012, p. 11)

Thus the locus of learning, in England certainly, seems to have come full circle. Rhetorically at least, the focus of pre-service teacher education and continuing professional learning has been relocated into the classroom. It is engagingly easy to slip conceptually into 'circle' metaphors: 'back to the future'; 'what goes round comes round'; and to reach the 'sitting by nelly' manual on workplace learning off the shelf and dust it down. Yet, is it the same work? The same place? The same learning?

When we sought to answer these questions, England seemed to be an interesting test-bed for workplace learning, because of the very radical nature of the proposed changes, but also because of the qualitatively different and more complex context that the workplace presented, compared to its nineteenth century counterpart. It seemed to provide a context where the nature of the work, the professional learning, the ecologies and communities of teacher practice, and the learning spaces themselves, were conceptually, pedagogically, intellectually and even architecturally in an evolutionary state. A key question that this book attempts to answer is how the components of the complex multi-disciplinary and cross-professional jigsaw that has come to frame teacher professional learning in England mesh (in productive or not-so-productive tension) at their interfaces. And what are the new generative possibilities for theorising and action, and how are they opened up at the boundaries?

Context

The international interest in teacher learning over the last decade has been generated by the intense and increasing importance vested in national and international league tables of pupil performance, located within the endemic audit culture (Power 1994, 1997). Pupil performance, considered to be of strategic significance in the development of an effective and appropriately skilled labour workforce, is claimed to be linked to international economic competitiveness. Fuller et al. (2004, p. 1) observe that policy-makers internationally, who are 'preoccupied with finding ways of strengthening the relationship between education systems and the economy are increasingly focusing on workplace learning as a way of improving organisational performance and, at an aggregate level, national economic success'. In England this agenda is manifest in the foreword to the White Paper 'The Importance of Teaching: Schools White Paper' (DfE 2010) where Cameron and Clegg, the Prime Minister and his deputy, observed:

> what really matters is how we're doing compared with our international competitors. That is what will define our economic growth and our country's future. The truth is, at the moment we are standing still while others race past. In the most recent OECD [Organisation for Economic Co-operation and Development] PISA [Programme for International Student Assessment] survey in 2006 we fell from 4th in the world in the 2000 survey to 14th in science, 7th to 17th in literacy, and 8th to 24th in mathematics. The only way we can catch up, and have the world-class schools our children deserve, is by learning the lessons of other countries' success. (DfE 2010, p. 3)

In the international quest for growth, made all the more acute by the current global economic crisis, teacher learning has become an area of strategic importance in the debate; most recently because current thinking positions teachers, and specifically teacher professional learning, as key to the effectiveness of school systems. The highly influential McKinsey Report (2007), in an analysis of data from 25 systems worldwide, identified three factors common to ten of the world's highest performing school systems. Two of these three factors relate directly to the training and professional learning of teachers: (1) getting the right people to become teachers; (2) developing them into effective instructors; and (3) ensuring the system is able to deliver the best possible instruction for every child (ibid: 5).

This unequivocal claim has directed a high level of international interest towards the Finnish education system, which—since 2000 when the Organisation for Economic Co-operation and Development (OECD) first established the Programme for International Student Assessment (PISA)—has consistently been identified as a high performing school system. In terms of performance in reading, in science and in mathematics, pupil achievement in Finland has remained consistently in the three highest-ranking countries internationally, although in recent years it has often been challenged for the top position by Hong Kong-China and Korea. There has also, unsurprisingly, been considerable scrutiny of teacher education systems in Finland, in a quest to find the elusive 'magic bullet'. This has been bolstered by the McKinsey Report's claim that:

> These systems demonstrate that the best practice for achieving these three things work irrespective of the culture in which they are applied. They demonstrate that substantial improvements in outcomes is possible in a short period of time and applying these best practices universally could have enormous impact in improving failing school systems, wherever they might be located (ibid.: 5).

Teacher education in Finland has at least four distinguishing qualities, according to the OECD report from Schleicher (2012). It is: (1) research-based and teachers, trained to master's level, undertake a research-based dissertation and are expected to engage in disciplined inquiry in the classroom throughout their teaching career; (2) strongly focused on developing pedagogical content knowledge; (3) effective in preparing teachers to diagnose students with learning difficulties and adapting instruction to their learning needs and styles; (4) effective in delivering a strong and extensive clinical experience component in a model school, including reflection on experiential learning and innovative research-based pedagogical theory (ibid.: 39). A teaching profession educated to master's level is identified as one key factor in its success; a position towards which an increasing number of other European school systems are moving (ibid.). A second factor is the role of the University Practice Schools which operate a clinic training model for pre-service teachers, and in which practising teachers engage in disciplined research-based enquiry throughout their teaching career (as we will see in Chap. 16).

These features together are conducive to nurturing the conditions for McKinsey's third factor: 'ensuring the system is able to deliver the best possible instruction for every child'. The report suggests that, to generate change in school systems, the levers need to be at individual teacher level and involve: (1) self-awareness of beliefs and practices; (2) gaining understanding of best practice through 'demonstration of such practices in authentic settings'; and (3) 'high expectations and a shared sense of purpose' (McKinsey and Company 2007, p. 27).

Twenty years ago a comparative review of European teacher education noted that, at the time, England and Wales were on their own in attempting to erode both the length, and the university-based academic rigour, of pre-service teacher training, whilst most other European countries were moving in the other direction (Holyoake 1993). In the intervening 20 years, as noted above, England in particular has continued on the inexorable path to a more extensively 'relevant' school-based initial training. Fundamental changes in regulations have introduced 'partnership' models between higher education training providers and schools, to varying degrees, in all the UK home nations—and indeed internationally (Brisard et al. 2005). Key questions are whether increasing the proportion of pre-service training undertaken in the workplace necessarily implies a lack of academic rigour or, as we asked earlier, whether increasing workplace learning will inevitably lead to better practice, and finally whether there is a distinction to be made between pre-service and continuing professional learning in this respect.

One fleeting attempt to increase the academic standing and early professional learning of teachers in England was the introduction of the Master's in Teaching and Learning. It was also a key strategy in New Labour's agenda for raising standards in education, and was championed by Ed Balls, the then Secretary of State for Education, in the policy document 'Being the Best for our Children: Releasing talent for teaching and learning', which set out the plans for developing the school workforce to meet to challenges of a twenty-first century school (DCSF 2008). The flagship Master's in Teaching and Learning was to make teaching a master's level profession, and in this they sought to emulate the Finnish model. The initiative displayed all the hallmarks of decontextualised 'educational policy borrowing' (Philips and Ochs 2004), albeit supported by McKinsey's claim (above) that, 'these three things work irrespective of the culture in which they are applied' (McKinsey and Company 2007, p. 5).

The Master's in Teaching and Learning was a professional master's programme, developed within a nationally agreed framework and based in the workplace, where the teacher would be supported by a more senior school-based coach and her learning would be contextualised to her and her school's needs. It was premised on a belief that it would offer professional development for early career teachers and significant improvements for schools. Frankham and Hiett (2011, p. 803), however, argue that contrary to the impression that the Master's in Teaching and Learning was an attempt to increase academic rigour whilst maintaining relevance,

> the MTL [Master's in Teaching and Learning] marks a new and significant step in expanding the utilitarianism of the English education system. The MTL represents a deepening hold on education by the state and a growing scepticism about the value of higher education in the CPD [continuing professional development] of teachers. It also aspires to a changing culture in schools as the workplace becomes the locus for the CPD of teachers. . . . The MTL, then, can be seen as part of a global phenomenon; in this case the policy lever of CPD is employed to support performative and audit policy agendas via a rigid accountability system. The MTL also represents a particular form of neo-liberal governmentality where increasing centralisation is "masked" by a "simulacra of care".

The pilot of the Master's in Teaching and Learning was abandoned after the first cohort, a victim of the cuts in education spending implemented by the Coalition Government upon taking up power in 2010. Retrospectively, it was found to have been effective in the way in which it helped teachers to reflect on their practice and develop a deeper critique into their teaching and learning strategies and engagement with theoretical perspectives (Castle et al., 2013). The initiative has, however, re-emerged in Wales as the Master's in Educational Practice. Voluntary for all newly qualified teachers in 2012, it is a three-year progamme which links to the Welsh Government's priorities. External mentors scaffold newly qualified teachers through the induction process and three master's modules a year. Delivered as a distance programme by an alliance of Welsh higher education institutions, the programme uses a Virtual Learning Environment with asynchronous online discussion, collaborative peer enquiry and action research (Salisbury and Morris 2012).

The Genesis and Structure of the Book

The Master's in Teaching and Learning is particularly pertinent to the narrative of this book because it was piloted on all newly qualified teachers in 2010–2011 in the North West of England. And it was designed, as we have noted, to be a professional master's award studied and supported in the workplace.

Workplace learning in teacher education specifically, and most particularly workplace learning undertaken in pursuit of postgraduate level study, is not well theorised compared to the extent and depth of theorisation on workplace learning in other fields (Rainbird et al. 2004a; Hager 2011). Little work has been done to understand what insights might be offered about alternative conceptualisations of learning and induction, or what might be learned from the substantive knowledge bases from other professions.

It was for this reason that workplace learning, and specifically the Master's in Teaching and Learning, was one of the research themes identified originally by the Teacher Education Research Network (TERN), a collaborative network of all seven North West universities involved in teacher education. TERN was initially funded by Economic and Social Research Council (ESRC), 2008–2009, (Murray et al. 2011) as a capacity-building initiative, and its early- and mid-career researcher participants developed an active community, enhanced individual research profiles and impacted on their institutional research cultures. The gap in the research literature on workplace learning was adopted as a common focus for TERN in its second year of operation, and a successful proposal for an ESRC seminar series was submitted in 2010. The seminars hosted by TERN in 2011 offered further capacity building potential and the opportunity to foster cross-institutional networking and research capacity building in the area of multi-professional policy and practice, and also additionality in terms of opportunities for professional learning, knowledge generation/exchange and user engagement.

The seminar series, planned as five one-day seminars, sought to explore the formal and informal teacher professional learning opportunities, including the higher-level study offered to individual teachers, their colleagues and the school community as a whole. It looked to critically engage with current policy agendas, to generate a more theoretically informed and robust model of workplace learning and teaching; and sought to cross-fertilise these across policy and practice in other professional fields (e.g. medicine and educational psychology). Generated from the seminar series, this book aims to explore teacher workplace learning in pre-service and continuing professional learning from four perspectives: social policy in respect of teacher professional learning and its enactment in the workplace, international comparators of pre-service teacher education, multi-professional perspectives on workplace learning, and finally socio-cultural theory.

The resulting book begins by offering a number of theoretical perspectives to frame workplace learning. The remainder of this chapter considers work and place and learning, and in doing so highlights contemporary debates around binary ways of thinking (about for example knowledge and learning) and around dichotomies (such as theory/practice). This leads to a discussion of the possibilities offered by 'third space' thinking, which draws on hybridity theory, and situates binaries and dichotomies in productive dialogue. From third spaces the discussion moves to nomadic spaces guided by the theoretical lens of Deleuze and Guattari. The theoretical focus moves in Chap. 2 to a socio-cultural theme as Childs, Edwards and McNicholl cross-fertilise research and practice in the field of education, by drawing on activity theory to analyse the theoretical and pedagogic underpinnings of teacher workplace learning.

In order to get a more diverse intellectual and theoretical purchase on workplace learning the next three chapters extend the discussion by drawing on cross-professional examples offering different models and ways of articulating their professional knowledge bases. In Chap. 3 Eraut draws on examples from engineering, accountancy and nursing to conceptualise growth of expertise, theorised in 'learning trajectories' which track progression along the continuity/discontinuity of lifelong learning. Dornan and Morcke in Chap. 4 apply Eraut's trajectories in the context of medicine. They problematise the possibility of 'making the complexity of practice teachable and testable' through the competency-based education which has been enthusiastically adopted by a medical profession and in which accountable and performativity have become fundamental. In Chap. 5 Woods focuses on workplace learning for trainee educational psychologists and identifies that the university-workplace learning partnership has been affected by the recent market driven reforms in the educational psychology sector, which has developed models of 'service trading' and statutory registration. Woods argues that as socio-political factors shape the context, organisational understanding of workplace learning opportunities for trainee educational psychologists will become vital.

The third section of the book explores education policy and practice in respect of professional learning. In Chap. 6 Burstow and Maguire undertake a historical review of teacher continuing professional learning policy under successive governments, and develop a useful model to track changes in policy and how it variously positions the teacher. They conclude by considering whether continuing professional learning is 'worth doing' and ask what a values-based continuing professional learning programme might look like. Cordingley and Buckler focus on the support of professional learning in the classroom in Chap. 7, and in doing so draw on work carried out to evaluate the effectiveness of schools as professional learning environments and to underpin the National Framework for Mentoring and Coaching which was used in the design and delivery of the coaching element of the Master's in Teaching and Learning. The next two chapters present and critique very different models of professional learning in mathematics. Chap. 8, by Barnes and Solomon, is grounded in a government-funded continuing professional development programme, the Mathematics Specialist Teacher programme, which created 'maths champions' with a view to them becoming agents of change in their schools. Chap. 9 by Williams, Ryan and Morgan considers the professional learning environment created by the endemic audit and performativity culture and conjectures how it impacts upon a research-led development project which uses a lesson study approach to 'generate and sustain an inquiry discourse within the wider school community'. The research theme is continued in Chap. 10 when Campbell considers the policy and practice context of teacher continuing professional learning in England, and the inherent tensions it reveals between individual, school and government priorities. She argues that practitioner inquiry is a powerful tool in workplace learning for engendering teachers' professional learning, most particularly when it is linked to postgraduate study.

In the final part of the book, attention turns to considering UK and international policy, research and practice regarding pre-service teacher education. It begins in Chap. 11 by returning to reflect upon the impact of the recent radical reforms in England, rehearsed briefly in Chap. 1. Following this, in Chap. 12, Conroy, Donaldson and Menter review the policy context for teacher education in Scotland and consider how a recently developed 'clinical model' of teacher education addresses the location of professional learning and the contested space between theory and practice. In Chap. 13 Conway, Murphy and Rutherford, consider policy and practice in pre-service teacher education in Ireland. They contend that 'work' not 'learning' has hitherto been fundamental to placement activity and argue for teacher education reform which reframes the school as a 'learning place'. Somewhat further afield in Portugal, Flores turns her attention to the implementation of the European wide Bologna process and its impact on pre-service teacher education. And most particularly, the place of workplace learning in the curriculum, which although valued is found not to articulate well with other university-based components. The final two chapters in this section originate from Scandinavia. In Chap. 15 Smith and Ulvik discuss a growing awareness in Norway that pre-service teacher education is a shared responsibility amongst policy-makers, higher education institutions and schools. However, on a pragmatic level the realisation of such a vision and its integration into current practice is still seen as a challenge. In Chap. 16 Kansanen describes Finland's 'conceptual' teacher education programmes that have, as an organising principle, a research-based approach which incorporates teachers' engagement with and in research, pedagogical thinking, and a symbiotic theory-practice relation.

Overall then the book offers a number of contexts for exploring how best to conceptualise and theorise teacher learning in the workplace in order to generate evidence to inform policy and improve practice. The final chapter draws together these international and cross-professional themes and concludes by reflecting what they may have to offer as a way forward for England, where the dominant political discourse is that the school, as the immediate practice setting, is the principal and most effective place in which knowledge of how to teach can be developed. It argues that other settings for workplace learning include universities and, increasingly for the future, virtual spaces which allow for the simulation of practice. Promoting multiple perspectives on teacher workplace learning by transcending national, cultural and professional boundaries can perhaps help us to understand what 'other' places and spaces might help us support learning, as we will go on to consider.

Framing Workplace Learning

Defining Workplace Learning

In framing teacher learning in the workplace, we craft our definition to include systematic planned opportunities for learning in the workplace and attendant experiential learning, where learning takes place but is not the primary goal of the activity. We also encompass structured learning in settings beyond the workplace, but drawing on knowledge and understandings derived from the workplace. In this we make no implicit assumption that learning would be resultant from the systematic planned learning opportunities, or about the qualities or value of any of the learning that does take place. In relation to pre- and in-service teachers, the purpose of the learning is often significantly different. For pre-service teachers, practicum experiences are part of the learning process about the nature of teacher work, and their induction and socialisation into the communities of practice (Wenger 1999). This induction process is often about the re-production of social and pedagogic practices. For in-service teachers, schools are both places of work (often hard and heavily regulated) and of learning (although not all learning is necessarily good) (cf VITAE study,

Day et al. 2006a). Workplace learning for serving teachers is less about induction (unless the teacher is newly qualified or an experienced teacher new to the school or phase) and more about—with appropriate support structures—the broadening and deepening of existing experience and knowledge or the learning of new instructional practices or curriculum content.

In our conceptualising of teacher learning, however, we recognise that schools are not designed with teacher learning in mind (notwithstanding categories such as the newly designated Teaching Schools mentioned at the beginning of the chapter), and that the core business of the education system, and specifically the school, is pupil learning. Similarly, patient care, we shall observe later in this volume, is the core business of the hospital (notwithstanding Teaching Hospitals upon which, in part, the Teaching Schools were modelled) and the educational psychology service. Yet, for these three public sector services, the up-skilling and re-validation of experienced staff and the training of new staff is vital for sustaining an effective and proficient workforce. This tension is common across the economy. Evans et al. (2006, p. 164) observe that, in private sector business and industry, 'For most employers, workers' learning is not a priority and represents a third-order decision'. (The first being the 'market and competitive strategy', the second 'work organisation and job design' (Mayhew and Keep 1999).)

The issue of where the responsibility lies for providing and sustaining a skilled workforce relates to earlier discussions about the role of the state in the provision of an appropriately skilled labour workforce and its relationship with validating and employing bodies in the public and private sectors. Ashton (2004), in an international analysis of the political organisation of workplace learning, identified three ideal typical models. Ordered in terms of an increasing degree of political control exhibited over the certification of learning in the workplace, they were: free market, corporatist and developmental state. In free market models, such as the UK, Ashton observed that the state had little or no input into workforce development, considering it best left to employers and individual workers. In all three models, state intervention was primarily in relation to initial workforce training.

Yet even with the most paternalistic of employers, access to learning opportunities at work is often problematic and inequitable. Rainbird et al. (2004a, p. 38) observe that 'theories of situated learning tend to stress the participative and consensual nature of learning at work rather than the constraints on individual and collective capacity for action'. They neglect to consider the social and cultural power relations in which access to the learning is negotiated. This can be particularly thorny where elements of initial training are undergone in the workplace, as in the case of teachers, doctors and educational psychologists. Tensions between the agendas of training providers, validating bodies/the state and employers are a very real possibility, as we shall see later in this volume.

Conceptualising Work and Place and Learning

In considering the phenomenon of teacher workplace learning, our first and most obvious analytical move was to disaggregate it into its constituent parts—work and place and learning. Not, we claim, an original move, for in this we have mirrored other workplace learning literature (see Malloch et al. 2011). It was, however, a necessary step along the way to developing a theoretical purchase on workplace learning.

Work

Before considering teacher workplace learning, it is important to consider schools as workplaces, teachers as workers and employees, and teaching as work. Cains and Malloch (Malloch et al. 2011, p. 6) begin by defining 'work' in opposition to home, but broaden the parameters to acknowledge a twenty-first century conceptual shift of a 'paradigmatic manner from paid actions from an employer to a broader range of activities' which they define as:

> an enabled purposive effort by an individual to initiate an activity or respond to an issue or a problem in a range of situations for some perceived (by them) productive end. This emphasises that the action is intentional engagement by an individual.

In comparison to such a definition, teachers' work appears to be, at one and the same time, both more clearly defined and more complex (see, inter alia, Day et al. 2006b, 2008; Sammons et al. 2007; Webb 2006; Webb and Vullamy 2006, 2008; Hodkinson and Hodkinson 2005). It has been argued by some that fundamental aspects of teachers' work have changed little since the nineteenth century (see, inter alia, Hunter 1994; Darling-Hammond 1994). It is certainly the case that the concept of 'the school' as a social structure is broadly unchanged. Schools still comprise: children and young people whose purpose in being there is 'to learn'; a staff who teach or support that learning; and the parents and the wider communities that the schools serve. Within these highly structured social regimes in which teachers work and pupils learn (Holland et al. 2007), the space—for example the design of classrooms and corridors—often contributes to the surveillance and regulation of pupils, both in terms of academic work and social behaviours (Hunter 1994). Those spaces are both structured by, and structuring of, social practices (Giddens 1984; McGregor 2003).

We shall consider space in greater depth in the next section of this chapter, but for now the 'traditional' spaces within schools, particularly classrooms, are important to understand as the predominant locations for teachers' work (and therefore for the workplace learning opportunities which that work might offer for both pre- and in-service teachers) and for the construction of teacher identities through their work (McGregor 2003). This is particularly so in secondary schools in the UK (for learners aged 11–16 or 18), which facilitate the creation of hierarchical and differentiated social relationships between groups of staff teaching different subjects (McGregor 2003). Daily and weekly timetables construct learning, distributing time to different subjects and modes of learning; bells segment time into lesson-sized units and mark off the day into different activities to which learners and teachers conform. In many ways then, both time and space contribute to limiting and controlling teachers' work and pupils' learning, creating regulated routines for school life which all follow. These include communally agreed and pre-determined timetabled periods of learning, interspersed with time for meals and social interactions (in playgrounds and staffrooms). These highly regulated and routinised social structures are part of both teachers' work and the learning which may take place within them; they may therefore both construct opportunities for learning and constrict them.

Teachers' work in schools, under some degree of national and/or local control (over 90 % in England), is also a casualty in the struggle of schools to gain autonomy from the state. This is particularly so in the attempt to establish ethos, values and curricula which reflect community needs, as opposed to national imperatives. In common with schooling systems in many developed countries, and set within in a pervasive performativity and audit culture across the whole of the public sector, teachers have been positioned by successive governments as failing to deliver strong national test results in international comparisons of pupil achievement, such as PISA. As Ingersoll (2003) notes, one way of understanding such perceived inadequacy is to see schools as malfunctioning organisations which fail to oversee the effectiveness of teachers' work in ensuring high levels of pupil achievement. One solution is to increase centralised control and hold teachers more accountable for learners' attainment as a proxy for the quality of their work. An alternative way of understanding the perceived inadequacy of the schooling systems is to assert that teachers' work is overly controlled and effectively de-professionalised (Mahony and Hextall 1998; Troman 1996) by the multiple imperatives of school and state, and that a greater degree of autonomy and flexibility for teachers would be the key to improving the school system.

In England, as in many other countries, the former path has been adopted, giving rise to increased regulation and surveillance of teachers' work, which has brought a steep increase in management and accountability related tasks (Ball 2001, 2003). These changes have impacted significantly on teachers' work, as shown by research conducted from the time of the introduction on the National Curriculum and National Testing in the late 1980s/early 1990s (see, inter alia, Troman 1996; Helsby 1999; Galton 1995), and in response to major reforms such as the introduction of the National Literacy and Numeracy Strategies in the late 1990s (Earl et al. 2003).

This barrage of state-imposed changes to curricula, testing regimes and pedagogy clearly changed the context of teachers' work in England and many of its imperatives. Prior to that, it could be argued, that the fundamental pedagogical relationships for the imparting of knowledge from teacher to learner had remained, and in some ways still does remain, relatively unchanged since the inception of formal schooling in the 1880s (Hunter 1994). This continuity of basic forms of pedagogy is often criticised by those who wish to see teachers keep pace with, and make more extensive use of, new technologies (e.g. Prensky 2001; Becta 2008). However, over and above such caveats, the point to be made here is that teaching, as enabling and facilitating learning, has always been the key task within most teachers' work.

In addition to the routinised rhythms and structures of school life identified above, however, teachers' work is often far from routine. The multiple roles performed by teachers today—as imparters of knowledge, facilitators of learning, curriculum managers and pastoral carers—illustrates the complex and multi-faceted nature of their work. Meeting diverse learning needs and ensuring progress, whilst helping learners develop appropriate values to negotiate the increasing complexity of their local and global world, requires teachers to have an extensive and multi-faceted knowledge base, high levels of pedagogical and inter-personal skills, as well as a commitment to the work of educating children and young people for an equitable and democratic society. Teachers' work can therefore be seen as complex, changing and changeable.

The high profile 'VITAE' [Variations in teachers' work lives and effectiveness] project (Day et al. 2006a, 2008; Sammons et al. 2007) is one of the few large-scale and cross-phase studies of serving teachers' work carried out in England in recent decades. Conducted with 100 schools and 300 case study teachers, the project reinforces our emphasis here on teaching as the core task within teachers' work, even in the age of audit, management overload and multi-professional working. VITAE identifies the factors that underpin teachers' initial motivation to teach and their sustained commitment to teaching as: working with children; 'making a difference'; and, for secondary teachers, interest in their subject (Day et al. 2006a, p. xviii). All, in other words, are related to the core task of teaching. The project is also important for its identification of the emotional and intellectual investments which teachers make to their work, drawing upon 'personal and professional capacities and experience, knowledge and skills' (ibid.: xii). It also underlines the importance of a supportive school culture and of good, relevant continuing professional learning provision in maintaining teachers' effectiveness, motivation and professional resilience in their work, and updating the complex and multi-faceted knowledge base which all teachers need.

The only other large-scale and recent study of teachers in England was the 'Becoming a Teacher' project; a six-year longitudinal study of teachers from their pre-service courses through to the fifth year of teaching (Hobson et al. 2006, 2009). It was clear that, of the original sample of 4,790 students, the majority was motivated by the idea of working with pupils to develop learning and during pre-service education found school-based experience (practicum) to be the most valuable aspect of their courses, especially when their professional introduction to teachers' work was well supported by mentors and colleagues and they felt part of the school community. In years one to five of teaching, when the sample size was 1,443 teachers, the most rewarding aspects of work were identified as: promoting pupil learning; good relationships with pupils and colleagues; growing in confidence as a teacher, sometimes reflected in promotion or additional responsibility; and access to further professional development opportunities. Adverse aspects of work included heavy workloads and the amount of administration and paper work.

Additionally, the significant differences in the work and workplace learning opportunities of teachers in the primary (teaching children aged 5–11) and secondary phases, which accompany different structures, curricula and teacher roles, are not always acknowledged. Throughout the UK the distinction still holds that primary teachers are, in the main, generalist class teachers and teach all the national curriculum subject areas, despite a number of moves over the last 20 years to introduce an element of specialist teaching. Indeed, a further move to introduce specialist mathematics teachers to primary schools is currently underway. Secondary teachers, on the other hand, are nearly always subject specialists, despite a recent move in some schools to deliver an integrated curriculum for Years 7 and 8 (ages 11–13). With subject specialisation often comes a strong sense of subject loyalty and allegiance to a particular culture and colleagues within the school (Helsby 1999; McGregor 2003). Most secondary teachers in England work in large schools (on average 900–1,000 young people) and move around the school to teach different classes during the day. In contrast, primary school teachers' work is usually within relatively small schools (on average just over 200 children); teaching is multi-subject, as noted, and often conducted in one classroom with one class of pupils, with whom strong relationships are formed. These differences mean that work in primary teaching has some different characteristics from that in secondary teaching, and the knowledge bases required may be different (although equally demanding and complex). These factors mean that the professional learning opportunities through workplace learning in each phase of schooling also vary.

Place (and Space)

In many ways the physical locations of schools have remained fundamentally unchanged; many buildings still date back to the Victorian era and most modern 'new build' schools reproduce certain elements of traditional school architecture (classrooms, corridors and large meeting places) in their design. Learning in the workplace suggests that there is a designated space where opportunities for professional learning and growth exist. Although, as argued above, the main part of teachers' work is still conducted within the walls of the school, for teachers the workspace is not strictly limited to the place commonly associated with their work (that is, the physical environment of the classroom or the school where they engage with students, colleagues and parents on a day-to-day basis). Preparation and planning of lessons, development of resources, marking of students' work and other administrative chores are frequently undertaken outside school hours and off school premises. Thus, pre-service and in-service teachers' workplace learning must be conceived as occurring inside as well as outside the physical environment of the school, as well as across professional boundaries.

The concepts of boundary crossing and hybridity aptly capture the imperatives imposed on teachers, particularly in England, given the multiple roles they have performed since the introduction of the Every Child Matters agenda (DfES 2004) located the teaching profession firmly within a multi-agency and trans-professional context. Although there has been some degree of retraction from this position in the last few years of Coalition Government, teachers' work is no longer confined to the clearly defined environment of the classroom, but takes place in diverse physical, professional, and sometimes virtual spaces. From this complex and diverse learning landscape within its situated social practices, arise a multitude of imperatives which newcomers to the profession must navigate (Lave and Wenger 1991). This is complicated further by the myriad of competing knowledge bases, be they of a pedagogical, subject-specific or professional nature. However, before we examine the spaces and places we need to provide some background understanding of these two concepts and how we interpret them in the context of this book.

In this endeavour, Schultze and Boland's (2000) exploration of place and space in a knowledge-intensive learning organisation is helpful. They recognise the social construction of these two concepts as 'an ongoing source of dialectic tension for the individual worker' (ibid.: 187) and the organisation, and draw on Harvey's (1989) distinction between 'being' in a place and the process of 'becoming' through traversing a space. Drawing on Casey (1997) they also identify tensions within the boundedness of place, which on the one hand evoke safety and stability, but on the other, limitations in terms of restricted movement, growth and the capacity for change. Schools, in terms of their physicality and organisational structures, can be perceived as 'safe' places that generate a sense of belonging, identity and situatedness amongst those who inhabit them. In contrast, 'space' conceptually evokes images of blurred and shifting boundaries. Gadamer's (2004) 'fusion of horizons' metaphor is helpful here, affording as it does free movement for individuals and the potential for personal growth and professional development, whilst at the same time embracing an element of unpredictability. The intersection of space and time is complicated further in virtual spaces where the local merges with the global, where physical absence can mean virtual presence, and where individual subjectivities are freed from the historically evolved identity and situated practices and norms of behaviour.

For pre-service and in-service teachers in England, professional practice in the physical workplace has become increasingly rigorously monitored and controlled by government regulatory and inspection regimes, set in the encompassing audit and performativity culture as we have noted earlier. This has placed individual schools in competition with one another and drawn a sharper focus on the boundaries and identities of schools. But at the same time new virtual spaces have opened up, where teachers can look beyond the horizon of their workplace to engage in professional learning and development activities. The internet affords teachers limitless possibilities for professional and social networking and discussion, and for access to knowledge bases and resources. It enables individuals to choose their own personal and/or professional identity and engage freely in debate without being constrained by the situatedness, and the tacitly agreed norms of professional behaviour, prevailing in their school. Such learning experiences are by no means always effortless and positive but can be liberating and empowering, in contrast with the sheer physicality of place. Harrison and Dourish (1996, p. 69) observe that 'a place is a space which is *invested with understandings* of behavioural appropriateness, cultural expectations, and so forth. We are located in *"space"*, but we act in "place"' (quoted in Wahlstedt et al. 2008). Teachers, as workers, are both part of, and separate from, the workplace community but, as Wahlstedt et al (2008, p. 1025) observe, learners need to be able to achieve a sense of placeness/situatedness (Evans et al. 2006; Evans and Kersh 2006). Lisahunter et al. (2011), in their study of 'the staffroom as a space and place for workplace learning' identify several spaces (professional, social, organisational) within a physically defined place, which 'are inextricably and dialogically linked with teachers' practices and relations' (ibid.: 35) and with their individual 'biographies, life experiences and life trajectories' (Kersh et al. 2011, p. 7).

Learning

Ahead of her time, Murial Spark's eponymous hero Miss Jean Brodie played on the twofold derivation of the word education by presenting her girls a vision of learning as 'educo' (e + duco meaning 'out of I lead') opposed to 'educatum' (meaning 'to train'). The latter is a model of 'learning as acquisition', of abstract rather than applied knowledge, and is still very current in England. Indeed, as far as the UK Coalition Government is concerned, it is the model of choice for both pupil learning (Gove 2012, announcing a shake-up of A levels and GCSEs claimed that 'Tough exams and rote learning help inspire students'); and teacher professional learning, through the National Scholarship Scheme which funds teachers to deepen their subject (as opposed to pedagogic content) knowledge (DfE 2011b). This is a view not shared by the VITEA research project in which Sammons et al. (2007, p. 686) concluded that 'CPD [continuing professional development] alone is unlikely to exert a major impact on teacher effectiveness. It needs to take place within professional, situated and personal contexts'. However, learning as acquisition is, claims Hager (2004), the 'standard paradigm of learning' and assumes a '*focus on mind*' (that positions learning as both the process of acquisition and product acquired); '*interiority*' (that positions learning as internal to the mind and valuable in and of itself rather than seeing its value in its applicability to solve problems or transform into pedagogic content knowledge for the classroom); and '*transparency*' (that positions learning as clear and unambiguous) (Hager 2004, pp. 243–244).

'Learning as acquisition' is presented by Sfard (1998) as in opposition to the metaphor 'learning as participation'. This dichotomy, Engeström (2011, p. 86) claims, 'is derived from the question: Is the learner to be understood primarily as an individual *or* as a community?'. 'Learning as participation' is undoubtedly the dominant metaphor for workplace learning, whether it be learning as participation in a community of practice (Lave and Wenger 1991), or learning through workplace participatory practices (Billett 2001, 2004; Fuller et al. 2005), or learning from participation in activity systems (Engeström 2001, 2004, 2011). For teachers, Hodkinson and Hodkinson (2005, p. 111) claim, evidence indicates that 'a combination of construction and participation' provides the most effective approach to learning. This can be done through the creation of more expansive learning environments (Fuller and Unwin 2003, 2004; Fuller et al. 2007) that enable the integration of personal construction with participatory activities.

Characteristically, performance in the workplace involves the integration of a number of disparate skills and knowledge traditions, which often includes the transfer of knowledge between education and workplace settings. Eraut (2004) compares and contrasts cultural and socially situated knowledge and personal knowledge (in its widest sense to include academic and non-codified knowledge), and identifies a five-stage process by which formal educational knowledge is applied in the workplace and integrated with other knowledge and skills. He develops this analysis further in Chap. 3.

Whilst it is commonly acknowledged, as noted above, that teachers require an extensive, complex and multi-faceted knowledge base in order to teach effectively, the precise nature of that knowledge has proved hard to define. This is, in part, because it supports what Furlong (1996, p. 154) refers to as the 'endemic uncertainty' of professional work. In a similar vein, the knowledge base of teaching has often been located in the 'swampy lowlands of professional knowledge' (Schön 1987), in comparison to the 'hard high grounds' of knowledge (ibid.) in disciplines such as the sciences.

The work of Shulman (1986, 1987), particularly his concept of pedagogical content knowledge, has been very influential in attempts to define teacher knowledge. In Shulman's conceptualisation, pedagogical content knowledge involves the intermingling of deep subject knowledge and knowledge of how the subject is developed within school curricula, with expert pedagogical knowledge in order to form expert and subject-specific pedagogical knowledge which teachers use to guide their actions in the classroom. This concept has now been extended by other researchers, including Ball (2000), Munby et al. (2001) and Shulman himself (2005). It has also spawned a number of detailed typologies of teacher knowledge, like that offered by Capel et al. (2009, p. 14), which defines teacher knowledge to include: pedagogical content knowledge; subject content knowledge; curriculum knowledge; general pedagogical knowledge; knowledge of educational contexts; and knowledge of educational 'ends', such as aims, purposes values.

Despite such attempts to define professional knowledge explicitly, much of it remains tacit and elusive because of its genesis in individual reflection in and on the highly contextualised actions involved in teaching (Schön 1987). This knowledge might well be seen as some of the most sophisticated and valuable teacher knowledge in dealing with the surprises, uncertainties and challenges of classroom life. But the ongoing lack of definition of such tacit knowledge can be seen as part of the reason why it often proves easy for policy-makers to reduce teacher knowledge to subject knowledge (gained during degree level study) and basic skills needed to achieve classroom 'competence', as a narrowly conceived form of professional knowledge and teacher professionality (Hoyle 1974). Such narrow and instrumental formulations, of a degree followed by an apprenticeship with a 'master' teacher in schools, can be seen to underpin many of the current 'reforms' of pre-service teacher education in England (see above, Gove 2010).

A further unhelpful factor in defining and defending teachers' knowledge as complex, is a series of enduring bifurcations—including academic/professional and theoretical/practical (Maguire 2000)—which haunt teaching and teacher education. In the binary of theory versus practical, two 'types' of knowledge—theoretical and practical—are simplistically conceived of as distinct and separated, rather than holistic and integrated. Furthermore, theoretical knowledge is often positioned as belonging to an 'academic' domain remote from and of little immediate use for teachers' work, and practical knowledge is reduced to a technical-rational model of basic knowledge for classroom 'competence'.

Cochran-Smith and Lytle (1999) develop this argument further by defining three common conceptions of knowledge: knowledge *for* practice (formal knowledge), knowledge *in* practice (practical knowledge), and knowledge *of* practice ('working within the contexts of inquiry communities to theorise and construct their work and to connect it to the larger social, cultural and political issues') (ibid.: 250). It is this last conception that they believe offers the potential for thinking about teacher learning in the twenty-first century, and they develop the notion of 'inquiry as stance' which, 'as a construct for understanding teacher learning in communities relies on a richer conception of knowledge than that allowed by the traditional formal knowledge-practical knowledge distinction' (ibid.: 289). The latter they claim, in the US at least, works to:

> maintain the hegemony of university generated knowledge for teaching... These implications serve to reify divisions that keep "teachers in their place"—the separation of practitioners from researcher, doers from thinkers, actors from analysts, and actions from ideas (ibid.: 289).

These binaries also play out in past and contemporary struggles around the construction, content, form and locations of pre- and in-service programmes.

Third Spaces

Underpinning this brief mapping of work and place and learning have been a significant number of binary oppositions. Most particularly, as we have seen, they have been central to the conceptualisations of '*knowledge*' as abstract or theoretical, versus applied or practical; and '*learning*' which is characterised, on the one hand, as formal or structured (systematic planned opportunities) and, on the other hand, informal or unstructured learning (where learning is not the primary goal). Learning does not, however, fall neatly into a workplace/non-workplace dichotomy. 'Systematic planned opportunities' do not equate perfectly with a non-workplace learning category, any more than 'learning is not the primary goal' equates to a workplace learning category. For Billett (2004), the binary oppositions formal/informal and structured/unstructured are not helpful because they privilege formal and structured learning, and informal and unstructured learning is positioned as deficit, defined by what it is not. Cairns and Malloch (2011, p. 11) offer an extensive list of 'Binaries that Bind' and recommend that they should be discontinued.

Our next analytical move is to do just that! Indeed a commitment to third space, asserts Moje et al. (2004),

> demands a suspicion of binaries; it demands that when one reads phrases such as "academic versus everyday literacies or knowledge", one wonders about other ways of being literate that are not acknowledged in such simple binary positions. One also wonders about how and when these forms of literacy overlap and whether everyday practices might, at times, look more like academic literacies than they do like everyday literacies (Moje et al. 2004, p. 42).

In third space, what hitherto seemed to be binary oppositions, can work productively together to generate new knowledge. Third space thinking draws on 'hybridity theory', which recognises the complexity of people and spaces and places. Bhabha (1994) articulates this as in-betweenness and uses the metaphor of 'fold' to represent a 'hybrid liminality' in a way that places the relational possibilities of the pre- and post-liminal states in a non-exclusive way (Stronach 1996 in McNamara 2002). Various authors have sought to do this in various ways:

- Soja (1996) examines the architecture of the physical and social to explore how physical space frames human interaction and how social practices shape the physical space. In Soja's third space, for example, new types of knowledge can be generated, as a bridge between community/home-based discourse and school-based discourse.
- Kozleski (2011) sees it as a space in which 'we can understand multiple perspectives, honour our differences, and find ways of improving how teachers learn and impact on their students'.
- Zeichner (2010) sees third space as an opportunity to integrate practitioner and academic knowledge in new ways: to enhance pre-service teachers' ability to learn in and from practice.
- Kalmbach Phillips (2002) see teachers' subjectivity as a 'battle site of discourses', spaces of openness that have not yet been colonised by existing orthodoxies and ideologies, but also spaces of hybridity, where multiple identities challenge binary orthodoxies (Bhabha 1994).
- For Gutiérrez et al. (1999, pp. 286–287), third space is a hybrid space, where 'competing discourses and positionings transform conflict and difference into rich zones of collaboration and learning (Gutiérrez et al. 1995, 1997)'. They see it as conveying 'the complexity of learning environments and their transformative potential' (ibid.: 287) affording 'expanded activity' (Engeström 1999) in a 'zone of proximal development' (Vygotsky 1978).

Reviewing the literature on third spaces, Moje et al. (2004) identify three different perspectives. The first uses third space to 'build bridges' between the discourses of home/community and those of school, and more generally between dominant and marginalised practices. The second uses third space to 'navigate' between different discourses and academic registers, to cross boundaries between discursive practices. The third is 'a space of cultural, social, and epistemological change in which the competing knowledges and discourses of different spaces are brought into "conversation" to challenge and reshape' (ibid.: 43).

It is this latter articulation that speaks best to our needs, a space where *theoretical and practical knowledge* and *personal and official discourses and aspirations* can enter into productive dialogue and, hopefully, effect an epistemological reconciliation. For a pre-service or beginning teacher this may be a reconciliation between: (1) personal and professional identities; (2) university privileged and school privileged pedagogies and practices, e.g. between (university-based) discourses of the ideal and (school-based) discourses of the real; (3) individual and official representations of an outstanding teacher, e.g. between their phenomenological understandings of what it is to be a teacher against the official version in the Teachers' Standards (DfE 2012); (4) current self-evaluation and personal aspirations, e.g. their understanding of the kind of teacher they are, compared to the kind of teacher they want to be; (5) personal understanding of a subject and its representations for teaching, e.g. between subject knowledge and pedagogic content knowledge; and (6) mathematics as a social practice (their personal articulation) and as a school subject (the discourse of the National Curriculum) (see Brown and McNamara 2005, 2011, for a more detailed articulation).

Nomadic Spaces

In our examination of place and space above we alluded to the distinction between a state of 'being' in a place and the process of 'becoming' through traversing a space (Harvey 1989). Pre-service teachers, in particular, can experience teaching practice as a recurrent shifting between positions of 'being' and 'becoming' whilst they engage in the ritual practices and symbolic acts of the teacher (McNamara et al. 2002). This provokes our third and final (and perhaps capricious) analytical move from *third spaces* to *nomadic spaces* guided by the theoretical lens of Deleuze and Guattari (2004, p. 419) who argue that:

> the nomad has territory; he follows customary paths; he goes from one point to another; he is not ignorant of the point (water points, dwelling points, assembly points etc). But the question is what in Nomad life is a principle and what is only a consequence. To begin with, although the points determine paths, they are strictly subordinate to the paths they determine. . . the nomad goes from point to point only as a consequence and as a factual necessity: in principle, points for him are relays along a trajectory.

According to Deleuze and Guattari (2004) then, although the nomad connects space she is not fundamentally defined by movement. To illustrate this the authors use the metaphor of the rhizome. A rhizome is a botanical term meaning 'mass of roots' (from rhízōma), as in a non-hierarchical root system, rather than a taproot system. The rhizome, not a conventional root but the main stem of a plant, is also know by the term 'rootstem'. In most cases the rhizome propagates underground disrupting the stem (above ground growing upward) and root (below ground growing downwards) order of things. It is thus a root system designed principally not to fix the organism in place but to propagate organically through space in neural-like pathways.

Nomads, like rhizomes, occupy space only in the sense that they traverse through space but they do not own the space or regulate that space. Deluze and Guattari (2004) compare the characteristics of *nomadic space* as opposed to *state space*. The former they note is smooth, unbounded and uncontrolled, the latter, on the other hand, is 'striated', it is gridded, coded and regulated:

> One of the fundamental tasks of the State is to striate the space over which it reigns, or to utilise smooth spaces as a means of communication in the service of striated space. It is a vital concern of every State not only to vanquish nomadism but to control migrations and, more generally, to establish a zone of rights over an entire "exterior," over all the flows traversing the ecumenon. (ibid.: 425)

State regulation of 'smooth' space is not irreversible, however; nomads have the potential to deterritorialise the striated space: 'a new nomadic potential has appeared, accompanied by the reconstitution of a smooth space or a manner of being in space as though it were smooth' (Deleuze and Guattari 2004, p. 426). Importantly then, the possibility of nomads disrupting or subverting the annexing of space by the State is opened up, and we are immediately drawn to contemplate how, as teacher educators we can support pre-service teachers in England to learn to be and become teachers in State-regulated space 'as if it was smooth'. And how individual teachers can reclaim control of their professional learning trajectory by privileging their understanding of their knowledge and skills and their perceptions of their personal development needs and aspirations over that articulated for them in the Teachers' Standards (DfE 2012) and the Framework for School Inspection (Ofsted 2013). This tension can be seen to mirror the now familiar debate over the redefining of professionalism. The 'new professionalism', observes Hoyle, is one in which 'status' has ceded to 'improvement in the quality of service' and 'autonomy' has ceded to 'accountability': 'It is implied that enhanced teacher 'status' will flow from a professionalism which adopts managerialism, technological innovation, competition, and rigorous accountability' (Hoyle 2001, p. 148). Evans (2008, p. 21) claims 'The common thread tying these 'new professionalisms' together—and which is the essential basis of their being categorised as 'new'—is generally perceived as a shift of power; whoever used to call the shots no longer does so (or, at least, does so to a lesser extent)'. She draws upon Ozga's (1995, p. 22) 'Critical analyses of professionalism', which 'do not stress the qualities inherent in an occupation but explore the value of the service offered by the members of that occupation to those in power'.

St. Pierre (1997, p. 378) explores this same tension to be found at the interface of nomad and State as she revisits the mental, textual and theoretical spaces in her research, to better understand the methodological problems she faced. Using the image of 'deterritorialisation' she concludes that:

> each researcher will have to struggle in this unintelligible space, taking note of the features of the landscape in order to tell us about the spikes and chasms and rhizomes of the map that precedes her territory. All I can say is that even though disjunction is a place of discomfort, it is also a site of affirmation, since there is the possibility of living differently.

In our endeavour to understand better workplace learning, and how 'living differently' might feel for pre- and in-service teachers, we will return briefly to the questions we posed at the beginning of the chapter: Is it the same work? Is it the same place? Is it the same learning? We will consider these questions in more detail in Chap. 11, but reviewing the evidence already presented we believe that, in England at least, teachers are already 'living differently', and in great need of an alternative and integrated way of conceptualising and articulating their work-place-learning. A 'multiplicity of interrelated practices' shape the 'complex landscape' that is their 'social learning system' (Wenger 2009), and this has become enmeshed in a fluid nexus of global, national and local agendas which have left teachers' experiences of their professional selves increasingly 'split, plural and conflictual' (Stronach et al. 2002, p. 109).

Engeström (2004, p. 145) argues that there is 'a new generation of expertise around, not based on supreme and supposedly stable individual knowledge and ability, but on the capacity of working communities to cross boundaries, negotiate and improvise'. Collaboration in meeting constantly changing challenges of a workplace, which is unstable and even in a 'state of radical discontinuous change', involves an expertise he dubs 'knotworking and expansive learning' and his 'integrative charac-terization' for the new type of expertise is 'collaborative and transformative expertise' (ibid.: 161).

But our nomadic professional not only has to cross boundaries to learn, but in the act of learning also creates boundaries (for others); 'Learning as the production of practice creates boundaries ... because sharing a history of learning ends up distin-guishing those who were involved from those who were not' (Wenger 2009). Such boundaries may not be geographic, but delineate territory and involve individuals working across multiple interacting communities and in serial boundary crossing. Workplace learning thus, takes place in and across different territories, and involves processes of territorialisation, de-territorialisation and colonisation; it helps us 'to open petrified borders, as well as to look for the possibilities of gaps and fissures, and in-between spaces, where learning takes places in usual and discontinuous ways' Kaustuv (2003, p. 13). Understood as a 'nomadic space' such a learning landscape could offer pre- and in-service teachers, and perhaps even teacher educators, a way of thinking about their positioning in respect of the regulatory power of the State that would empower them to reject the victim mentality of the oppressed. Kalmbach Phillips (2002, p. 25) notes that 'While smooth space does not promise "liberty" and is constantly being reversed to striated space, it "always possesses a greater power of deterritorialization than striated" (St. Peirre 1997, p. 369)', and asks:

> How would this be different from the paved, wished-for straight freeways of becoming a teacher, legislated through institutional discourse? Can such a nomadic space exist in a profession guided by national standards, checklists of teacher characteristics, and historically imbued definitions of gender? Is it possible to resist such forces and re-create space within the coded places of the academy where preservice teachers could explore subjectivities as nomads wandering across shifting sands? (ibid.: 25)

Concluding Thoughts

It may be that the very fluidity of the workplace learning landscape in England—where striated and smooth space exist side-by-side, and striated space is relentlessly being rendered smooth and then re-striated—offers our nomad possibilities for en-hanced criticality. If so, such affordances have to be recognised, accepted and traversed, for workplace learning is not always, or even perhaps not usually, part of a structured programme and thus is not always easily discernible. The extent to which learners are inclined or able to adopt a nomadic identity will not only be influ-enced by the structural, social and cultural boundaries inherent in a specific workplace learning environment. They will also be mediated by individuals' past and ongoing formal and informal, structured and unstructured educational experiences, and the extent to which these represent smooth or fractured 'learning territories' (Evans et al. 2006). In enacting their identity as learners in the workplace, new and experienced teachers need to be able to demonstrate agency in order to articulate their specific learning needs and to seek access to relevant knowledge bases and support systems.

This can best be achieved in environments where a symbiotic relationship between the multiple discourses about theory and practice, teaching and learning can be facilitated, and where disciplinary, institutional and professional boundaries are not perceived as restrictive, but as an infra-structure for the facilitation of dialogue as a basis for mutual understanding.

In times of increased government control and surveillance and an all pervasive performativity culture, mentoring and coaching (which we will consider in greater detail later) can perhaps provide one such space: where critical discussion about professional practice and policy can take place freely; where individual, collective and hybrid professional identities can be developed and enacted outside the constraints of tacitly agreed institutional or externally prescribed standards of effective teacher behaviour; where a profession's knowledge base is owned by those who represent it; where 'playing the game' and 'putting on a good show' do not determine the agenda of professional practice; and last but not least, where identifying a concern is recognised as an opportunity to bring about improvement through collaborative action. The unpredictability and diversity of such experiences are aptly captured by Deleuze's and Guattari's (2004) metaphor of the rhizome, which has no specific entry point, no privileging of one access route to learning over another and no one truth to follow.

References

Ashton, D. (2004). The political economy of workplace learning. In H. Rainbird, A. Fuller & A. Munroe (Eds.), *Workplace learning in context* (pp. 21–37). London: Routledge.

Ball, D. (2000). Bridging practices: Intertwining content and pedagogy in teaching and learning to teach. *Journal of Teacher Education, 51*(2), 241–247.

Ball, S. (2001). Performativities and fabrications in the education economy: Towards the performative society. In D. Gleeson & C. Husbands (Eds.), *The performing school: Managing teaching and learning in a performance culture* (pp. 210–226). London: Routledge.

Ball, S. (2003). The teacher's soul and the terrors of performativity. *Journal of Education Policy, 18*(2), 215–228.

Becta. (2008). Get on board next generation learning. www.nextgenerationlearning.org.uk. Accessed 25 June 2008.

Bhabha, H. (1994). *The location of culture*. London: Routledge.

Billett, S. (2001). *Learning in the workplace: Strategies for effective practice*. Sydney: Allen & Unwin.

Billet, S. (2004). Learning through work: Workplace participatory practices. In H. Rainbird, A. Fuller & A. Munroe (Eds.), *Workplace learning in context* (pp. 109–125). London: Routledge.

Brisard, E., Menter, I., & Smith, I. (2005). *Models of partnership in programmes of initial teacher education: A systematic literature review commissioned by the General Teaching Council Scotland*. Edinburgh: General Teaching Council Scotland.

Brown, T., & McNamara, O. (2005). *New teacher identity and regulative government: The discursive formation of primary mathematics teacher education*. New York: Springer.

Brown, T., & McNamara, O. (2011). *Becoming a mathematics teacher: Identity and identifications. Mathematics Education Library*. New York: Springer.

Cairns, L., & Malloch, M. (2011). Theories of work, place and learning: New directions. In M. Malloch, L. Cairns, K. Evans & B. O'Connor (Eds.), *The Sage handbook of workplace learning* (pp. 3–16). London: Sage.

Capel, S., Turner, T., & Leask, M. (Eds). *Learning to teach in the secondary school: a companion to school experience*. (5th edn 2009, 6th edn in press 2013) London: Routledge.

Casey, E. S. (1997). *The fate of place: A philosophical history*. Berkeley: University of California.

Castle, K., Peiser, G., Smith, E. (2013). Teacher development through the masters in teaching and learning: a lost opportunity. *Journal of Education for Teaching, 39*(1), 30–38.

Cochran-Smith, M., & Lytle, S. (1999). Relationships of knowledge and practice: Teacher learning communities. *Review of Research in Education, 24*, 249–305.

Darling-Hammond, L. (1994). Will 21st-century schools really be different? *The Education Digest, 60*, 4–8.

Day, C., Stobart, G., Sammons, P., Kington, A., Qing Gu, Smees, R., & Mujtaba, T. (2006a). Variations in teachers' work, lives and effectiveness. Research Report RR743. London: DfES. http://dera.ioe.ac.uk/6405/1/rr743.pdf. Accessed 2 Oct 2012.

Day, C. W., Kington, A., Stobart, G., & Sammons, P. (2006b). The personal and professional selves of teachers: Stable and unstable identities. *British Educational Research Journal, 34*(4), 601–616.

Day, C., Sammons, P., Gu, Q., Kington, A., & Stobart, G. (2008). Committed for life? Variations in teachers' work, lives and effectiveness. *Journal of Educational Change, 9*(3), 243–260.

DCSF. (2008). *Being the best for our children: Releasing talent for teaching and learning*. Nottingham: DCSF Publications (DCSF-00246-2008)

Deleuze, G., & Guattari, F. (2004). *A thousand plateaus: Capitalism and schizophrenia (B. Massumi, Trans.)*. Minneapolis: University of Minnesota Press. (Original work published 1980 copyright 1987).

DfE. (2010). *The importance of teaching: Schools white paper 2010*. London: DfE.

DfE. (2011a). The school workforce in England: November 2011. www.education.gov.uk/rsgateway/DB/SFR/s001062/sfr06-2012v7.pdf. Accessed 2 Oct 2012.

DfE. (2011b). Hundreds of teachers awarded national scholarships. www.education.gov.uk/inthenews/inthenews/a00200774/hundreds-of-teachers-awarded-national-scholarships. Accessed 2 Oct 2012.

DfE. (2012). Teachers' standards. London: DfE. https://www.education.gov.uk/publications/eOrderingDownload/teachers%20standards.pdf. Accessed 10 Oct 2012.

DfES. (2004). *Every child matters. Green Paper*. London: Department for Employment and Skills.

Earl, L., Watson, N., Levin, B., Leithwood, K., Fullan, M., Torrance, N., Jantzi, D., Mascal, B., & Volante, L. (2003). *Watching learning 3, final report of the external evaluation of England's National Literacy and Numeracy Strategies*. Toronto: Ontario Institute for Studies in Education, University of Toronto (OISE, UT).

Engeström, Y. (1999). Activity theory and individual and social transformation. In Y. Engeström, R. Miettinen & R. Punamaki (Eds.), *Perspectives on activity theory* (pp. 19–38). Cambridge: Cambridge University Press.

Engeström, Y. (2001). Expansive learning at work: Towards an activity-theoretical reconceptualization. *Journal of Education and Work, 14*(1), 133–156.

Engeström, Y. (2004). The new generation of expertise: Seven theses. In H. Rainbird, A. Fuller & A. Munroe (Eds), *Workplace learning in context* (pp. 145–165). London: Routledge.

Engeström, Y. (2011). Activity theory and learning at work. In M. Malloch, L. Cairns, K. Evans & B. O'Connor (Eds.), *The Sage handbook of workplace learning* (pp. 86–104). London: Sage.

Eraut, M. (2004). Transfer of knowledge between education and workplace settings. In H. Rainbird, A. Fuller & A. Munroe (Eds), *Workplace learning in context* (pp. 201–221). London: Routledge.

Evans, K., & Kersh, N. (2006). *Adults learning in, for and through the workplace: The significance of biography and experience*. Paper presented at the British Educational Research Association Annual Conference, University of Warwick, 6–9 September 2006.

Evans, K., Hodkinson, P., Rainbird, H., & Unwin, L. (2006). *Improving workplace learning.* London: Routledge.

Evans, L. (2008). Professionalism, professionality and the development of education professionals. *British Journal of Educational Studies, 56*(1), 20–38.

Frankham, J., & Hiett, S. (2011). The Master's in teaching and learning: Expanding utilitarianism in the continuing professional development of teachers in England. *Journal of Education Policy, 26*(6), 803–818.

Fuller, A., & Unwin, L. (2003). Learning as apprentices in the contemporary UK workplace: Creating and managing expansive and restrictive participation. *Journal of Education and Work, 16*(4), 407–426.

Fuller, A., & Unwin, L. (2004). Expansive learning environment integrating organizational and personal development. In H. Rainbird, A. Fuller & A. Munroe (Eds.), *Workplace learning in context* (pp. 126–144). London: Routledge.

Fuller, A., Munro, A., & Rainbird, H. (2004). Introduction and overview. In H. Rainbird, A. Fuller & A. Munroe (Eds.), *Workplace learning in context* (pp. 1–13). London: Routledge.

Fuller, A., Hodkinson, H., Hodkinson, P., & Unwin, L. (2005). Learning as peripheral participation in communities of practice: A reassessment of key concepts in workplace learning. *British Educational Research Journal, 31*(1), 49–68.

Fuller, A., Unwin, L., Felstead, A., Jewson, N., & Kakavelakis, K. (2007). Creating and using knowledge: An analysis of the differentiated nature of workplace learning environments. *British Educational Research Journal, 33*(5), 743–759.

Furlong, J. (1996). Do student teachers need higher education? In J. Furlong & R. Smith (Eds.), *The role of higher education in initial teacher education* (pp. 151–165). London: Kogan Page.

Gadamer, H.-G. (2004). *Truth and Method. 2nd revised edn.* London: Continuum International Publishing Group.

Galton, M. (1995). *Crisis in the primary classroom.* London: David Fulton.

Giddens, A. (1984). *The constitution of society.* Cambridge: Polity Press.

Gove, M. (2010). Speech to the annual conference of the National College for Leadership of Schools and Children's Services. Birmingham, 16 June. http://www.education.gov.uk/news/news/nationalcollege. Accessed 12 July 2012.

Gove, M. (2012) Tough exams and rote learning inspires pupils. www.theweek.co.uk/uk-news/50095/gove-tough-exams-and-rote-learning-help-inspire-students#ixzz2DGbwlHav. Accessed 12 Oct 2012.

Gutiérrez, K., Rymes, B., & Larson, J. (1995). Script, counterscript, and underlife in the classroom: James Brown versus Brown v. Board of Education. *Harvard Educational Review, 65,* 445–471.

Gutiérrez, K., Baquedano-López, P., & Turner, M. G. (1997). Putting language back into language arts: When the radical middle meets the third space. *Language Arts, 74,* 368–378.

Gutiérrez, K., Baquedano-López, P., & Tejeda, C. (1999). Rethinking diversity: Hybridity and hybrid language practices in the third space. *Mind, Culture, and Activity, 6*(4), 286–303.

Hager, P. (2004). The conceptualization and measurement of learning at work. In H. Rainbird, A. Fuller & A. Munroe (Eds.), *Workplace learning in context* (pp. 242–258). London: Routledge.

Hager, P. (2011). Theories of workplace learning. In M. Malloch, L. Cairns, K. Evans & B. O'Connor (Eds.), *The Sage handbook of workplace learning* (pp. 17–31). London: Sage.

Harrison, S., & Dourish, P. (1996). *Re-place-ing space: The roles of space and place in collaborative systems.* Proceedings of CSCW '96 (pp. 67–76). New York: ACM.

Harvey, D. (1989). *The condition of postmodernity: An enquiry into the origins of cultural change.* Oxford: Blackwell.

Helsby, G. (1999). *Changing teachers' work: The 'reform' of secondary schooling.* London: Taylor Francis.

Hobson, A., Malderez, A., Tracey, L., Giannakaki, M., Pell, R., Kerr, K., Chambers, G., Tomlinson, P., & Roper, T. (2006). Becoming a teacher: Student teachers' experiences of initial teacher training in England. *Research Report* RR744. London: DfEE. www.education.gov.uk/publications/eOrderingDownload/RR744.pdf. Accessed 2 Oct 2012.

Hobson, A., Malderez, A., Tracey, L., Ashby, P., Mitchell, N., McIntyre, J., Cooper, D., Roper, T., Chambers, G., & Tomlinson, P. (2009). *Becoming a teacher: Teachers' experiences of initial teacher training, induction and early professional development.* Research Report DCSF RR115. London: DCSF. www.education.gov.uk/publications/eOrderingDownload/DCSF-RR115.pdf. Accessed 2 Oct 2012.

Hodkinson, H., & Hodkinson, P. (2005). Improving schoolteachers' workplace learning. *Research Papers in Education, 20*(2), 109–131.

Holland, J., Gordon, T., & Lahelma, E. (2007). Temporal, spatial and embodied relations in the teacher's day at school. *Ethnography and Education, 2*(2), 221–237.

Holyoake, J. (1993). Initial teacher training—the French view. *Journal of Education for Teaching, 19*(2), 215–226.

Hoyle, E. (1974). Professionality, professionalism and control in teaching. *London Education Review, 3*(2), 13–19.

Hoyle, E. (2001). Teaching: Prestige, status and esteem. *Educational Management & Administration, 29*(2), 139–152.

Hunter, I. (1994). *Rethinking the school.* St. Leonards, New South Wales: Allen and Unwin

Ingersoll, R. (2003). *Who controls teachers' work? Power and accountability in America's schools.* Cambridge: Harvard University Press.

Kalmbach Phillips, D. (2002). Female preservice teachers' talk: Illustrations of subjectivity, visions of 'nomadic' space. *Teachers and Teaching: Theory and practice, 8*(1), 9–27.

Kaustuv, R. (2003). *Teachers in nomadic spaces: Deleuze and Curriculum.* New York: Peter Lang.

Kersh, N., Waite, E., & Evans, K. (2011). *The spatial dimensions of skills for life workplace provision.* Centre for learning and life chances in knowledge economies and societies, Research Paper 24. www.llakes.org. Accessed 12 July 2012.

Kozleski, E. (2011). Dialectical practices in education: Creating third space in the education of teachers. *Teacher Education and Special Education, 34*(3), 250–259.

Lave, J., & Wenger, E. (1991). *Situated learning.* Cambridge: Cambridge University Press.

Lisahunter, Rossi, T., Tinning, R., Flanagan, E., & Macdonald, D. (2011). Professional learning places and spaces: the staffroom as a site for beginning teacher induction and transition. *Asia-Pacific Journal of Teacher Education, 39*(1), 33–46.

Maguire, M. (2000). Inside/outside the ivory tower: Teacher education in the English academy. *Teaching in Higher Education, 5*(2), 149–165.

Mahony, P., & Hextall, I. (1998). Social justice and the reconstruction of teaching. *Journal of Education Policy, 13*(4), 545–558.

Malloch, M., Cairns, L., Evans, K., & O'Connor, B. (2011). *The Sage handbook of workplace learning.* London: Sage.

Mayhew, K., & Keep, E. (1999). The assessment: Education, training and economic performance. *Oxford Review of Economic Policy, 4*(3), 1–15.

McGregor, J. (2003). Making spaces: Teacher workplace topologies. *Pedagogy, Culture and Society., 11*(3), 353–377.

McKinsey, &C. (2007). How the world's best-performing school systems come out on top. London: McKinsey. www.mckinsey.com/locations/UK_Ireland/Publications.aspx Accessed 10 Oct 2012

McNally, J., Blake, A., & Reid, A. (2009). The informal learning of new teachers in school. *Journal of Workplace Learning, 21*(4), 322–333.

McNamara, O. (Ed.) (2002). *Becoming an evidence-based practitioner.* London: Routledge Falmer.

McNamara, O., Roberts, L., Basit, T., & Brown, T. (2002). Rites of passage in initial teacher training: Ritual, performance, ordeal and numeracy skills tests. *British Educational Research Journal, 28*(6), 861–876.

Moje, E. B., McIntosh-Ciechanowski, K., Ellis, L., Carrillo, R., & Collazo, T. (2004). Working toward third space in content area literacy: An examination of everyday funds of knowledge and discourse. *Reading Research Quarterly, 39*(1), 38–70.

Munby, H., Russell, T., & Martin, A. K. (2001). Teachers' knowledge and how it develops. In V. Richardson (Ed.), *Handbook of research on teaching* (4th ed, pp. 877–904). Washington, DC: American Educational Research Association.

Murray, J., Jones, M., McNamara, O., & Stanley, G. (2011). The Teacher Education Research Network (TERN): Building research capacity in the North West Region of England. ESRC Project Final Report: RES-069-25-0008. Swindon: ESRC.

National College for School Leadership. (2012). *System leadership prospectus*. London: National College.

Ofsted. (2013). The framework for school inspection. www.ofsted.gov.uk/resources/framework-for-school-inspection-january-2012. Accessed 22 Dec 2012.

Ozga, J. (1995). Deskilling a profession: Professionalism, deprofessionalisation and the new managerialism. In H. Busher & R. Saran (Eds.), *Managing teachers as professionals in schools* (pp. 21–38). London: Kogan Page.

Philips, D., & Ochs, K. (2004). Researching policy borrowing: Some methodological challenges in comparative education. *British Educational Research Journal, 30*(6), 773–784.

Power, M. (1994). *The audit explosion*. London: Demos.

Power, M. (1997). *The audit society: Rituals of verification*. Oxford: Oxford University Press.

Prensky, M. (2001). Digital native, digital immigrants. *On the Horizon, 9*(5), 1–6.

Rainbird, H., Fuller, A., & Munro, A. (2004a). *Workplace learning in context*. London: Routledge.

Rainbird, A., Munro, A., & Holly, L. (2004b). The employment relationship and workplace learning. In H. Rainbird, A. Fuller & A. Munro (Eds.), *Workplace learning in context* (pp. 38–53). London: Routledge.

Salisbury, J., & Morris, K. (2012). *Beyond the border: Perspectives on teacher education in Wales*. Paper presented at the UCET Annual Conference, November.

Sammons, P., Day, C., Kington, A., Gu, Q., Stobart, G., & Smees, R. (2007). Exploring variations in teachers' work, lives and their effects on pupils: Key findings and implications from a longitudinal mixed-method study. *British Educational Research Journal., 33*(5), 681–701.

Schleicher, A. (Ed.) (2012). Preparing teachers and developing school leaders for the 21st century: Lessons from around the World. OECD Publishing. http://dx.doi.org/10.1787/9789264xxxxxx-en. Accessed 10 Oct 2012.

Schön, D. (1987). *Educating the reflective practitioner*. San Francisco: Jossey Bass.

Schultze, U., & Boland, R. J. Jr (2000). Place, space and knowledge work: A study of outsourced computer systems administrators. *Accounting, Management and Information Technologies, 10*, 187–219.

Sfard, A. (1998). On two metaphors for learning and the dangers of choosing just one. *Educational Researcher, 27*(2), 4–13.

Shulman, L. (1986). Those who understand: Knowledge growth in teaching. *Educational Researcher, 15*(2), 4–31.

Shulman, L. (1987). Knowledge and teaching: Foundations of the new reform. *Harvard Educational Review, 57*(1), 1–22.

Shulman, L. (2005). Signature pedagogies in the professions. *Daedalus, 134*(3), 52–59.

Soja, E. (1996). *Thirdspace: Journeys to Los Angeles and other real-and-imagined places*. Oxford: Wiley Blackwell.

Stronach, I. (1996). Fashioning post-modernism, finishing modernism: Tales from the fitting room. *British Educational Research Journal, 22*, 359–375.

Stronach, I., Corbin, B., McNamara, O., Stark, S., & Warne, T. (2002). Towards an uncertain politics of professionalism: Teacher and nurse identities in flux. *Journal of Educational Policy, 17*(1), 109–138.

St. Pierre, E. (1997). Nomadic inquiry in the smooth spaces of the field: A preface. *International Journal of Qualitative Studies in Education, 10*(3), 365–383.

Troman, G. (1996). The rise of the new professionals: The restructuring of primary teachers' work and professionalism. *British Journal of Sociology of Education, 17*(4), 473–487.

Vygotsky, L. S. (1978). *Mind in society: The development of higher psychological processes.* Cambridge: Harvard University Press.

Wahlstedt, A., Pekkola, S., & Niemela, M. (2008). From e-learning space to e-learning place. *British Journal of Educational Technology, 39*(6), 1020–1030.

Webb, R. (Ed.) (2006). *Changing teaching and learning in the primary school.* London: Open University Press.

Webb, R., & Vulliamy, G. (2006). *Coming full circle? The impact of new labour's education policies.* London: ATL.

Webb, R., & Vulliamy, G. (2008). *'On a treadmill' but 'the kids are great': Primary teachers' work and wellbeing.* London: ATL.

Wenger, E. (1999). *Communities of practice: Learning, meaning, and identity.* Cambridge: Cambridge University Press.

Wenger, E. (2009). Communities of practice and social learning systems: The career of a concept. http://wenger-trayner.com/resources/publications/cops-and-learning-systems/. Accessed 10 Oct 2012.

Zeichner, K. (2010). Rethinking the connections between campus courses and field experiences in college- and university-based teacher education. *Journal of Teacher Education, 61*, 89–99.

Chapter 2
Developing a Multi-Layered System of Distributed Expertise: What does Cultural Historical Theory Bring to Understandings of Workplace Learning in School-University Partnerships?

Ann Childs, Anne Edwards and Jane McNicholl

Introduction

Teaching is difficult and learning to teach in the public arena of classrooms is extraordinarily difficult. There is no safety net for the pre-service teacher, no opportunity to be tentative, and huge risk of witnessed failure. Not the least of the flaws in an apprenticeship model of teacher education, as currently seen, is that pre-service teachers very rarely work alongside more expert professionals while attempting to teach in classrooms (Edwards and Collison 1996; Edwards and Protheroe 2003, 2004). One may then wonder whether teacher education would be better described as workplace performance rather than workplace learning.

In England, the development of a coherent response to these flaws has been inhibited by a discourse marked by aggression and defensiveness. The aggression has come from those involved in teacher education policy who point to the weaknesses of a model of professional learning which, they wrongly believe, relies on the simple application of research-based knowledge to practices by those who are novices in the practices. The defensiveness comes from university-based teacher educators who are doing all they can to ensure that learning through participation in school practices aligns with training expectations such as achieving the standards needed for qualification (Ellis et al. 2012). The battle-lines were drawn over 20 years ago (DfE 1992, 1993), and skirmishes between teacher educators and policy-makers have continued with almost every new Secretary of State for Education ever since.

A. Childs (✉) · A. Edwards · J. McNicholl
Department of Education, University of Oxford,
Oxford, UK
e-mail: ann.childs@education.ox.ac.uk

A. Edwards
e-mail: anne.edwards@education.ox.ac.uk

J. McNicholl
e-mail: jane.mcnicholl@education.ox.ac.uk

O. McNamara et al. (eds.), *Workplace Learning in Teacher Education,*   29
Professional Learning and Development in Schools and Higher Education 10,
DOI 10.1007/978-94-007-7826-9_2, © Springer Science+Business Media Dordrecht 2014

In part the impasse has arisen because the pre-service teacher education university-school partnership arrangements set up in the early 1990s happened too rapidly, without a fundamental questioning of whether the existing institutional structures were fit for the new purposes. Consequently, even the most robust partnerships can resemble marriages of convenience that are politely held together without any fundamental questioning of their bases. The recent Work of Teacher Education study (Ellis et al. 2012, under review) has shown that the paper over the cracks in the partnerships that were established in the early 1990s—and which were described in the 1990s Modes of Teacher Education study (Furlong et al. 2000)—is wearing thin. Meanwhile, the only alternative to these kinds of partnership that is available in public discourse is the self-improving school system (Hargreaves 2011), which has little place for university involvement. We therefore suggest that it is time to pick up the challenge that should have been given to university-based English teacher educators in 1992, and examine how we might help build learning environments that draw on the strengths of both universities and schools to create thinking, decision-making professionals.

To that end we are currently, with local schools, developing what we are describing ambitiously as a multi-layered system of distributed expertise and a new version of partnership. The layers are research, continuing professional learning and pre-service teacher education; and the expertise is that to be found both in schools and across the university. One of the origins of the initiative lies in Burn, Childs and McNicholl's delving into the black box into which pre-service teachers disappear when on school practice (Burn et al. 2007; Childs et al. in press). In the process they uncovered what and how pre-service teachers learned while interacting with teachers in humanities and science departments, in what Britzman describes as behind-the-scenes work (Britzman 1986). Their studies have revealed a hitherto hidden, but fascinating, picture of the pedagogic expertise that was distributed across some of the departments, and how the pre-service teachers in those departments were, at times, able to recognise, draw on it and contribute to it. It therefore made sense to us to increase opportunities for university-based staff to enter, and perhaps enrich, those conversations to strengthen the learning opportunities available to pre-service teachers and those who support them. At the same time, closer links with practices in schools would allow the pedagogic research undertaken by university-based colleagues to be more strongly connected with the purposes and anticipations of practitioners (Edwards et al. 2007).

Stimulated by that research, and our consequent intention to work even more closely with schools, we have begun to reconceptualise pre-service teacher education in what we are calling an Education Deanery, and are drawing on a strong theory of learning to do so. The theory is the configuration of approaches that gather under the label of 'cultural historical' understandings of learning and practice, which draw their inspiration from Vygotsky's research in Moscow in the 1920s and early 1930s. At their core is the recognition of a dialectic between learner and learning environment: we are shaped by the practices we inhabit, but also shape them. But this is no simple notion of person-context interaction. These dialectical relationships stretch, as Lave puts it, 'among semiotic systems, social structure and political economy'

Table 2.1 Planes of analysis (after Hedegaard 2012)

Entity	Process	Dynamic
Society	Political economy	Societal needs/conditions
Institution	Practice	Values/motives/objectives
Activity setting	Activity/situation (with potential for individual learning)	Motivation/demands
Person	Actions (learning arising from individual engagement in the activity)	Motive/intentions

(Lave 1988, p. 187). The re-thinking is therefore radical, and we hope far more productive than the skirmishes that have shaped teacher education of late.

Lave's cultural analysis arose from her study of cognition in everyday practices, where she observed that cognition is 'distributed—stretched over, not divided among—mind, body, activity and culturally organized settings (which include other actors)' (Lave 1988, p. 1). The argument underpinning the multi-layered system of distributed expertise that we are to discuss, is that interventions to enhance pre-service teachers' learning should be at the level of workplace practice. We also recognise that intervening and reshaping practices cannot be done independently of broader institutional concerns, therefore connections need to be based on the mutual aligning of at least some institutional purposes across organisational boundaries. Indeed, because of the intertwining of semiotic systems, social structure and political economy, any intervention may have a better chance of success if it occurs when social structures and political economies are being disrupted.

Current Disturbances and Disruptions in Teacher Education

Hedegaard's modelling of the relationships between societal purposes and values, institutional practices, activities in activity settings and personal actions helps explain the importance of timing. Like Lave, Hedegaard has taken a cultural analysis as her starting point and recognises the need to capture the connections and discrepancies in these relationships. Also like Lave, her focus is practices and how people think and act in the activities that constitute them. What she adds to Lave's analysis is a strong focus on motives at the analytic levels of society, institution, activity setting and person.

Table 2.1 is a slight adaptation of the analytic heuristic Hedegaard offers for studying children's learning within different practices. We suggest that it is an equally useful heuristic for examining pre-service teachers' workplace learning and considering when, where, how and why changes in the infrastructure of teacher education should occur. The responses to these questions are, of course, interlinked. For example, we may argue that we need changes in institutional practices to place *strong outcomes for pre-service teacher education* as a core value for schools so that school practices are, in part, shaped by the motive of creating the next generation of practitioners.

But, as Table 2.1 indicates, unless societal conditions are conducive to these motives, placing pre-service teacher education centrally in school practices may be experienced as going against the grain.

Relevant changes at the societal level are currently happening. Boundaries around schools are being disrupted to encourage school leaders to think systemically about professional learning and capacity building. Recently, policy-makers have consistently pointed to the apparent advantages of school-based routes into teaching. Michael Gove, the English Secretary of State for Education, bases his argument for school-based teacher education on the belief that:

> Teaching is a craft and it is best learnt as an apprentice observing a master craftsman or woman. Watching others, and being rigorously observed yourself as you develop, is the best route to acquiring mastery in the classroom. (Gove 2010)

Though, as we have observed, that kind of classroom-centred apprenticeship rarely happens.

In November 2011, the English government's teacher education implementation plan—'Training our Next Generation of Outstanding Teachers' (DfE 2011)—outlined how the shift to school-led, school-based teacher education would be achieved. School Direct is a new route into teaching which allows schools to select their own trainees and employ them at the end of the one-year training. School Direct (salaried) has also been introduced to replace an earlier, also salaried, Graduate Training Programme. Alongside School Direct, a network of Teaching Schools is being created with a focus on continuing professional learning. The intention is that it 'will lead the school system in training and developing outstanding teachers' (DfE 2011, p. 12).The implementation plan indicates that there will be 100 Teaching Schools in 2011/2012, rising to '500 schools and their alliances by 2014/2015' (ibid.: 12). The DfE website describes them as follows:

> Teaching schools give outstanding schools a leading role in the training and professional development of teachers, support staff and head teachers, as well as contributing to the raising of standards through school-to-school support. (DfE website: www.education.gov.uk/ nationalcollege/index/support-for-schools/teachingschools.htm).

The government is locating responsibilities for continuing professional learning in collaborations between Teaching Schools and academies. Nick Gibb, a recent Minister for Schools, explained the vision as follows:

> [b]y encouraging school-led professional development, we believe schools can strengthen the bonds that exist between them and allow for more opportunities for teachers and schools to collaborate with each other. So, more freedom, more and better professional development, and more collaboration. (Gibb 2011a)

The involvement of universities, professional associations and other bodies, currently involved in continuing professional learning in England, appears limited. Gibb (2011b) elaborated on the kinds of collaborations to be emulated:

> Many schools in the independent sector have already established successful partnerships with neighbouring institutions through the Independent State School Partnership scheme. And we want that sort of collaboration to continue through the new national network of

Teaching Schools; our Education Endowment Fund; and the National and Local Leaders of Education programme. (Gibb 2011b)

We agree that systemic approaches to teachers' professional learning are worthwhile, but can be limited by a reliance on what Huberman described as closed collective cycles, where the same knowledge is merely recycled (Huberman 1995). We are also concerned that the versions of systemic change we have briefly outlined are not premised on an understanding of the practices that comprise the systems of schooling, or how learning occurs in them. In the context of the policy churn that is reshaping the conditions of teachers' professional learning, (the first row under the headings in Table 2.1), we shall attempt to make visible the part to be played by university-based partners in workplace elements of pre-service teacher education.

Starting with Practices

The 'why' and 'how' of pre-service teachers' learning, within a broad notion of a locally collaborating education system, is a major strand in our discussion. Pursuing it has involved examining the semiotics of the situations in which pre-service teachers learn and the discursive environments that are conducive to learning. Our way into the why and how of teachers' learning is a conceptual analysis of what happens in the activities that appear to promote learning, and which are part of the institutional practices that teachers, at all stages of their career, inhabit. From that analysis we shall present evidence from studies we have undertaken to examine how university-school relationships may be reconfigured within a more systemic notion of teachers' professional learning.

Let us therefore start by clarifying how, with reference to Table 2.1, we are using the term practice. One of us has elsewhere described practices as '... [h]istorically accumulated, knowledge-laden, emotionally freighted and given direction by what is valued by those who inhabit them' (Edwards 2010, p. 5). Institutions, like schools and families, are made up of practices which value some knowledge over others, help shape identities and sense of belonging, and have purposes such as good examination results or being politically aware. What matters, i.e. the knowledge, values and motives in these practices, are made visible in the activities that take place within them, such as a teacher's planning meeting or a family's conversation over breakfast. The actions that occur during these activities give insight into the purposes of the activities, and in turn those of the institutional practices. The semiotics of the particular situation therefore open up the wider practice for scrutiny (Mäkitalo 2003, 2006).

Our concern is not simply to observe and report, but to consider how learning might be enabled, as people engage in activities in workplace practices. Cultural historical theory can help here. Vygotsky's learner is agentic in an important way: she or he works on and with what Vygotsky described as the social situation of their development. Writing of the social situation of development in the terms of children and their learning, Vygotsky described it as '[a] system of relations between a child of a given age and social reality' (Vygotsky 1998, p. 199). These relations are built as a learner takes forward her or his intentions, but they are also shaped by the possibilities for interpretation and action in any setting. There is, therefore, a dynamic that is sustained over time in which the learner engages in activities and creates and recreates his or her relationship with the practices in which the activities are located. Van Huizen, van Oers and Wubbels, in their analyses of a Vygotskian teacher education, refer to Leont'ev's notion of that relationship as a 'middle link' which mediates the 'connection of subject and world' (van Huizen et al. 2005, p. 271), and point to how the link positions person and practices as mutually constituting.

The dynamic tension between the agency of the learner and the affordances of the practice, as played out in each activity, is where learning occurs. The intentional agency of the beginning teacher needs to be sustained if she or he is to work on and with the system of relations they are building within school practices; whether practices are conducive to the exercise of that agency therefore becomes a crucial concern. We have long known from studies of early child development (Lewis and Brooks-Gunn 1979; Trevarthen 1977) that even young children are intentional and approach activities with the purpose of having an impact of some kind. Indeed, Vygotsky talked of learning as being a cycle of internalisation and externalisation, i.e. we not only take in, but act on what matters in our worlds.

But we should not downplay the part played by practices in this dynamic. Recently, Hedegaard has elaborated the cultural historical learning dialectic and argued that we should shift our attention from a primary focus on how development arises from a child's needs, and recognise more fundamentally the importance of the demands that practices make on learners (Hedegaard 2012). From this perspective the demands and affordances of practices, as recognised by the learner, become central to understanding learning. We suggest that, in teacher education, the practice which is making the demands on the pre-service teacher should be the practice of being a teacher; rather than the practice of being a student teacher. This suggestion is an important element in our case for rethinking pre-service teacher education partnerships. Our argument is that, in order to increase the demands on teachers and provoke and promote their learning, we need to attend to the demands that within-school practices make on them as teachers who are also learners. It then follows that interventions in school work practices, their demands and affordances, can be helpful in enabling social situations of development through which pre-service teachers can move forward in learning to be teachers.

As we have already indicated, pre-service teachers need to be receptive to the demands in practices, recognise and respond to them. At this point, cultural historical approaches to learning help us to see one of several possible roles for university-based teacher educators in preparing pre-service teachers for recognising and working with the resources for learning that are available to them in school practices. One of the main arguments against university-based teacher education has been the weak validity of notions of the application of university-acquired knowledge while working in schools (Hagger and McIntyre 2006). Researchers in the cultural historical field would agree with these criticisms, and would instead argue that we need to think more clearly in terms of peoples' transitions between settings (Beach 1999, 2001);

enabling pattern-seeking and recognition across settings (Greeno 1997, 2006) and developing an outward looking mind which is attuned to recognising the resources for action in a setting (Edwards et al. 2002). These alternative and compatible views of how knowledge moves and filters interpretations of the potential for action across the boundaries of settings, mean that university-based teacher educators need to prepare pre-service teachers for pattern-seeking and the use of the resources that will support their intentional actions when they make the transition from university to the workplace and back again. Teacher educators' familiarity with school practices is, we suggest, an essential pre-requisite for that role; and entering the black box of school practices is a fruitful way of gaining that familiarity.

In making the case for focusing on and intervening in school practices, we are therefore not suggesting that all teacher education should take place in schools. Indeed, we agree with Goodlad when he wrote of the role of teacher education in ratcheting up pre-service teachers' everyday understandings of what goes on in schools (Goodlad 1990). The Vygotskian cultural historical line adds to Goodlad's arguments with a particularly strong focus on the importance of language in re-fining everyday situated understandings so that they become more powerful and generalisable concepts that guide and regulate actions in activities.

Vygotsky, for example, argued that '[I]nternal regulation of goal-directed activity arises initially from external regulation' (Vygotsky 1999, p. 63), i.e. our actions become goal-directed and self-regulated through the use of language and the concepts carried in it. Recognising that, in the case of young children, the initial act takes place before the child knows how to describe it and control it, he observes that '[t]he act is usually overvalued to the detriment of the word' (ibid: 65). For Vygotsky, language is the primary tool with which we can regulate our relations with the practices we inhabit and create a productive social situation of development. He went on to argue that the effective use of language as a tool for regulating intentional action requires the ability to abstract from situations in order to begin to generalise and make meaning. It follows from this analysis of language and self-regulation that teacher education needs to include the opportunity for abstraction, for pattern-seeking and for looking beyond experiences of the everyday situated practices which the novice is navigating and trying to make sense of.

But, we suggest, it also needs to do more than that. It needs, as Goodlad also observed, to make visible and hold up for scrutiny the motives and values that shape the professional practices of teachers. As Vygotsky explained, '[t]he sense of the words is changed by the motive' (Vygotsky 1997, p. 136), i.e. by the orientation that we take to the phenomenon under discussion and our intentions in working with it. By understanding the motive, the 'why' of practice, scrutinising the purposes of our actions and those of others, we can achieve a conceptual distance that allows for self-regulation and purposeful action. It is not easy to do this and our experience as teacher educators over decades has demonstrated that beginning teachers need help in achieving that distance.

More recently, Wertsch has suggested to us that the explicit form of mediation we have just described, in terms of guided and demanding reflection on practices, is only one of the ways that learners are introduced to what is valued in a practice.

He proposes that we should attend also to what he calls 'implicit' mediation. He describes it in the following way:

'[i]t is part of an already ongoing communicative stream that is brought into contact with other forms of action' and it involves 'signs, especially natural language . . . (which) are not purposefully introduced into human action, and they do not initially emerge for the purpose of organizing it. Instead, they are part of a preexisiting, independent stream of communicative action that becomes integrated with other forms of goal directed behaviour.' (Wertsch 2007, pp. 180–181)

Wertsch's signalling of the potential mediational power of everyday talk in activities returns us once more to the importance of teacher educators' engagement with the everyday practices of schools. As we hope is already clear, we are not suggesting, as Wertsch appears to be doing, that simple immersion in the communication stream will lead to learning to be an informed teacher. We would instead agree with Derry's critique of Wertsch, that being part of the flow of everyday communication is not enough to guarantee learning. Derry's argument is that learning occurs best when learners are involved in making judgements which are tested within a system of inferences that constitutes the meaning systems they are engaging with.

[a] Vygotskian approach doesn't depend simply on individuals being placed in the required environment where they discover meaning for themselves. The learning environment must be designed and cannot rely on the spontaneous response to an environment which is not constructed according to, or involves, some clearly worked out conceptual framework. For Vygotsky concepts depend for their meaning on the system of judgements (inferences) within which they are disclosed. (Derry 2008, pp. 60–61)

Drawing on Brandom (1994, 2000), Derry suggests that making claims and asking for reasons enables learners to access the meaning making that is valued in the discourse in which they are participating. Her explanation of Vygotsky's concern with learning as a growing understanding of the inferences that comprise currently accepted meaning, not only has strong implications for how pupils are engaged as learners; it also connects with our argument for stronger teacher education engagement in the practices of schooling. That engagement, we suggest, has the potential to enable specialist teacher educators to weave research-based knowledge into the ongoing communicative stream to be found in schools and departments, and to sustain ways of interacting that privilege the making of claims and the asking for and giving of reasons.

Our analyses therefore lead us to proposing a dual strand approach to pre-service teacher education. The approach requires specialist teacher educators to hold fast to their role in guided reflection and abstraction from the everyday; but also to reframe how they work in schools to support teacher education more broadly. It is the latter that is the focus of what follows in this chapter. Our premise for a broadly systemic approach to teacher education and professional learning is that the values and motives that shape the practices of university-based teacher education and school-based teaching differ little. Indeed the proponents of transferring all teacher education to schools would agree, and suggest therefore that specialist university-based teacher education is unnecessary. That is not our argument; instead we suggest that working with similar 'whys' is a strength which enables alignments of institutional purposes.

These alignments mean that interventions in practices are able to go with the grain of school purposes, while at the same time offering moments of disruption that raise questions and open up language and intentions to scrutiny.

Sustained attention to the 'why' of teaching and therefore teacher education is, we believe, central to recognising teaching as a profession. Evetts, writing generally about the public sector professions, distinguishes between organisational profession-alism and occupational professionalism, with the former orientated to monitoring and controlling professional work and the latter led by the professions, knowledge, values, relationships (Evetts 2009). We suggest that weaving these aspects of pro-fessionalism into the system of relationships that are created between the beginning teacher and the reality of the workplace is one of the crucial roles of the professional teacher educator.

This analysis has focused on pre-service teacher education, but also runs right through the multi-layered system of distributed expertise that we are currently devel-oping, informing the development of continuing professional learning and research relationships as well. Van Huizen and his colleagues concluded their account of a Vygotskian perspective on teacher education with the following challenge.

> Implementing a Vygotskian perspective on teacher education will put demands on the environment in which trainees will be training and teaching.... and with a view to im-plementation, the theoretical approach in this paper will need elaboration into a research programme centred on the relation between a pedagogy supporting the professional de-velopment of trainee teachers and the institutional conditions that have to be fulfilled for realizing such a pedagogy. (Van Huizen et al. 2005, p. 285)

In the rest of this chapter we discuss the first stages in a programme that aims at creating the institutional conditions for such a pedagogy.

The Evidence Base

The arguments we have made so far have been based on a cultural historical reading of what is required if we are to present a coherent response to some of the weaknesses in teacher education we indicated earlier. The evidence base we are drawing on in making these arguments is: a completed series of studies on the learning that occurs in humanities and science departments (Burn et al. 2007; McNicholl and Childs 2010); and an ongoing study of what teachers and teacher educators expect from the multi-layered system of distributed expertise that we are developing. In addition, we draw on evidence from two demonstration interventions: an intervention in a school science department where we are interweaving research, continuing professional learning and pre-service teacher education; and a series of action research based learning sets alongside teachers in schools which are part of our pre-service teacher education partnership. We first outline the Department Study and then the demonstration project that builds on it. We next describe the Deanery Implementation Research Project and summarise a demonstration project that is supporting that development. We then assess what we are learning from these initiatives in order to create the institutional conditions for a pedagogy for teachers' professional learning that privileges teacher agency and continuous learning in the workplace.

The Department Study The data to be discussed in this chapter were gathered during one stage of a three-year departmentally funded study of interactions in science and humanities department staff rooms (Burn et al. 2007; Childs et al. in press). In the stage of the study under discussion, the first and third author spent two weeks in each of two secondary school science departments which had, over several years, proved to be particularly supportive to pre-service teacher learning. The initial aim was to identify the features of these workplaces that proved to be so conducive. The principal data collection methods were continuous participant observation in the science team room and semi-structured interviews with all department members. Departmental meetings and in-service training sessions were also observed. The researcher took descriptive notes of all conversations that occurred in the team room, at meetings and in training sessions. All interviews were recorded, with the permission of the teacher, and then transcribed. Analysis focused on how expertise in science teaching was made visible in teachers' conversations in which both explicit and implicit mediation took place. This talk made expertise accessible to pre-service teachers and to teachers who, as is typical in science departments, are required to teach topics not covered by their specialist subject knowledge.

The Demonstration Project: Internship development in a science department This innovation draws on earlier work by Ellis (2010), and places six science pre-service teachers—who are called interns in the programme in which they are enrolled—in one pre-service teacher education partnership school for the first two terms of their one-year PGCE programme. The need for the project arose from a shortage of places in schools for science pre-service teachers. An important feature is that the school and university collaborate on a small-scale research project in an area of priority for the school. The outcomes of the collaboration between teachers, pre-service teachers and university-based tutors are intended to meet the professional learning needs of the science department and enhance the research base of the initial teacher education partnership. Currently underway, evidence is being collected through regular focus group interviews with the six interns; two interviews with the six mentors and two teacher educators will be held over the course of the project. The interviews are exploring the purposes of the arrangement. There is also content analysis of documentation and interns' school-based research projects.

The Deanery Implementation Research Project This research study is funded by the charitable arm of Citigroup to examine what different stakeholders, university-based teacher educators, school colleagues, school students and university colleagues see as the purposes of tighter, more institutionally oriented links between schools and the university. It is currently underway, co-led by the second author. Here we draw only on data from university-based colleagues, i.e., departmental tutors and university administrators concerned with university-community links. Ten people in this group were interviewed using a schedule based in the analytic heuristic provided in Table 2.1. The schedule explored their motives for engaging with the Deanery and what they understood as the motives for others in their participation. The project has involved parallel interviews with three senior teachers in each of four partnership school. It has also carried out focus groups with Year 9 students in the four schools, followed by tracking two of these students in each school to understand their motives for aiming or not aiming at university study while selecting subjects for public examination.

Demonstration Project: Action research learning sets These started in 2011 and were run by the second author in two secondary schools which are also involved heavily in the pre-service teacher education partnership. In each school, groups of four teachers met with Edwards every six weeks, between October and July, to take forward their evidence-based action research enquiries into student self-assessment, self-regulation and problem-solving in Biology, Chemistry, English, History, Religious Education and vocational preparation. Classroom and online data were gathered and discussed. Notes were taken at each six-weekly meeting, and in one school a feedback session to staff was recorded. These learning sets are currently being extended to include all secondary schools to be involved in the Deanery we are developing.

Creating a Social Situation for Development Within the Demands of Practices

The Department Study focused on the interactions between teachers and between teachers and pre-service teachers in the science team rooms. It attempted to identify how the dialectic, created during pre-service teachers' agentic pursuit of solutions to problems in teaching and the demands of the practices of the departments, was leading to pre-service teachers' learning. Social structures that were conducive to teachers' professional learning had been created. These structures were not just the materiality of sitting on chairs around a table to eat and work, that biscuits were always available and that resources for sharing ideas (such as a white board) were to hand. Our analysis of the (inter)actions in the behind-the-scenes activities of lesson planning revealed that a discursive structure had been established, where the expertise of others was recognised as a resource to be drawn on to help children learn science (McNicholl and Childs 2010), and that everyone—technicians, pre-service teachers, senior staff—was expected to contribute to this distributed expertise by asking questions and giving answers.

Here is an extract from field notes taken by the first author in a team room at the end of a school day. Bridget is in her first year of teaching and needs to rethink her teaching plans.

> **Bridget** (newly qualified teacher) Says she will now have to plan for an optics lesson instead.
>
> **Nick** (head of science) Starts to talk about teaching optics and experiments she can do using lasers. He gives Bridget some safety advice about lasers and some principles of safety to follow. He talks about a visit he did with students to the local university on lasers and how lasers can make eye fluid boil. He moves on to the recent craze for pen lasers and also indicates that they don't have any safety information on power laser so they can't use them in school.

Bridget Talks about safety issues when she was at university. She moves on to sound and how using two speakers you can regulate beats.

Nick Draws a diagram about microwaves and says you ought to be able to do the same things with sound waves as you can with microwaves. They then talk about standing waves on a string.

Bridget Asks what order she should teach the concepts interference, diffraction and standing waves.

Nick Says it doesn't matter they all come under the heading of interference and then outlines some experiments on interference.

William (head of physics) brings in a speaker.

Nick Explains how you can use an IT package with Excel to show the wave equation (Audacity). He draws three graphs to show Bridget.

Bridget Says she finds the practical aspects of teaching Y12 more tricky.

Nick Talks about Y13 work and explains about practical work and four experiments and explains what pupils have to do in advance of the practical work.

Bridget Explains what she will do on Thursday—she will go over interference and then do experiments.

Nick Shows Bridget the Audacity Excel programme.

William now has signal generator working and speakers and we (Nick, Bridget, William and Ann) go into Bridget's lab to actually try things out and to show her how to set things up. In the lab the signal generator and the two speakers are set up.

Nancy (chemistry specialist) and **Julia** (biology specialist) join us to view the demonstration and we all walk across the classroom and lay down bits of paper to indicate the loud and soft areas to show patterns of interference.

In Derry's terms, this extract reveals a clear conceptual framework of what is regarded as good science pedagogy within which meanings are disclosed and openly discussed; and in Hedegaard's terms we can see that the demands on Bridget were those of being a teacher who should use every resource available to get ideas across to pupils. These discursive features did not arise spontaneously. The two team rooms were sites where the asking and answering of questions about how to present scientific ideas in lessons were customary, for example, the heads of department would produce artefacts to stimulate discussions, such as an exercise book from their own school days. This structuring of an environment where judgements were made against criteria which demanded an intertwining of science and pedagogy, ensured that student teachers were engaging with the meanings that shaped being a science teacher in those departments.

In the next extract from field notes taken by the third author, we can see how the expectations of framing and demands are echoed in an exchange between Ginny, a pre-service teacher, and Roger, a very experienced chemistry teacher—about teaching dynamic equilibrium.

Roger "Have you used troughs—you get two different sized troughs to model dynamic equilibrium." Roger is scribbling and drawing to help his explanation here using water troughs and beakers to demonstrate reversible reactions—the forward and backward reactions to get to equilibrium.

Ginny "What level do you need to go to at GCSE?" Ginny says that she doesn't know how to explain this idea at this level . . . she says that her subject knowledge is just not good enough.

Roger Simplifies his demonstration so that Ginny can understand better and be aware of the key points she needs to make at GCSE.

Ginny Do you refer to it as . . . in the classroom—what language do you use with pupils?

Later during an interview with Ginny, JM asked about the conversation.

JM The demonstration of equilibrium did you try that in the classroom?

Ginny Well the thing is I'd used it before, but the way Roger was explaining it was like a different way of using it. So I was trying to find out how he used it and adapted it. And I did use it with my top set and my mixed ability set, . . . I think it really did help them understand the idea.

These departments had created learning environments where it was expected that questions would be asked and answered, and gaps in knowledge should not be hidden. The field notes consistently revealed the team rooms as places where apprenticeship was happening, where learners were taken into the meaning systems of the more expert. However, as helpful as they were for beginning teachers, these were tightly bounded systems and similar to Huberman's closed collective cycles. Huberman summarised the weakness of this kind of network as follows: 'We are relying, as it were, on the collective wisdom—or lack thereof—of individual participants' (Huberman 1995, p. 201).

The action research learning sets, in attempting to address this weakness, more closely resembled Huberman's open collective cycles where external people '[a]re there at specific moments for specific purposes, to discuss cases or to provide conceptual foci. They are resource people, not group leaders.' (Huberman 1995, p. 202). Huberman's arguments are seminal and we recognise our debt to him. We simply hope to add to them by providing a conceptually based rationale for intervening in the practices inhabited by teachers and pre-service teachers.[1]

All the action research interventions undertaken by the teachers aimed at developing pupil capacity for self-regulation, through enhancing their learning strategies and, to greater or lesser degrees, engaging them in the self-assessment aspects of *Assessment for Learning*. The role of the university-based tutor was threefold: to advise on how to collect evidence; to provide research-based readings that helped take forward the interpretations of evidence; and to challenge the interpretations offered in meetings. The intention was to expand the repertoire of inferences against which judgments were made, through increasing the demands on how participants made sense of their actions in activities in classrooms.

---

[1] Note the work reported here did not constitute a research study. The second author was merely an external guide in the action learning process.

After three months both groups of teachers reported the same phenomenon, using the same form of words, within a week of each other. In brief, they found that they had to "reposition themselves as teachers". We are not claiming that this is a unique occurrence; but instead try to explain it in terms of cultural historical understandings of a learning dialectic. One of the teachers later described the change, when talking to colleagues who had not been involved in the action research, by explaining that he now put himself on the 'resource list' that was given to students to help plan their problem solving. He then went on to describe changes in how he taught as follows: "you physically reposition yourself. You change physically and conceptually where you are".

Table 2.1 indicates how changes in actions can be analysed in terms of motives, and how activities can be analysed in terms of the demands that they make. When teachers change their actions in activities, for example, by becoming a resource to support the learning of pupils who are working in more self-regulated ways, the demands made on the teacher by the activity reconfigures the dialectic that exists between teacher as actor and the practices in which the activities are located. Learning new ways of being a teacher arises from changes in the demands that are recognised and welcomed. The welcoming is important and occurs because the new demands are scrutinised in terms of what kinds of learners the department is trying to produce. The 'system of judgments (inferences)' (Derry 2008, p. 61), within which they were evaluating, is expanded to include valuing pupils' learning strategies, self-regulation and so on.

Here is another action research teacher doing such an expansion in a meeting of interested colleagues that he had convened. "You'll see on the reading list a paper on student planning and self-regulated learning. It's inspiring reading. It records students' discussions about their own learning. It's really good." These are not trivial examples. The expansion of the system of inferences by someone who is working within the familiar practices of the institution is recognised, implicitly at least, by recent emphases on the self-improving school. There the emphasis is on knowledge sharing within and between schools. Our argument is that knowledge exchange is not enough. Departments also need to work with the lessons of Lave's analyses of the cognition to be found in practices (Lave 1988) and to work systematically to enrich the intelligence that is 'stretched' across them. We are suggesting that the sustained involvement of university-based teacher education specialists can usefully augment that intelligence.

Implications for Enhancing Workplace Learning in Pre-service Teacher Education

In developing the Education Deanery as a multi-level system of distributed expertise, we are first unpacking and then building on some of the truisms of pre-service teacher education practice. One respondent in the Deanery Implementation Research Project explained "It is always an advantage to have a large number of students [pre-service teachers] in a department. It is terribly well known and definitely true that if you are a teacher working with a student teacher you look at what you are doing in a different way." She continued "If you put six student teachers in a department with six teachers you work on ideas together and reflect on what you are doing as a department. It is fantastic CPD [continuing professional development]." We agree, but to repeat ourselves, are arguing that it is not enough. We are with Derry when she says that 'the learning environment must be designed' (Derry 2008, p. 61), and have been suggesting that the 'system of inferences' must be enriched whenever possible.

The head of the science department in the internship development demonstration project summarised the importance of systematic department–university collaboration for her department:

> I think that the university input and input from the interns [pre-service teachers] brings in fresh ideas which re-invigorate the teaching in the school. I want a more research-informed perspective on key development challenges for the department and see working in partnership with [the university department] and drawing on their research expertise is a good way to work. It means that their visits to schools, rather than rushing in and out observing interns, can be for longer and more sustained periods working with the department and the interns on all of their key development priorities.

Our intention is to establish the Deanery as a framework within which university-school partnerships in research, continuing professional learning and pre-service teacher education can be formed and sustained. These partnerships will see teacher development as a continuum, with pre-service teachers immediately experiencing carefully regulated versions of the demands of being a teacher; rather than being, as one of us once put it, 'a guest bearing gifts' (Edwards 1997). They will enter workplaces where the system of inferences they encounter is not insular and limited to local historically accumulated knowledge, but open to question and development. As a result, the dialectic of demand and agentic enquiry will produce social situations of development that create teachers as 'occupational professionals' (Evetts 2009), who are carried forward by continuous attention to the purposes of their work as teachers.

We are seeing, in the evidence gathered in the studies and demonstration projects, that there is an appetite for the changes we are taking forward. Goodlad, reflecting on the decade of teacher education since his 1990 report, concluded in a 2002 article:

> [T]here will come a day, surely, when the social, economic, and political context of schooling and teacher education will engender and support the conditions necessary to a flourishing discipline of pedagogy joined to the preparation of superb pedagogues. (Goodlad 2002, pp. 220–221)

Between us we have 60 years of experience as teacher educators. We are therefore not naïve enough to believe that this day will arrive in England as a result of a sudden government policy *volte face* about the value of university involvement in the professional learning of teachers. But we believe that the kinds of arguments we have been making do provide a robust foundation for a response to the van Huizen et al. call for work on the connections between 'the professional development of trainee teachers and the institutional conditions that have to be fulfilled for realizing such a pedagogy' (van Huizen et al. 2005, p. 285).

References

Beach, K. (1999). Consequential transitions: A sociocultural expedition beyond transfer in education. *Review of Research in Education, 24*, 101–139.

Beach, K. (2001). Transitions between school and work: Some new understandings and questions about adult mathematics. In M. Schmitt & K. Safford-Ramus (Eds.), *Adults learning mathematics-7: A conversation between researchers and practitioners*. International Conference of adults learning mathematics. Downloaded from ERIC 13.5.07.

Brandom, R. (1994). *Making it explicit: Reasoning, representing, and discursive commitment*. Cambridge: Harvard University Press.

Brandom, R. (2000). *Articulating reasons: An introduction to inferentialism*. Cambridge: Harvard University Press.

Britzman, D. (1986). Cultural myths in the making of a teacher. *Harvard Educational Review, 56*(4), 442–456.

Burn, K., Childs, A., & McNicholl, J. (2007). The potential and challenges for student teachers' learning of subject specific pedagogical knowledge within secondary school subject departments. *The Curriculum Journal, 18*(4), 429–446.

Childs, A., Burn, K., & McNicholl, J. (in press). *What influences the learning cultures of subject departments in secondary schools?* A study of four subject departments in England. Teacher Development.

DfE. (1992). *Initial teacher training: Secondary phase—Circular 9/92*. London: Department for Education.

DfE. (1993). *The initial training of primary school teachers: New criteria for courses—Circular 14/93*. London: Department for Education.

DfE. (2011). *Training our next generation of outstanding teachers*. London: The Stationery Office.

Derry, J. (2008). Abstract rationality in education: From Vygotsky to Brandom. *Studies in the Philosophy of Education, 27*, 49–62.

Edwards, A. (1997). Guests bearing gifts: The position of student teachers in primary school classrooms. *British Educational Research Journal, 23*(1), 27–37.

Edwards, A. (2010). *Being an expert professional practitioner: The relational turn in expertise*. Dordrecht: Springer.

Edwards, A., & Collison, J. (1996). *Mentoring and developing practice in primary schools*. Buckingham: Open University Press.

Edwards, A., & Protheroe, L. (2003). Learning to see in classrooms: What are student teachers learning about teaching and learning while learning to teach in schools? *British Educational Research Journal, 29*(2), 227–242.

Edwards, A., & Protheroe, L. (2004). Teaching by proxy: Understanding how mentors are positioned in partnerships. *Oxford Review of Education, 30*(2), 183–197.

Edwards, A., Gilroy, P., & Hartley, D. (2002). *Rethinking teacher education: An interdisciplinary analysis*. London: Falmer.

Edwards, A., Sebba, J., & Rickinson, M. (2007). Working with users: Some implications for educational research. *British Educational Research Journal, 33*(5), 647–661.

Ellis, V. (2010). Studying the process of change: The double stimulation strategy in teacher education research. In V. Ellis, A. Edwards & P. Smagarinsky (Eds.), *Cultural historical perspectives on teacher education and development* (pp. 95–114). London: Routledge.

Ellis, V., McNicoll, J., & Pendry, A. (2012). Institutional conceptualisations of teacher education as academic work in England. *Teaching and Teacher Education, 28*, 685–693.

Ellis, V., McNicoll, J., Blake, A., & McNally, J. (under review). *Academic work and proletarianisation: A study of higher education-based teacher educators*

Evetts, J. (2009). New professionalism and new public management: Changes, continuities and consequences. *Comparative Sociology, 8*, 247–266.

Furlong, J., Barton, L., Miles, S., Whiting, C., & Whitty, G. (2000). *Teacher education in transition—reforming professionalism?* Buckingham: Open University Press.

Gibb, N. (2011a). 20th April 2011 Association of Teachers and Lecturers 2011 Conference. www.education.gov.uk/inthenews/speeches/a0076831/nick-gibb-to-the-association-of-teachers-and-lecturers-2011-conference. Accessed 7 Jan 2013.

Gibb, N. (2011b). Speech at Deputy Heads' Conference 7th June 2011.www.education.gov.uk/inthenews/speeches/a0077697/schools-minister-nick-gibb-to-the-2011-hmc-deputy-heads-conference. Accessed 7 Jan 2013.

Goodlad, J. (1990). *Teachers for our nation's schools*. San Francisco: Jossey-Bass.

Goodlad, J. (2002). Teacher education research: The outside and the inside. *Journal of Teacher Education, 53*(3), 216–221.

Gove, M. (2010). Speech at National College Annual Conference 16th June 2010. www.education.gov.uk/inthenews/speeches/a0061371/michael-gove-to-the-national-college-annual-conference-birmingham. Accessed 7 Jan 2013.

Greeno, J. (1997). On claims that answer the wrong questions. *Educational Researcher, 26*(1), 5–17.

Greeno, J. (2006). Authoritative, accountable positioning and connected general knowing; progressive themes in understanding transfer. *The Journal of the Learning Sciences, 15*(4), 537–547.

Hagger, H., & McIntyre, D. (2006). *Learning teaching from teachers*. Buckingham: Open University Press.

Hargreaves, D. (2011). *Leading a self-improving school system*. Nottingham: National College

Hedegaard, M. (2012). The dynamic aspects in children's learning and development. In M. Hedegar, A. Edwards & M. Fleer (Eds.), *Motives, emotions and values in the development of children and young people* (pp. 9–27). Cambridge: Cambridge University Press.

Huberman, M. (1995). Networks that alter teaching: Conceptualizations, exchanges and experiments. *Teachers and Teaching: Theory and practice, 1*(2), 193–211.

Lave, J. (1988). *Cognition in practice*. Cambridge: Cambridge University Press.

Lewis, M., & Brooks-Gunn, J. (1979). *Social cognition and the acquisition of Self*. New York: Plenum Press.

Mäkitalo, Å (2003). Accounting practices as situated knowing: Dilemmas and dynamics in institutional categorization. *Discourse Studies, 5*(4), 465–519.

Mäkitalo, Å (2006). Effort on display: Unemployment and interactional management of moral accountability. *Symbolic Interaction, 29*(4), 531–556.

McNicholl, J., & Childs, A. (2010). Taking a sociocultural perspective on science teachers' knowledge. In V. Ellis, A. Edwards & P. Smagarisnky (Eds.), *Cultural historical perspectives on teacher education and development* (pp. 45–52). London: Routledge.

Trevarthen, C. (1977). Descriptive analyses of infant communicative behaviour. In H. R. Schaffer (Ed.), *Studies in mother infant interaction*. London: Academic press.

van Huizen, P., van Oers, B., & Wubbels, T. (2005). A Vygotskian perspective on teacher education. *Journal of Curriculum Studies, 37*(3), 267–290.

Vygotsky, L. S. (1997). *The collected work of LS Vygotsky. Vol 3 The Problem of the Theory and History of Psychology*. New York: Plenum Press.

Vygotsky, L. S. (1998). *The collected work of LS Vygotsky. Vol 5 Child Psychology*. New York: Plenum Press.

Vygotsky, L. S. (1999). *The collected work of LS Vygotsky. Vol 6 Scientific Legacy*. New York: Plenum Press.

Wertsch, J. V. (2007). Mediation. In H. Daniels, M. Cole & J. V. Wertsch (Eds.), *The Cambridge companion to Vygotsky* (pp. 178–192). New York: Cambridge University Press.

Chapter 3
Developing Knowledge for Qualified Professionals

Michael Eraut

Introduction

The approach we take is to start with the experience of workplace learning. This means putting the individual employees centre stage and working outwards to learn from work groups, and other colleagues. This approach leads naturally to seeking how organisations can better facilitate workplace learning. In reviewing the research presented in this chapter, it is important to recognise that workplace learning is multi-faceted. Eraut and Hirsch (2007) highlight that, for individuals, there are four key factors to consider in relation to workplace learning:

- The capabilities an individual has in the broadest terms, including personal attributes, skills, knowledge, experience, and understanding;
- Their performance at work and how this is perceived by others and themselves;
- The formal and informal learning which takes place for that individual, and the processes by which this happens. Such learning is not necessarily planned or conscious;
- The context in which the individual is working and learning. This includes both the job and its wider context, especially the workplace culture, social interactions and management processes.

These four factors which interact with each other are illustrated in Fig. 3.1.

Different Types of Knowledge

The complexity of learning, and the contextual variations that sustain individuals at work, draw us to understand learning from both personal and social perspectives, although separating these types of knowledge is not always easy.

M. Eraut (✉)
University of Sussex, East Sussex, UK
e-mail: michael@eraut.eclipse.co.uk

O. McNamara et al. (eds.), *Workplace Learning in Teacher Education,*
Professional Learning and Development in Schools and Higher Education 10,
DOI 10.1007/978-94-007-7826-9_3, © Springer Science+Business Media Dordrecht 2014

Fig. 3.1 Key aspects of workplace learning

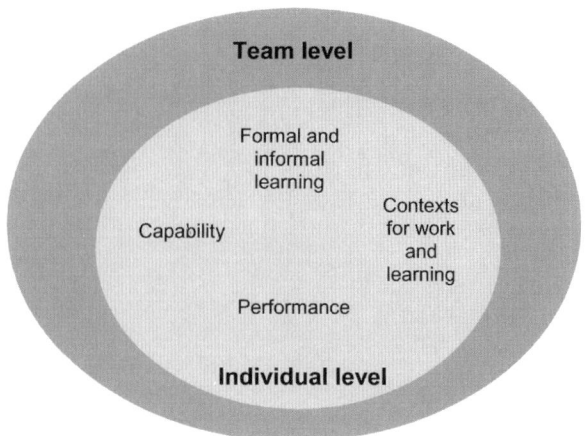

A personal perspective on knowledge and learning enables us to explore: what people know, what people can do, how they learn, and how different people interpret and use what they learn. A social perspective on knowledge highlights the social nature of most contexts for learning, the social origins of knowledge that is shared or passed on, the cultural practices that provide knowledge, and resources for learning.

'Knowledge', of course, has various meanings and interpretations. In perhaps its narrowest interpretation we have 'codified knowledge'—the kind stored in books, and believed to be 'true' or 'fact'. Creating and using codified knowledge requires skills (reading, writing, reasoning, etc.), which form 'practical knowledge'. In all workplaces, to varying degrees, workers need to use codified and practical knowledge—some of which they will learn through formal education, and some of which will be 'implicit knowledge' (they will learn it from their family, community, on-the-job, etc.). 'Cultural knowledge' also plays a role in the workplace. This is usually uncodified and acquired, for instance, through participation in working practices.

Personal knowledge is defined as what a person brings into new situations that enables them to think and act in those situations. This definition is not based on its truth but on its use. Looking more closely at personal knowledge we can say that it comprises:

- Codified knowledge ready for use;
- Knowledge acquired through acculturation;
- Knowledge constructed from experience, social interaction and reflection;
- Skills developed through practice with feedback;
- Episodes, impressions and images that provide the foundations for informal knowledge;
- Self-knowledge, attitudes, values and emotions.

The evidence of personal knowledge comes mainly from observations of performance, and this implies a holistic rather than fragmented approach to knowledge because, unless one stops to deliberate, the knowledge one uses is already available in an integrated form and ready for action. The challenge for professional learning is finding the balance between, on the one hand, developing separate aspects of performance, or on the other, focusing on simple holistic cases of performance, and then increasing their difficulty.

Memory

In understanding workplace learning it helps to be aware of memory, and of how we remember and use knowledge. Tulving's Theory of Memory (1972) distinguishes between *episodic memory* (for specific personally experienced events), and *semantic memory* (for generalised knowledge that transcends particular episodes and is associated with public codified knowledge). Linking these two types of memory depends on the use of reflection, to connect personally experienced episodes with codified semantic knowledge.

Our performance and behaviour may be influenced by either our episodic memory of practical experiences, or our semantic memory of codified knowledge—or both. The tacit knowledge we have via our episodic memory may be more quickly accessed and used than our semantic memory—so when a quick solution or action is needed in a situation, we are more likely to draw on our tacit knowledge from our episodic memory, because our knowledge from our semantic memory may not be quickly useable without more learning to make it 'fit' the situation.

Towards an Epistemology of Practice

Three significant research projects on workplace learning, conducted over a ten-year period, have informed our understanding of workplace learning and the concepts above. The first project was a three-year study for the English National Board for Nursing and Midwifery Education, within which the main project was *Learning to Use Scientific Knowledge in Education and Practice Settings*. The second was an Economic and Social Research Council (ESRC) project which interviewed managers and business, engineering and health professionals. The third project, from ESRC's *Teaching and Learning Research Programme*, allowed us to follow work in three different professions: nursing, engineering and chartered accountancy.

The English National Board for Nursing and Midwifery Education project ran from 1993 to 1995 and focused on the question of how best to learn how to use scientific knowledge in education and practice settings. It involved the evaluation of learning on biological, behavioural and social sciences for pre-registration nursing and midwifery programmes, and showed that most nurses failed to receive learning that connected their formal work with their practical work (Eraut et al. 1995). The research focused on three areas of professional practice—midwifery, general adult surgical wards, and mental health nursing—and six areas of scientific knowledge—fluids and electrolytes, nutrition, acute pain, shock, stress and self-esteem.

The researchers observed many different approaches to linking scientific knowledge with practice. They found, however, that only some teachers accepted responsibility for linking scientific knowledge with professional practice; and even they had insufficient opportunity to pursue this goal, since curricula provided little time for teaching in hospital environments. Few managers appeared to recognise that there was a conflict between the amount of scientific knowledge that was taught, and the time and teaching resources needed to help teachers learn how to use such scientific knowledge.

The second project, funded by the ESRC, involved a group of 11 teams studying aspects of The Learning Society. The project focused on: (1) learning from other people at work; (2) the impact of managers on learning in the workplace (120 interviews focused on business, engineering and health care, and 90 interviewees participated in second interviews 6–12 months later); and (3) from 1999 onwards, Eraut's work focused on non-formal learning and tacit knowledge in professional work.

Performance

Emanating from the research, Eraut et al. (2000) developed a generic model on mid-career learning of managers and professionals comprising four distinct but interacting elements of 'performance':[1]

1. Assessing clients and/or situations, sometimes briefly, sometimes involving a long process of investigation and consultation;
2. Deciding what, if any, action to take, both immediately and over a longer period, either on one's own or as a leader or member of a team;
3. Pursuing an agreed course of action, modifying, consulting and reassessing as and when necessary;
4. Meta-cognitive monitoring by individuals and/or groups of the people involved, whether agents or clients of the general progress of the case, problem, project or situation and, sometimes, also learning through reflection on the experience.

Each element of performance can take many different forms, according to the context, the time available and the types of technical and personal expertise being deployed. Although analytically distinct, they are often combined into an integrated performance that does not follow a simple sequence of assessment, decision and

---

[1] 'We use the term "performance" in a broad sense that includes thoughts and actions that take place within a chosen performance period, and those involved in preparing for, or reflecting on, that period.' (Eraut and Hirsch 2007).

Table 3.1 Types of process and modes of cognition (Eraut 2000)

Thought/action	Mode of Cognition		
	Instant/reflex	Rapid/intuitive	Deliberative/analytic
Reading of the situation	Pattern recognition	Rapid interpretation	Review involving discussions and/or analysis
Decision-making	Instant response	Intuitive	Deliberative with some analysis or discussion
Overt activity	Routinised actions	Routines punctuated by rapid decisions	Planned actions with periodic progress reviews
Metacognitive processes	Situational awareness	Implicit monitoring Short, reactive reflections	Conscious monitoring of thought and activity Self-management. Evaluation

action. Instead, the research findings provide a much more complex picture of the decision-making process and the nature of good performance in the workplace:

- Experts frequently generate and evaluate a single option rather than multiple options.
- Experts are distinguished from novices mainly by their situation assessment abilities, not their general reasoning skills.
- Because most naturalistic decision problems are ill-structured, decision-makers choose an option that is good enough, though not necessarily the best.
- Reasoning and acting are interleaved, rather than segregated (Weick 1983).
- Instead of analysing all facets of a situation, making a decision and then acting, it appears that in complex realistic situations people think a little, act a little, and then evaluate the outcomes and think and act some more (Connelly and Wagner 1988).

The implications for a manager's decision-making practice are that: (1) the relationship between knowledge and decision-making is rarely simple; (2) good decision-making is critically dependent on how the decision is framed by the decision-makers in the light of their situational understanding; and (3) the balance is tilted towards the personal knowledge of the decision-maker(s) and less towards any codified knowledge that might be available. When time is scarce, searching the literature or consulting a colleague is only tried when there is a high expectancy of getting a valuable pay-off very quickly.

Time and Cognition/Performance

Table 3.1 illustrates how the time variable affects the mode of cognition and/or mode of consultation of those involved. The model divides the time-continuum into three columns, whose headings seek to describe modes of cognition used by decision-makers, although the timescale may differ according to the way they work. For example, in one context rapid/intuitive might refer to a minute, while in another context it might include periods of up to ten minutes or even half-an-hour. The critical feature is that the decision-makers have limited time to deliberate or think in any depth.

The instant/reflex mode of cognition describes routinised behaviour that, at most, is semi-conscious. The rapid/intuitive mode of cognition indicates greater awareness of what is going on, and is often characterised by rapid decision-making within a period of continuous, semi-routinised action. Typically, it involves recognition of situations by comparison with similar situations previously encountered, then responding to them with already learned procedures (Klein 1989; Eraut et al. 1995). The time available affects the degree of mismatch that is tolerated, because rejection of familiar actions based on prior experience leads to deliberative problem-solving, and hence to a more time-consuming approach. As workers become more experienced, they acquire a wider range of precedents and recognise them more quickly and more accurately. The deliberative/analytic mode is characterised by explicit thinking of individuals or groups, possibly accompanied by consultation with others. It often involves the conscious use of different types of prior knowledge, and their application to new situations. These areas of knowledge may be either used in accustomed ways, with familiar adaptations, or combined in novel ways that require a significant period of problem-solving.

The relationship between time and cognition is probably interactive: shortage of time forces people to adopt a more intuitive approach, while the intuitive routines developed by experience enable people to do things more quickly. Crowded contexts also force people to be more selective with their attention and to process their incoming information more rapidly. Even when a group has some time for discussion, individual members may feel that their contributions have to be short, to the point and rapid. Hence meta-processes are limited to implicit monitoring and short, reactive reflections. But as more time becomes available, the role of meta-processes becomes more complex, expanding beyond self-awareness and monitoring to include the framing of problems, thinking about the deliberative process itself and how it is being handled.

Experienced people typically prefer to do many things quickly and smoothly if they are confident in their own proficiency. However, there are also situations where even proficient workers, who routinely work with crowded contexts, feel forced by pressure for productivity. Then quality falls, the level of risk is higher, and job satisfaction plummets. Both the development of proficiency, and learning to cope with pressures for rapid action, involve routinisation and further work; but whereas the routines associated with proficiency lead to improvement in both quality and productivity, coping routines increase productivity at the expense of quality. In either case, routinisation leads to knowledge becoming less explicit and less easily shared with others, i.e. more tacit. Tacit knowledge of this kind is also likely to lose value over time because circumstances change, new practices develop and people start to shortcut routines without being aware that they are reducing their effectiveness.

The greatest benefit of routinisation is that it reduces workers' cognitive load, and thus enables them to give more attention to monitoring the situation or communicating with clients and colleagues, hence becoming both more productive and more effective. We would not survive for long if we could not take for granted many aspects of what we see and do in everyday activities. Not everyone, however, takes the opportunity to take a more evaluative perspective on their practice. It is often difficult to disentangle routines from the practices in which they are embedded; and this makes it difficult, if not impossible, to describe them. Indeed, the main purpose of routines is to avoid having to think about them. The exception to this is when routines lead to coping mechanisms for dealing with work overloads with little regard for quality.

Routines are very difficult to change, not only because this would imply a negative evaluation of the previous practice, but also because such change involves a period of disorientation, while old routines are gradually unlearned and new routines are gradually developed. During this period, practitioners feel like novices without having the excuses, or discounts on performance normally accorded to novices. The pain of change lies in the loss of control over one's own practice, when one's tacit knowledge ceases to provide the necessary support and the resultant emotional turmoil is reducing one's motivation.

The Tacit Dimension of Performance

Getting to know other people typically involves the absorption of a great deal of incidental information, acquired by being a participant observer when others are present. While some of this knowledge may be explicit, much more will be gathered through impressions of their behaviour and character. Stories are normally regarded as an explicit form of communication, but they also carry implicit cultural and personal knowledge. We learn more about the people we meet than we are able to explain, and some of that knowledge may be so provisional that we are reluctant to make it explicit. Eraut (2004a) shows informal learning in the workplace. What influences our behaviour is our aggregated knowledge of that person, and that is usually a largely tacit process to which memories of incidents, encounters and episodes contribute in ways we cannot fully apprehend.

Another factor is the way we tend to organise our knowledge of people: this affects how we perceive their behaviour, as well as how we structure our memories of them, and neither is a fully conscious process. Managers have an additional problem, because their memories of occasions when they interacted with their subordinates are based on atypical samples of their subordinates' behaviour, caused by their own managerial presence. Many situations, for example, are largely characterised, not only by the differing perspectives of the participants present, but also by the assumed behaviour of 'significant others' off-stage. Knowledge of these perspectives depends not only on what people do and say, but also on how their actions are interpreted by others in the context of what they already 'know' about the people concerned. Thus tacit understandings or misunderstandings contribute not only to relationships and assumptions within an organisation, but also to transactions with external clients, customers, suppliers and stakeholders.

In the previous section, we discussed the tacit nature of rapid intuitive decision-making in terms of situational recognition and prior experience. When deciding what to say and how, or when asked for advice or giving feedback, decision-makers may discuss the options, then eventually decide on what seems to them to be 'the best fit'. This final decision will often be intuitive, drawing on the tacit aggregation of knowledge when there is less time or motivation to collect evidence or construct and clarify arguments. When there is even less time, decisions will be described as 'backing a hunch'.

A great deal of monitoring also involves tacit knowledge. A key issue concerns finding space for monitoring: how does one give any attention to self-monitoring when there are many apparently more urgent things demanding your attention; and how does one set up, or take advantage of, informal meetings to pursue one's monitoring agenda with others. A second issue relates to what one notices during conversations and observations. Whether one relies on spotting problems or more systematically scanning the environment, one still has to notice any relevant evidence; and this is particularly difficult if it is not very salient or rarely appears. Thirdly, one may also have to decide, often very quickly, whether or not to ignore, make a note for later consideration or make a rapid intervention. More explicit monitoring is only likely when seeking to avoid previous mistakes, and even then it may be only temporary.

Early Career Learning at Work

The ESRC Teaching and Learning Research Programme—the third project to have significant influence on our understanding of workplace learning—allowed us to follow three years of professional work in very different professions: nursing, engineering and chartered accountancy. Our three main questions were: what did the participating professionals learn; how was it being learned; and what were the factors that affected learning in a wide range of workplace settings?

We found that our participants learned much more through their work than through formally organised learning events, even in accountancy which included a substantial programme of formal training and examinations. We distinguished between (1) *work processes*, such as working with clients, working with colleagues or tackling challenging tasks, from which they learned as they went along; (2) *specific formal learning*, such as being coached, taking a course, or using other formal ways of working; and (3) *shorter learning activities* such as asking questions, giving and receiving feedback, negotiation, or using mediating artefacts. The full repertoire is shown in Table 3.2.

Our conclusion was that, given favourable conditions, learning in the workplace can be enhanced by improving opportunities for productive engagement in a wide range of work processes. Moreover, working alongside a colleague for a while enables someone to learn by asking questions and receiving feedback about shared activities and events as and when they happen. It also allows the learner to see how a colleague reads situations, monitors them and takes decisions. These activities are largely tacit and difficult to explain, even by experienced professionals. Working in

Table 3.2 Implications for learning at work

Work processes with learning as a by-product	Formal learning processes located at or near the workplace	Learning activities located within work or learning processes
Participation in group processes	Being supervised	Asking questions
Working alongside others	Being coached	Getting information
Consultation	Being mentored	Locating resource people
Tackling challenging tasks and roles	Shadowing	Listening and observing
	Visiting other sites	Negotiation
Problem-solving	Conferences	Reflecting
Trying things out	Short courses	Learning from mistakes
Consolidating, extending and refining skills	Working for a qualification	Giving and receiving feedback
	Independent study	Use of mediating artefacts (see
Working with clients		explanation below)

groups, whose members have different kinds of expertise, helps people to understand the nature of that expertise and make better use of it; but then the expertise becomes so normal that work processes cover 80 % or more of the learning at work (Eraut and Hirsh 2007), and they cease to talk about their 'well known' day-to-day work.

Work processes with learning as a by-product might involve:

- Participation in group processes covers team-working towards a common outcome, and groups set up for a special purpose, such as discussing a client, problem-solving, reviewing some practices, planning ahead, or responding to external changes.

- Working alongside others allows people to observe and listen to others at work and to participate in activities; and hence to learn some new practices and new perspectives, to become aware of different kinds of knowledge and expertise, and to gain some sense of other people's tacit knowledge. This mode of learning, which includes a lot of observation as well as discussion, is extremely important for learning tacit knowledge or the knowledge that underpins routines and intuitive decisions. When people see what is being said and done, explanations can be much shorter and the fine detail of incidents is still in people's minds; and multi-sensory engagement over some time enables the gradual development of tacit as well as explicit situational understanding.

- Consultations within or outside the working group, or even outside the organisation, are used for co-ordinating activities or getting advice. The act of initiating a consultation, however, depends on the relationships between the parties, the extent of a worker's network and the culture of the workplace. For newcomers the distinction between a consultation and being mentored or supervised is not always clear, as part of a mentor's or supervisor's role is making oneself available for consultation.

- Tackling challenging tasks and roles requires on-the-job learning and, if successful, leads to increased motivation and confidence. However, people are less inclined to take on challenges unless they feel confident, both in their ability to succeed as a result of previous experience and in the support of their manager and/or colleagues. Without such previous experience and support, challenges pose too high a risk.

- Problem-solving, individually or in groups, necessarily entails learning; otherwise there would be no problem. Such problems are not just technical, they may involve acquiring new knowledge before one can start, searching for relevant information and informants, imagination, persistence and interpersonal negotiation.
- Trying things out is distinguished from less purposeful behaviour by the intention to learn from the experience. It requires some prior assessment of risk, especially where other people might be affected, and may require special arrangements for getting feedback, as well as time for subsequent reflection and evaluation.
- Consolidating, extending and refining skills are particularly important when entering new jobs or taking on new roles, when these processes are sometimes supported by episodes of supervision, coaching or feedback. They are greatly helped by informal personal support and some sense of an onward learning trajectory.
- Working with clients also entails learning about the client, from any novel aspects of the client's problem or request, and from any new ideas that arise from the encounter. Some workers have daily experiences of working with clients, which may or may not be recognised as learning opportunities. Some progress from less to more important clients, or from those with simple needs to those with more complex needs. There can also be a strong emotional dimension, when a client arrives in a distressed state or is about to receive bad news. This is a context where sharing experiences can be helpful. Another factor is the extent to which client contact gives the work meaning and value, and thus enhances workers' sense of collective purpose.

'*Mediating artefacts*' feature in Table 3.2, and are worth explaining in a little more detail. They play a very important role in structuring work and sharing information, by mediating group learning about clients or projects in progress. Some artefacts in daily use carry information in a standard way that novices soon learn to understand. In both nursing and engineering, these include measurements, diagrams and photographs. For example, patient records cover temperature, fluid intake and output, drugs administration, biochemical data and various types of image. These refer both to the immediate past and to plans for the immediate future, and salient features considered important are prioritised for the incoming shift at every handover. Understanding the thinking behind the handover rituals is essential learning for newly qualified nurses.

Designated mentors were provided by all employers involved in our research, but most mentoring and coaching was provided by 'helpful others', who were already on the spot. This was strongest in the audit teams on client premises, where novice accountants learned from those just ahead of them. In engineering, new graduates, usually working in open-plan offices, were strongly encouraged to seek advice, and soon learned who could help them most with each area of expertise. Only in nursing did designated mentors play a significant role; but while some official mentors provided a lifeline for their novices, others were either allocated to a different shift or

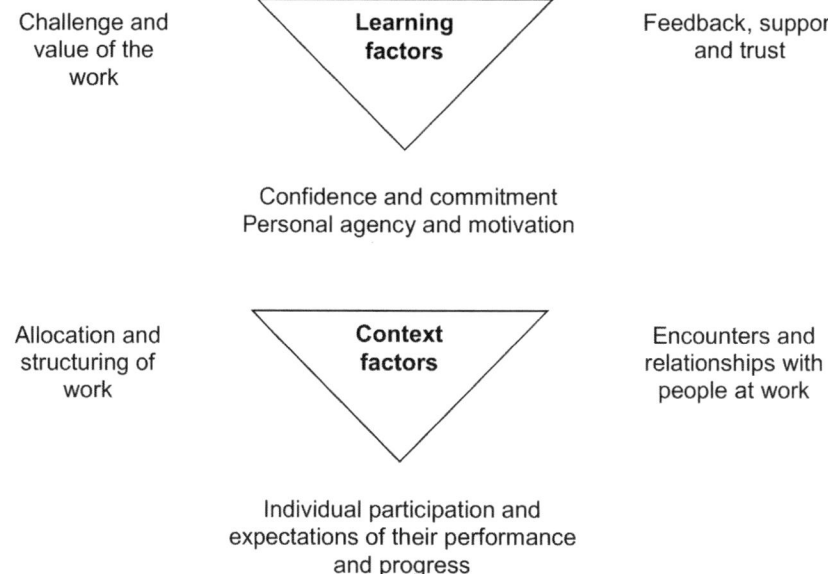

Fig. 3.2 Factors affecting learning at work: the two triangle model

unwilling to take the role seriously. Formal learning was strongest for accountants, who still needed to get a relevant qualification. Engineers had considerable access to continuing professional learning opportunities, but only rarely received any mentoring or coaching. Nurses found it difficult to get release for continuing professional learning and received less coaching from the wards than they needed, because it was difficult to release them.

We found that *feedback and support* were critically important for confidence and commitment, especially during the new employees' first few months, when the feedback and support were best provided by the person on the spot. This happened within the distributed apprenticeship approach used by our accountancy partners, and in other professions where the local workplace had developed a positive learning culture of mutual support. In the longer term, more normative feedback on progress and meeting organisational expectations also became important.

Equally important for developing confidence after the first few months were the right level of challenge and the perceived value of the work. This led us to a Two Triangle Model (Eraut 2007)—one for *learning factors* and one for *context factors* that affect learning at work (see Fig. 3.2). This diagram helped us to organise factors affecting workplace learning in each profession.

The research findings, as organised in the diagram, indicated for instance that confidence plays a big part in learning at work, and that this confidence is affected by the challenges a person is able to meet, and the support available to them. There is a triangular relationship between challenge, support and confidence. Similar triangular relationships were identified between allocation/structuring of work, relationships at work, and an individuals' participation and expectations for performance.

To illustrate this with specific examples, we found that newly qualified nurses were *over*-challenged physically, mentally and emotionally by their sudden increase in responsibility and the unceasing pressure of work in most ward environments. While some engineers progressed through a series of challenging assignments with remarkable rapidity, most were *under*-challenged and many were seriously under-challenged. Nearly all the accountants, however, were *appropriately* challenged for the majority of their traineeship.

Factors affecting participants' commitment to work, to colleagues, and to their employers included the quality of the support and feedback received, appreciation of the value of their work, and their personal sense of agency, which was not necessarily aligned with their employer's priorities.

For novice professionals to make good progress, a significant proportion of their work needed to be sufficiently new to challenge them, without being so daunting as to reduce their confidence. Their workload needed to be at a level that allowed them to respond to new challenges reflectively, rather than develop coping mechanisms that might later prove ineffective.

Thus, managers and/or senior colleagues had to balance the immediate demands of the job against the needs of the trainees to broaden their experience. This usually worked well in our two accountancy organisations; but in engineering the appropriateness of the allocated work differed hugely according to the company and the specialty. Very few graduate engineers in electronics or computer science had sufficiently challenging work, and nobody appeared to take any responsibility for addressing this problem. In nursing the quality of learning was mainly influenced by the ward manager and her senior nurses; some of the best and worst learning environments we observed co-existed in the same departments of the same hospitals.

The allocation and structuring of work was central to our participants' progress, because it affected:

- The difficulty or challenge of the work;
- The extent to which it was individual or collaborative;
- The opportunities for meeting, observing and working alongside people who had more or different expertise, and for forming relationships that might provide feedback and support.

Both the significance and the importance of the categories shown in the triangle diagrams changed markedly over the three years of the study, as the nature of the work changed. These changes included:

1. *Dealing with more difficult and complex problems,* e.g. sicker patients, larger sections of an audit, more flexible use of protocols, designing discrete components, and use of formal knowledge;
2. *Widening their range of competence,* e.g. budgets, value for money, liaising with clients, other professions or agencies, secondments, and giving presentations;
3. *Acquiring greater responsibility,* e.g. being 'in charge', becoming a team leader or manager, dealing with personnel, supporting other people's learning.

Figures 3.3, 3.4 and 3.5 illustrate the Two Triangle Model using the specific examples of the early career learning for chartered accountants, engineers and nurses. In each

Allocation and structuring of work
Audit teams (temporary)
Scaffolded progression
Contact with range of clients
Formal professional training for examinations

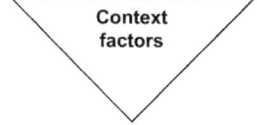
Context factors

Relationships at work
Strong mutual support in teams
Strong organisational culture
Sensitivity to client differences
Develops peer group interaction

Participation and expectations
Clear apprenticeship route
Pay your way
Must pass examinations

Challenge and value of the work
Good progression and client variation
Audit is a legal requirements
Value for clients is clear

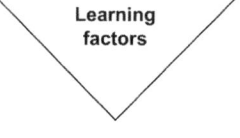
Learning factors

Feedback and support
Good on-the-spot feedback and support
Feedback on evaluation forms too late
Normative feedback weak

Confidence and commitment
Short-term confidence
Commitment to audit teams
Concerns about general progress
Less commitment to organisation
Range of career choices

Fig. 3.3 Accountants: context factors and learning factors

Allocation and structuring of work
Project teams (long term)
Open-plan offices
Social links around workplace intranet
Strong CPL programmes
Little direct client contact
Work suitable for trainees is scarce

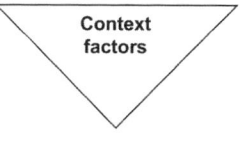
Context factors

Relationships at work
Ask anything culture
Loose links in large teams
Informal contact with neighbours
Develops wider networks
Hunter-gatherers of resources and expertise
Broader context of project often missing

Participation and expectations
Learning is serious business
Work expectations often unclear
Have to do whatever turns up
Limited peripheral participation within their project

Challenge and value of the work
Variable types and levels of challenge
Depends on work available
Isolation from clients resented
Chartered status valued only by some engineers

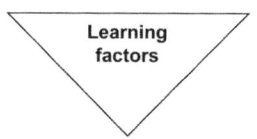
Learning factors

Feedback and support
GEs find out most helpful people in close range
GEs track down company expertise beyond their office
Many designated support roles, few of them active
Quality of support varies with immediate locality
Normative feedback is weak

Confidence and commitment
Confidence ebbs with lack of challenge
Commitment to chartered status ebbs if not valued in local workplace
Concerns about general progress
Range of career choices

Fig. 3.4 Graduate Engineers (GEs): context factors and learning factors

Allocation and structuring of work
Ward-based shift work
Full responsibility on arrival
Pressure cooker environments
Prioritisation critical
Multiple brief contacts with other health professionals

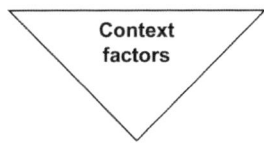

Relationships at work
Variable want climates
Ward leadership critical
Variable contact with peers
Delegating to healthcare assistants

Participation and expectations
Unreasonable expectations
Transition problems underestimated
Ultimate responsibility
Overwork is the norm

Challenge and value of the work
High levels of challenge
High value for patients
Complex relationships with other workers and professionals
Complex relationships with patients and their families

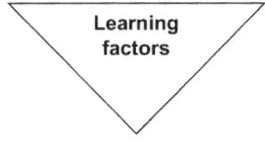

Feedback and support
Variable close support
Variable mentor support
Occasional skills coaching
Variable back-up
Emotional support critical
Access to training
Learning culture of ward

Confidence and commitment
Strong commitment to patients
Commitments to colleagues varies
Early loss of confidence
Concern about general progress
Rebuilding confidence depends on support

Fig. 3.5 Newly qualified nurses: context factors and learning factors

profession, we started from the perspective of looking at context factors before learning factors.

Points of Interest (Fig. 3.3)

- Accounts act as mediating artefacts, around which knowledge is shared;
- Audit work involves translation between accounts (professional discourse) and business processes (client discourse), and much of it is done on client premises;
- Trainees learn about several different kinds of business;
- Only a small minority of trainees are graduates in accountancy;
- A lot of the support comes from other trainees only a year or less ahead.

Points of Interest (Fig. 3.4)

- Sketches and designs often function as mediating artefacts;
- Lack of site experience reduces the understanding, morale and value of graduate engineers;
- Big differences between engineering disciplines, with electronic and computing work offering the least challenge.

Points of Interest (Fig. 3.5)

- Learning culture mainly determined at ward level;
- Considerable cross-professional work;
- Strong interest in gaining higher qualifications.

The Role of Learning Trajectories

We conceptualised our participants' learning as progressing along 'learning trajectories'; in order to accommodate both continuity and discontinuity of lifelong learning where:

- *Explicit progress* was being made on several trajectories simultaneously;
- *Implicit progress* could be inferred and later acknowledged on some trajectories;
- *Lack of use* on some trajectories usually meant that further learning would be required.

The research confirmed that newly qualified professionals have remarkably varied profiles across most relevant learning trajectories, as a result of both their individual agency and the different opportunities offered by the learning contexts through which they passed. Table 3.3 shows a typology of learning trajectories (Eraut and Hirsh 2007) which both encourages continuity of learning and counteracts the widespread delusion that a professional qualification properly represents a person's capability. Since it is unusual for an episode of work to use knowledge from only one trajectory, the seamless integration of personal knowledge from several trajectories is an important additional learning challenge. Thus the complexity of expertise is best represented by combining accounts of holistic performance episodes with trajectories of different types of knowledge.

The 'points' on these learning trajectories are best considered as windows on episodes of practice, and should include information about:

- The *setting* in which it took place, and features of that setting that might have affected the availability of resources;
- The *conditions* under which the performance took place, e.g., degree of supervision, pressure of time, crowdedness and conflicting priorities;
- The *situations* shown in Table 3.3 help to find the most important aspects of the assignment, and the other *categories of expertise* involved;
- Any differences from previously recorded episodes;
- Indicators of *expertise in the domain of the trajectory* having been maintained, widened or enhanced.

Sharu (2012) added several further points needed for Advanced Nurse Practitioners' professional learning:

- Fighting one's corner;
- Self-promotion;

Table 3.3 A typology of learning trajectories

Task Performance	*Role Performance*
Speed and fluency	Prioritisation
Complexity of tasks and problems	Range of responsibility
Range of skills required	Supporting other people's learning
Communication with a wide range of people	Leadership
Collaborative work	Accountability
	Supervisory role
Awareness and Understanding	Delegation
Other people: colleagues, customers, managers, etc.	Handling ethical issues
	Coping with unexpected problems
Contexts and situations	Crisis management
One's own organisation	Keeping up-to-date
Problems and risks	
Priorities and strategic issues	
Value issues	
Personal Development	*Knowledge of the Field*
Self evaluation	Knowing the repertoire of practices
Self management	Evidence of their effectiveness in particular contexts
Handling emotions	
Building and sustaining relationships	Using knowledge resources and networks
Disposition to attend to other perspectives	Knowing what you need to know
Disposition to consult and work with others	Making practices more explicit
Disposition to learn and improve one's practice	Conceptual and theoretical thinking
Accessing relevant knowledge and expertise	Use of evidence and argument
Ability to learn from experience	Writing appropriate documents
Teamwork	*Decision-making and Problem-solving*
Collaborative work	When to seek expert help
Facilitating social relations	Dealing with complexity
Joint planning and problem-solving	Group decision-making
Ability to engage in and promote mutual learning	Problem analysis
	Formulating and evaluating options
	Managing the process within an appropriate timescale
	Decision-making under pressure
	Judgement
	Quality of performance, output and outcomes
	Priorities
	Value issues
	Levels of risk

- Becoming a change agent;
- Developing a new professional persona

and role performance:

- Pioneership;
- Negotiating one's own role;
- Self-auditing;
- Autonomy.

Our own research recognises the need to develop a learning culture, based on confidence and trust in managers and colleagues, giving and receiving feedback without blame, and mutual learning and support. This requires:

- Learning from experiences, positive and negative, at both group and individual level;
- Learning from colleagues, clients and visitors;
- Locating and using relevant knowledge from outside sources;
- Giving attention to the emotional dimension of work;
- Discussing and reviewing learning opportunities, and their appropriateness;
- Reviewing work processes and opportunities for quality improvement.

This use of learning trajectories need not be a rival to the use of competences; because competences can be used in current situations, while learning trajectories focus on how they arrived and what is coming next. Thus, competence is the ability to perform the tasks and roles required to the expected standard, while learning trajectories are preparing for future developments. Both are needed for ongoing work.

The problem with most competency-based learning is not primarily with the competencies themselves, but with how they are used and understood. Many of the items in our Typology of Learning Trajectories, especially working in groups and personal feelings and qualities (McKee and Eraut 2012), are given little attention in either education or workplace settings. The need for good holistic performances, which combine several skills, is critical for developing good work; and examining learner pathways over time gives much better evidence than single assessment events. Hence, discussions about learning trajectories and learning goals should become generally available across the population, regardless of age and formal qualifications.

Broad representations of competence are often too vague for any practical use, and specific representations tend to become too numerous to handle, as lists of competencies approach the size of telephone directories. Formal assessments need detailed learning objectives, but assessors rarely agree with this, unless there is a past history of developing a consensus by discussing individual cases. Moreover, the half-life of such a consensus is usually very short, because people change who influence the implicit social agreement on what counts as competence. Both listing important attributes of competence and describing their integration into performance is a part-whole problem, for which nearly all previous representations have focused only on the parts. The changing and conditional nature of what counts as competence over time and between contexts may be understood and work well with one group, but not so well with another.

The Role of Managers in Supporting Learning Most of the examples of the use of mediating artefacts involve groups rather than individuals, and this is crucial for their effective use. When artefacts are seen as mediating tools rather than reified knowledge, we come to recognise that much of our knowledge lies in the discussions we have around the mediating artefacts rather than in the artefacts themselves. It is these crucial discussions that are missing from competency-based assessment and training. Examples of good practice identified through our research included:

- Protocols for deciding when a patient needs urgent attention;
- The contents of the nursing matrix on causes of acute pain;
- Engineers discussing virtual design 'drawings' on the screen over the telephone;
- Learning to translate business processes into audited accounts;
- Using still pictures rather than videos for discussing operations, so they can be more easily explained by patients and medical students.

This did not mean that managers had to do most of the work themselves, because much of what is needed can be done by people other than managers. However, it did mean that professional workers should be involved in change, whether it came from their own ideas or those of their colleagues. We found that many workers learned from others without being aware of their own growing knowledge, because they did not count informal discussions as new knowledge. Often the manager's role is to set the climate and encourage their staff to develop new ideas. To fulfil this role managers need to know that:

- Being over-challenged or under-challenged is bad for learning and morale. So providing an appropriate level of challenge is important for developing confidence and making good progress.
- The quantity and quality of informal learning can be enhanced by consulting with and working alongside others in teams or temporary groups. Hence good opportunities are needed for meeting and working with others to develop mutual trust and co-operative relationships.
- They may need skills in conflict resolution and addressing bad relationships that threaten the group climate and/or achievement.
- Support and feedback are critical, so it is important for managers to develop a positive learning culture of mutual support, both among individuals and across whole work groups.
- More traditional feedback on progress, strengths and weaknesses, and meeting organisational expectations, is also needed and this is discussed at some length below.
- Upsetting feedback, anxiety about one's status or performance, client behaviour, and relationships or events outside the workplace can all influence the emotional dimension of a person's working life. This may require ongoing attention for a period.

Workplaces are complex inter-personal environments, where managers need to be well informed about relationships and personal or collective concerns without being unduly intrusive. They also need to delegate and to work through other people as well as by direct action. Otherwise, they will never have enough time to realise their good intentions, and those they manage will have less opportunity for self development. It is increasingly recognised that frequent informal conversations with individuals and small groups create good settings for preparing people for coming issues, listening to their problems and concerns, seeking their advice, and asking them to consult others about a problem and come back with suggestions. In this context their personal interests need as much attention as the collective interest, if they are not to feel exploited. This means being supportive both when they have personal problems and in developing their future careers.

The Institute of Employment Studies report, *Managers as Developers of Others* (Hirsh et al. 2004), was based on managers' roles in developing their workers in four organisations, two in the private sector and two in the public sector. The authors interviewed givers and receivers of good and bad development support. They found that good development was delivered through a supportive relationship, sometimes short-lived but often over a period of months or years. It was typically characterised by the following features:

- Managers set a climate in which they are easy to approach, and where development is an important part of working life.
- They build developmental relationships with individuals in their teams and more widely. These relationships are often fostered by frequent, informal conversations about work, listening to concerns and the offer of positive support.
- Good development support is quite focused through a clear, shared analysis of development needs, frequent review and honest but constructive feedback.
- They often engage in informal coaching, make good use of formal training offered by the organisation, and focus heavily on finding the right kinds of experience, both within the job (often through delegating developmental tasks) and outside the job (through projects etc.).
- They offer active career development and work to help individuals have a realistic sense of their own potential and readiness for possible job moves. They see the individual in the context of their previous work experiences and their interests and obligations outside work.

Individuals in receipt of good development support reported increases in motivation and behaviour at work resulting from the increased sense of interest in work. So it seems that attention to development can both improve the capability of individuals and improve their motivation and engagement.

A survey by the Career Innovation Group (Winter and Jackson 2004) asked over 700 high performers in a small sample of large, mostly global, organisations to comment on the conversations they had at work that had high impact on them. Not surprisingly, these high performing employees are the kinds of people who get a lot of attention, and they had quite a lot of conversations about their work, especially with their managers. However they were not always getting the types of conversations they most needed:

- They had far more high impact conversations about their performance than about their development.
- The lack of development conversations also correlated with intention to leave. The big conversation gap was about career development, rather than skills and training for the current job.
- Forty per cent of respondents had an issue about work without any opportunity to discuss it, and were three times more likely than other respondents to be planning

to leave the organisation in the next 12 months. The study concluded that the best leaders were those who addressed both performance and development.

We conclude that managers have a major influence on workplace learning and culture that extends far beyond most job descriptions. Doing nothing about learning and development will have a strong negative effect (Winter and Jackson 2004, quoted in Eraut and Hirsh 2007, pp. 36–37). Thus managers need to: (1) have greater awareness of the modes through which people learn in the workplace; (2) recognise and attend to the factors which enhance or hinder individual or group learning; and (3) take the initiative in the longer-term development of their staff. The justification for giving this high priority is that what is good for learning is also good for retention, quality improvement and developing the skills and people that will be needed in the future.

Most of the research on learning by groups relates to intact social systems with clear boundaries and one or more common tasks to perform. In order to improve the effectiveness of such groups there is a need to understand group behaviour and to identify the factors that most powerfully enhance or depress its task effectiveness. These issues were clearly presented by Hackman's (1987) Normative Model of Group Effectiveness, which is briefly summarised below. Hackman starts with a broad definition of team effectiveness based on three criteria, all of which are socially defined:

- 'The productive output of the work group should meet or exceed the performance standards of the people who receive and/or review the output.'
- 'The social processes used in carrying out the work should maintain or enhance the capability of members to work together on subsequent team tasks.'
- 'The group experience should, on balance, satisfy rather than frustrate the personal needs of group members.'

He observed that 'The challenge for researchers and practitioners is to develop ways of understanding, designing and managing groups that help them to meet or exceed these modest standards' (ibid.: 323).

Two important distinctions were:

1. Expecting teams to 'in some way shape the future of the organisational strategy and development of the business', i.e. to generate new knowledge or synergistic learning;
2. Differences between teams integrated into the organisation as a semi-permanent structure and those organised as a largely separate project.

Continuing Professional Learning Most continuing professional learning activities are initiated by higher education or professional associations. Some more generic activities are developed by education or adult education departments, and many specialist concerns are covered by relevant charities, particularly in education, health and social care. Most organisations, managers, professional workers and safety workers get some support; but continuing professional learning is still dominated by short events with an emphasis on updating university-based courses linked to potential career advancement. This section therefore starts by considering what helps and what hinders workplace learning, and summarise the points in Table 3.4 (Eraut and Hirsh 2007).

Table 3.4 What helps and what hinders workplace learning?

What helps workplace learning?	What hinders workplace learning?
Individual factors	*Individual factors*
Learning with challenging work	Limited opportunity for challenging work
Frequent and constructive feedback	Excessive pressure and stress
Time for learning with others	
Team level factors	*Team level factors*
Supportive relationships and mutual respect	Work issues not discussed with others
Frequent discussions with colleagues	Unsupportive or threatening behaviour
Formal team meetings and reviews	Social isolation at work
Learning opportunities through allocating and designing work processes	
Support for and from line management	*Defensive approach from managers*
Role for managers and experienced workers in supporting the time and learning of others	Line managers who are unwilling to resolve work issues constructively
Attention to emotional aspects of work	Lack in giving employees meta-skills and confidence in learning
Tolerance, diversity and alternative ideas	
Support managers to give feedback, develop coaching, and delegate more to others	Leaving managers to develop their staff, when they lack the skills or motivation to do so
Select managers with an interest in, and aptitude for, developing others	
Approach to learning and development	*Approach to learning and development*
Employees motivated and supported to take responsibility for their own learning	On-the-job learning may not be used if there is little time allocated for it
Accessible learning advisers for both managers and employees, and a flexible capacity to design bespoke learning interventions and work with teams	Courses may be seen as the main, or only, means of learning
	The learning and development function may miss key aspects for line managers or business needs
Learning interventions linked closely to the work context, with careful consideration of learning transfer to the job	Bureaucratic approaches to competence and assessment may miss important aspects of learning
Organisational context, processes and leadership behaviour	*Organisational context, processes and leadership behaviour*
Performance and reward systems which pay attention to knowledge sharing	Promotion and reward mechanisms which emphasise the short-term and individual performance, instead of investing in medium-term or collective performance
Clear organisational values underpinning work and personal behaviour	
Behaviour at the top which discusses problems and issues	Senior management contexts in which people avoid change to protect their job security or power
Encouragement of networking and wider development of the social workplace	

Learning Focus

Learning is viewed as occurring across organisation levels (individual, group, organisation), and also as impacting performance and possibly values. This emphasis on learning is shared within continuing professional learning, but it is often given less priority than knowledge. Moreover, continuing professional learning gives far less attention to learning at group and organisational levels. One reason for this may be the ambiguous position of those who have the dual role of professional practitioner and manager. The prevailing tendency is for practitioner learning to be the main focus of continuing professional learning, with some management learning being provided by employers, in large organisations under the auspices of their human resource development function. However, there are a number of processes which can be used to encourage both managers and employees. For example, managers can, and should, be partly assessed on how they develop their subordinates. Individuals can have personal development objectives built into their job objectives, and teams can also be given performance targets that include a learning dimension. Perhaps the most critical issues at any level are those which determine and prioritise learning needs; for example using what kind of consultation and at what level of detail.

Human resource development has tended to use a training needs model focused on performance, in which the contribution of employees to the learning needs analysis varies widely according to the organisational culture and the area of concern. Continuing professional learning provides opportunities for sharing practitioners' experiences across organisations. The most neglected aspect of continuing professional learning is the problem of transfer. This covers four distinct processes with some important common aspects:

- Transfer of formal knowledge into performance in a specific context;
- Transfer of performance from one context to another;
- Transfer of practices from one person to another person;
- Transfer of practices from one group to another group.

Eraut (2004b) has argued elsewhere that this fundamental difficulty can be attributed to two problems: the narrow conception of practical knowledge used in most formal education, and the lack of any significance or ownership of the transfer process itself. This transfer process can be deconstructed into five inter-related stages:

- The extraction of potentially relevant knowledge from the context(s) of its acquisition and previous use;
- Understanding the new situation, a process that often depends on informal social learning;
- Recognising what knowledge and skills are relevant;
- Transforming the relevant skills to fit the new situation;
- Integrating the relevant skills with other knowledge and skills in order to think, act or communicate in the new situation (Eraut 2004b).

The problem that remains is that of how best to help those who have learned knowledge appropriate for their field of work and how to use it in a range of potentially relevant situations. This process can be greatly accelerated if another person with relevant expertise can share the development and offer appropriate advice. The difficulty here is that proficient workers cannot easily communicate their taken-for-granted local practices, and may not even be aware of their more tacit aspects. Those with recent experience of using relevant knowledge in two or more contexts will be better prepared to help newcomers. For others, approaches to sharing tacit knowledge that we have used or encountered in the literature (Eraut et al. 2004) include:

- Demonstrating skills with a voice-over commentary—this may not be an authentic account of normal thinking in action, but can still communicate much useful tacit knowledge;
- Discussing common episodes at which the participants were co-present;
- Recordings of episodes, with the possible addition of a voice-over commentary (Holmstrom and Rosenqvist 2004);
- Describing incidents or telling stories, followed by discussion (Fairbairn 2002);
- Discussing cases and/or problems, real or fictional;
- Use of mediating artefacts.

Over time, it also becomes possible to develop new vocabulary and practices for discussing expertise, and gradually to introduce concepts and theories that may help people to make more sense of their experience.

Performance Focus

The importance of a smooth boundary between management and professional expertise is exemplified by Hoag's (2001) account of skills development in his engineering company. His group constructed a set of five proficiency levels, a paragraph for each of 15 areas of engineering; they could rely on self-assessment of these because any discrepancies soon become apparent. These levels could then be used for assigning people to projects and reviewing the match between the company's anticipated skill mix and its anticipated future demands. This covered:

- Providing a clear snapshot of department deficiencies;
- Succession planning for retirements, transfers or resignations;
- Rapid and intelligent staffing of new projects;
- Ensuring that the best choices are made in internal staffing selections (employer transfers);
- Ensuring that staff selections fully consider employee diversity.

Another human resource development intervention is personal support through coaching, mentoring and enriched feedback. Carter's (2001) report on executive coaching sees this as responding to three problems: the isolation of many managers; the increasing demand for 'soft skills' which are not amenable to formal teaching; and the failure of organisations to give managers enough feedback. Both coaching and mentoring have proved exceptionally popular with employees, as well as being perceived as effective by human resource professionals.

Eighty-eight per cent of respondents to the Chartered Institute of Personnel and Development (CIPD) 2005 survey of training and development reported using internal coaching, 72 % mentoring, and 64 % external coaching: a pattern extending well into the smaller firms in the sample. However, coaching was rarely offered to anyone other than managers.

Historically, continuing professional learning has given less attention to performance issues, partly because providers have little knowledge of the factors within the organisational system that might affect an individual's performance in any particular workplace. Nevertheless, continuing professional learning is now beginning to be asked to measure its ultimate impact on service users. This is an absurd idea because, although a well-conceived course can be an excellent learning event, it cannot be a complete learning package that delivers the desired outcomes. That normally requires a considerable further amount of on-the-job learning, and this will only happen if the learning is treated as a high priority by the participants' work group. That is why research has consistently reported that courses are only effective when delivered 'just in time' (Eraut et al. 2000).

Strategic focus

This focus involves strategic human resource development being integrated into an organisation's mission or purpose and incorporated into all major planning initiatives. Case study-based research by the Institute of Employment Studies (Hirsh and Tamkin 2005) found that many large organisations do not have a single formal training plan, but a range of plans and budgets at varied locations. The study identified five main mechanisms which influence training plans and priorities:

1. *Formal business planning both at top level and more locally*, leading to training priorities. Either a training plan or set of priorities can be produced on the basis of business plans or targets, or the two processes of business planning and workforce development planning are wrapped together.
2. *Links from human resource strategy to training implications*. The Institute of Employment Studies study did not find many cases in which human resource strategies gave clear indications of training needs. Competence frameworks were often used in training and development, but there was little evidence that they mapped onto *real* skill gaps.
3. *Plans for key workforce groups*. Organisations often have a specific plan and budget for management and leadership development, partly because this aspect of learning tends to be co-ordinated by a centralised, corporate team. Some have specific early career entry and training schemes at graduate level.
4. *Major business issues or changes* often lead directly to major training interventions, usually with extra funds from the corporate centre. Typical of these would be re-organisations, mergers or acquisitions, or major changes in technology or products. In a similar way, specific changes in work at local level can lead to the identification of learning needs which may not have been foreseen on the normal annual planning cycle. But responding to such needs may depend upon the local unit being able to set aside specific funding.
5. *Take-up of training provision* is a strong influence on future plans. Training courses or other interventions which are well used and receive positive feedback through evaluation are often repeated. Learning provision which is not well used tends to be dropped. This effect is particularly strong where local managers have to pay for the training, whether provided in-house or by external suppliers.

Continuing professional learning has given much less attention to strategic issues, and this causes many problems for professional workers. In particular it needs to address the issues of specifying and providing a quality service and giving greater priority to user perspectives. This will require both close alignment with strategic development and a greater focus on learning at group and organisational levels. This is especially important in health care organisations because of their multi-professional character. Not only is there lack of alignment with human resource development but there are separate continuous professional learning policies and practices for each professional group.

References

Carter, A. (2001). *Executive coaching: inspiring performance at work.* IES Report 379. Brighton: Institute of Employment Studies.

Chartered Institute of Personal and Development (CIPD). (2005). *Training and development, annual survey report.* London: CIPD.

Connelly, T., & Wagner, W. G. (1988). Decision cycles. In R. L. Cardy, S. M. Puffer & M. M. Newman (Eds.), *Advances in information processing in organizations. (Vol 3, pp. 183–205).* Greenwich: JAI Press.

Eraut, M. (2000). Non-formal learning and tacit knowledge in professional work. *British Journal of Educational Psychology, 70,* 113–136.

Eraut, M. (2004a). Informal learning in the workplace. *Studies in Continuing Education, 26*(2), 247–273.

Eraut, M. (2004b). Transfer of knowledge between education and workplace settings. In H. Rainbird, A. Fuller & H. Munro (Eds.), *Workplace learning in context* (pp. 201–221). London: Routledge.

Eraut, M. (2007). Learning from other people in the workplace. *Oxford Review of Education, 33*(4), 403–422.

Eraut, M., & Hirsh, W. (2007). *The significance of workplace learning for individuals, groups and organisations.* Commissioned by SKOPE, ESRC Centre on Skills, Knowledge and Organisational Performance.

Eraut, M., Alderton, J., Boylan, A., & Wraight, A. (1995). *Learning to use scientific knowledge in education and practice settings.* London: English National Board for Nursing, Midwifery and Health Visiting.

Eraut, M., Alderton, J., Cole, G., & Senker, P. (2000). Development of knowledge and skills at work. In F. Coffield (Ed.), *Differing visions of a learning society: Research findings* (Vol 1). Bristol: The Policy Press.

Eraut, M., Maillardet, F. J., Miller, C., Steadman, S., Ali, S., Blackman, C., & Furner, J. (2004). *Learning in the professional workplace: Relationships between learning factors and contextual factors.* San Diego: AERA 2004 Conference.

Fairbairn, G. J. (2002). Ethics, empathy and storytelling in professional development. *Learning in Health and Social Care, 1,* 22–32.

Hackman, J. R. (1987). The design of work teams. In J. Lorsch (Ed.), *Handbook of organizational behavior* (pp. 315–342). Englewood Cliffs NJ: Prentice-Hall.

Hirsh, W., & Tamkin, P. (2005). *Planning training for your business.* Report 422. Brighton: Institute for Employment Studies.

Hirsh, W., Silverman, M., Tamkin, P., & Jackson, C. (2004). *Managers as developers of others.* IES Report 407. Brighton: Institute for Employment Studies.

Hoag, K. (2001). *Skills development for engineers: An innovative model for advanced learning in the workplace.* London: The Institution of Electrical Engineers.

Holmstrom, I., & Rosenqvist, U. (2004). Interventions to support reflection and learning. *Learning in Health and Social Care, 3*(4), 203–212.

Klein, G. A. (1989). Recognition-primed decisions. In W. B. Rouse (Ed.), *Advances in man-machine systems research* (pp. 47–92). Greenwich: JAI Press.

McKee, A., & Eraut, M. (2012). *Learning trajectories, innovation and identity for professional development.* (Edited book with 3 chapters). Springer.

Sharu, D. (2012). From nurse to advanced nurse practitioner: Mid-career transformation. In Learning trajectories, innovation and identity for professional development. In A. McKee & M. Eraut (Eds.) *Learning trajectories, innovation and identity for professional development innovation and change in professional education*, (Vol 7 pp. 175–192). Springer.

Weick, K. E. (1983). Managerial thought in the context of action. In C. Srivastva (Ed.), *The executive mind.* San Francisco: Jossey-Bass.

Winter, J., & Jackson, C. (2004). *The conversation gap.* Oxford: Career Innovation Group.

Chapter 4
Work-based, Accredited Professional Education: Insights from Medicine

Tim Dornan and Anne-Mette Mørcke

Introduction

Medicine is a health care profession which has much in common with the teaching profession. Health care professionals make the care of patients 'their first concern' (General Medical Council 2006) just as teachers put the education of students first. Health care, like teaching, may be practised in for-profit organisations or not-for-profit ones, but professional ethics are expected to transcend the business model of the institution that employs a doctor or teacher. There is an element of risk to being a health care professional, just as actions by teachers on behalf of students may threaten their licensure or health. Medicine differs from other health care professions, but perhaps not from teaching, in that practice is expected sometimes to be standard and sometimes non-standard. Doctors are expected to adhere to protocols, but they are also expected to forge solutions to unique problems, which is a justification for it being such a 'knowledge-rich' health care profession. Teaching, also, is knowledge-rich.

Parallels between medicine and teaching do not end there. Medical professional ethics make it explicit that doctors should be teachers of other doctors and medical students (General Medical Council 2006). But it is there that differences between medicine and teaching become apparent. Clinical teachers are almost always medical practitioners first, so the parallel would be with a chemist or physicist who did a bit of secondary school teaching as a 'spin-off' of their practice, rather than a typical chemistry or physics teacher. From a communities of practice theoretical perspective

T. Dornan (✉)
Maastricht University, Maastricht, Netherlands
e-mail: t.dornan@maastrichtuniversity.nl

The University of Manchester, Manchester, UK

A.-M. Mørcke
Centre for Medical Education, Aarhus University,
Aarhus, Denmark
e-mail: amm@medu.au.dk

O. McNamara et al. (eds.), *Workplace Learning in Teacher Education,*
Professional Learning and Development in Schools and Higher Education 10,
DOI 10.1007/978-94-007-7826-9_4, © Springer Science+Business Media Dordrecht 2014

(Wenger 1998), we have recently framed clinical teachers as having two practices: a practice of patient care and an educational practice (McLachlan et al. 2012). Different doctors give those two practices different priorities and are more or less successful at aligning them with one another (Bell et al. 2013). To make matters more complicated still, doctors may also be managers and/or researchers, in which case teaching can be the 'safest' of several practices. Education is all too often 'at the bottom of the food chain' in medicine as it can be in universities, but hopefully not in schools.

Teachers and teacher educators reading this chapter may find medicine a confusing exemplar because there are two strands in our narrative which can easily get tangled round one another: learning how to do the job of a doctor 'on the job'; and learning to be a medical teacher (which may be on or off the job). The first is the more obviously relevant so we will concentrate on it in this section, turning to the training of doctors as teachers later. Learning how to do the job of a doctor and 'remaining up to scratch' is often referred to as a 'lifelong learning continuum'. In reality, the supposed continuum has separate phases, with 'transitions' between them. The first stage, which lasts 4–7 years, prepares medical students to perform doctors' jobs after qualifying. At this stage, people who are not yet part of the workforce learn by shadowing those who are whilst enrolled in higher education courses. The second stage, which lasts 5–10 years, is learning as a 'resident' (foundation or specialist trainees in UK parlance). Learners are now part of the workforce but not yet independent practitioners. The third stage, the continuing education of fully trained doctors, helps them keep their skills up to date and finely honed. It starts in their middle age and continues to retirement. For all the effort that has gone into developing work-based medical education, people consistently report that one stage fails to prepare learners adequately for the next stage (Teunissen and Westerman 2011). The result is that people feel as though they are learning the job from scratch when they enter a new phase, despite all their earlier studies; a problem that we suspect is to be found in other professions, perhaps including teaching.

Doctors(-to-be) are not only taught by doctors. Scientists dominate medical students' early, university-based undergraduate education and contribute at other times as well. Other health professionals and social scientists teach in clinical skills laboratories, where learning is supported by simulation technology. Patients also teach, sometimes in 'expert' roles (Hendry et al. 1999), but more often in the passive role of 'object' from whom students learn (McLachlan et al. 2012). However, doctors are doctors' most important teachers because the medical education that has the greatest impact takes place in workplaces, either closely linked to or as part of patient care. A result of having such a variety of teachers in medical schools is that medical students are boundary crossers, learning on both sides of boundaries, which only they ever cross.

The next two sections on codified and uncodified knowledge explore how the medical profession frames and articulates its knowledge base and what types of knowledge it values in order that readers can compare and contrast medicine with their own practice. It treats the education of medical students and young doctors as a 'theory-in-use' of medical knowledge. After these two sections, we return to the strand of how doctors learn to be teachers.

Codified Knowledge

Meet Sarah

Sarah is a (fictional) junior resident; in other words, she is in the second of the three stages of a medical lifetime described above. When she was a medical student, teachers frequently tested her knowledge during teaching sessions. She also passed a number of high stake exams: five 100-item multiple choice questionnaires, ten short written answer exams, a few oral question-answer exams, a long essay exam, three large project reports that were followed by a defence (viva), and three long case clinical exams. She did well in medical school based on her grades from all those assessments and qualified. Recently, she passed the first part examination for specialist certification, which was a multiple-choice assessment of declarative knowledge, including the basic biomedical sciences.

Erudite, Codified Knowledge

Medicine established its powerful position amongst health professions by developing an erudite corpus of knowledge and making high academic performance an entry requirement. Codified knowledge has been valued over practice-based, tacit knowledge since medieval times, when doctors left barber-surgeons and apothecaries to do the menial work of treating patients. The high value given to codified knowledge is apparent in modern medical education practice as well. In his institutional ethnography of a medical school, Sinclair identified a question-answer routine as an archetypal feature of medical students' learning (Sinclair 1997). Typically, such questions demand a single 'right answer', which Biggs and Tang (2007) described using the cognitive term declarative knowledge. Medical textbooks, which students and young doctors are expected to learn more-or-less by heart, provide the answers to such questions, often in long lists. Declarative knowledge is acquired, also, in state-of-the-art lectures given by revered experts and grand rounds, when doctors pit their erudition against one another around an exemplar patient case. Declarative knowledge is demanded when medical students and young doctors give case presentations at patients' bedsides. It is a criterion of success in long case clinical examinations, a time-honoured genre in which students are asked to examine a patient and answer questions about anatomy, physiology, pathology, medical terms, expected symptoms, clinical findings and their frequencies, plausible and rare diagnoses, complications, treatments and prognosis. Thus the medical profession espouses a broad and deep corpus of codified knowledge, though a new discourse of curriculum has led to widespread adoption of competency-based medical education.

Competency-based Education

The competency discourse signals a change in how the medical profession frames the knowledge it values. Competency-based curricula are written as sets of learning outcomes or competencies, which must be clearly stated and unambiguous. They are expressed as behaviours that learners must be able to demonstrate, the subject matter those behaviours pertain to, and the contexts in which the behaviours must be demonstrated (Biggs and Tang 2007). Competency-based education was trumpeted as a new approach to medical education at the turn of the millennium (Harden et al. 1999), though we have been able to trace a more or less unbroken line of inheritance from behaviourist psychology of the 1940s down to its recent revival (Morcke et al. 2012). The revival reasserted a view expressed in earlier years that an outcome specification could benefit curriculum design, assessment, programme evaluation, and accountability. So, the competency movement progressed quickly from advocacy to worldwide implementation (Harden 2007; Frank and Danoff 2007; Cooke et al. 2010).

> **Back to Sarah and her education**
> Sarah, who is now three years on from qualifying as a doctor, has chosen to follow a specialty education in general internal medicine. She followed a competency-based curriculum in medical school and continues to do so during specialist training. To add to her exam successes, she has passed an objective structured clinical examination testing her behaviour in 20 different standard-ised and simulated settings, which was a requirement for entry into higher specialist training. She did well on that one as well. Furthermore, she has dutifully filled out her learning portfolio, documenting her competence as a communicator, co-operator, leader, health promoter, academic, and profes-sional. Her ability to perform certain clinical procedures has been assessed in workplaces and she has been through a multi-source feedback (anonymous rat-ings of professional attributes by ten co-workers) and a 'case based discussion', where she explained the clinical reasoning that lay behind her management of a patient. The specialist physician she currently works for is her 'educational supervisor'. Sarah recently had an appraisal when her supervisor reviewed her acquisition of competence to check she is progressing satisfactorily.

One reason competency-based education was avidly adopted is that performance outcomes offered medicine an escape from an unhappy marriage to declarative knowledge. As can be seen from Sarah's story, competencies broadened doctors' abilities from giving right answers to possessing and being able to enact skills, func-tional knowledge, and attitudes. Those broader types of learning outcome aligned better with vernacular experiences gained in workplaces than a theory of knowledge that valued the abstract and the abstruse, and yet they are still codified.

Competency-based education, we suggest, has made medicine seem clearly de-fined and safe. Society has put doctors' accountability for delivering safe and effective care high on the agenda of medical schools. Testing the competencies of medical students and doctors is an attractive way of demonstrating social accountability and ensuring the profession upholds its own high professional standards. With the shift to competency-based education and its focus on demonstrable behaviours, a shift towards more performance assessment and an assumption that such assessments can test professionalism has followed. The snag, however, is that performance assessment of skills and functional knowledge cannot truly distinguish good from less good doctors. Society wants professional competence to include affective qualities like empathy, altruism, confidence, self-reflection, an ability to cope under stress, and upholding professional values. Long before the recent advocacy of competency-based education began, it was acknowledged that complex personal and professional attributes—being a good doctor—could not be broken down to demonstrable performance outcomes and assessed objectively. Competency-based education can meet society's demand for accountability but not, it is generally acknowledged, the demand for doctors to demonstrate humane qualities. The recent focus on measuring competencies in the name of patient safety will, inevitably, have unintended as well as intended consequences. It is distinctly possible that what is gained in training and assessing safe doctors may be lost in not educating doctors to be 'good' ones.

To summarise this section, we have reviewed two ways of framing and codifying medical competence, both of which are heavily weighted towards assessment. The first reflects a professional culture, which dates back many years. It frames competence as being able to give the right answer to questions testing declarative knowledge. The second frames competence as the ability to demonstrate proficiency. The first derives from medicine's long cultural history. The second is a response to society's call for doctors to be more socially accountable for their competence. Neither, however, is based on careful scrutiny of the attributes that will enable doctors to perform effectively in practice, as opposed to test conditions. The next section introduces an alternative perspective on professional proficiency and explores how it applies to medicine.

Uncodified Knowledge

emWe précis here some key points made by Eraut in Chap. 3, which describes the type of professional knowledge called upon in workplaces as ill-structured, in distinct contrast to the codified knowledge valued by medicine's assessment culture and presented in textbooks. The information available to professionals, according to Eraut, is incomplete, ambiguous, and changing. And the goals of professionals are ill-defined, in competition with one another, and shifting. Decisions, which occur in multiple event-feedback loops, are taken within time constraints. The stakes are high, many stakeholders contribute to decisions, and decision-makers balance personal choice with organisational norms and goals. So, the relationship between knowledge and decision-making is not simple. Problems have to be framed in terms of decision-makers' situational understanding. Codified knowledge is less important than personal knowledge, which includes uncodifiable cultural knowledge. Uncodified knowledge is acquired informally through participation in working practices and tends to be taken for granted.

Some harsh realities of medical work

It is Sarah's first 'on call' shift at a district hospital during her third year of residency. A senior resident, who is supervising her, is also working in the hospital but at the end of a phone, and the specialist who is providing 'cover' to them both is doing so by telephone from home. It is a busy shift, not least because Sarah has repeatedly been paged by the nursing staff on a ward, where a patient who is not in command of his faculties has been abusing nurses. They are demanding that 'a doctor does something' to calm the patient down. That would pose the most experienced doctor, let alone Sarah, a practical and ethical challenge. Meanwhile, she is called to see a patient in the emergency department who has diabetes and a sore on his foot. She knows diabetic foot ulcers can ultimately lead to amputation if they are not handled quickly and appropriately on occasions like this one. She tries to recall teaching she received as a medical student. The action she must take is influenced by a judgment as to whether or not the blood supply to the patient's foot is seriously impaired but how, exactly, does one do that? She must also get an X-ray of the foot to determine if the underlying bone is infected; how, she tries to remember, will she make that judgement when she examines the X-ray? She is inexperienced at doing so. Should she call the senior resident now, later or not at all? The senior resident she is reporting to today has a reputation for making harsh judgements on juniors who 'bottle out' too quickly, but what will the specialist covering them both say if Sarah shows herself unwilling to call for help when in doubt? Should she go 'over the head' of the senior resident, or will that cause even more trouble? Perhaps there is a doctor on call for the diabetes department; how does she find that out? She should probably admit the patient to hospital, but should it be to a medical or surgical ward? If a surgical ward, is it the local practice for such patients to go to a general surgical, orthopaedic, or vascular ward? She should start antibiotics to treat infection in the foot. Is there a protocol that dictates which antibiotics are to be used in this hospital and how can she find that out? There goes her pager again from the ward with the abusive patient. You just don't learn in medical school how to manage patients with diabetic foot problems and you don't learn to do so properly 'on the job' unless you do a diabetic job, which not everyone does. Even then, you find Dr X likes his patients managed one way and Dr Y another. They don't get on well with one another so you get yelled at for making the wrong decision if you don't first find out if the patient's specialist is Dr X or Dr Y. Sarah knows that even people who've completed their accreditation exams are floored by problems they haven't done the right jobs to train them for. Why, oh why, did she have to get a diabetic foot, which she's clueless about, at a moment like this, rather than something straightforward like pneumonia? And **** that pager . . .

Eraut's choice of the term 'learning trajectories' (Chap. 3, this volume) well describes the continuous nature of clinical learning though, as he notes, it is not in conflict with the static term 'competencies', which describes a person's level of attainment at a particular point in time. Table 3.3 in Chap. 3 shows Eraut's eight categories of trajectory, which we now illustrate with clinical examples.

Task Performance

This is the trajectory along which learners develop their ability to perform a wide range of tasks fluently. Those tasks include psychomotor skills, intellectual tasks, and social ones, ranging from examining the blood supply of a diabetic foot, completing a form requesting an X-ray whilst simultaneously answering the telephone, to telling someone their spouse has died and allowing them to express their grief. Clinical tasks are always dialogical because they involve patients, vicariously if not in person, and usually involve collaboration with a range of other people.

Awareness and Understanding

The preceding vignette of Sarah and the diabetic patient with a sore on his foot demonstrates the degree of situational awareness that doctors must develop through experience in workplaces. It shows the broad range of considerations doctors have to take into account when framing clinical problems and the risks of not considering all the relevant factors. It illustrates the subtle nature of some values, priorities, and strategies that surround the solution of clinical problems and the need for learners to be strategic in solving them.

Personal Development

Much has been written about medical students' and young doctors' identity trajectories; they 'become' rather than accrete the attributes of trained practitioners (Monrouxe 2010). The vignette above shows how something so apparently simple as calling for help could construct a learner's identity as 'someone who bottles out too soon', 'goes over colleagues' heads', or 'is unwilling to call for help'. The self-management and emotional reactions entailed in making such a judgment call when your pager is harassing you are self-evident. Teunissen and colleagues have shown how trainee doctors faced with such choices have to balance their willingness to learn against their keenness to cut favourable impressions with senior colleagues (Teunissen et al. 2009).

Teamwork

Medicine cannot be practised without collaboration, and yet it is a competitive profession. Along the teamwork trajectory, junior doctors like Sarah must develop their ability to plan and solve problems jointly, which may be challenging when doctors of different grades of seniority work together, or members of different health professions join together to care for patients. The different priorities and competencies of all professionals involved in problems have to be reconciled and used to patients' benefit.

Role Performance

Readiness to take on a senior position as a fully trained doctor calls for trainees to take on a variety of roles. They progress over five years from being the most junior members of clinical teams to supervising and teaching more junior people. They must both lead and be accountable to others. They must be able to manage crises and handle ethical issues. They must learn to delegate.

Academic Knowledge and Skills

We have highlighted the divide between the type of knowledge tested in exams and the type of knowledge required in practice. A 'half-way house' between them is 'evidence-based medicine', which exhorts doctors to formulate questions arising from patient care in ways that are amenable to scholarly answers. The snag is that the espoused medical knowledge taught and tested in undergraduate and postgraduate education ill prepares doctors to solve clinical problems in scholarly ways, unless a patient's problem is an exotic one. There is also an ongoing debate about the true proportion of clinical problems that are amenable to the type of codified solutions on-line databases and the like can offer. Another disjoint is between the basic sciences taught in medical school and the way clinical problems present, which are so removed from one another that 'transfer' of knowledge is a substantial relearning task. Clinical reasoning is held to be a type of theoretical thinking, but experienced doctors make sophisticated diagnoses and choose treatments in ways that seem to novices more like black magic than logic, and which experienced doctors may put down to 'gut feelings' or 'experience'.

Decision-making and Problem-solving

If one takes into account the human dimension of illness, clinical problems are rarely entirely simple, though doctors-in-training may have to (over) simplify them to survive the pressures of workload and complexity they deal with every day. The ability to see problems in simple ways that lead to the most effective actions comes with experience, and challenges people's tolerance of uncertainty and ability to see problems in shades of grey rather than black and white. Consider, for example, the abusive patient about whom Sarah is repeatedly being paged. The hospital operates a 'zero tolerance' policy towards abuse of staff, which he is clearly breaching. He could be cautioned, sedated and/or physically restrained by security staff, which would allow Sarah to devote the requisite time to the patient with a sore on their foot. But the abusive behaviour could be due to physical illness that needs treatment. It could also result from the patient being afraid, and the nurses may be afraid too. A gentle and understanding approach to the people concerned could 'defuse' the problem or lead to some other less draconian solution than having a burly security guard sitting at the bedside and making the patient even more afraid.

Judgement

The last of Eraut's eight categories of learning trajectory may seem to have been covered in different ways under previous ones, but the times when doctors make their worst mistakes is when they fail to judge how sick a patient is. There are other judgement calls: one of us, for example, became aware that a doctor working under his supervision was dangerously unskilled. When the nurses and doctors on the ward were asked, individually, if they had any concerns, every one of them was seriously concerned about the doctor's performance, but neither individually nor collectively had they judged the person as unfit to practice, which was clearly the case.

To conclude our treatment of knowledge, it is ironic that medicine primarily values codified knowledge and its leaders are currently trying to reduce such complex attributes as doctors' humanity to competencies, while research in hairdressing (Billett 2006), nursing, accountancy, and engineering (Eraut; Chap. 3 in this volume) has arrived at more authentic descriptions of how learning occurs. We are not arguing that Eraut's typology should be formally adopted in medical education. We do find it informative, however, that it can be so easily populated with medical examples. Medicine, we conclude, has types of knowledge that defy codification. Eraut's concept that learning takes place along trajectories, moreover, sanctions the type of lifelong learning that makes specialist doctors experts rather than just competent people. The next section moves from how doctors become expert clinicians to how they learn to teach. It starts from a historical perspective and then considers some contemporary forces for change. It identifies a mismatch between how doctors are taught to support the on-the-job learning of junior colleagues and how medicine is actually learned on-the-job, which is consonant with misalignment in theories of knowledge discussed above.

Becoming a Medical Teacher

Teaching your future colleagues

Sarah's third year of residency is progressing and she is keeping her portfolio of evidence that demonstrates her competence up to date. Although her current hospital is not a university hospital, medical students rotate here to do clinical placements with the consultant she is working for. He has a management role and copes with his teaching responsibilities by unofficially delegating them to Sarah. She likes the idea of having contact with students, but the mandatory 'teach the teachers' workshop she attended in her last job was very much orientated towards teaching skills like blood-taking and examining students' proficiency on anatomical models in a clinical skills laboratory. One of the students asks if she can sit in with Sarah during this afternoon's outpatient clinic. Sarah is self-conscious about having someone watching her work and cannot imagine how, under the time pressures she faces, she can find time to teach as well as see patients.

The previously mentioned notion that doctors have a *duty* to teach suggests that education is embedded in medicine, which implies that doctors' basic skills-set equips them to be educators. That would have been a reasonable assumption in earlier years when postgraduate medical education was an apprenticeship and junior doctors learned practice skills under the tutelage of a master. That type of education is neatly summarised by the aphorism: 'See one, do one, teach one'. Assessment, feedback, appraisal and portfolios were nowhere to be seen! Now, education processes are much more formal and teaching roles are also more formal. In particular, there is an emphasis on instructing and assessing teaching skills. As young doctors' education has been formalised, teaching roles have been formalised and so has teacher development. Medical professional organisations, which formerly only acted as examining bodies, have constituted themselves as providers of teacher training. By doing so, they have retained their power and influence despite education becoming a practice distinct from medicine.

In order to examine how the role and education of medical teachers is constructed in 'the new order', Table 4.1 presents the syllabus for a course aimed at helping doctors take on workplace education roles, from supervisor of trainee doctors' daily work through to education leader. Rather than choosing one such course (many of which are run in the UK) entirely at random, we chose one provided in the part of England where the seminars on which this book was born took place. We have added subheadings to the table and clustered course content under them, but Table 4.1 is otherwise faithful to the online description of what is doubtless an effective course. It is striking that (summative) assessment is the strongest theme. The workplace-based assessments referred to in the upper section of Table 4.1 entail demonstrating clinical proficiency to a supervisor. Learners are responsible for asking trained doctors to perform such assessments at mutually convenient moments. A learner performs some

Table 4.1 Programme for a postgraduate certificate in workplace-based postgraduate medical education

Completion of this 20-credit module gives a doctor 'approved clinical supervisor status'—in other words, approval to supervise the daily clinical work of a doctor in training. Topics addressed in it include:	
Teaching learners medical practice:	Assessing learners:
Clinical skills teaching	Workplace-based assessment
Teaching in the clinical workplace	Feedback
Co-conducting clinical practice:	Portfolios
Supervision	Education theory:
Education practice:	Understanding adult learning
Reflective practice	Styles of learning
Peer observation of teaching	Styles of teaching
Fostering learning environments:	Philosophy of teaching
Educational climate	
Completion of this 20-credit module gives a doctors'approved educational supervisor status'—in other words, approval to act as an appraiser with responsibility for a trainee's learning for a defined period. Topics addressed in it include:	
Assessing learners:	Formal education roles/processes:
Assessing learning needs	Mentoring and coaching
Learning agreements and objectives	Quality management
Assessment and appraisal principles	Introduction to careers support
Annual review of competence progression (ARCP) reports	Supporting trainees in difficulty
Completion of this 20-credit module, together with the preceding two, qualifies doctors for award of a Postgraduate Certificate in Workplace Based Postgraduate Medical Education. Topics addressed in it include:	
Assessing learners:	Education practice:
Appraisal skills	Approaches to medical education, e.g. PBL, e-learning
ARCP cycle and structures	Educational leadership—principles and approaches
Formal education roles/processes:	Presentation skills
Managing the educational experience	Methods of medical education, e.g. presentations, group work
Advanced career management	
Recruitment and selection	
Curriculum planning and course design	

Adapted from: www.nwpgmd.nhs.uk/sites/default/files/PGCEOverviewJuly2012.pdf. The headings of the three sections of the table were adapted by us from the original course description, and the underlined subheadings and grouping of course content were done by us. The individual items of learning in the course are copied verbatim from the original site

authentic task for about ten minutes while a doctor observes and then completes a computer-based proforma. The doctor gives the learner verbal feedback on strengths demonstrated and areas for improvement. Fitness to progress through training is determined by cumulative performance over multiple such assessments so each one is 'low stakes'. All specialties include 'high stakes' assessments as well, which are provided by medical professional accrediting organisations. They typically assess practical proficiency in simulated settings and knowledge under standardised test conditions.

The middle section of Table 4.1 includes formal roles taken on by clinicians as assessors, appraisers, coaches, mentors, career advisers and supporters at times of difficulty. Trained doctors are, to some degree, both poachers and gamekeepers in their relationships with trainees. Poachers, because supervisor and supervisee practice together and are interdependent in running what are usually very hard-pressed clinical services. They may develop quite close and friendly relationships, in which a supervisor's instinct is to support their supervisee; or, at worst, turn a blind eye to their shortcomings or deny that such shortcomings exist. If subjectivity can bedevil supervision in a positive way, it can bedevil supervision in a negative way too; typically, when relationships between supervisor and supervisee are soured for some reason. But even within friendly relationships, one key professional duty of doctors is to give honest opinions about the proficiency of other doctors, particularly when the wellbeing of patients is at stake. So, supervisors must be gamekeepers as well as poachers.

It is striking to compare the rather formal and regulatory discourse of medical education presented in Table 4.1, with the findings of a detailed ethnographic survey of how trainee doctors actually learn. Shah and colleagues (Shah et al. 2012) found that trainee doctors learned primarily through informal learning that took place in the heat of, and was intimately linked to, clinical practice. Their learning began and ended with the care of individual patients, alone or supported by experienced practitioners. The formal educational system represented by Table 4.1, and captured by terms like assessment, appraisal, mentoring, portfolio, teaching and so on, was conspicuous by its absence in both teachers' and learners' narrative accounts. Just two items in Table 4.1—co-conducting practice and fostering learning environments—were strongly represented in the study of Shah et al. (2012). Trainee doctors learned best in warm, well-organised learning environments, where the workload was neither too great nor too small, and where there was time to step back from the rigours of patient care, ponder it, and discuss it with peers and experienced seniors. Learning was a social process. Their medium of learning was the informal communicative practices of workplaces, which allowed more experienced doctors to share cognitive processes and tacit knowledge with less experienced ones (Shah et al. 2012). Medical students, like the one who wants to sit in with Sarah, need more in the way of formal instruction than Sarah, whose learning is decidedly on-the-job, but it is only through on-the-job, experience that students can ever find out what doctors do, and what they will have to do when qualified.

Moving from the specific and regional instance of medical teacher education presented in Table 4.1 to wider generalities, 'faculty development' (training doctors and other staff of medical schools to be teachers) is the subject of much contemporary medical education research. A systematic literature review by Steinert and colleagues (Steinert et al. 2006) summarised research in the field. Faculty development, the review concluded, had positive effects, particularly when it used experiential learning, provision of feedback, effective peer and colleague relationships, well-designed interventions following principles of teaching and learning, and the use of a diversity of educational methods within single interventions. The review was bedevilled by having 'teaching' as the main dependent variable. The term 'teaching' is used in medicine as though it has some universally shared meaning, but the review of Steinert et al. (2006) showed it could mean anything from 'chalk and talk' pedagogy, to instructing clinical skills, to mentoring young doctors' professional development. It would be puzzling if investing resources in teaching teachers had no positive effects at all, so the results of the review are unsurprising, if encouraging. But it leaves us unsure how to help doctors most efficiently and effectively reconcile their practice of medicine with the education of less experienced colleagues, which is what Sarah has to do. We appeal to readers to consider parallels in their own practices; how much do we know about how experienced teachers in any field share their expertise with trainee teachers in present-day education?

To summarise this section, we have described how a centuries-old, informal process of learning to teach has rather quickly become formalised in line with a new discourse of faculty development. Formal courses, which have sprung up to support clinical teacher education, seem rather closely linked to assessment processes and implicitly linked to professional regulation. Meanwhile, research shows that most professional learning takes place informally, through social interactions between experienced and novice practitioners, and is distinctly unlinked to regulation. So, the official curriculum of teacher education in medicine is removed from the very educational practice it is supposed to support.

Summary and Conclusions

This chapter has reviewed a practice that puts the needs of patients ahead of profit or practitioners' personal ambitions, even if at some risk to their wellbeing. It has shown how theories of codified knowledge, which are rather far removed from everyday workplace realities, dominate the official discourse of education. Those theories serve two purposes. One is to make professional expertise susceptible to assessment. The other, which follows from being able to assess professional expertise, is to subjugate junior practitioners to senior ones. Reducing learning to measurable competencies is very much in vogue, despite earlier rejection of this approach to education. The subject matter of learning, as applied in practice, is far removed from competencies, particularly when it comes to subtle, humane ones like interpersonal skills and professional values. Eraut's taxonomy of trajectories along which professionals grow, that was developed in accountancy, nursing and engineering, could be applied also to medicine. This chapter arrived at those conclusions by a case-study of medicine as a professional educational practice, but we suggest there may be useful parallels with teaching. Workplace education allows practitioners to learn their profession in ways that would not be possible if learning was mainly based in university study, but a regulatory discourse of competency-based education, applied to workplace learning, threatens to trivialise the very professional values it seeks to support.

References

Bell, K., Wenger, E., Boshuizen, H., Scherpbier, A., & Dornan, T. (2013). How clerkship students learn from real patients in workplaces, Submitted

Biggs, J. A., & Tang, C. (2007). *Teaching for quality learning at University*. Maidenhead: Open University Press.

Billett, S. (2006). Relational interdependence between social and individual agency in work and working life. *Mind, Culture, and Activity, 13,* 53–69.

Cooke, M., Irby, D. M., & O'Brien, B. C. (2010). *Educating physicians: A call for reform of medical school and residency. Carnegie Foundation for the Advancement of Teaching*. San Francisco: Jossey-Bass.

Frank, J. R., & Danoff, D. (2007). The CanMEDS initiative: Implementing an outcomes-based framework of physician competencies. *Medical Teacher, 29*(7), 642–647. doi:10.1080/01421590701746983..

General Medical Council. (2006). *Good medical practice*. London: General Medical Council.

Harden, R. M. (2007). Outcome-based education: The future is today. *Medical Teacher, 29,* 625–629.

Harden, R. M., Crosby, J. R., & Davis, M. H. (1999). AMEE Guide No 14: Outcome-based education: Part 1—An introduction to outcome-based education. *Medical Teacher, 21,* 7–14.

Hendry, G. D., Schreiber, L., & Bryce, D. (1999). Patients teach students: Partners in arthritis education. *Medical Education, 33,* 674–677.

Mclachlan, E., King, N., Wenger, E., & Dornan, T. (2012). Phenomenological analysis of patient experiences of medical student teaching encounters. *Medical Education*, In press

Monrouxe, L. V. (2010). Identity, identification and medical education: Why should we care? *Medical Education, 44*(1), 40–49. doi:10.1111/j.1365–2923.2009.03440.x..

Morcke, A., Dornan, T., & Eika, B. (2012). Competence and outcome based education. An exploration of its origins, theoretical basis, and empirical evidence. *Advances in health sciences education† ↓: theory and practice*, In press.

Shah, P., Smithies, A., Dexter, H., Snowden, N., & Dornan, T. (2012). How do residents learn through work? *Case study in rheumatology*, In prepara

Sinclair, S. (1997). Making doctors. An institutional apprenticeship. In S. Sinclair (Ed.), *Making doctors. An institutional apprenticeship*. Oxford: Berg.

Steinert, Y., Mann, K., Centeno, A., Dolmans, D., Spencer, J., Gelula, M., & Prideaux, D. (2006). A systematic review of faculty development initiatives designed to improve teaching effectiveness in medical education: BEME Guide No 8. *Medical Teacher, 28,* 497–526.

Teunissen, P., & Westerman, M. (2011). Opportunity or threat: Ambiguity in the consequences of transitions in medical education. *Medical Education, 45,* 51–59.

Teunissen, P. W., Stapel, D. A., Van der Vleuten, C., Scherpbier, A., Boor, K., & Scheele, F. (2009). Who wants feedback? An investigation of the variables influencing residents' feedback-seeking behavior in relation to night shifts. *Academic Medicine, 84,* 910–917.

Wenger, E. (1998). *Communities of practice. Learning, meaning and identity*. Cambridge: Cambridge University Press.

Chapter 5
'In This Together': Developing University-Workplace Partnerships in Initial Professional Training for Practitioner Educational Psychologists

Kevin Woods

Introduction

For practitioner educational psychologists, there are two main areas of focus for workplace learning: the continuing professional learning of qualified psychologists (Health Professions Council (HPC) 2008a) and the initial training of educational psychologists (ITEP) (HPC 2008a).[1] This chapter focuses on ITEP, with a particular focus on the significance of partnership between universities and the settings for workplace learning. Notably, a recent wide-ranging government review of ITEP (Department of Education (DfE) 2011, p. 12) concludes that 'consistency in the quality of placements will need to be addressed', and highlights repeatedly the need for 'partnership working between HEIs [higher education institutions] and placement providers' (ibid.: 12). Historically, however, developments to promote effective workplace learning for psychologists, and for the mental health professions more generally, have tended to adopt a competence-based approach (Dunsmuir and Leadbetter 2010; cf. Gonsalvez and Milne 2010; Roth and Pilling 2007; Scaife 2001). Consequently, the organisational and socio-political context for the development of relevant competences for ITEP workplace learning, encompassing the university-workplace partnership, has been largely ignored in the literature, possibly on account of a perception that little can be done to influence it, or that issues within this context might be difficult to address constructively. The context for ITEP workplace learning, however, is of critical significance to educational psychology trainers who have responsibility for operationalising workplace learning quality assurance measures through their partnerships with workplace settings.

This chapter draws on the author's 15 years' experience as a university ITEP programme director, and on preliminary data from a national study of the supervision

---

[1] In the UK the title 'educational psychologist' refers to the practitioner role known in most other countries as 'school psychologist'.

K. Woods (✉)
School of Education, The University of Manchester, Manchester, UK
e-mail: kevin.a.woods@manchester.ac.uk

O. McNamara et al. (eds.), *Workplace Learning in Teacher Education,*
Professional Learning and Development in Schools and Higher Education 10,
DOI 10.1007/978-94-007-7826-9_5, © Springer Science+Business Media Dordrecht 2014

experiences of trainee educational psychologists,[2] to explore the significance of the organisational and socio-political context within which the university-workplace partnership has functioned and evolved within the context of ITEP in England. Two specific aspects of this context are considered: first, the developing role of educational psychologists within, and more recently outside of, local authority Children's Services;[3] second, development in the national arrangements for ITEP in England. The chapter then goes on to highlight specific facilitative strategies for the development of effective university-workplace learning provider partnership within the current ITEP context.

Context Aspect 1: The Role of the Practitioner Educational Psychologist

From a broad-ranging literature review, Fallon et al. (2010, p. 4) propose the following role definition of practitioner educational psychologists:

> Educational psychologists are fundamentally scientist-practitioners who utilise, for the benefit of children and young people, psychological skills, knowledge and understanding through the functions of consultation, assessment, intervention, research and training, at organisational, group or individual level across educational, community and care settings, with a variety of role partners.

The great majority of practitioner educational psychologists in the UK continue to be employed directly by local authorities; a central function of this role being concerned with support for children with special educational needs and their families, including the provision of psychological assessments and reviews relating to authorities' statutory obligations in relation to special educational needs. As indicated in the role definition above, most educational psychologists would consider the child and family to be their primary client, and indeed the statutory regulation of educational psychologists relates to the protection of the public. However, apart from direct requests for statutory assessment work from local authorities, the great

---

[2] This national Trainee Educational Psychologist Supervision project is a long-term collaboration between the government's UK Teaching Agency-funded ITEP programmes at the Universities of Manchester, Birmingham, Newcastle, and the London University Institute of Education. Building on the work of Atkinson and Woods (2007), the project aims to provide a comprehensive and contextualised evidence base on the elements and setting conditions for effective ITEP workplace learning. The multi-strand, multi-phase project runs from 2012 to 2015, utilising a range of data gathering methods across ITEP workplace settings within each region, including focus groups, online surveys and case studies with trainee psychologists, supervisor psychologists and managers within the workplace. The data presented within this chapter draws on 12 focus groups held with trainee educational psychologists, grouped by university and by year group (i.e. Year 1, Year 2 or Year 3). For further information about forthcoming publications from the project, please contact the project lead Professor Kevin Woods at the University of Manchester, kevin.a.woods@manchester.ac.uk.

[3] 'Children's Services' in England encompass all of the social care and education services to children and young people (e.g. social work, educational psychology, family support), which are provided by professionals employed by the local government county, district or borough.

majority of educational psychologists' work is contracted through, and supported by, consultations and direct work with professionals in schools and other settings, most often school teachers and school managers. Other professionals, therefore, are strongly positioned as the 'customers' or 'contractors' for educational psychology services (Baxter and Frederickson 2005), though it is significant to this aspect of the role that professional perceptions of educational psychologists have, for a variety of possible reasons, been observed to be ambivalent in some areas (e.g. Wood 1998; Farrell et al. 2006). Though the direct statutory assessment functions of the educational psychologist's role have tended to be seen as the essential core function by some local authority or school commissioners, it has also been acknowledged by researchers that educational psychologists' preventive, early intervention, ostensibly non-statutory work plays an important role in reducing the need for statutory work (Woods 2012; DfE 2011; Farrell et al. 2006).

In the UK, the profession of practitioner educational psychology is relatively small, with fewer than 4,000 registered practitioners (HPC 2011), serving a population of 0–25-year-olds of approximately 19.75 m (National Office of Statistics 2011). Accordingly, teams of educational psychologists located within each local authority in the UK are relatively small, with a ratio of practitioners to children/young people of up to 1:5,000. Educational psychology service evaluation therefore often gives a clear indication of insufficient quantity of available service (Farrell et al. 2006). As a result of educational psychology services being spread very thinly, educational psychologists often, though not always, work in relative isolation as lone practitioners covering a specific geographic 'patch' of primary, secondary and special schools. Whilst achieving some benefits of service continuity for both educational psychologists and school staff, this commonly used model of service delivery reduces the opportunities for educational psychologists to learn and develop practice by learning 'on the job' from each other. This geographic model of service delivery also requires that educational psychologist practitioners, whilst often developing a degree of specialism (e.g. autism, learning difficulties), need to retain a largely generic practice role which is supported by substantial ongoing continuing professional learning and access to supervision, both of which most often take place away from direct service delivery. It follows that continuing professional learning and professional practice supervision are both highly valued, but both place a significant demand on already stretched service resources (Dunsmuir and Leadbetter 2010; Cartmell 2011).

Within the last ten years, three factors have significantly influenced the educational psychologist practitioner role and/or the settings within which they work. First, the Every Child Matters[4] (Department for Education and Skills 2004) agenda introduced the need for all those working within local authority Children's Services to work in a more integrated way which allowed for flexible commissioning of services across health, social care and educational services. The effect of this has been to

---

[4] 'Every Child Matters' is an English government initiative, stemming from the Education Act 2004, which emphasises an integrated services focus on a range of outcomes for children. International comparisons can be made with other legislation and initiatives (such as 'No Child Left Behind' in the United States and 'Getting it Right for Every Child' in Scotland), which emphasise a focus on outcomes, particularly for vulnerable groups and groups at risk of underachievement.

place particular emphasis on the distinctiveness of the educational psychologist's contribution with respect to other service providers (Farrell et al. 2006). In practice, this has meant that educational psychologists have more recently provided a range of services to front line workers within Children's Services across social care and education (e.g. Association of Educational Psychologists (AEP) 2008; Woods et al. 2009). Whilst providing extended opportunities for professional practice, this shift has also required an increased flexibility and 'customer focus' by educational psychology services (Fallon et al. 2010).

A second significant change has been the introduction in 2009 of statutory regulation of all practitioner psychology professions by the Health and Care Professions Council (HCPC), replacing the previous non-statutory regulation by the British Psychological Society. As well as Standards of Conduct, Performance and Ethics, HCPC regulation introduced 109 Standards of Proficiency to be achieved and maintained by practitioner educational psychologists. Accordingly, these Standards, which were initially unfamiliar to both educational psychology trainers and practitioners, have come to form the developmental framework for the training of educational psychologists. It has also been significant that the Standards include a requirement to understand different models of professional practice supervision. Further to this, the HCPC also received a remit to apply its Standards of Education and Training to all ITEP programmes in the UK, which include requirements for universities to deliver training to all workplace supervisors and to monitor workplace resources and provisions. Consequently, ensuring the quality of workplace supervision for trainee educational psychologists is now, in England, a statutory requirement, as well as a quality benchmark for approved providers of training programmes (HPC 2008b; British Psychological Society 2010; cf. Gonsalvez and Milne 2010).

A third and most recent influential factor, local authority financial restrictions, has operated in interaction with the development of integrated Children's Services, serving to rapidly accelerate the move of psychological services towards a commissioning model (AEP 2011). Over the last two years, most local authority psychological services have moved towards a partial, or even fully, 'traded' model of service delivery, in which the service is required to generate income from local 'customers', such as schools, to cover its costs. In practice, this has meant that school managers can directly buy more or less of the services of educational psychologists. This has created the opportunity for many psychologists to leave local authority employment and set up independent psychological consultancies, or social enterprises, or as sole traders, to trade directly with schools and other commissioners, in competition with local authority services. This in turn, together with financially driven local authority schemes for voluntary redundancy/early retirement, has reduced the capacity of local authority services to respond flexibly within the commissioning context. One solution to this need for psychological services and consultancies to become quickly 'scalable' both in service range and volume, has been the appointment of practitioner educational psychologists on an ad hoc, often daily basis, as 'associates'. Such associate educational psychologists, often drawn from the increasing pool of voluntarily redundant or retired psychologists, may be less likely to be available for, or allocated to, any involvement in strategic, developmental or supervisory activity within the psychological service/consultancy.

Context Aspect 2: Arrangements for the Initial Training of Educational Psychologists

Notwithstanding the influence of developments in the qualified educational psychologist's role for the management of workplace learning, developments within ITEP have also been significant to workplace learning for trainee educational psychologists. The current structure for ITEP, which involves both academic and workplace teaching, learning and assessment, came about through the British Psychological Society's national transition in 2006 to a full-time three-year doctorate level initial professional training qualification. Proportions, and specific structures, of academic and workplace learning currently vary between the 16 ITEP university training providers in the UK. Prior to this, ITEP had been delivered through a full-time one-year master's level qualification, attracting government funding for university fees and a trainee bursary. The background to restructuring training to the three-year doctorate level is long and complex, though it is relevant to observe that professional opinion on the wisdom and necessity of this change was at the time divided, in part because the restructured training route no longer required psychology graduates entering training to have also qualified and worked as school teachers. With the benefit of hindsight, it may be that the motivation to address shortcomings in the previous master's level training programme (Farrell et al. 1998), overlooked the significance for professional training of the shift in emphasis towards research activity within a doctorate level programme. At the same time, it may be advantageous that the removal of teacher status requirement within restructured ITEP has allowed for a broader range of professional backgrounds for ITEP entrants. This, in turn, has perhaps provided a broader foundation for the profession, and some specific services, to deliver services within an integrated Children's Services model across education, health and social care.

Most significant perhaps to the experience of trainee educational psychologists in the change to a three-year training route was the assumed provision of student bursaries in Years 2 and 3 by workplace settings (e.g. services, consultancies), rather than by central government. This created a direct, high-stakes financial interdependency between university training providers and a range of individual educational psychology service providers (National Association of Principal Educational Psychologists (NAPEP) 2011). This means that a Year 2 or 3 trainee psychologist becomes, within their workplace setting, a significant draw on the relatively small service budget, and so their contribution to service delivery, in the short or longer term, must be accounted for at the level of the individual service provider. Notably, individual psychological service providers are not linked by any organisational or consortium structure, making difficult the development of regional strategic responses to this issue, such as the pooling of resources across service providers. Consequently, the challenges upon training providers and trainees themselves to obtain adequate student bursaries attached to workplace settings in Years 2 and 3, led in some cases to trainees withdrawing from training, or undertaking full-time work learning placement and study without the expected bursary income. Aside from this, there is considerable occupation-related stress and frustration, even for those whose search for funds ultimately ends successfully.

As a result of these pressures, together with the failure of the government's arm's length management organisation to secure sufficient centralised funds to meet government commitments to funding training, the government commissioned its own review of ITEP in 2011 (DfE 2011). As well as greater consistency of structure and quality of work learning placements, the review recommended a managed ('single interview') process for matching trainees in Years 2 and 3 to work learning placements, such that the trainees themselves did not have to be directly selected (or rejected) by the employer. This will, in future, require that ITEP work learning providers host bursary placements for trainee educational psychologists, not directly selected by themselves, which will direct scrutiny on initial selection of entrants to ITEP. Whilst this may promote a welcome degree of involvement and investment in ITEP entry selection by workplace learning providers, it may also reveal workplace learning providers' philosophical differences, for example, in relation to entrants' essential knowledge, skills or understanding, and in relation to ITEP/placement selection processes. It will also detract the already limited resources of both service and ITEP providers away from developing and assuring the quality of workplace learning experiences.

A final significant ITEP development since 2008 has been a competitive tendering process for ITEP funding, initially on a full economic costing basis, and from 2013 on the basis of a capped costing per trainee educational psychologist. This process has worked in a way that university ITEP providers have had to bid, in consultation with regional workplace learning providers, for a minimum number of funded ITEP places. This then further reduced flexibility to adjust ITEP numbers when funded workplace learning opportunities became scarce, creating a temporary surfeit of trainee educational psychologists in need of bursary funds for Years 2 and 3 of their workplace learning. Notably, the DfE (2011, pp. 7–8) found that 'It is becoming increasingly difficult for training providers to find suitable and timely placements for the trainees in years two and three of the doctorate', citing the economic climate as a factor in reducing the number of available workplace learning providers. Furthermore, the recent removal of full economic costing within the tendering process risks placing ITEP trainers in a position of being required to implement statutory standards and quality assurance benchmarks without the means to feasibly manage the resources for this.

Critical Implications for University-Workplace Partnership for ITEP

The contextual factors outlined thus far, relating to either the role of educational psychologists or the national arrangements for ITEP, have a significant bearing on the university-workplace learning provider partnership in relation to ITEP, which in turn shapes the structure and quality of workplace learning experience, including practice supervision, that trainee educational psychologists ultimately receive. Six critical implications for partnership and workplace learning experience are outlined below.

First, educational psychologists' access to their child or young person clients through local authorities, particularly under models of 'traded' services, means that psychological services must have keen regard for the perceptions of the value and management of their work. A particular issue relates to the dominance of requests for psychological assessments towards either local authority statutory assessment, or as part of a school's evidence towards a request for such (DfE 2011; Farrell et al. 2006). However, as part of their development of generic competence, trainee psychologists are required by universities to gain substantial practice experience of all role functions, including training, research and intervention. In some contexts, this range of practice experience may be perceived negatively by either school commissioners or even supervisory psychologists. For example, a trainee psychologist may find that the opportunity to monitor interventions, an essential part of hypothesis testing within casework, is limited. This may be because monitoring interventions may be perceived by school customers as using valuable time which could be better spent on assessment of new cases. A further recurrent issue relating to role perception has been the professional title given to the trainee psychologist within the workplace learning setting. Ethical standards require that all clients and commissioners of educational psychology services understand the trainee's unqualified trainee status, as well as the supervision arrangements for their work by registered practitioner psychologists. However, workplace learning supervisors or managers have often endeavoured to make ambiguous the trainee's status in order to avoid any challenge to the 'credibility' or value of services being provided. Accordingly, training providers have had to instruct both workplace learning providers and trainees themselves in the exact role title to be used and to proscribe use of any slightly obfuscating variations, of which there is a surprisingly high number.

Second, the thinly spread, lone practitioner nature of the educational psychologist's role significantly reduces the opportunity for trainee educational psychologists to learn through modelling and joint working. Whilst trainees can shadow individual qualified psychologists, it is often the case that the trainee's time, which is most often being paid for by the psychological service, has to provide services which contribute to the overall service delivery of the team. Therefore, a trainee psychologist's shadowing or joint working with a qualified psychologist is not cost neutral to the psychological service. The effect of this is that most of a trainee psychologist's practice supervision is delivered through the media of direct verbal report or role play. A contributory factor may also be the somewhat controversial view of some supervisors that if the role of a qualified psychologist is that of a lone practitioner then this is the role for which trainees should be prepared.

> I felt like when our tutors come and observe us in placement on the last day, that was like an experience that was really, really positive for me and I wish I would have had that more maybe from my supervisor in my placement. So that sort of observing, feeding back and really sort of thinking about different ways we could have done it. (Year 1 trainee educational psychologist)

> Is it about actually the kind of coaching and shadowing and that feedback? Should supervision encompass a lot more. . . the amount of times we've asked for joint work, you get a bit bored of actually asking the same question. (Year 3 trainee educational psychologist)

The thinly spread and highly accountable nature of educational psychology service delivery within the current movement to traded service delivery models may also risk compromising the regularity/quantity or quality of practice supervision to trainees:

> There is a pressure on you thinking that you're eating into somebody's time. (Year 2 trainee educational psychologist)
>
> My named supervisor is just very, very busy and I'm aware of that so I feel like I'm doing her a favour in a sense of being proactive about it and just getting on with it. (Year 2 trainee educational psychologist)
>
> I worry sometimes because my supervisor's so busy, I'm always very aware that I'm using her time. (Year 2 trainee educational psychologist)
>
> At the start of the supervision session they're thinking 'actually I've got x, y and z to do', how much they can attend to what your learning needs are? (Year 3 trainee educational psychologist)

In practice, supervisors often rely on the supplemental use of email and phone contact with the trainee, though this operates sometimes on the basis of a supervisor's goodwill. A response by the Association of Educational Psychologists to the issue of the additional time burden arising from trainee supervision was the stipulation that supervisors should receive additional remuneration for acting as a supervisor, which in the absence of available additional central funding tended to mean that the role of trainee supervisor more often was allocated to senior practitioners whose roles already attracted additional remuneration:

> How much they want to be a supervisor, if it's imposed on them to say 'you're senior, your role is to supervise such and such'... whether you actually kind of say 'actually I'd like this as a supervisor' depends on how much you actually want to do the job. (Year 3 trainee educational psychologist)

The highly accountable nature of educational psychology service delivery also has other consequences which may affect the delivery of effective workplace supervision to trainee psychologists. In line with HCPC regulation, training universities often stipulate that any proposed workplace learning setting for a trainee educational psychologist must have a nominated supervisor who has undertaken supervisor training at the relevant ITEP training university. The nominated supervisor's not unusual indication of unavailability to attend training, however, often throws up a dilemma because of factors such as: the nominated supervisor may have another critical appointment, such as attendance at court or tribunal; the desired workplace learning setting may be the only one which is geographically feasible for the trainee psychologist; the nominated supervisor may be a well-regarded senior practitioner with much expertise and experience to offer to the trainee. Faced with the decision to allow exemption from attending supervisor training, the training provider must also factor in the potential diplomatic effects on relationships with the workplace setting if they decline the exemption request, as well as the impression of deregulation that may be given by any conspicuous absences at the training programme. In practice, of course, solutions can often be found to isolated problems, though the view of the National Association of Principal Educational Psychologists (NAPEP 2011, p. 1) that 'the needs of services and of training courses can be different' may be worth further exploration when considering how training universities and workplace settings work together.

Third, the reduction in core local authority psychological services and corresponding increase in sole traders, psychological consultancies and social enterprises, has had several consequences. Universities have had to form workplace learning partnerships with a range of new organisations, some of which are in direct competition with other long-standing workplace partners within local authorities. In 2011, the National Association of Principal Educational Psychologists (within local authorities) formally signalled their opposition to workplace learning settings for trainee educational psychologists outside of local authority psychological services, despite a paucity of such workplace learning opportunities within local authority services (NAPEP 2011). At the time, furthermore, training contracts issued to trainees by the government sponsor required the trainee to take up local authority employment for two years post-qualification, which trainees themselves feared would be compromised by workplace experience outside of a local authority. Formally, this situation was short-lived, with the DfE (2011, p. 6, 12) acknowledgement that 'EPs [educational psychologists] are moving to a more varied pattern of employment – some with private sector providers of education services, and into private practice. . . All employers will have the potential to offer bursarial placements'. However, the realistic consequences of crossing between the self-employed and local authority employed contexts, for both trainees and qualified psychologists, perhaps remains to be seen. One further consequence of the use of sole trader, social enterprise or independent consultancies as workplace learning locations for ITEP may emanate from their potential to develop more specialist roles, for example, providing mainly training services, or types of specialist assessments, or intensive services to one school.

Fourth, the effect of restructured ITEP is that, since 2006, trainee educational psychologists have been, and will continue for several years to be, supervised by qualified psychologists who trained through a master's, rather than doctorate programme, and who were all qualified school teachers upon ITEP entry.[5] Without a full understanding, and to some extent acceptance, of the rationale for restructured ITEP, two implications of this are: that a supervisor may find a trainee's non-teaching background difficult to accommodate, or even to be an inherent disadvantage;[6] and that some one-year master's trained supervisors may consider a three-year doctorate trainee psychologist to be lacking in independence in the last two years of the training programme:

> And I wonder if there's a difference between people who supervise people on the masters course to the doctorate course because as a doctorate I've come in without the teaching background and from a health perspective which. . . and now I understand why I've hit such a dissonance between the medical model to the interactionist model and I suppose I think

---

[5] Approximately 30 % of current ITEP entrants are qualified school teachers.

[6] This particular issue is complex and may in any case relate as much to the context of the particular services being delivered as the educational psychologist role more generally. See Frederickson, Osborne and Reed (2001) for extended discussion of this issue.

that... it's a different... we're on a different journey, becoming a psychologist as to all the teachers who did the masters course. (Year 3 trainee educational psychologist)

I was a teacher but even so it's still very different and within my service people have said things, not in a nasty way to me, but they've said like 'when I was in your position I was qualified' kind of thing and I was going in as a second year trainee and they... in their experience they would have been going in as a newly qualified person at that time and I don't think there's always an understanding around the requirements of the thesis and the doctorate work and I think sometimes when... me and... like other trainee educational psychologists at the service are moaning about 'oh I've got to do this and I've got to balance this and that.' I don't think it's always understood quite... (Year 3 trainee educational psychologist)

A further implication of master's level qualified supervisors of doctorate trainee educational psychologists is that supervisors may, depending on the orientation of the particular ITEP programme, have significant knowledge gaps, in particular relating to breadth or depth of learning in professional practice models, supervisory models, therapeutic techniques, or research methodologies.

She [supervisor] just felt she was out of practice with it and the one day [supervisor training] wasn't enough to... like really explicitly practise those models and get an in-depth understanding of them. (Year 1 trainee educational psychologist)

I suppose there's quite a range of different EPs [educational psychologists] who might be supervisors and I know my supervisor qualified before a lot of these models were even out, so I don't even know what my current supervisor's knowledge is of those models. (Year 3 trainee educational psychologist)

Fifth, the regulation of educational psychology practice and training by the HCPC has required psychological service providers, in collaboration with university ITEP providers, to work within the HCPC standards frameworks. Notwithstanding the aforementioned issue relating to mandatory training for workplace learning supervisors, this has undoubtedly increased the cognitive and administrative load on supervisors in other ways. For example, pre-HCPC regulation, the Manchester ITEP programme was structured through 24 learning outcomes, whereas the HCPC stipulates 109 standards, many of which require careful interpretation and differentiation.

When I was doing the research on supervision in my service, that was something I kind of highlighted which is why they are now doing training around supervision, because it's actually an HPC[7] requirement. (Year 2 trainee educational psychologist)

HCPC regulation has provided a new context for conversations about adequate supervision of delegated work, about the material provisions for workplace learning (e.g. workspace), about being completely explicit to customers about the status of a trainee psychologist, and about accuracy and clarity of record-keeping in relation to the supervision of the work of the trainee psychologist.

Sixth, the lack of government funds for workplace learning bursaries for Year 2 and 3 trainees has required university ITEP providers to negotiate workplace learning bursaries on behalf of government-funded trainees. This has been particularly

---

[7] Until 31 July 2012, the HCPC was known as the Health Professions Council (HPC).

challenging at a time of local authority service contraction and the trading of services (DfE 2011). It has been necessary for university ITEP providers to demonstrate to psychological service providers how Year 2 and Year 3 trainees can provide good service delivery value for money, taking account of the costs of supervision. At the same time, trainee psychologists have required reassurance that they are professionally valued, and that workplace learning negotiations between the universities and psychological service providers, which are ongoing throughout the whole of Year 1, will certainly produce the required number of workplace learning bursaries.

Optimising University-Workplace Partnerships for ITEP

Not surprisingly, psychological service providers have, to a greater or lesser extent, been proactive in managing the ITEP partnership issues which have arisen from the aforementioned changes in the role of, and training arrangements for, educational psychologists. Some workplace learning providers have requested additional input from ITEP providers on novel aspects of training, such as research methods and professional practice models. In-house, several service providers have made adaptations to service delivery to accommodate trainee supervision within trading of services, even in some cases embedding a workplace learning bursary within the service core structure. Particular innovations have included using trainees' therapeutic skills to extend the repertoire of traded services; using trainees to backfill lower level work, enabling more experienced qualified colleagues to be available to trade more complex or higher level services; and using trainees' research capacity and skills to support evidence-based practice within the service.

At the same time, whilst a healthy supply of high quality new entrants to the profession is a concern to all service providers, the broader management of ITEP is not, and opportunities for developing solutions within the university-workplace learning partnership may be limited. Where ITEP providers serve a large geographic area, a small psychological service may traditionally have chosen to host a trainee psychologist on workplace learning once every three or four years, though restructured ITEP has, since 2008, trebled the number of trainees within the ITEP system. Therefore, university strategies to support workplace learning provider adaptations within the partnership have been developed; six of these are outlined below.

The first is to work from the general principle that university ITEP providers and psychological service providers are 'in this together', which has a surprisingly powerful depolarising effect within discussions. From this principle, either party is able to externalise the main change agents affecting the interdependent partnership: local authority contraction leading to trading of services, British Psychological Society transition to three-year doctoral level ITEP, the structuring of doctorates by university faculty boards, and the imposed professional regulation by the HCPC. This externalisation of contextual factors militates against viewing negotiations as a tussle from positions of 'different interests', and has more easily allowed space to jointly work on problem-solving strategies, often bringing secondary benefits within the partnership. For example, joint work on specification and differentiation of HCPC professional standards, and on practice supervision, have brought benefits for qualified psychologists' own workplace learning and continuing professional learning (cf. Atkinson and Woods 2007; Carrington 2004).

> I'm offering supervision a lot of the time because I do a lot of reflecting, and they talk through cases with me at those times and I've found that massive for my learning but also the self-efficacy of giving back... my own supervisor has started to come into my office after a session and he'll talk through his case with me while he's formulating and I'll be like reflective back to him. (Year 3 trainee educational psychologist)

Second is the importance of facilitating and allowing time for effective two-way communication. This has required university ITEP providers to negotiate their attendance at all regional meetings of psychological service managers and to request sufficient time on the agenda to discuss, rather than inform about, ITEP and partnership issues, such as exploration of interdependency. Within this, it has been crucially important that each partner's concerns from their own ITEP or service delivery contexts are listened to and accommodated, at the same time encouraging acceptance of what are 'givens' for both partners (e.g. doctorate level training; financial accountability within a traded psychological service model). It has been useful within discussions to hear from some service providers and managers that they have a strong degree of ownership of, and sustainability concern for ITEP, linked to values about the profession's distinctive contributions to positive outcomes for children (Fallon et al. 2010; Farrell et al. 2006).

Third, in order to avoid potential rivalry between training and practice sectors, it has been useful to frame university ITEP concerns in terms of the impact of workplace learning or supervision arrangements on the training experience and expectations of trainee educational psychologists themselves. Foregrounding the effects of dissonance in skill development expectations between university and workplace learning contexts, and of resistance to negotiate development of bursaried workplace learning opportunities, has enabled a joint focus on the learning and welfare of the trainees as future colleagues. Allied to this have been two sub-strategies. First, to place where possible more than one trainee within a single workplace learning provider, as this concentrates feedback on the adequacy and consistency of trainee experience to the workplace learning provider, as well as providing valuable mutual support to the placed trainees in communicating their needs within the workplace setting. Second, to place trainees in services where one or more of the qualified psychologists undertook their ITEP under the restructured doctoral route, which again serves to enhance the effective communication of feedback on the trainee experience within the service.

Fourth, it has been important for ITEP providers to be honest, as well as sympathetic and accommodating, in discussions with service providers, particularly on issues relating to restructured ITEP. In truth, restructured ITEP is an 'experiment'. It may be that entry to ITEP is significantly advantaged through experience gained as a school teacher, and it may be that the changing background of entrants to the profession significantly changes the scope of service delivery and the ultimate role of educational psychologists, for better or worse. This honest acknowledgement is supported by the first principle that ITEP providers and psychological services are partnered within a context which has been strongly shaped by socio-political factors which are largely independent of either partner's influence.

Fifth has been the strategy to develop workplace learning provider networking in relation to ITEP, since often small individual workplace learning providers are not organisationally linked, as might be individual health service trusts through a regional strategic health authority. As solutions to challenges relating to workplace learning and supervision have been creatively addressed by individual workplace learning providers, with more or less active support from ITEP providers, it has been productive to encourage connection to other workplace learning providers where similar challenges are being faced. In the present context, this has been a particularly useful strategy for the development of supervision structures and the inclusion of trainee psychologists within a traded service delivery.

The sixth partnership strategy, perhaps the most surprising in the context of this chapter, is that of simply promoting reflection on the university-workplace partnership. With the majority of ITEP and psychological service senior managers having entered and developed within the profession through a period of relative ITEP and local authority stability, the opportunities to critically reflect upon the nature of this partnership did not perhaps present themselves as readily in the past as in the present. With the range of described role and training factors affecting the context of the partnership, subtle issues have been raised around who leads or follows which aspects of the partnership, and where compromises might need to be considered and how these should be broached and acknowledged. Some psychological service managers strongly expect universities through ITEP to be taking a lead on developments in professional practice and for the trainee psychologists to be 'at the leading edge'; whereas other managers strongly consider the role of ITEP universities as serving to prepare individuals for the practitioner roles which psychological services currently require. Similarly, some university ITEP providers may strongly value a traditional doctoral research thesis, whereas others might be minded, or persuaded, to see the value or feasibility in practice of a more 'modular' thesis structure. Shared reflections on the nature of the university-workplace learning partnership within ITEP have been helpful in enabling each partner to make considered decisions about where they should lead, follow, or compromise within the partnership.

Conclusion

It has been argued that within initial professional training for educational psychology, the consistent quality of the workplace learning experience, and in particular of professional practice supervision, is significantly influenced by factors within the context of the university-workplace learning partnership. Recent developments in the context of the role of practitioner educational psychologists, and in the arrangements for initial professional training, have necessitated reflection on the interdependency within this partnership. This shared organisational learning (cf. Weick 2001; Argyris 1999) will be important in the next phase of partnership development, as economic and socio-political factors, including continued government spending restrictions and decentralisation, continue to shape the context in which workplace learning is negotiated.

References

Argyris, C. (1999). *On organisational learning* (2nd ed.). Oxford: Blackwell.

Association of Educational Psychologists (AEP). (2008). *Educational psychologists in multidisciplinary settings: Investigations into the work of educational psychologists in children's services Authorities.* Durham: AEP.

Association of Educational Psychologists (AEP) (2011). *The delivery of educational psychology services.* Durham: AEP.

Atkinson, C., & Woods, K. (2007). Effective fieldwork supervision of trainee educational psychologists: What is needed? *Educational Psychology in Practice, 23*(4), 299–316.

Baxter, J., & Frederickson, N. (2005). Every child matters: Can educational psychology contribute to radical reform? *Educational Psychology in Practice, 21,* 87–102.

British Psychological Society (BPS) (2010). *Accreditation through partnership handbook guidance for educational psychology programmes in England, Northern Ireland and Wales.* Leicester: BPS.

Carrington, G. (2004). Supervision as a reciprocal learning process. *Educational Psychology in Practice, 20*(1), 31–42.

Cartmell, H. (2011). *Evaluation of an educational psychology service's professional practice supervision arrangements.* University of Manchester, unpublished research assignment paper for D.Ed.Ch.Psychol.

Department for Education and Skills (DfES). (2004). *Every child matters: Change for children.* London: HMSO.

Department of Education (DfE). (2011). *Developing sustainable arrangements for the initial training of educational psychologists.* London: DfE.

Dunsmuir, S., & Leadbetter, J. (2010). *Professional supervision: Guidelines for practice for educational psychologists.* Leicester: British Psychological Society.

Fallon, K., Woods, K., & Rooney, S. (2010). A discussion of the developing role of educational psychologists within children's services. *Educational Psychology in Practice, 26,* 1–24.

Farrell, P., Gersch, I., & Morris, S. (1998). Progress towards three-year professional training courses for educational psychologists. *Educational Psychology in Practice, 14*(1), 44–51.

Farrell, P., Woods, K., Lewis, S., Rooney, S., Squires, G., & O'Conner, M. (2006). *Function and contribution of educational psychologists in light of the 'Every child matters: Change for children' agenda.* London: DfES.

Frederickson, N., Osborne, L. A., & Reed, P. (2001). Teaching experience and educational psychologists' credibility with teachers: An empirical investigation. *Educational Psychology in Practice, 17*(2), 93–108.

Gonsalvez, C. J., & Milne, D. L. (2010). Clinical supervisor training in Australia: A review of current problems and possible solutions. *Australian Psychologist, 45*(4), 233–242.

Health Professions Council (HPC). (2008a). *Your guide to our standards for continuing professional development.* London: Health Professions Council.

Health Professions Council (HPC). (2008b). *Standards of education and training.* London: Health Professions Council.

Health Professions Council (HPC). (2011). Profession and modality data—practitioner psychologists. Personal email communication to the author, 23 February.

National Association of Principal Educational Psychologists (NAPEP). (2011). Letter to Programme Directors' Group for educational psychology. Dated 7 December, 2011.

National Office of Statistics (NOS). (2011). 2011 Census: Population estimates for the United Kingdom. www.ons.gov.uk/ons/rel/census/2011-census/population-and-household-estimates-for-the-united-kingdom/stb-2011-census–population-estimates-for-the-united-kingdom.html. Accessed 28 Dec 2012.

Roth, A. D., & Pilling, S. (2007). *The competences required to deliver effective cognitive and behavioural therapy for people with depression and anxiety disorders.* London: Department of Health.

Scaife, J. (2001). *Supervision in the mental health professions: A practitioner's guide.* Hove: Brunner-Routledge.

Weick, K. E. (2001). *Making sense of the organisation.* Oxford: Blackwell.

Wood, A. (1998). OK then: What do EPs do? *Special Children*, May, 11–13.

Woods, K. (2012). The role and perspectives of practitioner educational psychologists. In L. Peer & G. Reid (Eds.), *Special educational needs: A guide for inclusive practice* (pp. 255–272). London: Sage Publications.

Woods, K., Bond, C., Farrell, P., Humphrey, N., & Tyldesley, K. (2009) *The role of educational psychology in the safeguarding of children in the UK.* Durham: AEP.

Chapter 6
Disentangling What it Means to be a Teacher in the Twenty-First Century: Policy and Practice in Teachers' Continuing Professional Learning

Bob Burstow and Meg Maguire

Introduction

Education researchers, education policy-makers, the mass media, teachers and their representative federations and unions seem to unanimously agree. Effective schools, and more specifically student success, are **dependent upon the quality of the teachers** in the school (Larsen 2010, p. 225, our emphasis).

The most 'simple' and immediate way in which to 'improve' schools and raise their effectiveness is to 'improve' teachers by reforming the way in which they are prepared for, and supported in their occupational role. For this reason, education policy-makers and politicians have turned their attention to this task. However, one of the fundamental dilemmas in teacher education policy work is that questions such as what should be, or what ought to be, the role of the teacher in contemporary society get left aside. For example, should teaching be a 'directed profession' (Bottery and Wright 2000) led by the demands of and overseen by various governments, where teachers are trained and prepared in the delivery of what is nationally mandated? Should teachers become 'agents of change' (Johnson and Hallgarten 2000) who take control of their professional destinies and influence policy in their area of expertise?

The work of teachers has always been subjected to criticism. If there are concerns about the attitudes and behaviours of young people, then teachers and teacher education are usually expected to respond in some way. If there are 'needs' for greater literacy and numeracy skills in the workforce, then teachers and teacher education have to be reformed to respond to this call for change. If the economy 'demands' a different kind of workforce, then again education, and by implication, teacher education, has to be changed to meet this requirement. The shape that these policy interventions take will be seen in changes in the pre-service preparation of teachers.

B. Burstow (✉) · M. Maguire
King's College London, London, UK
e-mail: bob.burstow@kcl.ac.uk

M. Maguire
e-mail: meg.maguire@kcl.ac.uk

O. McNamara et al. (eds.), *Workplace Learning in Teacher Education,*
Professional Learning and Development in Schools and Higher Education 10,
DOI 10.1007/978-94-007-7826-9_6, © Springer Science+Business Media Dordrecht 2014

However, and significantly for this chapter, it will also be seen in the provision of in-service education and training, what we refer to in this chapter as continuing professional learning, for this is the 'quickest' way to roll out educational change.

In this chapter, we will be thinking about how these reforming attempts are to be understood, specifically in the case of teachers' continuing professional learning. We begin by looking at continuing professional learning along three 'axes': the origin of the programmes, the beneficiaries of the programmes, and the implied view taken of the teachers in the construction and delivery of the programmes. Working from this base we will then develop and present a new tool for viewing the variety of major continuing professional learning programmes in England over the last 20 years. This, we believe, reveals something of both New Labour's and the Conservative Coalition's attitude to teachers and teaching in the light of the policy approaches that were taken.

Continuing Professional Learning Policy: Three Core Questions

Policy is always underpinned by sets of assumptions, propositions, beliefs, and, crucially, sets of values (Ozga 2000). As we have already signalled, in relation to the perennial 'problem' of the teacher, and the reform of the teacher, continuing professional learning is a key policy tool through which 'desired' changes can be attempted. For example, if a government sees levels of literacy as a policy problem, they could institute and roll out programmes for teachers to improve the teaching of reading. In this first section, we will uncover some of the value positions that underpin the provision of continuing professional learning, through a critical discussion of what we term the three core questions that pertain to it. First, where is the source of the initiative—where does the 'drive' for the continuing professional learning originate; second, what sort of continuing professional learning is needed; then finally, what do various versions of continuing professional learning programmes say about the position and power of the recipients? We will consider each of these in turn.

What is the 'Source' of the Continuing Professional Learning Programme?

It is hardly surprising, given the continuous stream of education reform of schools over the last 40 years, that continuing professional learning policy has stayed 'very much in the half shadows of the education debate' (Glover and Law 1996, p. 19). In the 40 years since the James Report on Teacher Education and Training (James Lord of Rosholme 1972) there is much evidence, in England, of the growth of professional development power-sharing between national governments and schools—and the resulting increasing isolation of the local authorities (McMahon 1998; Burstow 2011). The first diminution of the local authorities' influence was partly an effect of the 1988 Education Act, and later the introduction of the Grant Maintained Schools system, which, together with the introduction of a 'market forces' approach, allowed schools more choice as to where they spent their allocation of training funding. One key feature in the English context has been the growth of consultancies and private companies bidding for contracts to 'deliver' education services such as continuing professional learning; a veritable 'commercialisation of education' (Ball 2008, p. 203). It has been for schools to judge how effective these organisations are at delivering successful programmes—a move from local authority-inspired 'training menus', to the 'institutional accountability' focus of the 1990's, and onwards into private-public relationships (Glover and Law 1996; Dean 1991). In many cases the population of trainers and consultants has been made up of former teachers and senior managers, who often brought considerable expertise and experience to their new work. However, this shift was a further reinforcement of the externally innovated, top-down response to national policy demands—continuing professional development being 'done to' teachers rather than being 'done by' them.

Olson identifies three models which, he argues, characterise in-service training. Trainers might select from: a systems model concerned with the techniques of change; an ecological model which would address the environment needed to encourage change; and/or a cognitive model which would 'search for schemes teachers can follow to bring about learning' (Olson 1992, p. 1). These models are all externally imposed upon the teacher. Whatever their intended outcome, they are introduced by trainers who will use various techniques to create a new environment. At the time of writing, 20 years after Olson's typology of continuing professional learning provision was generated, professional development has become predicated on a shared and personalised viewpoint—at least in the rhetoric that surrounds this provision. There has been a strong sense of widening the range of continuing professional learning, from being taught courses usually offered by higher education institutes, to:

> 'job-embedded, collaborative professional development activities, such as common planning time, being formally monitored by another teacher or networking with other teachers outside the school, [which were viewed as] more helpful as professional development than the more traditional forms of development strategies.' (Boyle et al. 2004, p. 4)

(It will be useful to revisit Olson's models later on in this chapter in relation to the professional/craft spectrum of teaching as an occupation and the implicit view of the teacher that these models imply.)

However, in England, the growing domination of the Teacher Training Authority (which became the Teacher Development Agency, then the Teaching Agency and most recently the National College for Teaching and Leadership), and the demands of performance management, have also influenced professional learning (Bolam 2000) in the drive to reform the whole of teacher education (both initial and continuing) in order to 're-professionalise' teachers for the twenty-first century (Whitty 2000). This policy shift has contributed to a swing towards the centralisation of teacher education, aligning changes in professional practice to a set of new professional competencies; centrally mandated lists of requirements to be met by all intending teachers, containing implicit representations of the role of teachers and the task of teaching (Bird et al. 2005).

These moves to regulate, centralise and control teacher education have been echoed at an international level. Increasingly, education is viewed as central to economic success (Ball 2008). This produces a corresponding concern for the effective preparation, utilisation and development of a country's teaching force (Koçoğ lu 2011; Jones et al. 2011). In England this move was accompanied by some redefinition of the role of in-service training, 'bringing a stronger emphasis on lifelong learning and continuing development', as well as a recognition that professional development 'serves as a catalyst for the continuous adjustments which have to be made in dynamic systems' (Glover and Law 1996, p. 26). However, moves by an increasingly centralist style of government have further de-professionalised teaching (Toynbee and Walker 2012b). Specifically, an increasingly directed and specific style of training, focused on particular parts of the curriculum, such as literacy and numeracy, presents the 'trained' teachers with a set of lesson plans and the expectation that this is what will be followed during the working day. This inferred lack of trust in the teacher to work independently, reflected in a series of initiatives imposed from above, reflects a sense of teachers as workers in a trade or craft, in need of specific tools to do a particular task (see Fig. 6.1).

Along with the increase in political control of continuing professional learning courses for teachers, and as a positive outcome of the discouragement of local authority dominated training, has been the development in schools, as independent organisations, of their own views as to how they can best manage continuing professional learning themselves. This 'turn' is also a reaction to the change in model from an individualistic focus to a 'group focus on professional learning, based on the school and its collective needs' (Craft 2000, p. 12). Research supporting this development has also been a contributory factor. Some time ago, Dean (1991, p. 3) noted that there was dissatisfaction with 'some of the models of development which were current formerly, because we know a lot more than we once did about the way adults learn'. More recently, Hargreaves has noted the 'huge vacuums' in continuing professional learning that were an outcome of the increasing parochiality of self-managing schools divorced from the 'system level support' that had been provided by the local authority (Hargreaves 2000, p. 168).

Some time ago in the English context, Kirk had noted the move away from top-down initiatives 'imposed upon teachers', towards the bottom-up approach as 'a way of sustaining the creativity of the school, its capacity to solve its own problems through appropriate professional action' (Kirk 1988, p. 51). This approach was effectively reversed by the 1988 Education Act and the imposition of top-down, target-driven standards and expectations for the state education system that were generated, and which continued to dominate continuing professional learning provision into the twenty-first century. It is only in the last five years (MacBeath 2009) that heads and their schools have been offered the opportunity of a more rigorous bottom-up developmental opportunity for continuing professional learning. This move has been complemented by approaches to continuing professional learning in some of the more recent national programmes, notably the suite of management development courses developed by the National College for School Leadership: Leading from the Middle (Revell 2002) and Leadership Pathways (Barrett 2007). These have allowed the school organisation to regain some influence as a policy actor (through the effective use of a lead professional as an in-house coach for the participating staff members) where they had previously been rendered almost impotent.

However, there can be dangers if continuing professional learning only concentrates on practical day-to-day concerns. Goodson and Hargreaves (1996, p. 13) note that 'not all... practical knowledge is educationally beneficial or worthwhile' and that there is a risk that 'overzealous promotion [of this model] may actually redirect teachers away from broader moral social projects and commitments ... turning practical knowledge into parochial knowledge'. These arguments, and the evidence from specific schools that have too wholeheartedly embraced these concepts, should not be allowed to diminish the value of the move to validate the day-to-day working experiences of teachers as useful professional knowledge; rather it should reinforce the position of higher education as the disseminator of a validated and integrated *corpus*. Hargreaves neatly captures the tension between policy-makers and policy workers (teachers) as follows:

> What is being identified is a growing and developing tension between: the increasing desire of those concerned with national level planning and development to directly instruct and mould the teaching force into their current image of correctness and the increasing skills of individual professionals and a variety of groups—from department, to whole school— in internally diagnosing, managing and controlling their own developmental processes. (Hargreaves 1994, p. 10)

This 'growing tension' raises issues, and concerns, surrounding the emphasis that may be placed on the professional and craft aspects of the job done by teachers, interweaving with the dangers of 'learning-centred' being equated with 'school-focused' and becoming far too parochial in its thinking.

Continuing Professional Learning: Is it Needed? What Form Should it Take?

Turning to our second core question, Glover and Law (1996) were clear about the particular groups who might benefit from various forms of continuing professional learning. There are those individuals—adults working in the school—who wish to 'develop the skills and knowledge to teach effectively and to grow as a professional'. Then there are the teams within the school—typically departments or key stages— who are looking to 'develop approaches and share expertise within a team situation'. Third, the whole institution may need to 'establish common values which determine policies for the school' (Glover and Law 1996, p. 32). To this list, we should add national bodies—non-governmental organisations (NGOs) for example—who have recognised teachers as agents of reform (Al-Mutawa and Al-Furaih 2005) and who seek to bring this about by means of continuing professional learning. All these groups will have their own particular needs. There is a question, however, as to where the need for 'developing' itself originates. For our purposes here we will focus on the approaches taken by a succession of government-led initiatives in England.

The Macnair Report (1944) understood the need for teachers to go on 'refresher courses', but specified that these would be delivered by 'training colleges and university training departments, by local education authorities and by independent organisations' and also occasionally by Her Majesty's Inspectorate (HMI) (DES 1944, p. 49). The James Report (1972) acknowledged the growing theoretical background of education, and encouraged teachers to 'extend and deepen their knowledge of teaching methods and of educational theory' as well as 'refresh and extend their knowledge of their special interests' and keep up to date with educational technology (James Lord of Rosholme 1972, p. 2.7). The vision of the James Report is contained in its stated belief that 'in-service training should begin in the schools' (ibid.: 2.21)—alongside an expectation that 'some teachers of high quality . . . should have the option of returning to one of a few selected training institutions for a further year, to take a course leading to the award of an MA(Ed)' (ibid.: 2.18). Thus, while there has been a long-standing recognition of the need for and value of continuing professional learning, there was no specification of content. There was an implicit notion of teacher (and school) autonomy in selecting aspects of curriculum and pedagogy for further exploration, and no assumption that policy-makers would intervene into this essentially professional context—driven by teachers and educationalists, for teachers and educationalists—a policy vacuum waiting to be filled!

Moving rapidly forwards, the Education Act (1994) legislated for the foundation of the Teacher Training Agency which was charged with all matters relating to 'raising the standards of teaching' (DES 1994, p. 1.2); a statement which *de facto* moved the control of continuing professional learning more firmly into the hands of the central administration. Four years later, the Department of Education and Science (DES) stated that 'schools and teachers will set their own priorities, *bearing in mind the need for training on national initiatives*' (DES 1998, p. 7.14, our emphasis). This was distilled into a strategy by the Department for Education and Employment (DfEE) following consultation with the General Teaching Council (DfEE 2001) which led, in its turn, to research into teachers' own perceptions of their development (Hustler et al. 2003). Toynbee and Walker (2012b) remark on this trend as an example of apparent professional freedom of action being controlled in practice by centrally imposed criteria—and characteristic of educational policy shifts more generally (Ball 2008).

The increased emphasis on schools as the preferred delivery site for continuing professional learning, irrespective of alternative needs (which co-incidentally distanced the universities and colleges) was made clear by the 2020 Review Group (2006) when it stated that:

> much of the [continuing professional learning] activity should be school-based, with a sustained focus on improving learning and teaching. This is not to say that external courses have no place, rather, that such courses are not enough in themselves to effect transfer of knowledge and skills. (August et al. 2006, p. 32).

They also recommended that the Teacher Development Agency should 'promote the engagement of all schools in a reformed programme of CPD [continuing professional development]' (August et al. 2006, p. 34). This policy statement paved the way for the Schools White Paper (2010) which proposed 'a national network of Teaching

Schools on the model of teaching hospitals' (DfE 2010, p. 8) which, by implication, places the responsibility for continuing professional learning firmly with the senior teaching staff of each Teaching School.

This recent policy proposal appears to be a move away from centralised imposition. The White Paper regrets the ways that, in the past 'Government has tended to lead, organise and systematise improvement activity seeking to ensure compliance with its priorities' and demands recognition that 'the primary responsibility for improvement rests with schools'. However, somewhat contradictorily, unstated but nonetheless rigid rules of compliance will be centrally applied as 'the National College will be responsible for quality assurance of their [Teaching Schools] work, and will remove accreditation from any school not meeting the standards' (DfE 2010, p. 21, 22 and 2.24)—another example of alleged freedoms actually being centrally controlled (Toynbee and Walker 2012a). The findings of the Education Committee (2012) further confirm the setting of continuing professional learning: 'external training had had its day, and that in-house CPL [continuing professional learning] was often more valuable as it was easier for teachers to keep in touch after the event' (House of Commons Education Committee 2012, p. 96).

What we see in this brief overview of policy moves are a number of settlements, in the English context, around how continuing professional learning is to be 'taken': as general/professional needs for continuing professional learning to stimulate growth and facilitate a critical up-to-dateness with educational developments, to a centrally determined focus on systems-wide needs (often to 'bed-in' new government policies). We will now raise questions about what some of these versions of continuing professional learning implicitly (and explicitly) assume about the nature of teaching and the position of the teacher.

Models of Continuing Professional Learning and Their Construction of the Teacher

At the start of this chapter, we contrasted two views of the teacher; as a deliverer of policy mandated elsewhere or as a professional enquirer into an area where the individual has expertise and an ethical commitment: what Johnson and Hallgarten (2000) describe as 'agents of change'. Michael Gove, the current Secretary of State for Education in the Conservative Coalition government, has argued that 'teachers grow as professionals by allowing their work to be observed by other professionals' (Gove 2010) and that 'teaching is a craft and it is best learnt as an apprentice observing a master craftsman or woman' (Gove 2010). In many senses, teaching is far too complex to be limited in this manner; teacher education and the continuing professional learning of teachers needs to recognise the complexity, the situatedness and the role of theory in coming to decisions. Heilbron (2010, p. 7) has argued that teaching is undertaken in 'situations of complexity' that require practical judgements that in turn draw upon 'a number of elements, including applied theoretical knowledge'. She goes on, 'there can be no split between elements encountered in reading,

Fig. 6.1 Continuing
professional learning—Craft
view of teaching

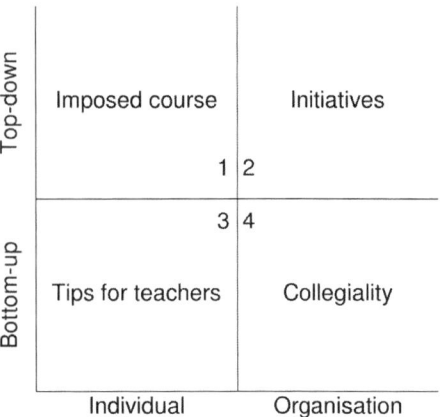

research, university and schools' (ibid.: 8). This is far richer, more complex and harder to bring off in pre-service provision and in continuing professional learning.

So far in this chapter we have been arguing that policy debates about the importance of and types of continuing professional learning that are needed and the tensions that characterise this provision are, to some extent, predicated on the way in which the teacher is being constructed. Is teaching a craft or profession, for example? Should the primary intention of continuing professional learning be for the benefit of the individual or the organisation, and what difficulties shape the tension between the source of the innovation or intervention—should this be top-down or bottom-up? Now, taking these questions as a framework for a typology of continuing professional learning, we propose that juxtaposing these in a succession of Carrell diagrams, may provide some means of extracting sense from confusion.

Consider first the view of teaching as predominantly a craft, and setting within that the 'benefit' and 'innovation' as axes. Populating the resulting four cells with the corresponding continuing professional learning would give the result illustrated in Fig. 6.1. A bottom-up generated continuing professional learning programme for the benefit of individuals (Fig. 6.1: cell 3) might well be at the level of tips for teachers, in practice the sort of emailed news-sheet that is now quite common, or a sharing of good practice session during a joint school in-service day.

A bottom-up generated continuing professional learning programme giving benefit to the organisation (Fig. 6.1: cell 4) might be a reflective practitioner programme, along the lines of the Teacher Learning Communities developed in London by Wiliam during 2008–09 (Thompson and Wiliam 2007)—where in-school groups of staff met regularly to consider their own practice in the light of that of others, and to trial possible alternative approaches (Buie 2009).

Continuing counter-clockwise (to Fig. 6.1: cell 2), the constant rain of initiatives from the education-related non-governmental organisations over the period of the New Labour Government sit well within the top-down imposed continuing professional learning that benefits the organisation cell and would seem to confirm the governmental view of teaching-as-craft.

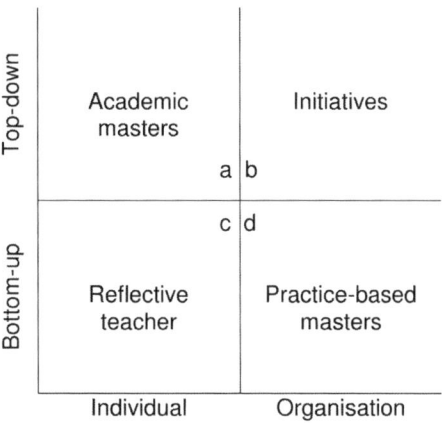

Fig. 6.2 Continuing professional learning—Professional view of teaching

The final cell (Fig. 6.1: cell 1) is a little more problematic. There is little immediately obvious continuing professional learning imposed from above for the 'benefit' of the individual. Updates by examining boards, and the like, might qualify, but the controlling effect of the individual actor by the organisation, that is implicit in this pairing, is best expressed by a school staff review that allows for this direction of the development of individual members by senior leaders.

Consider now the same axes, but set within the view of teachers-as-professionals. This generates the continuing professional learning matrix shown in Fig. 6.2. The logic imposed by this framework produces one identical cell population, the organisation still benefits from initiatives imposed from above (Fig. 6.2: cell b), but this is the sole carry-over.

Consider the individual from this viewpoint. A bottom-up approach to continuing professional learning (Fig. 6.2: cell c) may result in a reflective teacher programme, whereas a top-down professionally biased continuing professional learning programme (Fig. 6.2: cell a) would take the form of a university-based master's degree that would improve the individual's promotion chances.

Interestingly, the matrix suggests that the organisation might expect to gain more from their staff studying a practice-based master's than they would from a more academic version, which would benefit the individual more in their own professional development and thinking (Fig. 6.2: cell d). The collegiality inherent in many of the current practice-based degrees might be expected to generate a stronger coherent reflective and proactive workforce in comparison to the more isolated and individually centred study. In addition, in the form adopted by the Master's in Teaching and Learning that resulted from the New Labour White Paper 'Being the Best for Our Children' (DCSF 2008), the lead professional role (the in-school coach) provided an opportunity for direct influence on the specifics that are being studied by the individual (Daly et al. 2004). This argument also applies to the increasing number of master's degrees being commissioned by schools and particularly by clusters of schools to suit their particular needs and philosophies.

Using the Model: Tracking Changes in Policy

Now consider a few examples of previous continuing professional learning programmes for teachers in England. The 13-year-long New Labour administration showed a change in its attitude and opinion over time. At an early stage in that administration, the New Opportunities Fund cross-curricular information and communication technology programme (Pitkeathly et al. 2004, p. 21) was an example of a top-down course for the benefit of every individual teacher (Fig. 6.1: cell 1). Course materials were centrally produced and delivered, often on the school premises, by external agencies. Teachers were required to attend irrespective of their previous experience in the use of information and communication technology. A further example of this is the cascade approach adopted by the continuing professional learning programmes, developed to disseminate the National Literacy and National Numeracy Strategies to the teaching workforce. By the end of the same decade, the piloting of the Master's in Teaching and Learning (TDA 2009) looks, in comparison, to be a swing to a view of teachers as professionals—and further to the recognition of the potential benefits to the school and to the influence of the school on the degree itself (Fig. 6.2: cell d).

Further back in time we can also see other swings: the James report (James Lord of Rosholme 1972) maintained a consistent top-down view of continuing professional learning while accepting movement along the craft/profession axis (Fig. 6.1: cell 1 and Fig. 6.2: cell a). In contrast, the Cambridge Review of Primary Education (Alexander 2010) and the Rose Report (Rose 2009) led to a brief flowering of bottom-up teacher-led development, as teachers began to experiment with cross-curricular themes, echoing the Nuffield Primary Science ideals and philosophies (Nuffield Foundation 2012). So these implementations fit better into cell 4 of Fig. 6.1—of collegiality and shared good practice.

Now consider Fig. 6.3, the juxtaposition of the two figures (Fig. 6.1 and Fig. 6.2). Looking at this matrix, there is now a perceptible conflict at government level. If we accept that 'initiatives' (cells b and 2) often represent the government influence over both teacher-as-craft and of teacher-as-professional, then the introduction of any formal master's by government or school consortium (and indeed any government acceptance of teaching being a master's level job) may imply a release of control over continuing professional learning by the administration and hence of a large amount of fine control of teaching. This goes against the trend of all governments since 1988 in England, as shown by the record of schools-related legislation introduced in every year since then (Fig. 6.4).[1] Up until the arrival of the Conservative Coalition Government in 2010, the trend had been for an increasing volume of highly specific micro-legislation. The resultant fall in the number of individual items of legislation in the last three years has, however, been more than matched by the far-reaching nature of those instruments.

---

[1] The data displayed here was derived from www.legislation.gov.uk using the keyword 'school' and asking for all legislation in all regions so as to keep parity before and after devolution.

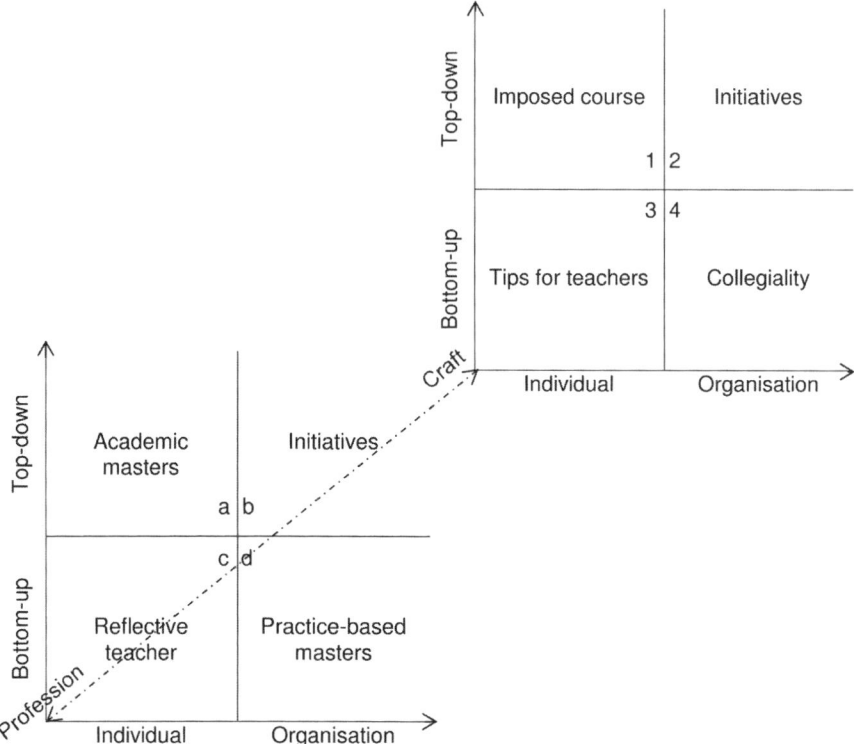

Fig. 6.3 Three axis view of continuing professional learning types

The balance between the need for any government to control the education of its future workforce and the dangers of over- and micro-management is clear from the sheer number of legislative items (peaking at nearly one-per-day in 1999). There was some evidence of the continuation of this conflict in recent statements by the current Secretary of State, where pre-service teacher training was referred to as an apprenticeship (a craft-related term with its implications of close control and programming into the status quo, for apprenticeship implies a stasis), while still viewing the job as being worth studying at master's level (with its suggestion of independence of thought and approach) (Gove 2010, p. 8). In terms of the framework, this represents a diagonal move from cell 3 in Fig. 6.3 to cell a, with no apparent awareness of the disjunction.

This conflict is another example of the prescience of Hargreaves' (2000) account of the tensions that might be expected between 'a widespread, postmodern professionalism that is open, inclusive and democratic' (which will be the result of social will), and a desire (by government) to de-professionalise 'by returning teachers to the hands-on, intuitive, learn-as-you-go approach of the pre-professional age' (Hargreaves 2000, p. 167). There is also the possibility of the academic world being able

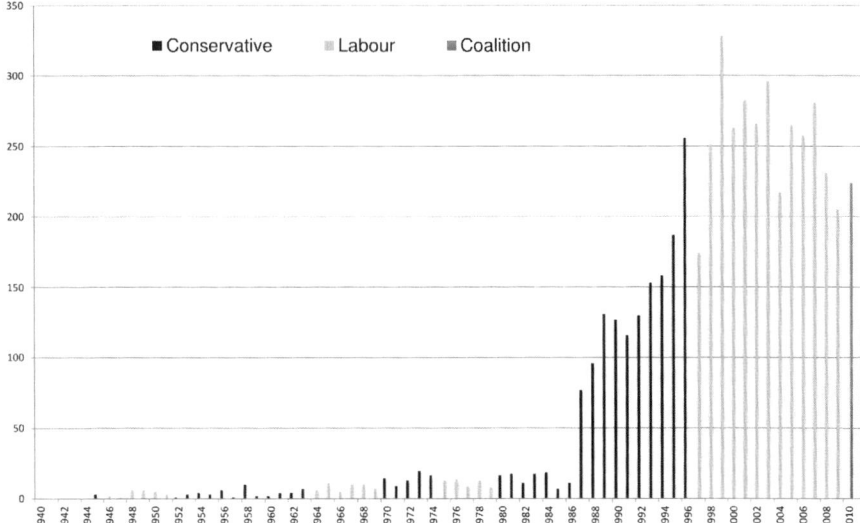

Fig. 6.4 Items of government legislation 1940–2011

to release its own monopoly of control over degree content and to allow other, qualified casts of policy actors some say over the direction of study. The accreditation of workplace study—a recognition of the 'scholarship of teaching' (Daly et al. 2004, p. 100)—as implemented in the Chartered Teacher scheme in Scotland and the Master's in Teaching and Learning in England (and now the Master's of Educational Practice in Wales), allows for the participation of the teacher in the direction of their studies, which the university tutors can then refine and extend. This potential to empower the school organisation may give heart to the Conservative Coalition, as it sits well within their expressed desire to move the training of teachers from the universities into the schools, but presents a difficulty in terms of their own loss of control.

Is Continuing Professional Learning Worth Doing?

Research into the effect of master's level work on pupils, staff and schools is patchy. Edwards was beginning to see 'evidence of the teachers' development in thinking about how theoretical models and research impact on professional life' (Edwards and Eacott 2008, p. 34), which, while hopeful is both vague and limited in impact. The literature review by McCormick (McCormick et al. 2008, p. 5) identified research which, while acknowledging the evidence of impact on pupil learning did not find convincing links to either pupil attainment or on whole-school change. As to the significance of accreditation as a factor in continuing professional learning effectiveness, the opinion in the literature seems to be 'case not proven', perhaps because this is too recent a development to be susceptible to any distanced analysis. The most positive response is dismissed as the data was collected entirely from a self-selected group who were already on an accredited course (McCormick et al. 2008, p. 22). The research content of the same report echoes these findings where '75 % of surveyed teachers indicate that accreditation is "not important" or "of limited importance" in their decisions to participate in CPL' (Pedder et al. 2008, p. 7).

In marked contrast, however, is the feedback from the Scottish Chartered Teacher scheme,[2] which predates English practice. Comments from evaluative research noted 'the positive effect that participation in the study programme had on practice', as well as understanding that 'participation in the programme emphasised the developing clarity of their actual and potential professional role' and how 'the programme in which these teachers engaged was seen as mainly positive, which may be unusual when CPL is not generally highly regarded' (Grieve and McGinley 2010, pp. 179–181). The report did, however, regret the finding that 'most participants in the programme reported a lack of interest and consequently a lack of support from school peers', which tends to support McCormick's finding.

Apparently, control of professional learning programmes by government carries its own risks, and now both this and the English Master's in Teaching and Learning (in its national form) have ceased to operate. It is of interest that, in addition to the Education Secretary of the Scottish Parliament proposing a replacement of the Chartered Teacher scheme with a master's level qualification (BBC 2012), the Welsh Assembly is implementing its own national Master of Educational Practice—hosted by Cardiff University, with Aberystwyth and Bangor Universities—which bears many similarities to the English Master's in Teaching and Learning. This draws attention to the very different ways in which teaching is currently regarded by the three national governments.

At the time of writing, schools and university departments are working to implement the latest move to place the responsibility and funding for continuing professional learning firmly in the hands of selected schools (DfE 2012b). At the same time, the revised Teachers Standards requires that all teachers should 'take responsibility for improving teaching through appropriate professional development' (DfE 2012a, p. 9). As this is factored into the next round of Ofsted inspections and reports, the meaning of 'appropriate' will become clear, and thus central control will be imposed. We can, however, hope that this may be the opportunity for schools, and teachers, to reclaim the developmental high-ground and begin to implement some values-based continuing professional learning programmes.

There is some sign of this in current practice. The development of learning communities (Wiliam 2012) in many schools (which may sit in cells c, 3 or 4 in Fig. 6.3, depending on the approaches taken by each staff and senior team) is a bottom-up

---

[2] The Scottish Chartered Teacher scheme was a system of qualification 'similar to a master's degree' which was also linked to a further set of six incremental points on a new pay scale. The awarding body was City and Guilds on a criterion referenced scheme. Like the Master's in Teaching and Learning it has now closed (in February 2012) although the Education Secretary for the Scottish Parliament said that it would be replaced by a new master's level qualification.

approach that may well be meeting the needs of both teachers and the wider school. There are also signs of a grass-roots change in the relationship between schools and universities. The school-focused, enquiry-led, practice-specific degrees—similar in style and content to the Master's in Teaching and Learning—allow for teachers and schools to meet their specific needs, supported by the university tutors' knowledge of the wider field. This may also occur without the accreditation aspect. Ainscow et al. have just published their account of facilitating teacher-initiated research within five schools in one town (Ainscow et al. 2012). In addition, as the population of higher degree holders on school staff increases, so too will schools' ability to deliver their own high-level professional learning programmes, for which they may then seek accreditation by a local university (presumably with some additional contribution from the university staff in terms of updating, tutoring and examination). A third development, most recently reported on by Scott (2012), recounts how the presence of significant (15 in the case study) Postgraduate Certificate of Education students in one placement school acted as an opportunity and incentive for existing members of staff to update their own pedagogical and subject knowledge, a fact that was recognised and then supported by the senior team in the school. However, despite all the incentives that may be provided by senior leaders, and regardless of how attractive and relevant the devised programme is, there will be no effect unless the teachers themselves are given the means to do the work, particularly some recovery of time in which to do the work. So, on the down-side, there are anecdotal accounts of senior teams offering their staff sponsorship to allow them to take on accredited professional learning, only to find zero take-up, apparently because of the extremely high demands being made on teachers. A head teacher who is also prepared to spend money on staffing above quota—so as to provide increased capacity among the teaching staff—is, on this basis, more likely to find a take-up for the offer. Finally, if the head and senior team are closely involved and investing in the success of the programme, rather than staying aloof and leaving it to their teachers and the university tutors, then this explicit sharing in the values of the professional learning programme will increase teacher involvement and commitment (Poekert 2012; Cordingley and Bell 2012).

Conclusion

In this chapter, we have talked about policy and teachers' professional learning. What we have seen is a story of indecision and confusion, born of a lengthy period of change and the complexity of disentangling what it means to be a teacher in the twenty-first century. The confusion is born of the multiple views of teaching and its place in society, and is reflected in the shifting purposes and outcomes of continuing professional learning. In this chapter, we have offered an approach towards analysing the types of continuing professional learning that are being produced, and hopefully, an approach that directs attention towards questions of values and questions about the role of the teacher—as a 'deliverer' of policy or as a critical interpreter. More and more, in pre-service teacher education and in continuing professional learning, the emphasis lies with successful in-school experience and technical skills. What we are arguing for in this chapter is an approach towards teachers' professional learning that reflects other equally important aspects. Issues of commitment, values and judgement are frequently side-lined, made optional or simply omitted, and in this way, teacher education is constructed as a skill where socio-cultural complexity is displaced or disregarded. Will teachers accept their role as increasingly directed professionals or should they become 'agents of change'—in control of their professional destinies and influential in polices that shape their professional world?

References

Ainscow, M., Dyson, A., Goldrick, S., & West, M. (2012). *Developing equitable education systems*. Oxford: Routledge.

Alexander, R. (2010). Cambridge primary review briefings: The final report. Cambridge. www.primaryreview.org.uk/downloads/revised_2011–02/FINAL_REPORT_BRIEFING_REVISED_2_11.pdf. Accessed 28 Sept 2012.

Al-Mutawa, N., & Al-Furaih, S. (2005). Evaluation of the in-service education and training programme for Kuwait army instructors. *Journal of In-Service Education, 31*, 373–392.

August, K., Brooks, R., Gilbert, C., Hancock, D., Hargreaves, D., Pearce, N., Roberts, J., Rose, J., & Wise, D. (2006). 2020 vision: Report of the teaching and learning in 2020 review group. Nottingham: Department for Education and Skills.

Ball, S. J. (2008). *The education debate*. Bristol: Policy Press.

Barrett, J. (2007). Reluctant to be No 1. TES. www.tes.co.uk/article.aspx?storycode=2332956. Accessed 18 Sept 2012.

BBC (2012). EIS attacks SNP move to end chartered teacher scheme. BBC. www.bbc.co.uk/news/uk-scotland-16963545. Accessed 9 November 2012.

Bird, M., Ding, S., Hanson, A., Leontovitsch, A., & McCartney, R. (2005). There is nothing as practical as a good theory: An examination of the outcomes of a 'traditional' MA in education for educational professionals. *Journal of In-Service Education, 31*, 427–454.

Bolam, R. (2000). Emerging policy trends: Some implications for continuing professional development. *Journal of In-Service Education, 26*, 267–280.

Bottery, M., & Wright, N. (2000). *Teachers and the state: Towards a directed profession*. London: Routledge.

Boyle, B., While, D., & Boyle, T. (2004). A longitudinal study of teacher change: What makes professional development effective? *Curriculum Journal, 15*, 45–68.

Buie, E. (2009). Much can be achieved with a bit of TLC. Times Educational Supplement Scotland. 16 October 2009.

Burstow, B. (2011). Initial teacher education: A consideration of tensions between schools, colleges and government. In I. M. Saleh & M. S. Khine (Eds.), *Teaching teachers*. New York: Nova Science Publishers, Inc.

Cordingley, P., & Bell, M. (2012). *Understanding what enables high quality professional learning: A report on the research evidence*. London: CUREE and Pearson.

Craft, A. (2000). *Continuing professional development: A practical guide for teachers and schools*. London, Routledge/Falmer.

Daly, C., Pachler, N., & Lambert, D. (2004). Teacher learning: Towards a professional academy. *Teaching in Higher Education, 9*, 99–111.

DCSF. (2008). *Being the best for our children: Releasing talent for teaching and learning*. Nottingham: DCSF Publications.

Dean, J. (1991). *Professional development in school*. Milton Keynes: Open University Press.
DES. (1944). *The McNair report: Teachers and youth leaders*. London: HMSO.
DES. (1994). *Education Act 1994: Teacher training*. London: HMSO.
DES. (1998). *Teaching and higher education act 1998: Teaching profession and general teaching councils*. London: HMSO.
DFE. (2010). *The importance of teaching: The schools white paper 2010*. London: DFE.
DFE. (2012a). *Teachers standards*. London: DFE.
DFE. (2012b). The teaching agency. London. www.education.gov.uk/aboutdfe/armslengthbodies/b0077806/the-teaching-agency. Accessed 21 Sept 2012.
DFEE. (2001). *Learning and teaching: A strategy for professional development*. London: DFEE.
Edwards, J.-A., & Eacott, J. (2008). The impact of masters level study on teachers' professional development. Proceedings of the British Society for Research into Learning Mathematics 28(3). Kings College, London.
Glover, D., & Law, S. (1996). *Managing professional development in education*. London: Kogan Page.
Goodson, I. F., & Hargreaves, A. (1996). *Teachers professional lives*. London: Falmer.
Gove, M. (2010). National College Annual Conference Speech. www.michaelgove.com/content/national_college_annual_conference. Accessed Oct 2010.
Grieve, A. M., & McGinley, B. P. (2010). Enhancing professionalism? Teachers' voices on continuing professional development in Scotland. *Teaching Education, 21*, 171–184.
Hargreaves, A. (1994). *Changing teachers, changing times: Teachers' work and culture in the postmodern age*. London: Cassell.
Hargreaves, A. (2000). Four ages of professionalism and professional learning. *Teachers and Teaching: Theory and Practice, 6*, 151–182.
Heilbron, R. (2010). *Critical practice in teacher education: A study of professional learning*. London: Institute of Education, University of London.
House of Commons Education Committee. (2012). *Great teachers: Attracting, training and retaining the best. Ninth Report of Session 2010–12*. London: The Stationery Office.
Hustler, D., McNamara, O., Jarvis, J., Londra, M., & Campbell, A. (2003). *Teachers' perceptions of continuing professional development. Report Brief: 429*. Manchester: Manchester Metroplitan University.
James Lord of Rosholme. (1972). *The James report: Teacher education and training*. London: Her Majesty's Stationery Office.
Johnson, M., & Hallgarten, J. (2000). *From victims of change to agents of change: The future of the teaching profession*. London: Institute of Public Policy Research.
Jones, M., Stanley, G., MCNamara, O., & Murray, J. (2011). Facilitating teacher educators' professional learning through a regional research capacity-building network. *Asia-Pacific Journal of Teacher Education, 39*, 263–275.
Kirk, G. (1988). *Teacher education and professional development*. Edinburgh: Scottish Academic Press.
Koçoğlu, Z. (2011). Emotional intelligence and teacher efficacy: A study of Turkish EFL pre-service teachers. *Teacher Development, 15*, 471–484.
Larsen, M. A. (2010). Troubling the discourse of teacher centrality: A comparative perspective. *Journal of Education Policy, 25*, 207–231.
MacBeath, J. (2009). *Self evaluation: Background, principles and key learning*. Nottingham: NCSL
McCormick, R., Banks, F., Morgan, B., Opfer, D., Pedder, D., Storey, A., & Wolfenden, F. (2008). *Literature review report: Schools and continuing professional development (CPD) in England—State of the Nation research project (T34718)*. London: Training and Development Agency for Schools.
McMahon, A. (1998). What teachers think of professional development. *Professional Development Today, 2*, 69–79.
Nuffield, F. (2012). Welcome to Primary Science and SPACE. www.nuffieldfoundation.org/primary-science-and-space. Accessed 28 Sept 2012.

Olson, J. (1992). *Understanding teaching: Beyond expertise*. Milton Keynes: Open University Press.

Ozga, J. (2000). *Policy research in education settings: Contested terrain*. Buckingham: Open University Press.

Pedder, D., Storey, A., & Opfer, V. D. (2008). *Schools and continuing professional development (CPD) in England—State of the Nation research project (T34718)*. London: TDA.

Pitkeathly, J., Bolton, E., Barrow, J., & Campbell, D. (2004). *New opportunities fund annual report: 2003/2004*. London: The Stationery Office.

Poekert, P. E. (2012). Teacher leadership and professional development: Examining links between two concepts central to school improvement. *Professional Development in Education, 38,* 169–188.

Revell, P. (2002). Leading from the middle. Times Educational Supplement. http://www.tes.co.uk/article.aspx?storycode=369100. Accessed 18 Sept 2012.

Rose, J. (2009). *The Rose report into primary education: Executive summary and conclusions*. London: DCSF.

Scott, H. (2012). *Multiple student placements in one partner school. Shaping the learning of teachers: Innovations in school-led teacher education*. Lancaster: TEAN, University of Cumbria.

TDA. (2009). *The national framework for masters in teaching and learning*. Nottingham: Teacher Development Agency.

Thompson, M., & Wiliam, D. (2007). *Tight but loose: A conceptual framework for scaling up school reforms*. Chicago: American Educational Research Association (AERA).

Toynbee, P., & Walker, D. (Sept 2012a). Cameron's coalition: A government with ominous intent. *The Guardian, 20,* 6.

Toynbee, P., & Walker, D. (2012b). *Dogma and disarray: Cameron at half-time*. London: Granta.

Whitty, G. (2000). Teacher professionalism in new times. *Journal of In-Service Education, 26,* 281–293.

Wiliam, D. (2012). *Sustaining formative assessment with teacher learning communities*. Kindle: Amazon.

Chapter 7
Pulling Learning Through: Building the Profession's Skills in Making Use of Workplace Coaching Opportunities

Philippa Cordingley and Natalia Buckler

Research Background

In 2008, a review of the literature on the nature of professional learning relevant to the goals and core requirements of the Government's Master's in Teaching and Learning policy was carried out by Centre for the Use of Research and Evidence in Education (CUREE), to explore the implications of the evidence for the development of coaching and professional learning within the Master's programme (Cordingley et al. 2011). The majority of research papers informing this review fell into one of three categories. The first category defined professional learning as synonymous with professional development. The second focused on what others do to professional learners and/or the conditions in which professional learning flourishes. The third, rather smaller, group explored the types of learning activities, the dispositions and the skills of professional learners. This section of the chapter synthesises across this literature to identify and explore the key dimensions of professional learning.

Professional Learning in Context

Teachers' professional learning is contextualised by their teaching practice and experiences; a phenomenon that is understood in different ways. In 1984, Buchmann highlighted that professional learning was concerned with the development of 'knowledge for action'. Referring to the development of professional knowledge, Eraut (1994, p. 20) pointed out that it was mainly 'constructed through experience and its nature depends on the cumulative acquisition, selection and interpretation of that experience'. Meanwhile, the English General Teaching Council's Professional

P. Cordingley (✉) · N. Buckler
Centre for the Use of Research and Evidence in Education,
Coventry, UK
e-mail: philippa.cordingley@curee.co.uk

N. Buckler
e-mail: natalia.buckler@curee.co.uk

O. McNamara et al. (eds.), *Workplace Learning in Teacher Education,*
Professional Learning and Development in Schools and Higher Education 10,
DOI 10.1007/978-94-007-7826-9_7, © Springer Science+Business Media Dordrecht 2014

Learning Framework (2003, p. 2) defined professional learning as a 'wide range of learning experiences, deepening and revitalising teachers' skills, abilities, values and knowledge'. More recently, Timperley et al.'s (2007) best evidence synthesis defined professional learning by contrasting it with professional development. *Professional development* refers to 'those processes and activities designed to enhance the professional knowledge, skills, and attitudes of educators so that they might, in turn, improve the learning of students' (Guskey 2000, quoted in Timperley 2007, p. 3), whereas *professional learning* implies an internal process through which individuals create professional knowledge; an umbrella term under which professional development of the 'delivery' kind is just one part. Hagger et al. (2008, p. 166) further emphasise the role of experience in professional learning: 'experience is vital since it is in the processes of planning, teaching and evaluation that all the other sources of knowledge on which one might draw come together in action and acquire meaning'.

For the purposes of this chapter, we define teachers' professional learning as the process of developing knowledge, actions, skills, abilities and values that is embedded in teachers' practice and experience and aimed primarily at developing and improving children and young people's learning. In this chapter we refer to continuing professional learning, to the support provided for continuing professional learning (i.e. continuing professional development), and to combinations of the two (continuing professional development and learning).

Lave and Wenger's (1991) study gave impetus to a number of models and theories of workplace learning. Their work challenged the prevailing orthodoxy which linked adult learning to participation in formal education or training.

Based on the ethnographic studies of how people learn at work, Lave and Wenger (1991) proposed two inter-related concepts—*legitimate peripheral participation* and *communities of practice*—which allowed them to explain how novices progress to full participant status. Their vision of learning as a 'collective and relational process involving the co-participation of newcomers with more experienced others' (Fuller 2006, p. 76) became a foundation for theories of apprenticeship and learning in non-specialist educational settings.

In addition to the exploration of the social context of learning, there is a substantial body of work that explores the impact of the workplace itself. Workplace learning in education, as Eraut (2001, p. 8) pointed out, 'arises naturally out of demands and challenges of work-solving problems, improving quality and/or productivity, or coping with change—and out of social interactions in the workplace'. Learning in the workplace involves a combination of 'thinking, trying things out and talking to other people' (Eraut 2001, p. 8). Teacher professional learning, as a form of adult learning, occurs over time; is reflective and experimental by nature, and fuelled by various sources of information; and is driven by the learner around meaningful issues (Wald and Castleberry 2000).

Eraut (2000) distinguishes between *formal* and *non-formal learning* in the workplace. He suggests that learning becomes formal if any of the following aspects are present in the learning situation:

- A prescribed learning framework;
- An organised learning event or package;
- The presence of a designated teacher or trainer;

- The award of a qualification or credit;
- The external specification of outcomes.

Formal professional learning can be appropriate in many contexts and its outcomes are not necessarily limited to propositional knowledge, as the latter could just as well be an outcome of non-formal learning (Eraut 2000). This suggests that non-formal learning refers to any kind of learning that 'does not take place within, or follow from, a formally organised learning programme or event' (Eraut 2000, p. 114).

Eraut (2000) also proposes a typology of non-formal learning, including *implicit* learning, *reactive* learning and *deliberative* learning. Building on earlier research into formal and informal workplace learning, Tynjälä (2008) similarly distinguishes between formal and informal learning and subdivides informal learning into incidental learning that arises as a side effect and intentional informal learning.

Whilst more recent research into learning at work suggests that it 'should not be seen as an inferior or limited form of participation' (Fuller 2006, p. 76), the opportunities and challenges of crossing the boundaries between the workplace and other sites for learning and sources of knowledge and expertise (e.g. higher education institutes in the case of teacher learning) also have a role to play. They can provide a broader range of learning opportunities and stimuli for learning (Fuller 2006; Eraut 2000). Young (2004) further argues that not all knowledge can or should be viewed as situated or context-specific. Some kinds of knowledge or models of understanding set out to offer more generic support to practitioners. For example, Fuller (2006, p. 77) proposed to provide access for professional learners 'to theories and concepts which go beyond the immediate, "know-how" required to perform tasks in particular workplaces', thus integrating workplace learning with learning from other sources.

A different aspect of crossing the boundaries between different sites of learning was highlighted by Wallace (1998, p. 16), who warned about 'the myth of automatic transfer: the assumption underlying many so-called "experiential" courses in professional learning that simulations are valid ways of conveying skills and that what is developed and practiced in the simulation context will, or should, naturally transfer back to the real life professional setting without much or any additional attention to learning'. Joyce and Showers (2002) found that theoretical input should be accompanied by demonstration, opportunities to try out new knowledge/theory in practice, getting feedback, and being supported by coaching to make the biggest impact on improving teachers' performance. Cordingley et al. (2007) also found that effective teacher learning and development comprised both the introduction of new knowledge and skills by specialists, and a range of measures for supporting and embedding their use—including coaching, collaboration, modelling and experimentation.

Professional Learners: Their Identity and Commitment to Continued Learning

Just as we have learned to focus specifically on how to encourage increasing independence in young people's learning, so the literature on continuing professional development and learning—encompassing both internal processes and external support aspects of teachers enhancing their professional knowledge, skills and practice[1]—suggests that we need to consider the ways that professional learners take an increasingly active role in their own learning. Zeichner (1996, p. 217) argued that without teachers taking control over their development and becoming committed to their learning '. . . it is miseducative, no matter how successful the teacher might be in the short run'.

Teachers' dispositions and commitment to continued learning are emphasised as factors to be taken into account in planning for professional learning, by both Hodkinson and Hodkinson (2005) and Burn et al. (2008). Amongst the factors that could have an impact on teachers' commitment to learning, Day et al. (2006) highlighted personal factors (values, beliefs, life events and circumstances and thus feelings); situated factors (school leadership, culture, colleagues, working conditions and pupils); and professional factors (roles, professional development arrangements and opportunities, external policies).

Exploring the issue of pre-service teachers' capacity to continue learning in new contexts, Hagger et al. (2008) found that their orientations towards risk and their aspirations played an important role in sustaining learning. Pre-service teachers whose aspirations for their pupils were limited, and who assumed that their practice and skills would automatically flow from increased experience, tended to 'plateau'. Hagger et al. (2008) suggested that encouraging new teachers to experiment in their own teaching and to take risks could counteract this and build secure foundations for their lifelong learning and professional development; as well as help them become competent classroom practitioners. Experimenting, taking risks and making decisions in the classroom are inevitably connected with teachers' feelings and emotions, which need to be considered and taken in to account along with their knowledge and behaviour when discussing issues of teacher competence and its development (Leat 1993). The full systematic reviews of the impact of continuing professional development and learning, based on the EPPI[2] methodology (Cordingley et al. 2003, 2005a, b and 2007), also highlight confidence in continuing to learn and tackle change, and commitment to do so, as an (often unforeseen) outcome of effective continuing professional development and learning.

Factors and Tools that Support Workplace Learning

There is a growing body of evidence about the skills, behaviours and characteristics of professional learners. Reflecting on evidence from teaching and learning practice and theory, and analysing and evaluating it, is highlighted as an important source of and goal for professional learning by many researchers. For example, Day (1993), and

---

[1] See Timperley's definitions of professional development and learning discussed earlier in the chapter.

[2] The Evidence for Policy and Practice Information and Co-ordinating Centre (EPPI-Centre), part of the Social Science Research Unit at the Institute of Education, University of London, is the centre for systematic review work in social science and public policy in the UK.

more recently Leat et al. (2008) and Lofthouse and Wright (2008), emphasise how working with colleagues, coaches and mentors, and using various tools (particularly video) can ensure the quality of professional learning and provide opportunities to develop educational theory rooted in practice. Eraut (2001) stressed the importance of developing self-awareness through collecting evidence from others on the effects of a practitioner's actions as a requirement for effective professional learning. The second systematic review of research about the effectiveness of continuing professional development and learning (Cordingley et al. 2005a) also found that reflective practice that is not coupled with experimentation is not linked with positive effects for pupils.

There is robust evidence that collaboration is a powerful tool in promoting, sustaining and supporting professional learning. A systematic review of the impacts of collaboration (Cordingley et al. 2003) found that in all but one of the 15 studies with high quality impact evidence, teacher collaboration was linked with improvements in both teaching and learning; many of which were substantial. The efficacy for professional learning of discussing and exploring beliefs, values, vision and practice highlighted here is supported by more recent research (e.g. Bolam et al. 2005; Hord and Sommers 2008). A review of the evidence about the impact of networking (Bell et al. 2006, p. 6) found that peer collaboration was widely used to support the transfer of knowledge and practice; while expert contribution 'ranged from training to strategic advice and facilitation'.

Cordingley et al. (2007) and Timperley et al. (2007) found that specialist input is an important catalyst in effective teacher learning. Specialists help teacher learners engage with the relevant theoretical and practical knowledge base and support them in a number of ways; most importantly by modeling, workshops, observation and feedback, and challenging orthodoxies, etc.

Connections and Parallels Between Workplace and Pupil Learning

It is understandable that there is more evidence about the support that is needed for professional learning and the contexts in which it flourishes, than about the learning process itself; it is a great deal easier to research inputs than contextualised outcomes. But the challenge of focusing on teacher professional learning has broader historical roots too. Just as for too many decades those who supported and researched teaching and learning for young people concentrated too much on the teaching and not enough on the learners and learning, so continuing professional development provision, and the underpinning research, concentrated on the continuing professional development interventions; on what was done to teachers. By making the teacher the object of the exercise, this type of work not only, unintentionally, reinforced a 'done to' model of professional growth; it also inserted teacher outcomes as an often impenetrable variable between professional learning support processes and goals, and pupil learning.

This problem was very effectively illustrated by some of the challenges encountered in carrying out early EPPI framed systematic reviews of the evidence about the effects of different kinds of continuing professional development on staff and pupil learning. The team of serving and retired teachers who had agreed to act as critical friends to this work were adamant that there was no point in carrying out a systematic review of evidence about professional learning if the connections with pupil learning were not made. The effect of this was to exclude from the review the great majority of studies of continuing professional development because almost none of these collected pupil outcome data. What emerged in their stead were studies of specific interventions in pupil learning that also problematised teacher development. The nature and complexity of the characteristics of effective continuing professional development and learning that emerged, whilst initially focused on continuing professional development, also began to shine a spotlight upon the professional learning processes.

The systematic reviews were used directly to shape a number of national policies in England including, for example, the National Strategies (2005), which made extensive and direct use of the findings. For instance, the findings were deeply embedded in the strategies' co-coaching publications and training. Similarly, the Department for Education and Skills (DfES), used the findings to shape their Continuing Professional Development Strategy, while the General Teaching Council (GTC 2005, 2006) used them to shape their continuing professional development policy and the Teacher Learning Academy (Lord et al. 2009).

At the same time, the work of the Economic and Social Research Council's Teaching and Learning Research Programme (TLRP) was gathering pace in highlighting the importance of pupil voice (Rudduck and McIntyre 2007) and pupil agency in their own learning (James et al. 2006). So, by 2008, the parallels between workplace professional learning for teachers and their pupils' learning were beginning to be made very explicit, for example, through Cordingley's (2008) 'sauce for the goose' metaphor and monograph, highlighting the parallels between pedagogy for continuing professional learning and for pupil learning, and some of the key distinctions. This increased awareness about the importance of the professional learning process, and experience became sufficiently high profile for it to feature as a major set of coaching-based policy requirements in the then Labour Government's Master's in Teaching and Learning policy programme.

Professional Learning Communities

The importance of collaboration was being increasingly revealed as an effective teaching and learning strategy for pupils; for example, from the work of the TLRP,[3] social contexts for teacher learning were emerging as key professional learning mechanisms, particularly in relation to professional learning communities. The 2005 report of the *Effective Professional Learning Communities* project—funded by the then DfES, National College for School Leadership and General Teaching Council (Bolam et al. 2005)—for instance, highlighted both the ways in which professional learning communities can make a difference to teacher and student learning, and

---

[3] See http://www.tlrp.org/.

the follow-up creation and free provision of a range of materials and tools to promote the development of professional learning communities in the UK. This report gained widespread recognition through, for example, the work of the National College for School Leadership's Networked Learning Communities Programme (Earl et al. 2006).

DuFour et al. (2004, p. 24) provide a useful summary of the functions of professional learning communities as 'groups of educators, administrators, community members and other stakeholders who collectively, systemically... identify and solve problems as they emerge; create places of action and experimentation; and are willing to test ideas that do seem to hold potential for improving student achievement'.

Professional learning in professional learning communities is, as the name implies, more often collective than individual (Bolam et al. 2005) and involves reflective enquiry, dialogues about reflection, and various other kinds of collaboration. Keay and Lloyd (2007) see the potential for self-regulatory quality assurance of professional learning and development in professional learning communities as an additional benefit.

Hodkinson and Hodkinson (2005, p. 120) suggest three dimensions which influence the professional learning of secondary school teachers: their dispositions; school (department) cultures and management; and frameworks. Two of these are contextual: 'the practices and cultures of the subject departments; and the management and regulatory frameworks, at school and national policy levels'. The evidence exploring the impact of frameworks and standards on professional learning is, at present, rather limited. However, it is possible to conclude that how the frameworks (e.g. performance management) are used and interpreted sets the context for, and influences, professional learning, and may have the effect of increasing or decreasing professional learners' sense of agency, self-regulation and accountability.

CUREE's own evidence (Cordingley and Buckler 2012) emerging from current research in 22 mixed primary and secondary schools in England (to date), explores the characteristics of effective staff learning environments and the ways that these connect staff and pupil learning. In doing so, it is starting to unpack some of the many drivers of and conditions for effective staff learning environments in relation to: how needs are assessed formatively and summatively; the ways in which collaboration is used as a strategic learning resource; the ways specialist expertise is recognised, sourced and used; how evidence of varying kinds is used; and a range of aspects of the leadership of continuing professional development and learning (modelling, prioritisation and alignment, the evaluation of and exploration of impact, and the use of tools and protocols to secure quality at scale).

Coaching as a Case Study

The characteristics of effective support for workplace professional learning are, as this chapter shows, complex, layered and highly contextualised. A range of different ways of integrating these into effective approaches to supporting professional learning and the growth of teacher agency has grown in parallel. Variously labelled 'coaching', 'conferencing', 'collaborative enquiry', 'action research' and 'research lesson study', these approaches share a number of characteristics. One of them was teachers' constant efforts to experiment with, adapt, and contextualise for specific pupils, approaches to teaching and learning developed in other contexts, always focused on achieving higher aspirations for pupils. Similarly common was use of evidence from pupils' responses to new approaches and from teachers' experiments as a springboard for learning, and as a driver for interrogating practice in order to enable teachers to develop an underpinning rationale or practical theory about why things do and don't work. Finally, learning from observing teaching and learning practice; and a combination of specialist expertise (in various forms, including research summaries, tools and protocols) to challenge orthodoxies and introduce high leverage, evidence-rich approaches and peer support to embed learning from specialists in day-to-day contexts, also emerged as key features of effective support for workplace learning.

In 2005, the National Framework for Coaching and Mentoring was published by the then DfES, following a year-long period of consultation, development and research by CUREE. The framework had been commissioned by the DfES to build upon the outcomes of the large-scale systematic reviews of the impact of continuing professional development and learning on students and on their teachers (Cordingley et al. 2003, 2005a, 2007), and to contextualise the outcomes of these reviews into coaching and mentoring practice in England.

The National Framework[4] arose principally from the evidence from three reviews of the research about the impact of collaborative and individually-oriented continuing professional development on teachers and teaching and on student learning and achievement. This encompassed a systematic procedure which collectively involved scanning over 4,000 titles and abstracts, retrieving more than 300 full studies and conducting at least 45 data extractions, before using a methodological weighting system to carry out three syntheses of the evidence. There was consistency across the reviews in relation to a number of positive links between collaborative, sustained continuing professional development and continuing professional learning and teachers' self-confidence (e.g. in taking risks); self efficacy (their belief in their ability to make a difference); willingness to continue professional learning; willingness and ability to make changes to practice; deeper knowledge and understanding of subject and pedagogy; and wider repertoire of strategies and ability to match these to their learning needs.

There were also positive links with pupils' motivation to learn; performance (e.g. test results); specific skills (e.g. maths and literacy, decoding, reading, problem solving); responses to specific subjects and curricula; organisation of work; use of collaboration as a learning strategy; questioning skills and responses; and skills in selecting and using a wider range of learning activities.

---

[4] http://www.curee.co.uk/files/publication/1219313968/mentoring_and_coaching_national_framework.pdf.

Although the Framework was built from the foundations of the evidence from these reviews, the findings from research of informed commentators, including Adey (2002) and Joyce and Showers (2002), were also brought to bear, as were the lessons from evaluations of national programmes such as DfES (2004) Primary National Strategy: Intensifying support programme (2004), and Earl et al.'s (2003) evaluation of the National Literacy and Numeracy Strategies. The experiences and development work of a number of national agencies in England (General Teaching Council, National College for School Leadership, Training and Development Agency for Schools, Specialist Schools and Academies Trust, DfES amongst them) were also investigated collaboratively with key representatives. All of these agencies subsequently adopted the principles outlined in the Framework.

In 2007, a fourth systematic review into continuing professional development and learning linked to positive student outcomes (Cordingley et al. 2007) focused explicitly on the nature of the expert or specialist contribution to teacher learning. The review identified three main contributions from specialists to initiate and embed professional learning in ways that benefit pupils as well as teachers:

- Specialist knowledge of a particular subject area and/or effective pedagogical approaches;
- Specialist knowledge and skills in framing, initiating and sustaining the continuing professional development and learning process;
- An understanding of the dynamics, challenges and facilitators of professional learning in practical ways within the fast paced dynamics of day-to-day school life.

The studies from which the evidence was drawn were all set within the context of continuing professional development and learning processes, which might well be described as a mix of (mostly in-school) specialist coaching supplemented by in-school peer and co-coaching.

The key finding in relation to the role of specialists was that they both introduced new knowledge and/or skills *and* they employed a repertoire of support mechanisms to help embed learning through collaboration and bring about changes in teachers' practice. From the instruction element, teachers gained new knowledge, skills and understanding. They learned more about their subject. They learned how to learn about teaching and learning and hence to widen their approaches to teaching. Specialist coaching-based contributions to support teachers' learning were present at many stages and in different contexts. They included the use of modelling, workshops, observation and feedback. They always sat alongside strategies for supporting peer working, usually via collaborative coaching between reciprocal learners working in the teachers' own schools and classrooms. These featured, in particular, as important strategies for motivating teachers to make changes and in building ownership. Some of the strategies highlighted in the reviews, as being used by professionals in coaching contexts (whether or not that is what they were labelled) for supporting teacher learning, included: support for engaging with underpinning rationale and exploring and refining beliefs in light of evidence; activities that structure and sustain discussion about experiments with new approaches; scaffolding growing independence;

encouraging, enabling and structuring peer support; focusing professional learning through the lens of needs of specific students; and enabling alignment with other priorities.

Timperley et al.'s (2007) parallel systematic review identified seven closely related elements as important for promoting professional learning in ways that impacted positively and substantively on a range of student outcomes. These included: providing sufficient time for extended opportunities to learn and using the time effectively; focusing on engaging teachers in the learning process rather than being concerned about whether they volunteered or not; challenging problematic discourses; providing opportunities to interact in a community of professionals; and ensuring content was consistent with wider policy trends, etc.

She found that 'experts' need more than knowledge of the content of changes in teaching practice that might make a difference to students; they also need to know how to make the content meaningful to teachers and manageable within the context of teaching practice. The review also found that external experts who expected teachers to implement their preferred practices were typically less effective than those who worked with teachers in more iterative ways, involving them in discussions and the development of meaning for their classroom contexts. 'Expecting teachers to act as technicians and to implement a set of "behaviours" belies the complexity of teaching, the embeddedness of individual acts of teaching, and the need to be responsive to the learning needs of students' (ibid., p. xxix). Effective support for continuing professional development participants involved support in processing new understandings and their implications for teaching. Sometimes this involved 'challenging problematic beliefs and testing the efficacy of competing ideas' (ibid., p. xxx).

Timperley et al.'s (2007) work also draws attention to the importance of challenging prevailing discourses: usually based on assumptions that some groups of students could not learn as well as others and/or emphasising limited curriculum goals. 'The challenge to discourses typically involved iterative cycles of thinking about alternatives and becoming aware of learning gains made as a result of changed teaching approaches' (ibid., p. xxvii).

Leadership was a strong feature of the Timperley review findings. It is clear from the literature that coaches will need to have strong school support. Bolam and Weindling (2006) identify the key role of heads and senior staff in promoting and supporting continuing professional development and learning. Ofsted (2006) found that resource allocation, performance management, balancing between national and school priorities and treating workforce development as continuing professional development and learning should be integrally planned. Continuing professional development and learning should have clearly specified outcomes, based on student learning and assessment mechanisms, and schools should recognise the need for specialist subject contributions. The provision of coaches and mentors, and tailoring development to the best possible sources (including in-school training), were all highlighted in the report.

Since the publication of the Framework, the importance of the role of coaching has been underlined, and the challenges it represents have continued to be highlighted in the research. For example, studies of the Collaborative Coaching and Learning (CCL) model in Boston (e.g. Donaldson and Neufeld 2006) found evidence that the CCL policy direction adopted by Boston public schools is effective in terms of a positive influence on student achievement, staff development, recruitment and retention. On the other hand, two national thematic studies of continuing professional development practices in England (Ofsted 2006, 2010) highlighted continuing problems in coaching practices, and emphasised in particular, schools' lack of understanding of the different forms of coaching and mentoring, leading to them being unable to use them to best effect. The 22 CUREE evaluation studies of the stage of maturity of continuing professional development and learning in schools during the 2011/2012 academic year (Cordingley and Buckler 2012) help to flesh out some of the reasons for these challenges. Very often schools who describe themselves as offering a coaching culture are simply referring to the style of discussion used by line managers in performance review meetings. Whilst many teachers value this, this model means that coaching occurs at most once a year (52 % of teachers say they experience coaching at most once a year, even though 75 % of schools describe coaching as a key continuing professional development and learning tool). Similarly, fewer than half of teachers say that the identification or refinement of learning goals features as part of coaching conversations. By and large, coaching is welcomed enthusiastically as part of leadership/executive development, but is, as a result, usually generic, stopping short of the infusion of deep specialist pedagogic content knowledge and of mobilising peer support/reciprocal vulnerability as a means of building ownership, sustainability and the development of a practical underpinning rationale or theory to give teachers increasing control over their own learning.

Other Approaches to Supporting Workplace Learning in Schools in England

CUREE's latest evidence about the state of maturity of continuing professional development and learning in schools in England (Cordingley and Buckler 2012) shows that the proportion of workplace learning in many of them is rising; partly due to recent cuts in schools' continuing professional development and learning budgets and partly due to disappointment in the quality of much of the external continuing professional development provision. For example, over half of school practitioners state that they do not participate in any external professional development and a further 29 % indicate that they do so only once a year or even less often. There is also growing recognition and support for workplace learning in building in-school capacity.

In this context, school activities focus on supporting their staff development via creating programmes of core formal workplace continuing professional development opportunities, the vast majority of which are aimed at all staff and focus on whole school issues. Over 50 % of the school practitioners involved in CUREE's work with 22 schools, reported that the bulk of the continuing professional development they participated in targeted whole-school priorities and was not aimed at them personally. Worryingly, nearly 20 % of practitioners found whole-school sessions largely irrelevant and another 50 % could only sometimes link them to their practice.

In secondary schools in particular, a significant proportion of formal school-based sessions had a strong emphasis on general pedagogy, as this was often easy to link to whole-school priorities and was largely applicable to all curriculum areas. At the same time, teachers' professional learning in areas of their subject specialism, which the majority of them saw as most relevant for their practice and progression as education professionals, was often pushed into the background. Primary schools generally found it easier to make whole-school sessions relevant for their staff but even there such sessions seem to focus on generic pedagogies and to be challenging environments for supporting personalised professional learning.

These emerging concerns are from a very small portion of our now extensive qualitative and quantitative evidence about workplace learning and the environments that shape it. Over the next six months we will be significantly increasing the number of schools included and starting to undertake a more in-depth analysis in order to help explore some of the issues and questions raised in this chapter.

Conclusions

In summary, the updating and review process underpinning this chapter reinforces and complements the historical evidence about effective professional learning and how strategies such as coaching can support it effectively. None of the evidence undermines in any way the previous findings or the content of the National Framework for Coaching and Mentoring. But what the chapter does point to is a need to expand the original boundaries of the Framework, to shift the attention of both practitioners and researchers towards exploring the notion of the professional learning process alongside consideration of what is offered to structure and support it. It also highlights the need for more fully developed principles for professional learning.

The evidence in this chapter suggests to the authors that such principles could usefully be organised under four broad headings: first, critically analysing and evaluating evidence, that is, collecting and analysing evidence of and feedback on their practice and their students' learning; second, taking and managing risks, involving, for example, exploration of the costs and benefits of changes to practice, and making informed judgements before taking action; third, collaborating with others, that is, making their beliefs and values, their knowledge and practice and their plans and ideas explicit and available for shared scrutiny and development; and fourth, growing in independence, that is, taking increasing responsibility for their own learning and reflection.

References

Adey, P. (2002). The role of in-service professional development of science teachers in large-scale changes in teaching practice: A look at Britain and Indonesia. In P. Fraser-Abder (Ed.), *Professional development of science teachers: Local insights with lessons for the global community* (pp. 158–171). London: Routledge.

Bell, M., Cordingley, P., & Mitchell, H. (2006). The impact of networks on pupil, practitioners, organisations and the communities they serve. Cranfield: National College for School Leadership (NCSL). http://www.nationalcollege.org.uk/download?id=133214 & filename=nlc-impact-of-networks-on-pupils-practitioners-organisations-and-communities.pdf.

Bolam, R., & Weindling, D. (2006). *Synthesis of research and evaluation projects concerned with capacity-building through teachers' professional development.* London: General Teaching Council for England.

Bolam, R., McMahon, A., Stoll, L., Thomas, S., Wallace, M., Greenwood, A., Hawkey, K., Ingram, M., Atkinson, A., & Smith, M. (2005). Creating and sustaining professional learning communities. Research report 637. London: Department for Education & Skills (DfES) and University of Bristol.

Buchmann, M. (1984). The priority of knowledge and understanding in teaching. In L. Katz & J. Raths (Eds.), *Advances in teacher education* (Vol. 1, pp. 29–48). Norwood: Ablex.

Burn, K., Hagger, H., & Mutton, T. (2008). *Strengthening and sustaining learning in the second year of teaching. Paper presented at: The annual conference of the British Educational Research Association, University of Edinburgh.* Edinburgh: 3–6 September 2008.

Cordingley, P. (2008). Sauce for the goose: Learning entitlements that work for teachers as well as their pupils. Coventry: Centre for the Use of Research and Evidence (CUREE). http://www.curee.co.uk/resources/publications/sauce-goose-leaflet-pdf-format. Accessed 1 Feb 2013.

Cordingley, P., & Buckler, N. (2012). Professional learning environments in primary and secondary contexts. Paper presented at BERA Annual Conference, University of Manchester, University of Manchester, 4–5 September, 2012. Session 3.29: 11.00–12.30 Wednesday 5 September 2012.

Cordingley, P., Bell, M., Rundell, B., & Evans, D. (2003). *The impact of collaborative CPD on classroom teaching and learning.* London: EPPI-Centre, Social Science Research Unit, Institute of Education, University of London.

Cordingley, P., Bell, M., Thomason, S., & Firth, A. (2005a). *The impact of collaborative continuing professional development (CPD) on classroom teaching and learning. Review: How do collaborative and sustained CPD and sustained but not collaborative CPD affect teaching and learning?* London: EPPI-Centre, Social Science Research Unit, Institute of Education, University of London.

Cordingley, P., Bell, M., Evans, D., & Firth, A. (2005b). *The impact of collaborative CPD on classroom teaching and learning. Review: What do teacher impact data tell us about collaborative CPD?* London: EPPI-Centre, Institute of Education, University of London.

Cordingley, P., Bell, M., Isham, C., Evans, D., & Firth, A. (2007). What do specialists do in CPD programmes for which there is evidence of positive outcomes for pupils and teachers? Technical report. In Research Evidence in Education Library. London: EPPI-Centre, Social Science Research Unit, Institute of Education, University of London.

Cordingley, P., Buckler, N., & Bell, M. (2011). Professional learning and the role of the coach in the new Masters in Teaching and Learning (MTL): Technical report. Coventry: Centre for the Use of Research and Evidence in Education (CUREE). http://www.curee.co.uk/files/publication/[site-timestamp]/CUREE%20MTL%20technical%20report%20FINAL%20rev.pdf. Accessed 12 Oct 2012.

CUREE (Centre for the Use of Research and Evidence in Education). (2005). Mentoring and coaching national framework. London: DFES. http://webarchive.nationalarchives.gov.uk/20110809101133/nsonline.org.uk/node/132345. Accessed 1 Feb 2013.

Day, C. (1993). The development of teachers' thinking and practice: Does choice lead to empowerment? In J. Elliott (Ed.), *Reconstructing teacher education: Teacher development*. London: The Falmer Press.

Day, C., Stobart, G., Sammons, P., Alison Kington, A., Gu, K., Smees, R., & Tamjid Mujtaba, T. (2006). *Variations in teachers' work, lives and effectiveness*. London: Department for Education and Skills (DfES) (Research Report 743).

DfES. (2004). Primary national strategy: Intensifying support programme. London: Department for Education and Skills. http://webarchive.nationalarchives.gov.uk/20110809101133/wsassets.s3. amazonaws.com/ws/nso/pdf/1c002e8d1a6baa8ec33d7c55c945ad7b.pdf. Accessed 1 Feb 2013.

DfES. (2005). Mentoring and coaching CPD capacity building project (2004–2005): National framework for mentoring and coaching. Coventry: CUREE & Department for Education and Skills. http://www.curee.co.uk/files/publication/1219313968/mentoring_and_coaching_national_framework.pdf. Accessed 1 Feb 2013.

Donaldson, M., & Neufeld, B. (2006). *Collaborative coaching and learning in literacy: Implementation at four Boston public schools*. Cambridge: Education Matters, Inc.

DuFour, R., DuFour, R., Eaker, R., & Karhenek, G. (2004). *Whatever it takes: How professional learning communities respond when kids don't learn*. Bloomington: National Education Service.

Earl, L., Watson, N., Levin, B., Leithwood, Fullan, M., Torrance, N., Jantzi, D., Mascall, D., & Volante, L. (2003). *Final report of the external evaluation of England's national literacy and numeracy strategies*. Ontario: University of Toronto.

Earl, L., Katz, S., Elgie, S., Jaafar, S., & Foster, L. (2006). How networked learning communities work: Volume 1—The report. Toronto: Aporia Consulting Ltd. http://networkedlearning.ncsl.org.uk/collections/network-research-series/reports/how-networked-learning-communities-work.pdf. Accessed 1 Feb 2013.

Eraut, M. (1994). *Developing professional knowledge and competence*. London: Falmer.

Eraut, M. (2000). Non-formal learning and tacit knowledge in professional work. *British Journal of Educational Psychology, 70,* 113–136.

Eraut, M. (2001). Teachers learning in the workplace. In A. Kesidou (Ed.), *Continuing teacher education and school development* (pp. 54–68). Greece: Aristotle University of Thessaloniki.

Fuller, A. (2006). Participative learning through the work-based route: From apprenticeship to part-time higher education. *European Journal of Vocational Education, 37,* 68–81.

GTC. (2003). *Commitment: The teachers' professional learning framework*. London: General Teaching Council for England (GTC).

GTC. (2005). Learning together: leading professional development (TPLF04) London: General Teaching Council for England. http://dera.ioe.ac.uk/8256/1/tplf_learntog_pltog0405.pdf. Accessed 1 Feb 2013.

GTC. (2006). *Professional learning framework: Peer observation*. London: General Teaching Council for England.

Hagger, H., Burn, K., Mutton, T., & Brindley, S. (2008). Practice makes perfect? Learning to learn as a teacher. *Oxford Review of Education, 34*(2), 159–178.

Hodkinson, H., & Hodkinson, P. (2005). Improving schoolteachers' workplace learning. *Research Papers in Education, 20*(2), 109–132.

Hord, S., & Sommers, W. (2008). *Leading professional learning communities: Voices from research and practice*. California: Corwin Press.

James, M., Black, P., McCormick, R., Pedder, D., & Wiliam, D. (2006). Learning how to learn, in classrooms, schools and networks: Aims, design and analysis. *Research Papers in Education, 21*(2), 101–118.

Joyce, B., & Showers, B. (2002). *Student achievement through staff development*. New York: Longman.

Keay, J., & Lloyd, C. (2007). Professional learning communities. Paper presented at: AARE 2007 International Educational Research Conference.

Lave, J., & Wenger, E. (1991). *Situated learning*. Cambridge: Cambridge University Press.

Leat, D. (1993). A conceptual model of competence. *Journal of In-Service Education, 19*(2), 35–40.

Leat, D., Lofthouse, R., Cummings, C., & Hall, E. (2008). Developing an analytical framework for coaching sessions for use by new teachers. Paper presented at: The British Education Research Association Conference, 3–6 September, 2008, Edinburgh, UK.

Lofthouse, R., & Wright, D. (2008). Enquiring into practice: a new method of lesson observation. Paper presented at: the British Education Research Association Conference, 3–6 September, 2008, Edinburgh, UK.

Lord, P., Lamont, E., Harland, J., Mitchell, H., & Straw, S. (2009). *Evaluation of the GTC's Teacher Learning Academy (TLA): Impacts on teachers, pupils and schools.* London: General Teaching Council for England.

National Strategy. (2005). *Coaching and assessment for learning.* London: Department for Education and Skills.

Ofsted. (2006). *The logical chain: CPD in effective schools.* London: Office for Standards in Education.

Ofsted. (2010). *Good professional development in schools.* London: Office for Standards in Education.

Rudduck, J., & McIntyre, D. (Eds). (2007). *Improving learning through consulting pupils. Teaching and Learning Research Programme (TLRP) Consulting Pupils Project Team.* London: Routledge.

Timperley, H., Wilson, A., Barrar, H., & Fung, I. (2007). *Teacher professional learning and development: Best evidence synthesis iteration (BES).* Wellington: Ministry of Education.

Tynjälä, P. (2008). Perspectives into learning at the workplace. *Educational Research Review, 3*(2), 130–154.

Wald, P. J., & Castleberry, M. S. (2000). *Educators as learners: Creating a professional learning community in your school.* Alexandria: Association for Supervision and Curriculum Development.

Wallace, M. (1998). When is experiential learning not experiential learning. In G. Claxton (Ed.), *Liberating the learner: Lessons for professional development in education* (pp. 16–31). London: Routledge.

Young, M. (2004). Conceptualizing vocational knowledge: Some theoretical considerations. In H. Rainbird, Fuller, A., & Munro, A. (Eds.), Workplace learning in context. London: Routledge.

Zeichner, K. (1996). Designing educative practicum experiences. In K. Zeichner, S. Melnick & M. L. Gomez (Eds.), *Currents of reform in preservice teacher education.* New York: Teachers College Press.

Chapter 8
Empowering Teachers as Learners: Continuing Professional Learning Programmes as Sites for Critical Development in Pedagogical Practice

Yvonne Barnes and Yvette Solomon

Introduction

In this chapter we describe our research on a continuing professional learning pro-gramme which began in 2009 as part of a national initiative to raise the standard of mathematics teaching in English primary schools by creating 'maths champions' who would influence mathematics pedagogy in their schools, thereby addressing a perceived deficit in teacher subject knowledge and pedagogic skill in the primary sec-tor (see Williams 2008). The version of the Mathematics Specialist Teacher (MaST) programme that we report on here aimed to provide teachers with the necessary skills and knowledge to be able to critically assess and construct pedagogical prac-tices for their own settings. Combining formal input focusing on recent research with participant-led discussion and reflection, it emphasised mathematical problem-solving and enquiry, and participants were required to undertake small research projects within their own school settings that involved posing different mathematical tasks to their pupils. They were then asked to reflect on the children's learning and their own teaching. Teachers were also required to undertake regular critiques of re-search literature. A reflection of their own practice and current research was assessed through the production of two 5,000 word essays at master's level.

The course was not intended to provide a model of 'best practice' or prototype blueprint for mathematics teaching. Rather, the intention was to provide enhanced reflective skills so that participants could evaluate their developing professional prac-tice to suit their own particular context needs. We know from previous research in continuing professional learning (e.g. Corbin et al. 2003; McNamara and Corbin

Y. Barnes (✉)
Faculty of Education, Manchester Metropolitan University,
Manchester, UK
e-mail: y.barnes@mmu.ac.uk

Y. Solomon
Education and Social Research Institute, Manchester Metropolitan University,
Manchester, UK
e-mail: y.solomon@mmu.ac.uk

O. McNamara et al. (eds.), *Workplace Learning in Teacher Education,*
Professional Learning and Development in Schools and Higher Education 10,
DOI 10.1007/978-94-007-7826-9_8, © Springer Science+Business Media Dordrecht 2014

2001; Brown et al. 2007) that it is neither realistic nor necessarily desirable to evaluate programmes in terms of the extent to which they impact on teachers' practice in pre-determined 'ideal' ways, without tension and negotiation. Elsewhere (Barnes et al. 2013) we have explored this issue, arguing that teachers engage with continuing professional learning in a variety of ways which build on their particular professional experiences and contexts, and that programme outcomes need to be understood against the background of teachers' developing professional identities. In this chapter we explore professional development in more detail, examining how the MaST continuing professional learning programme enabled teachers to become more reflective practitioners who are able to critically analyse curriculum and pedagogical practices within mathematics teaching.

Background: Continuing Professional Learning

Questioning the Impact of Continuing Professional Learning Programmes

Evaluating the impact of continuing professional learning programmes is difficult, not least because of the need to agree on what we might expect as a marker of success. Continuing professional learning in mathematics education is frequently assumed to have a goal of moving towards a pedagogic 'ideal' (Tzur et al. 2001), but identifying and measuring this presents a challenge. For example, Farmer et al. (2003) attempted to capture the complexity of improvement in instruction by considering the impact on teachers' fundamental dispositions and beliefs about teaching mathematics. They thus identified three different levels of engagement with continuing professional learning in terms of teachers' perceptions of it: as a source of useful concrete activities and additional mathematics content (level 1); as support or enhancement of their professional principles and understanding (level 2); and as a focus on and challenge to their attitudes and beliefs (level 3). Farmer et al. argued that it was at this third level that continuing professional learning had the most sustained impact on participants' future practice. However, it is worth noting that challenge does not thereby presuppose certain teacher behaviours; rather, it leads to reflection, an issue which we pursue later.

Much research into the effectiveness of continuing professional learning has shown that teachers do not always do what they 'should' in relation to course objectives, and that there is often a mismatch between what a programme recommends in relation to practice and what schools actually require, or what the teacher believes to be 'right' (see Barnes et al. 2013). There are many factors involved, including regulative government policy and teacher resistance to change, or the role of local contexts. As Cochran-Smith and Lytle (1999) suggest, prescriptive continuing professional learning programmes can often de-emphasise differences in local cultures, so failing to address the particular needs of that context or school. But there are more fundamental pedagogic factors at play too: many continuing professional learning programmes involve merely 'bolting on' new ideas to existing practice, leaving teachers' beliefs in relation to pedagogy unchallenged (McNamara and Corbin 2001). Even when teachers' beliefs about pedagogy *are* challenged, however, further difficulties arise in relation to making adjustments to practice when confronted by new discursive styles and understandings. Drawing on Bourdieu, Nolan (2012) points out that one cannot assume that there will be a straightforward substitution of practice, since changing practice is a matter of changing one's habitus—adopting new ideas and practices is not going to be a 'quick fix'.

In our earlier work (Barnes et al. 2013) we have built on this identification of complexity to argue that evaluation of continuing professional learning in mathematics education needs to involve more subtle measures which acknowledge teachers' professional agency and reflection. In what follows we consider in detail what this entails in practice.

Critical Reflection

Recalling John Dewey's (1916) idea that reflective thinking makes education an ongoing reconstruction of experience, we employ the concept of the reflective practitioner to acknowledge the expertise of the experienced teacher who develops and improves their teaching as a result of reflection on their own actions and practices. Recent development of this idea can be seen as a reaction against a view of teachers as mere technicians who service top-down approaches to education reform. As Zeichner and Lui (2010) maintain, if teachers are not to be seen in this way, they need to determine their own agency through a critical and continual evaluation of the purposes, consequences and social context of their work. For these writers, the reflective process not only needs a focus—such as social/personal and academic issues regarding children as learners, or wider social equality issues—but should also challenge rather than reinforce current practices. Thus, reflection should be an intentional act of systematic inquiry (Lyons 2010), an act that looks both backwards and to the future and leads to the learning of new things.

When it comes to actually implementing critical reflection as a practice, a number of researchers report on the importance of collaboration with practitioner colleagues in problematising the teaching and learning process (see for example Loughran 2010). Thus, Barnett and O'Mahony (2006) developed a reflective culture by presenting a 'problem' in continuing professional learning sessions which participants focused on in their own classroom contexts and then reflected on collaboratively in subsequent sessions, discussing and questioning existing practices and sharing collective reflections. Gimbert (2000) found that this kind of environment enabled teachers to develop a culture of challenge towards 'didactic arrangements' in which they were able to critique existing practices rather than accepting 'that is the way it is'. Similarly, Nissila (2005) and Park et al. (2007) report that reflection makes 'tacit assumptions' open to question, and so opens up access to new visions and perspectives as part of professional development.

Central to such reflective practice is practitioners' sensitivity to different elements of their practice. In order to understand the complexity of how teachers gain from professional learning opportunities, and to operationalise our interest in their development of reflective, critical analysis, our focus in this chapter, then, is on 'noticing' (Erickson 2011; Mason 2002, 2002; Sherin et al. 2011). What is noticed and indeed what is observed in the first place (Ghaye 2010), how it is noticed, and why it is noticed are important in shaping the nature of, and response to, reflective practice. We explore the implications of a focus on noticing in the following section.

Developing the Skills of Noticing

While noticing as a component of professional expertise is well documented in association with the multidimensionality, simultaneity and unpredictability of teaching (Doyle 1977), more recently Erickson (2011, p. 18) argued that 'mere years in the classroom did not have a straight relation to improvement in teaching practice', since noticing by teachers without reflection within action is not 'pedagogical experience'. Jacobs et al. (2011) researched 'in-the-moment instructional decision making' as a crucial element of building on children's thinking (Jacobs et al. 2007), and found that the expertise and skill required to focus on and remember pertinent features of particular situations grew only when teachers were engaged in two or more years of professional development experience. Thus, such expertise is not something that teachers routinely possess, requiring, as Mason (2002) argues, the acquisition of a practice (or discipline) of noticing.

However, recognising the impact of teachers' individual trajectories and beliefs introduces a further complexity. Erickson (2006) found that attending to noticing enabled teachers to question habitual or taken-for-granted assumptions about their teaching and the classroom environment, but that the judgements they brought to their noticing were influenced profoundly by their prior experience. Experienced teachers, he found, connected details of the moment to wider issues such as curriculum structure and annual cycles. In addition, however, they sometimes used this ability to combine discrete items of information to construct a coherent interpretive picture that sometimes resulted in unwarranted inferences, since they viewed events through the lens of their own 'philosophy of practice'. These beliefs were concerned with the nature of learners, about important aspects of their subject matter and about the nature of learning.

Returning to the issue of change, then, we note Mason's (2011) argument that noticing involves the development of a *collection of practices* designed to sensitise oneself to the teaching and learning context, so as to notice opportunities for future actions which are new rather than automatic and determined by habit. Echoing other research on noticing and reflection, he thus underlines the importance of noticing as an intentional act which challenges current practice. It is active rather than passive, and reflexivity (reflection) necessarily concerns what we focus our energy and attention on. As Sherin et al. (2011, p. 3) ask 'where do teachers look, what do they see and what do they make of what they see?'.

Applying Noticing in Mathematics Education and the MaST Programme

There are multiple benefits for mathematics education of developing teacher noticing. It has become a central tool in the implementation of mathematics teaching which aims to engender a greater depth of understanding in a subject which has been prone to rote learning and transmission teaching. As recommended by the National Council of Teachers of Mathematics (NCTM 2000), mathematics teaching needs to be adaptive and responsive to pupils' needs, such that teachers are required to make decisions as the lesson unfolds. This style of teaching is therefore reliant on what teachers notice on a moment-by-moment basis. Furthermore, Sherin et al. (2011) argue, noticing supports teachers' own professional development as they learn to learn from the cycle of noticing/paying attention to a particular aspect of their teaching, responding to it, and attending to the results. At the micro-level, noticing provides a language of description for 'decomposing' practice (Sherin et al. 2011, p. 6), that is, for being able to identify and describe salient features.

Exploiting this latter idea, Mason's (1988) approach used video as a stimulus for recall and analysis of related incidents from teachers' own practice (thus avoiding direct normative analysis of the video material itself). Teachers were asked to choose a salient moment and describe it to colleagues, reducing judgements or emotive terms to a minimum. Participants developed a 'collective vocabulary' and a 'rich web' of shared incidents which provided a foundation for recognition of similar incidents in their practice and enabled them to avoid habitual responses and act in a different way, drawing on a collection of alternative actions. Mason felt that this was the essence of the discipline of noticing, in which an 'inner witness or monitor' is developed. Through the development of an 'awareness of awareness' (Gattegno 1987), the practitioner may start to ask themselves such questions as 'Why are we doing this?'.

The philosophy of the MaST continuing professional learning programme as it was designed and delivered at this particular university—whereby the practitioner acted as a researcher identifying, reflecting and reporting back on problems within their own context—provided an opportunity for the teachers to practise the act or discipline of noticing. The programme employed Barnett and O'Mahony's (2006) 'reflective culture design', and instead of using video required participants to carry out and discuss short teaching research projects in their own locations. Session time was then given to analysing reflections on these short teaching sessions. This process of withdrawing from action, and then intentionally reflecting on and reconstructing the action and its effects, is advocated by Simon and Tzur (2004) as increasing the possibility of a fresh response rather than a habitual reaction (Korthagen and Vasalos 2010). In the rest of this chapter we focus on the impact of MaST on participants in terms of their empowerment as learning professionals, as opposed to passive receivers of a 'MaST philosophy'. In researching their responses to the programme through the lens of noticing, we were interested to enquire whether they were seeing the previously 'invisible' elements within their practice and the classroom, and if this resulted in a shift in their perspective and practice. More fundamentally, however, we were also interested in exploring whether the MaST programme had provided them with a new, empowering language of description, which would take them beyond their immediate context and personal histories, rather than a series of 'tricks and tips'.

Methodology: Researching Noticing

In researching noticing in our programme, we note Sherin and Star's (2011) comment that teacher noticing has multiple meanings in the literature, and that trying to capture and analyse teacher behaviour and reasoning is a complex process. Focusing on infrequent events is one strategy, when teachers see something that stands out because it is surprising or seems important—'noticing as recognising noteworthy classroom phenomena' (ibid., p. 68). Using this approach, however, narrows the focus to the non-routine, while in fact it is the routine aspect of teachers' work which may be precisely what needs to be captured. An alternative is a 'focus on a subcomponent of the larger systems'(ibid., p. 69), in which the teacher—who is bombarded with what the psychologist and philosopher William James famously described as 'blooming, buzzing confusion' (James 1890)—attends to, and selects, particular element(s) which become the 'noticed thing'. Having interpreted and made sense of the 'noticed thing', in relation to its connection with broader principles of teaching and learning and current context, the teacher takes some action leading to modification of the 'blooming, buzzing confusion' (Sherin and Star 2011, p. 70).

There are difficulties associated with noticing 'intuitive' behaviours, however. For example, Sherin and Star (2011) note that all teacher noticing is active—because what the teacher sees in the world is strongly driven by their knowledge and expectations. In addition, since perception is active, the teacher does not just see but actively *looks*. Furthermore, the teacher has an active role in shaping what occurs within the classroom to produce certain kinds of events, and for some of these events, may have established interpretations in advance.

Ten of the 170 MaST course participants from the first cohort of the programme were involved in the study. All participated in interviews with the authors which were designed to encourage them to talk about their personal beliefs about mathematics education and their confidence and subject knowledge about mathematics, together with the impact of MaST on these issues and on their practice in general. We discuss these interviews in terms of the impact on their practice in Barnes et al. (2013). In this chapter, we focus on classroom observation and post-observation interviews with two teachers, Liz and Bernie, whom we selected for follow-up on the basis that they demonstrated a high level of enthusiasm and motivation during the MaST taught sessions and were interested in participating further in our discussions. Although

Bernie and Liz are representative of the MaST participants, we cannot say that these teachers are representative of primary teachers in general as they were part of a group of teachers who self-selected to take part in the two-year MaST programme and were therefore particularly committed to improving their maths teaching. The observations and interviews were conducted by the first author, a tutor on the MaST programme and well known to both as a fellow professional and practitioner. Each teacher's lesson was videotaped and used as a prompt in the interview, in which they were invited to discuss their changing practices, what they noticed in their classes, and how they responded to children in terms of enhancing their mathematics understanding.

In terms of our ultimate focus on teachers' acquisition of an empowering discipline of noticing and language of description, we aimed to analyse the interview and video data to find answers to a range of questions: Were they more reflective and reflexive? What, and how often, were they noticing about their own practice and children's thinking and understanding? Were they (more) aware of how they responded to questions or devised activities? How were they responding to what they noticed? In short, were they demonstrating an 'awareness of awareness'?

Data Analysis

We analysed the video material in order to establish teaching style and content, in terms of the type of activities which the children were set, the particular concepts which were modelled in the lesson, the use of resources, the teacher's exposition of the concept and tasks, the type of questions which were asked, and the content and nature of responses made to children's answers. We also looked for instances where the teacher's responses appeared to demonstrate increased critical reflection in relation to their own practice and student understanding. Our analysis acknowledges the close relationship between noticing and reflection and teachers' subject knowledge and beliefs about mathematics, and their professional identities. We thus aimed to take into account, and make part of our analysis, the fact that their attention would be focused on issues that they believed to be important and of high priority. In particular, we sought to address this issue in part by noticing ourselves any matches and mismatches between the teachers' reports on their practice, and our own observation of it. We thus begin with their reports of noticing.

Reporting Noticing

Like the other teachers in our study, both Liz and Bernie reported that the MaST programme had led to changes in their practice as a result of critical reflection which involved noticing how and what the children were learning. For example, Bernie explained that she had developed a more experiential teaching approach, so that:

> . . . now I back off, I just give them an opportunity, I let them talk about it and they teach each other and I only input where necessary. I just provide a forum and I provide the materials they need, basically, to do that.

Liz told us that her use of mathematical vocabulary and language had developed so that she was more aware of highlighting and explaining possible misconceptions during her teaching:

> I have been prompted from MaST to use the 'language' of maths—'what is an angle?' 'What are parallel lines?' I wouldn't have gone down the route I did today had it not been for listening to other people. . . . [I] would have said before MaST 'It is an angle' 'an obtuse angle is over 90 and less than 180' and left it at that. When discussing parallel lines I wouldn't have done the little diagram and asked 'is this a parallel line?'. I wouldn't have explored it to that extent.

However, in addition to reporting these new developments in their practice, both Bernie and Liz told us that they saw MaST as providing validation for their pre-existing pedagogic approaches and beliefs, thus fitting with Erickson's (2011) and Sherin and Star's (2011) observation that noticing is filtered through the lens of prior experience. Bernie therefore talks about her development of noticing children's skills as something which builds on her prior beliefs:

> Because I have developed my own practice now. I've always been interested in the fact that I really believe that children have skills that we don't really take notice of when we're teaching them. We don't build on the knowledge, we try to impose knowledge on them. . . The fact that I can recognise in them that they've got skills of their own that I've got to develop and channel, so not me telling them, it's them the person they are, they bring a lot to the classroom.

Liz also reported that the MaST course had provided her with the evidence to develop a pedagogical style which she already believed in:

> The lesson today was really broad and I did know that I wanted to get certain vocabulary in and I did know that I wanted to do measuring with protractors, but the rest of it the children took that learning and that's something that I wasn't as comfortable with prior to doing MAST . . . Trying it and doing it for myself has proven this—actually they have learnt more than if I had done it my 'old' way and having the confidence to do that more often.

Both teachers' reports of their new reflections on teaching and the role of MaST in their practice led us to look closely at these particular aspects of their lessons when the interview was over. In the next section we describe the lessons and explore what turned out to be mis-matches between their reports and our own understanding of what we observed.

Exploring Practice: Observing Bernie and Liz

Bernie's Lesson: Developing Experiential Learning?

As we have seen, Bernie had stated that her teaching philosophy encompasses the belief that the children bring to the context their own skills and understanding which need to be channelled and built upon. During her lesson, all the children were required to work on a real life investigation. The more able children within the higher ability groups were presented with the task with minimal intervention by Bernie. They worked collaboratively within small groups, coped well with the tasks and articulated their findings clearly to the rest of the class. For other ability groups, however, Bernie introduced the investigative tasks with a more direct teaching approach, providing explicit instructions for the children to follow whilst undertaking the tasks. We also observed that these children found the tasks extremely challenging, both in terms of understanding what was required within the investigations and also being able to cope with the mathematical procedures that the tasks demanded. Clearly, providing suitable investigative tasks for a class of children working at a wide range of ability levels is very challenging for any teacher. In some instances they may not be able to meet the demands of noticing children's responses to questions, or how they approach and tackle a particular problem, and important aspects regarding children's understanding can go unnoticed. As a consequence, although an experiential style of teaching was adopted for the higher ability children, the rest of the children were presented with a more direct transmission teaching approach which did not appear to build on their existing knowledge.

This appears to indicate a mismatch between Bernie's account of her practice, and what was actually observed. From this point of view, we might conclude that the MaST programme had not had the impact that Bernie claimed, or that we had hoped for. However, Bernie herself was under no illusions about this. Commenting on this part of her lesson, she recognised that not all of the children had been involved in experiential learning. In addition, she also observed that her aim to provide opportunities for experiential learning did not mean that she did not employ direct teaching of skills: "I'm not saying that every day I do that [experiential learning] because I teach them skills". She was reflective about why she had included skills teaching, arguing that this was a particular area where some of her children need further input: "A lot of the children have spends, they know what money is, they know what change is but they can't always record it. So you have to teach them how to record it...". She was, then, aware that she had to make compromises and was unable to practice what she advocated in every instance.

Liz's Lesson: Focusing on the Language

Liz's expressed interest lay in what she had learned about mathematical language during the MaST course, and her lesson—about the properties of 2D shapes—reflected this. The structure of the lesson involved an extended exposition in which she modelled various 2D shapes by folding a piece of paper. The children followed throughout, copying with their own pieces of paper. A short independent group activity followed, in which the children were required to construct a 2D picture or pattern from their folded 2D shapes. In line with her interview, Liz paid attention to the mathematical vocabulary and language used both by herself and the children. She also paid careful attention to her own questioning and the children's answers in order to anticipate

Fig. 8.1 Parallel lines
example drawn by teacher

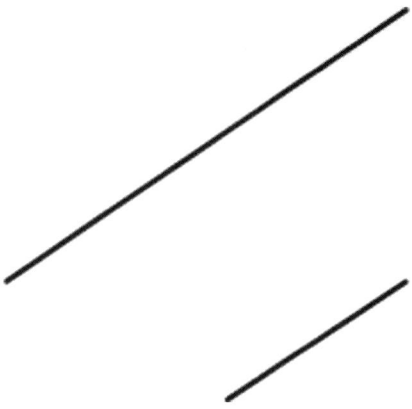

opportunities to uncover typical misconceptions. Thus, when a child responded to her question 'What is meant by parallel lines?' by providing the answer 'it means that they look the same', she responded by drawing two lines of different lengths on the whiteboard and inclined at the same angle of 45 degrees, as shown in Fig. 8.1.

In whole-class discussion, Liz elicited agreement that these lines were parallel, but that they were in fact *not* the same as they were of different lengths.

Although the activity was practical in nature and allowed for a focus on mathematical vocabulary, Liz's teaching was highly structured, with each step carefully teacher-led. The children had very few opportunities to discover concepts for themselves and, in contrast to Liz's interview responses, did not in fact 'lead the learning'. When this opportunity did arise, their task was to design a picture or pattern with their shapes, but this appeared to be a fairly low level task for the children to undertake, given that they had demonstrated a very competent level of the understanding of properties of 2D shapes throughout the lesson. However, during the plenary, Liz identified further mathematical ideas, one of which arose from the children. This consisted of identifying where children had constructed 'new' 2D shapes (hexagons) which had not been modelled during the teacher input. She also pointed out to the class where a series of shapes had fitted together without gaps and had therefore tessellated.

Although Liz's teaching could be said to be in the 'batch processing' style identified by Erickson (2011), based on the questionable assumption that learning is taking place just because the class is working in an orderly way or is 'raising their hand enthusiastically', she was careful to pay attention to the responses made by children to her questions. Liz also carefully checked their understanding by probing for further clarification where necessary and taking the opportunity to highlight possible misconceptions. Again, while Liz's teaching appears on the face of it not to be following the 'MaST way', it nevertheless illustrates a type of noticing defined by Erickson (2011) as 'instrumental', in that the noticing was made in order to act—something was done right away by Liz regarding what she noticed.

Noticing Noticing

Examining teaching through the discipline of noticing allows for fine-grained changes in practice to be uncovered. It provides evidence that a continuing professional learning programme has had some impact, but these changes are necessarily small and subtle. While changes did not occur 'across the board', both of these teachers were reflective and were 'noticing' more about their practice. In order to unpack this more, we return to Liz and Bernie's interviews, to look more closely at what they say about how they have changed. As we have seen, both have paid attention to issues which are central to their particular pedagogic beliefs—in Liz's case to the importance of language, in Bernie's to the idea of recognising and developing children's existing knowledge. We know from research such as Erickson's that we should not be surprised by this. However, one way of understanding these patterns, and Liz and Bernie's references to having new confidence as a result of MaST, is in terms of the programme as providing an explicit language of pedagogy which in turn legitimises ideas which they have, until now, been unable to reflect on or articulate. This effect is clearly described by Bernie:

> I needed a mirror for myself and it allowed me that opportunity...it gave me that forum...I'm not always the most confident person but I've got ideas, you know what I mean, and it just gave me that opportunity to use them.

Some of the language and legitimacy was provided by MaST requirements to read academic journals and research literature, which also gave Liz the opportunity to be more reflective:

> I have always been quite reflective but the good thing about MaST is that it gave you time to really think about it.

Participation also enabled teachers to think about practice as individual; Liz did not see MaST as prescriptive, but, rather, as being about developing one's own practice and pedagogical style:

> It taught me a lot in terms of other peoples' teaching styles... Every time we came it was a different challenge that we all took on board but in different ways. So it just makes me think that people going back to school won't teach like I do and I don't teach like they do so we don't have to conform to any methods so they weren't going back to school and thinking 'Well I've got to achieve the same as everyone else'.

Having worked with Bernie and Liz over the course of the two-year continuing professional learning programme and during the research process, it was apparent to the first author that their pedagogical commitments differed. Bernie's belief that teaching mathematics through challenge and real life situations, with the teacher as a force moving the children on from behind rather than leading from the front, was evident throughout the interview process. She reported that the MaST course had provided her with the validation to embrace this pedagogical approach more fully. Liz exhibited a preference for a more direct, instructional, pedagogical commitment in the lesson observation. She reported, however, that the MaST programme had allowed her to appreciate that pedagogical practice is very individual and that there is no one best practice model that can be advocated and followed. It had also provided her with the confidence to take more risks within her own teaching and develop flexibility in her own teaching approach. Despite the mismatch which we have seen for both teachers between their lessons and interviews, we would argue that both demonstrated that, through the discipline of noticing, their skills in critical self-reflection had developed. They now had a language that allowed them to articulate the choices they made.

Conclusion

Assessing the impact of continuing professional learning is difficult, and expecting a clear 'before and after' picture over-simplifies the complex process of teaching development. Our research has sought to focus on teachers' development of an empowering discipline of noticing to develop critical reflective skills. In the interview and observation process, both Bernie and Liz's reflections demonstrated an increased awareness of their own pedagogical practice and student thinking and understanding. This led to small, incremental changes being made to their practice, which included such things as the attention paid to mathematical language and vocabulary, deepening understanding of pupil learning and misconceptions, and the confidence to embrace a more experiential teaching approach. While we recognise the difficulty in disentangling the particular impact of the MaST programme from that of engagement in our research process, we suggest that a major source of development for both teachers was the integration of a research process into the MaST programme itself—to some extent, MaST participants are working in a 'third space' (see Williams and Ryan 2013) in which teacher and researcher roles are hybridised. The programme gave them an opportunity to reflect with others (fellow teachers and their university tutor), with that reflection built around a small research task in every formal session. Our later discussions with Bernie and Liz undoubtedly acted as further stimulus for development, but we see this as part of an ongoing process which clearly began during the programme.

What this suggests about workplace learning is that programmes need to provide opportunities to research one's own practice and to reflect, stand back and question over a period of time, with a knowledgeable other or group. Although there was some mismatch between what was reported at interview and what we observed during classroom episodes, both teachers demonstrated that they had developed a 'language' that allowed them to articulate and critique the choices they made within their practice. This particular development is perhaps indicative of an internalisation of the reflective process—their ways of explaining their particular practice foci were unique to them, and tailored to their concerns. Most importantly, we consider that through the exercise of their ability to critically self reflect—described by Mason (2002) as an 'awareness of awareness'—they had gained agency as professional decision-makers as part of ongoing practitioner development. Any claims regarding the 'success' of the programme, in terms of its stated aim of impacting directly on mathematics pedagogy at school level, would need to go beyond Williams' (2008) original goal of enhancing deep subject knowledge. Our research shows the more fundamental and sustainable role of continuing professional learning as addressing the teacher as researcher-practitioner.

References

Barnes, Y., Cockerham, C., Hanley, U., & Solomon, Y. (2013). How do mathematics teaching enhancement programmes 'work'? Re-thinking agency in regulative times. In V. Farnsworth & Y. Solomon (Eds.), *Reframing educational research: Resisting the 'what works' agenda.* London: Routledge.

Barnett, B. G., & O'Mahony, G. R. (2006). Developing a culture for reflection: Implications for school improvement. *Reflective Practice, 7*(4), 499–523.

Brown, T., Hanley, U., Darby, S., & Calder, N. (2007). Teachers' conceptions of learning philosophies: Discussing context and contextualising discussion. *Mathematics Teacher Education, 10,* 183–200.

Cochran-Smith, M., & Lytle, S. L. (1999). Relationship of knowledge and practice: Teacher learning in communities. In A. Iran-Nejad & C. Pearson (Eds.), *Review of research in education (Vol. 24, pp. 249–306).* Washington, DC: American Educational Research Association.

Corbin, B., McNamara, O., & Williams, J. (2003). Numeracy coordinators: 'brokering' change within and between communities of practice? *British Journal of Educational Studies, 51*(4), 344–368.

Dewey, J. (1916/1944). *Democracy and education: An introduction to the philosophy of Education.* New York: The Free Press.

Doyle, W. (1977). Learning the classroom environment: An ecological analysis. *Journal of Teacher Education, 28*(6), 51–55.

Erickson, F. (2006). Studying side by side: Collaborative action ethnography in educational research. In G. Spindler & L. Hammond (Eds.), *New horizons for ethnography in education* (pp. 235–257). Mahwah: Erlbaum.

Erickson, F. (2011). On noticing teacher noticing. In M. G. Sherin, V. R. Jacobs & R. A. Philipp (Eds.), *Mathematics teacher noticing seeing through teachers' eyes* (pp. 17–34). New York: Routledge.

Farmer, J. D., Gerretson, H., & Lassak, M. (2003). What teachers take from professional development: Cases and implications. *Journal of Mathematics Teacher Education, 6,* 331–360.

Gattegno, C. (1987). *The science of education: Part I. Theoretical considerations.* New York: Educational Solutions.

Ghaye, T. (2010). A reflective inquiry as participatory and appreciative action and reflection. In N. Lyons (Ed.), *Handbook of Reflection and Reflective Inquiry.* London: Springer.

Gimbert, B. G. (2000). Nurturing an intern learning community in a professional development school culture: Spaces for voice and multiple perspectives. Paper presented at the American Educational Research Association, New Orleans, LA.

Jacobs, V. R., Franke, M. L., Carpenter, T. P., Levi, L., & Battey, D. (2007). Professional development focused on children's algebraic reasoning in elementary school. *Journal for Research in Mathematics Education, 38,* 258–288.

Jacobs, V. R., Lamb, L. L. C., Philipp, R. A., & Schappelle, B. P. (2011). Deciding how to respond on the basis of children's understandings. In M. G. Sherin, V. R. Jacobs & R. A. Philipp (Eds.), *Mathematics teacher noticing seeing through teachers' eyes* (pp. 97–116). New York: Routledge.

James, W. (1890). *The principles of psychology.* New York: Holt.

Korthagen, F., & Vasalos, A. (2010). Going to the core: Deepening reflection by connection. In N. Lyons (Ed.), *Handbook of reflection and reflective inquiry (pp. 531–554).* New York: Springer.

Loughran, J. (2010). Reflection through collaborative action research and inquiry. In N. Lyons (Ed.), *Handbook of reflection and reflective inquiry (pp. 401–416)*. New York: Springer.

Lyons, N. (2010). Reflection and reflective inquiry: What future? In N. Lyons (Ed.), *Handbook of reflection and reflective inquiry* (pp. 573–580). New York: Springer.

Mason, J. (1988). Fragments: The implications for teachers, learners and media users/researchers of personal construal and fragmentary recollection of aural and visual messages. *Instructional Science, 17,* 195–218.

Mason, J. (2002). *Researching your own practice: The discipline of noticing*. London: Routeledge-Falmer.

Mason, J. (2011). Noticing roots and branches. In M. G. Sherin, V. R. Jacobs & R. A. Philipp (Eds.), *Mathematics teacher noticing seeing through teachers' eyes* (pp. 35–50). New York: Routledge.

McNamara, O., & Corbin, B. (2001). Warranting practices: Teachers embedding the National Numeracy Strategy. *British Journal of Educational Studies, 49*(3), 260–284.

National Council of Teachers of Mathematics. (2000). *Principles and standards for school mathematics*. Reston: Author.

Nissila, S.-P. (2005). Individual and collective reflection. How to meet the needs of development in teaching. *European Journal of Teacher Education, 28*(2), 209–219.

Nolan, K. (2012). Dispositions in the field: Viewing mathematics teacher education through the lens of Bourdieu's social field theory. *Educational Studies in Mathematics, 80,* 201–215.

Park, S., Oliver, J. S., Johnson, T. S., Graham, P., & Oppong, N. K. (2007). Colleagues' roles in the professional development of teachers: Results from a research study of National Board Certification. *Teaching and Teacher Education: An International Journal of Research and Studies, 23*(4), 368–389.

Sherin, B., & Star, J. R. (2011). Reflections on the study of teacher noticing. In M. G. Sherin, V. R. Jacobs & R. A. Philipp (Eds.), *Mathematics teacher noticing seeing through teachers' eyes* (pp. 66–78). New York: Routledge.

Sherin, M. G., Jacobs, V. R., & Philipp, R. A. (2011). Situating the study of teacher noticing. In M. G. Sherin, V. R. Jacobs & R. A. Philipp (Eds.), *Mathematics teacher noticing seeing through teachers' eyes* (pp. 3–13). New York: Routledge.

Simon, M., & Tzur, R. (2004). Explicating the role of mathematical tasks in conceptual learning: An elaboration of the hypothetical learning trajectory. *Mathematical Thinking and Learning, 6,* 91–104.

Tzur, R., Simon, M., Heinz, K., & Kinzel, M. (2001). An account of a teacher's perspectives on learning and teaching mathematics: Implications for teacher development. *Journal of Mathematics Teacher Education, 4*(3), 227–254.

Williams, P. (2008). Independent review of mathematics teaching in early years settings and primary schools. DCSF-00433–2008.

Williams, J., & Ryan, J. (2013). Research, policy and professional development: Designing hybrid activities in third spaces. In V. Farnsworth & Y. Solomon (Eds.), *Reframing educational research: Resisting the 'what works' agenda*. London: Routledge.

Zeichner, K., & Lui, K. Y. (2010). A critical analysis of reflection as a goal for teacher education. In N. Lyons (Ed.)., *Handbook of reflection and reflective inquiry* (pp. 67–84). London: Springer.

Chapter 9
Lesson Study in a Performative Culture

Julian Williams, Julie Ryan and Siân Morgan

Introduction

Lesson study originated in Japan as an inquiry-based approach to the professional development of teaching and teachers. It involves teachers' groups jointly planning and analysing special lessons in real classrooms, usually involving a focus on some innovation. Mathematics lessons in particular have often been studied, usually developing conceptual mathematics through the children's active problem-solving (Hart et al. 2011). Lesson study is widely recognised as powerful for mathematics education reform, and has been adopted—with adaptations—around the world. But every such adaptation in non-Japanese cultures inevitably involves a local effect. We ask, what can happen when lesson study is introduced in the particular English conditions where performance management and performativity are so dominant in schools and in professional learning? We report two case studies of our lesson study work with primary and secondary teachers in England.

International League Tables and Performativity

We live in an era of international comparison studies of children's educational achievement, where participating countries are placed in league tables in terms of their children's performance on written tests in key curriculum areas. Such results

J. Williams (✉)
School of Education, The University of Manchester, Manchester, UK
e-mail: julian.williams@manchester.ac.uk

J. Ryan
Faculty of Education, Manchester Metropolitan University,
Manchester, UK
e-mail: J.T.Ryan@mmu.ac.uk

S. Morgan
School of Education, The University of Manchester, Manchester, UK
e-mail: sian.morgan@manchester.ac.uk

O. McNamara et al. (eds.), *Workplace Learning in Teacher Education,*   151
Professional Learning and Development in Schools and Higher Education 10,
DOI 10.1007/978-94-007-7826-9_9, © Springer Science+Business Media Dordrecht 2014

have captured the imagination of politicians and social commentators and are generally focused in these terms: 'Are we doing better than before?', 'Have we improved our *position*?', and 'Why can't we be more like Singapore, Finland. . . ?'. Children here in the UK have been thus been characterised as 'performing for Britain' or 'doing their sums for England'.

The International Association for the Evaluation of Educational Achievement (IEA) has conducted such comparative studies in mathematics and science since 1995, and subsequently every four years. Its Trends in International Mathematics and Science Study (TIMSS) measures fourth- and eighth-grade children's[1] achievement on written tests, and gathers background information about the contexts for learning from the children, their teachers, and their school principals, and information about the mathematics and science curricula in each country (IEA 2012).

The most recent TIMSS study (Sturman et al. 2008, pp. 1–2)[2] summarised England's 'grade 4 mathematics (year 5)' score in these terms:

> England's score, 541, was again very high, and significantly higher than in 2003. Only four countries outscored England: Hong Kong (607), Singapore (599), Chinese Taipei (576), and Japan (568).There is a larger gap between England and the highest scoring Pacific Rim countries in grade 4 mathematics than in grade 4 science. Four countries produced scores not significantly different from England's: Kazakhstan (539), the Russian Federation, Latvia and the Netherlands (535). Countries outperformed by England included the United States, Germany, Denmark, Italy, Sweden, Scotland, Australia and New Zealand. England improved on its level of performance in 2003: the 2007 score of 541 was 10 points higher than the 531 achieved in 2003. This was continued improvement as the 2003 score was much higher than in the earlier 1995 survey (484). As in science, England's performance in mathematics at year 5 is amongst the best in the world and continues to improve.

England's performance for 'grade 8 (Year 9)' was similarly described in terms of improvement from 2003 and noted better and similarly performing countries.

The Organisation for Economic Co-operation and Development (OECD) has conducted another international study, first in 2000 and subsequently every three years. Its Programme for International Student Assessment (PISA) measures 15-year-old students' scholastic performance in mathematics, science and reading. It too produces a league table of performance of participating countries.

The position of England in such league tables has been used by politicians to motivate and justify re-direction in educational policy. A recent exchange in the UK parliament in 2011 began with a question from Andy Burnham, Education Secretary in the former Labour Government but now in opposition:

> Can the Secretary of State tell the House on what research or evidence he has based his selection of subjects in the new English baccalaureate?

The Education Secretary for the current government, Michael Gove said in reply:

> The research and evidence that I undertook was to look at what the highest performing education jurisdictions do. When the OECD published its table on how our country had been doing in education over the past 10 years, I was struck to see that under Labour's stewardship we had slipped in the international league tables for English, for mathematics and for science.

---

[1] Year 5 (9- and 10-year olds) and Year 9 (3- and 14-year olds) in England.

[2] The TIMSS 2011 study was due to be published in December 2012.

Andy Burnham replied:

> ... let me quote from last year's PISA-programme for international student assessment-report, which says: "Most successful school systems grant greater autonomy to individual schools to design curricula and assessment policies".

The Secretary of State replied:

> I am surprised that the right hon. Gentleman has the brass neck to quote the PISA figures when they show that on his watch the standard of education which was offered to young people in this country declined relative to our international competitors. Literacy, down; numeracy, down; science, down: fail, fail, fail.' (Parliamentary report, 7 February 2011)

The political view here, that the UK is *competing* in an international education performance league, places great pressure on politicians and the teaching profession. 'Fail, fail, fail' is a summary political judgement passed down to those whose daily work is in classrooms—the teachers. England's 'performance' in such international league tables is also widely reported in the media, and political and public discourse refers to a 'driving up of standards' through external agencies. The teacher is exhorted to 'improve', and 'poor teaching' is to be 'rooted out'. This discourse comes to infect schools, staff rooms, and performance management: England is very good nowadays at getting rid of failing local authorities, failing schools, failing head teachers and teachers, and of course failing children. Arguably we are much better at this than most other countries in the league!

However, we, the authors, take a different view. There are more positive professional benefits to be gained from international studies and in particular consideration of cultural differences in pedagogical practice: for example, what can we, in the teaching profession, learn from other 'jurisdictions' and their practices? Some of those countries are also studying what they can learn from ours. There is also more to be gained from creating spaces to examine and share evolving local practice: How can we develop new cultural practices? Or, as Barrow (1984, p. 261) asked: How can we give teaching back to teachers? Give them ownership of their professional learning.

The English Culture of Performativity

We live in an era of performativity and performance management, where measures of performance are used as evidence in both policy formation and professional management. In a sense it was always so: throughout industry there was always a 'bottom line' calculation that equates essentially to money equivalence. In the public sector, however, this is relatively new. The spread of the 'New Public Management' has been charted by Strathern (2000) for the academy and by Power (1997) for the entire public sector. It originated in a combination of accountability, audit and discourse of best-value. Who can argue against holding management to account for tax payers' money, and who can argue against requiring evidence of delivery to specifications?

We theorise the education system as a production system of the commodity Marx called labour power, and the education of future labourers as enhancing this power, which has exchange value (it can be sold for money) and use value (it is useful in production, and even in consumption). In the education system, the work of educating done by teachers is paid for by the State, and the value produced as certificates of a Boudieusian 'cultural capital', a cultural 'commodity' that will one day have economic value when the student enters the labour market (see Williams 2012). Thus, the audit and accountability economy in schooling is mediated by the State; but we refer to the knowledge learned by students as having an educational form of exchange value (the enhancement of their status or CV) as well as use value (to the extent they understand the knowledge well enough to make use of it).

However, evidence has accumulated of performativity's unintended consequences: research has uncovered some of its pernicious, presumably unintended, effects. Hospitals have adopted dangerous practices to 'deliver' required waiting time limits.[3] Police fail to record times of calls in order to reduce their 'response times',[4] and schools persuade students to make 'early exam entry' decisions that enhance a school's profile, even while damaging a student's future educational prospects (Advisory Committee on Mathematics Education 2011). Most of these practices involve responding to measures of performance rather than the quality of the performance itself. Teaching-to-the-test is quite successful short term in 'driving up standards', yet an accumulating body of research suggests that, while we have been working hard to drive up standards for many years, the outcomes for learners are not much better in terms of students' understanding or dispositions. In fact, teaching-to-the-test seems to be associated with a long-term decline in students' enjoyment of the subject and their choosing to study a subject in the future (see Pampaka et al. 2012a, b).

In particular, we suggest, performance management based on students' test grade outcomes (i.e. management that rewards teachers and head teachers in one way or another for the test performance of their learners) can be particularly pernicious if: (i) it applies to a combination of short-term gains, for example, to a period of teaching of less than several years; and (ii) it applies competitively to individual teachers or head teachers. Short-term measures undermine long-term work, while individual performance management measures undermine the professional culture (see Williams 2011). Finally, we have a problem with assessment of learning designed for formative purposes being used as summative evidence and vice versa (see Black and Wiliam 1998; Williams and Ryan 2000). Although it is possible to do both, they do pull in different directions:

> Summative assessment is usually motivated by the need to sum up what has been learnt over a period of time, by a need for accountability to the wider community or simply for the purposes of selection. Formative assessment is motivated by the need to identify children's strengths and weaknesses so as to inform the next steps in teaching. (Williams and Ryan 2000, p. 51)

---

[3] See for example, 'Independent inquiry into care provided by Mid Staffordshire NHS Foundation Trust January 2005—March 2009, Volume 1 & 2', chaired by Robert Francis QC, at http://www.midstaffsinquiry.com/pressrelease.html. Accessed 10 December 2012.

[4] BBC Panorama: 'Dial 999. . . and Wait?' BBC One, Monday, 3 September, 2012 http://www.bbc.co.uk/news/health-19455784. Accessed 10 December 2012.

In sum, we would argue that England's policy on schooling and school management has evolved all the worst features of the 'magic bullet' that kills the joy of learning and teaching.

What can we do? One approach is to argue that policy requires an accountability practice such that it can, in its turn, hold policy to account. The policy-makers and politicians, in their turn, then must also explain themselves to the public and the media when—apparently as a consequence of, and on account of their policies— things go wrong. What if it is shown that teaching-to-the-test is not working, as many teachers say they believe but feel obliged to practice?

One opportunity might be to develop measures that more faithfully reflect the significance of a broad range of educational objectives: measures of learners' dispositions such as confidence, or intention to further study (see Pampaka et al. 2012b), metacognitive awarenesses (Schraw 2002) or even 'performance assessment' (Bell et al. 1992). These might be particularly important to policy-making if the evidence shows that teaching for dispositions and metacognition has long-term gains over shorter-term teaching-to-the-test, such as the evidence collected by cognitive acceleration research (e.g. Adey and Shayer 1994).

We argue that the rhetoric of policy might be used sometimes to good effect. The reference to learning from the 'world's best systems'[5] might be a case in point, especially as reform movements grow in other relatively high performing education systems, such as Singapore and the Pacific Rim. Furthermore, in some systems the relationship between professional development and research is much better articulated than in England and the rest of the UK. In particular, Japanese lesson study has a growing worldwide reputation, with apparently successful variants in the Pacific and in English-speaking countries (Australia and the USA). We favour lesson study for many reasons, but not least because it places deep learning outcomes and life-long professional development in the centre, and because it pursues this through a systematic partnership involving researchers with professionals developing practice.

Lesson Study

Lesson study is based on a long-established Japanese model of continuous improvement of teacher professional learning, and it has become popular in the US and Australia over the last decade. The Japanese approach studies the art of teaching, which is seen traditionally as practice that all teachers must learn, and continue to learn collectively, throughout their professional careers.

Interest in lesson study in mathematics education circles outside Japan grew out of the 1995 TIMSS Video Study and its contrast of mathematics instruction in Japan, Germany and the US (Stigler and Hiebert 1999), where comparisons in children's performance *and also* classroom practice were stark. Some ten years later, Stigler and Hiebert (2009) reported that many of the US readers of their earlier report had found the Japanese pattern of teaching both foreign and intriguing. Their readers had

---

[5] See statement of the current UK Education Secretary earlier in this chapter in relation to 'highest performing education jurisdictions'.

been particularly struck by the 'elegance with which Japanese teachers engage[d] their students in doing important mathematical work, work that focuses on core mathematical ideas and their applications' (ibid, p. 32). However, Stigler and Hiebert (2009) cautioned their readers to beware of concluding that Japan's teaching methods had 'anything at all to do with their high levels of achievement' (ibid, p. 33); they claimed, for example, motivation may be a more important factor.

Lesson study is based on the principle that change/improvement in teaching and learning in classrooms is best achieved by teachers themselves, empowered to make their own decisions through collaborative research-informed practice.

> Improving something as complex and culturally embedded as teaching requires the efforts of all the players, including students, parents, and politicians. But teachers must be the primary driving force behind change. They are the best positioned to understand the problems that students face and to generate possible solutions. (Stigler and Hiebert 1999, p. 135)

Lesson study is a dynamic research model whereby teachers work together to forge ongoing learning of both their subject matter knowledge and pedagogical content knowledge, and to share professional knowledge. It is a cyclical model of collaborative planning, observation, review, refinement and re-teaching of a research-lesson, and has many organisational possibilities. This collegial professional activity impacts on individual practice and, through participation and dissemination, informs the system as a whole.

> Through live research lessons, written reports, videos and sharing of experiences with colleagues, lesson study spreads thoughtfully-designed lessons on a wide-range of topics, creating a system that learns. (Lewis 2002, p. 11)

Teachers in the US have reported that their subject matter knowledge has been strengthened through lesson study, as they became aware of missing knowledge that was needed to inform their pedagogical practice.

> Lesson study alone does not ensure access to content knowledge. But teachers are likely to build their content knowledge as they study good lessons, anticipate student thinking, discuss student work with colleagues, and call on outside specialists. Lesson study can help educators notice gaps in their own understanding and provide a meaningful, motivating context to remedy them. (Lewis 2002, p. 31)

The key principle of the Japanese model is that teachers are the most pertinent and effective 'drivers' of their professional practice. This is in stark contrast to practice in England over the last decades, where change in classroom practice, and particularly in mathematics and literacy teaching, has been directed and monitored by central government through prescription, not only of content but also of style. Compliance has been ensured by external inspection of classroom practice and public reporting of schools' results in national league tables.

We argue that such external control leads to teacher alienation and dissatisfaction, and disempowerment leads to an impoverished professional practice. Transplanting professional practice from one culture to another of course is not the answer. Teaching practice is embedded in existing local culture and knowledge, but examining alternatives may open up new possibilities if the new perspective is adopted and adapted by the teachers themselves.

The practice of lesson study is generally evolving as it disseminates globally from Japan, and we now describe and analyse how lesson study can develop in a different culture, where teacher professional learning in England is dominated by graded lesson observations and league tables of children's performance on national tests.

Case Study 1: Primary School Project

Our current work with teachers in a small primary school in Manchester (authors Ryan and Williams) is part of a three-year project to develop dialogic pedagogy in mathematics. The teachers in the school already shared our interest in the productive use of children's mathematical errors and misconceptions to provoke classroom dialogue, and were enthusiastic about further developing mathematical talk and reasoning in all their classes, from reception to Year 6 (Ryan and Williams 2012).

We introduced all the staff (head, deputy head, eight teachers, seven teaching assistants) to Japanese lesson study, and described it as an ongoing, continuous improvement research model that used collaborative planning to design mathematical activity to give teachers insight into their children's mathematical development. We noticed that they were particularly engaged by the shift in focus from the teacher to the children, and there was palpable relief that we were not presenting yet another form of inspection for performance management.

As an introduction, we played a lesson study video of an actual 60-minute lesson from Japan on the 'Multiplication Algorithm'[6] for grade 3 children, led by Mr. Hideyuki Muramoto. This lesson had been designed by the Mathematics Group at Maruyama and it was being observed by a large number of Japanese and international visitors. The classroom, though large by England's standards, was thus very crowded. The lesson was presented by Mr. Muramoto and the visitors stood around the edges of the room; they would move around observing the children's work when the teacher had set them to work. We also gave our project teachers the detailed lesson plan (and the outline of the rest of the unit of 13 lessons) which had been drawn up by the Maruyama Group in their lesson study cycles.

The teachers found this lesson 'foreign but intriguing', just like Stigler and Hiebert's US teachers. They initially found the apparent 'chaos' and noise in the classroom surprising and almost shocking in contrast to expectations of Japanese practice and in comparison to accepted teacher-led (and dominant) practice in England. The large class size was also noted. The teachers remarked that as the lesson unfolded they began to see how artfully Mr. Muramoto had held back, had let the children talk and had skilfully orchestrated the development of ideas. The use of a large traditional blackboard to comprehensively track the lesson development was also seen as surprising. The electronic whiteboard is now a normal feature of classrooms in England, and blackboards have long since disappeared. Yet, in the Japanese classroom, the teacher was able to present and review the 'journey' of the children's work towards the lesson goal, with the trace of the lesson evident on the blackboard.

---

[6] 'Multiplication Algorithm' lesson video: http://hrd.apec.org/index.php/Multiplication_Algorithm_ Grade_3_%28Japan%29. Accessed 10 December 2012.

The Japanese lesson plan and the more generalised nature of lesson goal-setting were also discussed in terms of cultural difference. For this particular unit, the overall goal and then particular lesson goals are stated quite differently to that in England:

> The goal of the Mathematics Group at Maruyama is to develop students' ability to use what they learned before to solve problems in the new learning situations by making connections. In addition, we want to provide 3rd grade students with experiences in mathematics that enable them to use what they learned before to solve problems in new learning situations by making connections. This lesson, "The Multiplication Algorithm (1)," is designed to utilize prior learning to make connections and solve problems in new learning situations. (Mathematics Group at Maruyama 2006, p. 1)

The Japanese teachers here appear to be focusing on developing the third grade children's metacognitive strategies through 'authentic' mathematical experiences—perhaps the model is to encourage children to act like mathematicians. The process of 'making connections' and the use of 'mathematical experiences' were considered too broad for a lesson objective in a classroom in England. The Maruyama Group also had a clear research focus for their lesson study: 'What kinds of lessons develop students who can use what they learned before to solve problems in new learning situations by making connections?' This makes the action research focus explicit and shows a more holistic approach to lesson design, affording a broadening of the professional conversation.

After the first meeting with our project group, the staff decided that we would start with two groups of teachers in the school working with us, with the goal of developing mathematical talk and dialogue. Together we would develop a *variation* of the Japanese lesson study model and report back to the whole staff on our progress.

The model was to identify a mathematical topic or process area currently seen as important for a particular class of children, jointly plan a lesson, identify roles and what we are looking for to report and discuss, and have one teacher leading the session but have the rest of the lesson study team actually working with a group of children rather than simply observing (as in the Japanese model). Two of us worked with two groups of three teachers. Both groups comprised two 'neighbouring' teachers and a teaching assistant. Thus, at any one time, there were five of us involved in each lesson study cycle and present in the classroom.

The teachers leading the lessons (with their own class) were initially apprehensive about being watched and judged in 'performance', but this seemed to fade as the collaborative nature of the lesson planning took hold and we developed a shared research focus on the children's responses rather than on the teacher leading the lesson. We were all engaged as active participants in *every stage* of the lesson study cycle: planning, preparing resources, participating in the actual lesson, contributing in the debriefing analysis, and deciding the next steps and refinement of practice. So our team differed significantly from the Japanese practice in that we were all engaged in the actual lesson; talking with our group of children, indicating to the lead teacher that a child had something to offer, and also asking questions, through the lead teacher, of children who were presenting ideas. The lessons were therefore not as tightly 'scripted' as the Japanese lessons.

The two teacher groups reported their work on developing mathematical dialogue to a whole staff dissemination event, held mid-year on campus at one of our universities. They re-visited the purpose of the project, showed their colleagues how the practical tasks that had been designed in the lesson study cycle had supported the children's mathematical reasoning in peer and class discussion, and drew some conclusions about their curriculum. The use of mathematical models and tools was a particular theme, as were the verbal prompts that the teachers had been developing in literacy lessons, e.g. "I agree with … however … I think … because … ". The teachers displayed some of the children's work (the children's own video recordings and transcriptions of peer and class interactions, the children's photos, drawings, and written explanations) and these were discussed with obvious enthusiasm and professional engagement by all their colleagues.

The Year 6 group had used measurement activity to develop understanding of place value, and several teachers were surprised by the evidence shown and noted: "The children could not explain tenths and hundredths", "I think we teach place value unrelated to reality" and "We need to be teaching in a context". The Year 4 group had focused on the use of models in particular to develop multiplicative reasoning (for division), and their teacher reported that it had been a revelation to see how the children used the models to reason and, under the teacher's challenge, to "prove it!". The teacher said "It's about shared understanding (in the classroom)". Another lesson study teacher who used ideas from the project lesson back in their own class said "Repeated activity is magic", "We don't give children credit for listening".

The teachers orchestrated a professional discussion around their conclusions about pedagogy drawn from their lesson study. One teacher presented the following points:

> The adult should 'sit back' for 60 % of the time in group discussions and guide for 40 % of the time.
> The word 'model' should be in our maths curriculum from Reception.
> Having an established role in a group is important to enable discussion.
> There needs to be evidence in maths books of the way in which a child logically works though a problem.

In summary, we draw the following observations from our lesson study development. The 'space' created by the project for experimentation and risk-taking was essential. The commitment of management to risk a different type of development, and the involvement of the research team as an outside stimulus that gave the work a certain kudos, helped to establish this.

- The lesson study practice evolved in local conditions to the point, perhaps, where a Japanese teacher/researcher might deny this was lesson study proper. Yet the systematic and collaborative inquiry based on the children's mathematics was a common characteristic: with consequences for the growing trust and professional solidarity of those involved.
- The focus on dialogue in classrooms was supported by the lesson study research practices of listening to, recording, and analysing children's mathematical arguments and reasoning in dialogue; we claimed this is a hybrid research-teaching practice (see Williams and Ryan in press);
- Discussion and analysis in the lesson study group entered the staff room, and other teachers became informally involved in trying out activities and discussing

findings; these reflections and discussions entered formal staff meetings too, and were believed to be a significant outcome of the project impact for the school.

- While test outcomes are said to be improving, we are puzzled as to whether or how evidence of causal connection can be found.

A key result for this work seems to be the ways in which the lesson study project fitted into the particular English performative culture: the lesson study's freedom to take risks was hedged by:

1. A commitment to risk due to the personal beliefs of and articulation of a convincing rationale by the school's head teacher, deputy head teacher, senior management and subject co-ordinator (in part the reason why the researchers chose to work there);
2. The risk being somewhat limited in time (there was, to some degree, a move 'back to the usual' when the lesson study was over, and nearing tests in assessment week);
3. An enrichment of resources due to the outside commitment.

Case Study 2: Secondary School Project

Our work with secondary schools (authors Morgan and Williams) began with a successful bid for a government–funded (TDA)[7] project. Teaching Schools[8] were invited by the TDA to bid for funding for a pre-service teacher education research and development project. When writing the bid the school had to identify an outstanding pre-service teacher education provider to work in partnership with. This enabled the Teaching School to work with colleagues from the university, with one colleague (one of the authors, Morgan) previously appointed to a joint role in both the school and the university. Additional schools were invited by the Teaching School to participate in the Lesson Study Project with the aim of enhancing questioning and dialogue in mathematics classrooms. The six additional schools involved with the project were either part of the Teaching School alliance or were university pre-service teacher education partnership schools.[9] The project involved pre-service teachers, as well as experienced teachers and colleagues from the university. This was initially a two-term project, but it is envisaged that colleagues may wish to extend this project in the future, and some are already doing so.

The project funding allowed colleagues to meet on two occasions, initially for a full-day conference to outline the project, and then for a half-day conference (two months later) for reporting back and planning next steps. Facilitated lesson study

---

[7] The TDA (Training and Development Agency for schools) became the Teaching Agency in April 2012 and then the National College for Teaching and Leadership in April 2013.

[8] Teaching Schools: a government designation that gives outstanding schools a leading role in professional development.

[9] Teaching School alliance: a group of schools and other partners supported by the leadership of a Teaching School (Department for Education). University partnership schools: schools that work in partnership with universities to provide placements for pre-service teacher education students.

work took place in between. Most participating schools involved two mathematics teachers and, where possible, two pre-service teachers. These lesson study groups were expected to engage in at least one round of lesson study together (joint lesson planning, joint teaching the lesson, and joint analysis and review), between the conferences so they would have findings to report.

An article was provided, prior to the April conference, to give colleagues some background to lesson study in Japan—'A lesson is like a swiftly flowing river' (Lewis and Tsuchida 1998). The initial conference was attended by two teachers and two pre-service teachers from each school, with more from the host school. Colleagues from the university and Teaching Agency also attended. The day started with an initial mathematical activity that modelled a classroom strategy to encourage dialogue, and colleagues were introduced to Japanese lesson study through video snippets of a Japanese lesson that had been studied. Also, video footage of a lesson study lesson taught at the Teaching School was shown and discussed. Colleagues then discussed strategies to enhance dialogue and questioning in the mathematics classroom, and they began their joint lesson planning for lesson study before leaving the conference. The atmosphere was very positive and colleagues seemed enthused and eager to start.

All lesson study groups were facilitated by a colleague from either the university or the Teaching School. Care was taken to ensure that this colleague remained a member of the group and did not take a lead. This was more difficult in certain instances, where some colleagues expected the facilitator to lead because of their experience and role; in some cases they were the university tutor for the pre-service teacher(s) in their groups. The complexity of this role is discussed by Corcoran (2011); in the lesson study groups that she convened, with third-year Bachelor of Education students, she feared that power relations would be counterproductive to the process. The groups all did at least one lesson study cycle, with some managing to repeat the lesson one or two times with different classes, refining the lesson each time. All focused on enhancing dialogue and questioning, but in a variety of different ways, involving various mathematics topics. It was interesting that some lesson study groups chose to share learning objectives with their classes that were not topic-based but that focused on skills linked with questioning and dialogue.

The focus on dialogue and questioning was, for some colleagues, quite different to the norm, and the legitimacy of this style of teaching was questioned with reference to government inspections. Colleagues were somewhat reassured when a school that had taught in this way was inspected and came out of it positively. Ofsted (the external inspectorate) and performance management are prevalent in teachers' minds. We therefore expected these issues to be raised at some point during the initial conference. Both teachers and pre-service teachers were concerned about the pace of progress when planning these lessons. This related to Ofsted requirements that teaching should show that all students have made progress, even in the 20 minutes or so in which they were to be observed.

For schools that had many teachers and pre-service teachers in the lesson study classroom (where each adult worked individually with a group of learners) there was a concern that the lesson would be difficult to replicate with just the one teacher present, as would normally be the case. In future lesson studies, they thought this would need to be considered during the planning or when reviewing the lesson.

In the final conference, the teachers reflected that they had gained from working with colleagues, from having a focus on questioning and dialogue, and from reflecting on their own practice, in a non-threatening way. The following comments in their reports were indicative of the reflections we collected:

> Other members of the department were involved in the delivery process as well as people from outside the school—this collaboration allowed the exploration of ideas and processes.
> Running a lesson study allowed me to see how much this kind of activity benefits the pupils, therefore the dialogue and questioning techniques are something that I will focus on in planning lessons.
> The chance to step out of my comfort zone and have whole class discussion for the entire lesson.

Similarly, the pre-service teachers commented that they valued both working collaboratively with their experienced colleagues and the sharing of ideas and approaches. Some also commented on an increased confidence to try out new ideas.

> Good lesson suggestions from other schools. Motivation to try these out!
> Got to plan with experienced staff and tweak things. Enabled me to make sure all my pupils made contributions in a lesson.
> A chance to explore new teaching methods. An opportunity to see how pupils reacted to this kind of teaching. Evaluation with colleagues.

As with the primary school lesson study, these reflections suggest that lesson study is valued as a collaboration in which professionals can discuss together, free from inspection and threats of grading of performance. The freedom to take risks was again here hedged by the three factors: the support from senior management, an externally-resourced project, and a time-limited commitment. The experiences of one of the seven schools involved with lesson study through this project will now be described below in more detail.

The Radcliffe Lesson Study Group

In one lesson study group at Radcliffe school,[10] the group chose to develop an 'investigative' lesson on number patterns. Examples in the syllabus include linear sequences like 4, 7, 10,... and 2, 5, 10, 17,... (see Fig. 9.1). The university tutor suggested: (i) that such patterns should also reveal and be supported by geometric representations, and (ii) an old pack of materials from the Nottingham Shell Centre could be used which included such examples, teaching plans, computer programmes and videos.

The lesson was planned by an experienced teacher, who is used to more dialogic pedagogic practices, with three pre-service teachers and the first author. As an investigative lesson it was perhaps not that risky for this experienced teacher in the school, but was atypical for many teachers and for the pre-service teachers in that school. The group decided to use matchstick models for the first sequence, and growing squares for the second. The teacher was to lead the lesson, and decided to try

---

[10] The name of the school has been changed.

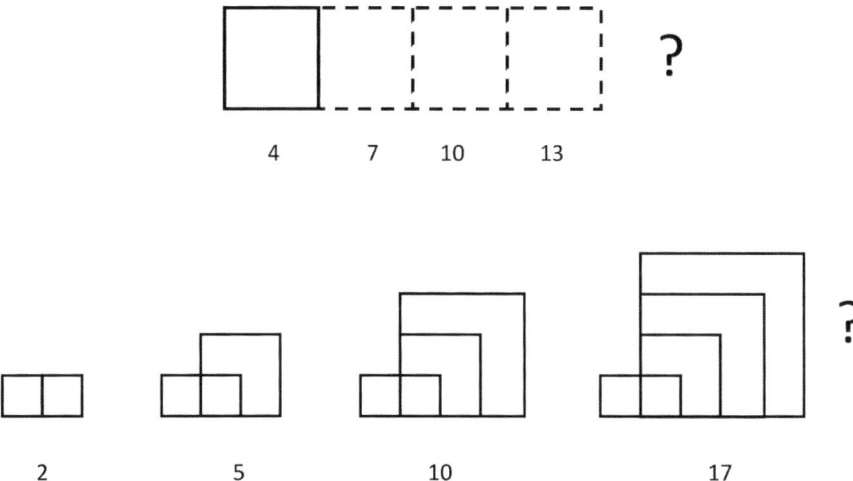

Fig. 9.1 Match-stick and squared-grid patterns for number sequences

'not to tell', but rather to 'ask for reasons', and even 'suggest wrong answers if necessary' to get the children to reason and argue.

Post-lesson analysis included the suggestion that the two different contexts of sticks and squares might not be as clear as if a similar context was used in linear and quadratic cases. It was suggested that the linear case using squares might provide a dramatic contrast to the quadratic pattern, facilitating the point that quadratic patterns look more like growing two dimensional square-ish objects, while their differences are growing like linear patterns. As a result the team tried out this suggestion, and found this did not work well, because the linear pattern appeared too obvious and uninteresting to the learners.

A further interesting observation was made by pre-service teachers who tried out this lesson on other classes. They said when they tried it that they had many difficulties in keeping 'order and discipline', with children chatting and being difficult to 'bring back' to attention for class discussion. This was regarded by them as a real threat, as they felt their own grades for such lessons would be poor. A major factor in this seemed to us to be the fact that pre-service teachers were placed in the position of taking the lead in changing established, traditional practice in experienced teachers' classrooms. This seemed a decisive threat, and made us question whether pre-service teachers in such a situation could benefit fully from lesson study in the English context unless they had the full support and indeed leadership of their mentors and more experienced colleagues. In the event that pre-service teachers lead in taking such risks, at least the lesson study must relieve them of perceived threats of evaluations of their success, in conditions where evaluations of classroom management of their lessons appear to them often paramount.

Additionally, it should be noted that the report of this lesson study to the wider lesson study seminar (with teachers and pre-service teachers from other schools) drew attention to the way such lessons might be evaluated by inspectors: it seemed important that the teacher leading this class had been recently formally inspected teaching 'lessons like this' and had been highly graded. Thus we could say that the value of this commodity lies not only in its 'use' as a means of teaching for understanding, but has to establish its exchange value in the school cultural economies of surveillance and inspection.

Lessons Across the Study

In sum, we drew the following lessons from these lesson studies:

First, the lesson study practices varied from school to school, and occasion to occasion, and was very different from those reported in Japan and in some other countries. This suggests we are in a period in which systematic practice is still unsettled and uncertain, and its place within the culture is being formed.

Second, there was an almost universal perception that this work provided a very different development opportunity, relatively free from the performance management threats teachers normally experience from classroom observations and feedback. This was perhaps less so for the pre-service teachers in this context, which we attributed to the power relations with their lesson study colleagues (school mentors and university tutors) as Corcoran (2011) previously observed. It would be important in future to explicitly insulate their lesson 'grading' from their experimentation with the lesson study practice.

Third, there seemed to be special reasons in each case that persuaded school management to take part in the projects, and we suspect this will only be sustainable if a case can be made that helps management justify the resource in performance terms. There is a real threat to the way lesson study might develop within a performance management context, here, given the first two points.

We conclude that the future of lesson study in this cultural context is wide open: the tension between the self-organising elements of professional development on the one side and the accountability of professionals to performance management on the other will no doubt continue to shape its course and the way it settles into the professional culture in England. We must anticipate the need not only to establish the use value of lesson study, but also manage the culture of performance management, from which it requires some value. No doubt this value (we call exchange value) is related to its use value in teaching and learning, but not necessarily always directly so, since it is mediated by a wider cultural economy in schooling (see Williams 2011, 2012).

Discussion and Conclusion

We began with a view that there is much to be gained from consideration of different cultural practices in teaching development and teacher learning. Over the last decade, the ascendancy of international comparisons of *children's performance* in mathematics, and inferential judgements of *teacher performance*, had resulted in political interference/direction and external 'fixes' that, we believe, had impoverished classroom practice and demoralised the teaching profession. Teaching development had been effectively taken from the teachers.

However, we thought that examination of another cultural practice—Japanese lesson study—provided an opportunity to see what *could be* if teachers were in control. This professional practice reverses the top-down flow of authority and crucially involves teacher collaboration and research-based practice. We did not seek to import the practice but rather to use it as a frame which could evolve under local conditions in the hands of teachers.

We have described and analysed what lesson study is beginning to look like in England's primary and secondary schools, where the performativity agenda still rules and where teacher professional learning has been dominated by graded lesson observations and scrutinised in the light of national league tables. We theorised this performativity in social terms, using the concept of commodification of education and the use and exchange value of knowledge. It does no harm to the lesson study cause to observe that mathematics learning in Japan scores well, for instance, even though we have no evidence of causal connection.

We noted teachers' initial fears that lesson study could involve yet another watch on their performance. However, these concerns were allayed once the nature of lesson study was shown to involve professional practice that the teachers created, evaluated and controlled. The joint practice of inquiry, the formulation of different types of lesson goals, the focus on what children do and think, and the opportunities to develop professional conversations were all reported by them as new and engaging. The teachers began to take a wider view of a curriculum informed by their research in their classrooms.

However, the support of the system (e.g. from senior management) was shown to be crucial in providing the 'space' for lesson study practice to evolve, and in allowing risk-taking and investment in time to support long-term change in practice that was owned and directed by the teachers. We 'outside' mathematics educators were able to provide research evidence from the wider field, key readings and activities, and another viewpoint to add to the professional conversation. We see such provision of resources as vital if we are to move from performativity to giving teaching back to teachers.

Our work with teachers in schools shows that there is potential to change the 'cultural script' through the evolving lesson study practice that values ongoing collaboration and research, and that works to improve children's engagement with *inquiry and dialogue* in mathematics in their classrooms.

> Within a culture, people have common mental pictures of what teaching is like, what teachers in a classroom do, and what students do. These mental pictures are scripts. These cultural scripts, which are often implicit, guide students and teachers to know what role each is to play in a classroom. But cultural scripts are social constraints or affordances and only guide, not determine, actions on the parts of individuals. (Corey et al. 2010, p. 439)

We are learning much from these lessons about the performance culture and what Wenger (2009) describes as the 'vertical' component of accountability it demands (i.e. as opposed to the horizontal accountability to know-how that our professional community of practice demands, perhaps including our fellows, peers and students/children). We argue that the lesson study culture can respond to the performativity agenda by pointing to the policy failure of teaching-to-the-test in the long term, and of the need to address and broaden the range of learning outcomes. In particular, it responds to the need for a lifelong professional learning culture of improvement that stands up to onslaughts of political short-termism and robustly asks 'where's your evidence?'.

References

Adey, P., & Shayer, M. (1994). *Really raising standards*. London: Routledge.
Advisory Committee on Mathematics Education. (2011). ACME Position paper on early and multiple entry to GCSE mathematics. http://www.acme-uk.org/news/news-items-repository/2011/5/position-paper-on-early-and-mutiple-entry-to-gcse-mathematics. Accessed 10 Dec 2012.
Barrow, R. (1984). *Giving teaching back to teachers: A critical introduction to curriculum theory*. London: Wheatsheaf Books Ltd.
Bartalo, D. B. (2012). *Closing the teaching gap: Coaching for instructional leaders*. London: Sage.
Bell, A., Burkhardt, H., & Swan, M. (1992). Balanced assessment of mathematical performance. In R. Lesh & S. Lamon (Eds.), *Assessment of authentic performance in school mathematics* (pp. 119–144). Washington DC: American Association for the Advancement of Science.
Black, P., & Wiliam, D. (1998). Assessment and classroom learning. *Assessment in Education, 5*(1), 7–74.
Corcoran, D. (2011). Learning from lesson study: Power distribution in a community of practice. In L. C. Hart, A. S. Alston & A. Murata (Eds.), *Lesson study research and practice in mathematics education: Altogether* (pp. 251–267). London: Springer.
Corey, D. L., Peterson, B. E., Merill Lewis, B., & Bukarau, J. (2010). Are there any places that students use their heads? Principles of high-quality Japanese mathematics instruction. *Journal for Research in Mathematics Education, 41*(5), 438–478.
Hart, L. C., Alston, A., & Murata, A. (Eds.). (2011). *Lesson study research and practice in mathematics education: Learning together*. London: Springer.
IEA. (2012). Trends in international mathematics and science study 2011. http://www.iea.nl/timss_2011.html. Accessed 3 Oct 2012.
Lewis, C. C. (2002). *Lesson study: A handbook of teacher-led instructional change*. Philadelphia: RBS.
Lewis, C., & Tsuchida, I. (1998). A lesson is like a swiftly flowing river. *American Educator, 22*(4), 12–17.
Mathematics Group at Maruyama. (2006) 3rd Grade Mathematics Lesson Plan: 'Multiplication Algorithm (1)' led by Hideyuki Muramoto, Sapporo City Maruyama Elementary School. http://hrd.apec.org/index.php/Multiplication_Algorithm_Grade_3_%28Japan%29#Lesson_Overview. Accessed 10 Dec 2012.
Pampaka, M., Williams, J. S., & Hutcheson, G. (2012a). Measuring students' transition into university and its association with learning outcomes. *British Educational Research Journal, 38*(6), 1041–1070.
Pampaka, M., Williams, J. S., Hutcheson, G., Wake, G., Black, L., Davis, P., & Hernandez-Martinez, P. (2012b). The association between mathematics pedagogy and learners' dispositions for university study. *British Educational Research Journal, 38*(3), 473–496.
Parliamentary, R. (2011). http://www.publications.parliament.uk/pa/cm201011/cmhansrd/cm110207/debtext/110207-0001.htm#1102076000004. Accessed 3 Oct 2012.

Power, M. (1997). *The audit society: Rituals of verification*. Oxford: Oxford University Press.

Ryan, J., & Williams, J. (2012). Children's argumentation in primary school mathematics: the use of models and tools to support reasoning and explanation. Paper presented to the Annual Conference of the British Educational Research Association, September 2012.

Schraw, G. (2002). Promoting general metacognitive awareness. In H. J. Hartman (Ed.), *Metacognition in learning and instruction: Theory, research and practice* (pp. 3–16). Dordrect: Kluwer.

Stigler, J., & Hiebert, J. (1999/2009). *The teaching gap: Best ideas from the world's teachers for improving education in the classroom*. New York: Free Press.

Stigler, J. W., & Hiebert, J. (2009). Closing the teaching gap. *Phi Delta Kappan, 91*(3), 32–37.

Strathern, M. (Ed.). (2000). *Audit cultures: Anthropological studies in accountability, ethics and the academy*. London: Routledge.

Sturman, L., Ruddock, G., Burge, B., Lin, Y., & Vappula, H. (2008). England's achievement in TIMSS 2007: National report for England. Slough: NFER.

Wenger, E. (2009). Social learning capability: Four essays on innovation and learning in social systems. Social Innovation, Sociedade e Trabalho booklets, 12—separate supplement. Lisbon: MTSS/GEP & EQUAL.

Williams, J. (2011). Audit and evaluation of pedagogy: Towards a cultural-historical perspective. In T. Rowland & K. Ruthven (Eds.), *Mathematical knowledge in teaching* (pp. 161–178). Dordrecht: Springer.

Williams, J. (2012). Use and exchange value in mathematics education: Contemporary CHAT meets Bourdieu's sociology. *Educational Studies in Mathematics, 80*(1), 57–72.

Williams, J., & Ryan, J. (2000). National testing and the improvement of classroom teaching: Can they coexist? *British Educational Research Journal, 26*(1), 49–73.

Williams, J., & Ryan, J. (in press). Research, policy, and professional development: designing hybrid activities in third spaces. In V. Farnsworth & Y. Solomon (Eds.), *What works in education? Bridging theory and practice in research*. London: Routledge.

Chapter 10
The Policy Context of Teachers' Workplace Learning: The Case for Research-based Professionalism in Teacher Education in England

Anne Campbell

Introduction

This chapter will address the recent and current policy and context of professional learning in teacher education, with particular reference to professional master's level provision. The importance of teachers' and schools' perceptions of improvement, development and learning and the inherent tensions between individual, school and government priorities will be explored (Hustler et al. 2003; Opfer and Pedder 2010b). The chapter will discuss the lack of theorisation in this field (McCormick et al. 2008; McCormick 2010) and draw upon the work of Little (1982, 2002) on workplace conditions for successful schools, Day (1999) on lifelong learning, and relevant research in the field of vocational education (Anderson 1982; Billet 1996, 2006). Finally, it will trace the evolution of teacher as researcher, from Stenhouse's work in 1975 and the move from curriculum research and development, through a focus on professional development, to the current focus on professional learning involving coaching, inquiry and research in the workplace. It will argue that inquiry and research form powerful tools in workplace learning for master's level provision and teachers' professional learning.

The Professional Development Landscape: Policy and Context

During the last 20 years or so, education in England has been subject to intense accountability: the implementation of a National Curriculum and the introduction of a national programme of testing, more detailed and demanding than any other national programme (Furlong et al. 2009; Mahony and Hextall 2000). Teachers have, at times, felt a lack of self-worth, as measures to inspect schools and appraise teachers have been introduced under the banner of 'modernising'. Professional learning steadily

A. Campbell (✉)
Edinburgh, Scotland
e-mail: annejcampbell66@gmail.com

O. McNamara et al. (eds.), *Workplace Learning in Teacher Education,*
Professional Learning and Development in Schools and Higher Education 10,
DOI 10.1007/978-94-007-7826-9_10, © Springer Science+Business Media Dordrecht 2014

became something that was 'done to' teachers—often on the so-called 'Baker Days' named after the Secretary of Education in the late 1980s—and initiatives seemed unbalanced, being more heavily weighted towards central control and prescription than locally identified needs. This is not the case in all parts of the UK. The General Teaching Councils and governments in Scotland, Wales and Northern Ireland have each taken different stances, more measured and less intense than in England, on policies for the professional development of teachers.

In England, as the professional development of teachers gained a high profile, it seemed to be like a political football, subject to constant shifts and changes. Civil servants, politicians, professional associations, private sector companies, universities, schools, parents and local authorities, all became stakeholders. Teachers had a quasi-statutory requirement to engage in professional development; to identify, document, record and evaluate it as they crossed through the barriers of induction standards and threshold and grappled with targets for performance management. There was a plethora of documentation relating to: professional standards; curriculum priority areas; guidance for effective professional development; and impact evaluation. Teachers' professional learning became part of government policy, encapsulated in the first national strategy, 'Learning and Teaching: A Strategy for Professional Development' (DfES 2001). It was then further reviewed in the then Teacher Training Agency's extended remit to include continuing professional learning, (TTA 2005) and recently envisioned in the 'Strategy for the Development of the Children's Workforce in Schools', produced by the Training Development Agency (TDA 2009). There has been a gradual recognition over the last ten years or so of the importance of continuing professional learning related to curriculum change, as initiative after initiative has been launched, and teachers have tried to adjust to rapid change. The content of the policy documents above has hinted at ownership and choice in the identification and meeting of perceived needs, but the reality is that teachers have been subjected to a great deal of prescription, both in the content and format of professional development and in particular through 'training' linked to the National Strategies (Day et al. 2007).

Public accountability has been increasingly visible, in league tables, inspections and media coverage. Individual schools and classrooms were to become 'learning communities' and the sites of future professional development (DfES 2001). Despite the rhetoric of teacher control of their own professional learning, the raising standards agenda still dominated the professional preparation and development of teachers, not least in initiatives such as Best Practice Research Scholarships, Education Action Zones and Networked Learning Communities, and most recently the Master's in Teaching and Learning. However, despite the prescription in these initiatives, there was much evidence of high quality professional learning with regard, particularly, to Best Practice Research Scholarships (Furlong et al. 2003) and Networked Learning Communities (Day and Hadfield 2004; McLaughlin 2009).

However, in addition to this prescription, it may also be that a lack of understanding of the nature, processes and purposes of professional development initiatives had influenced teachers' ability to take a more leading role in their learning, and I will consider that later. Pedder et al. (2010, p. 7) note that a lack of theorising about teachers' continuing professional learning is common, but mention some notable exceptions, such as Putnam and Borko (2000), looking at teacher learning from a situated perspective, which is by its nature a social view of learning. Borko (2004), in reviewing the research on what is known about continuing professional learning, argues that both a cognitive and a social perspective are needed to understand teacher learning. McCormick (2010, p. 407) notes:

> First, it is evident that we just need more research into what is happening in schools with regard to CPD [continuing professional development] and the views of teachers and school leaders about that activity. Second, CPD needs to be theorised more, not just in terms of views of professionalism and professional autonomy (the most common form of theorising), but in relation to what happens with regard to the CPD processes . . . Third, there is a need for the details of these learning processes to be investigated both at the point at which teachers are "creating" practices and also where they are "sharing" them.

This contrasts with the more general literature on workplace learning, where many types of work situations are theorised in terms of types of knowledge and learning (e.g. Anderson 1982; Billett 2006), including that in schools (e.g. Hodkinson and Hodkinson 2004). Much of the theory about workplace learning comes from the vocational educational and adult learning fields, although research into pre-service teacher education and partnership practices can offer valuable insights into workplace learning in teacher education (McIntyre et al. 1993; Furlong and Maynard 1995; Edwards and Collinson 1996).

In the 1980s, local authorities used to receive funding to support teachers on full-time master's degrees, and teachers had to apply for these generous awards covering salary, replacement costs and fees. Whilst the recent climate would appear to offer flexibility of provision, it can also result in inequalities and lack of entitlement for pupils, teachers and schools. In 2003, Department for Education and Skills (DfES) pronouncements indicated a change in policy for funding continuing professional learning. Most of the core funding for continuing professional learning went straight into school budgets, for schools to decide how it should be spent. Some schools spent substantial amounts on continuing professional learning, others, for a variety of reasons including other budgetary constraints, spent very little. The demise of many of the central funds for innovative teacher research and development between 2003 and 2008 (e.g. Practice Research Scholarships, Education Action Zones and Networked Learning Communities) heralded a decrease in activity, as schools used the devolved funding for teachers' and teaching support staff's salaries. As can be seen by the recent Schools White Paper (DFE 2010), this current government aims to continue to fund the schools and cease any central funding and ring-fencing of funds in what they hope will give schools more power to decide what they spend it on. Arguably, this is a robust strategy, but it may, as in 2003, be subject to individual school priorities which are not always about professional learning.

A recent policy statement on continuing professional learning or Professional Development (PD), a term borrowed from America and used in the document, is contained in the 'Strategy for the Professional Development of the Children's Workforce in Schools 2009–2012' (TDA 2009) and outlines the main challenge for provision as being the development of a 'world class workforce'. Its vision, informed by a number of TDA commissioned projects in continuing professional learning (Robinson et al. 2008; Bubb et al. 2009; Earley and Porritt 2009; and Pedder et al. 2010), is to 'embed a learning culture, within and across all schools, that maximises the potential of all members of the school workforce and enables children and young people to achieve the best outcomes possible'. The widening of the lens to include all who work with children in schools and a firm focus on outcomes extends the trend started in the first national strategy in 2001. Entitlement and the rights and responsibilities of continuing professional learning for all members of the workforce were identified and highlighted. The list of effective features includes some likely suspects: coaching; workplace learning balanced by external activity; impact; accountability through performance review and feedback from children and community. It looks as though the ball is firmly in the schools' court, with responsibility for identifying, providing and evaluating PD, but as Pedder et al. (2010, p. 368) argue:

> A key policy goal of successive governments has been to enforce the compliance of teachers to the national reform agenda by harnessing their day-to-day practices, how they think about their work, and what they aspire to achieve through their work to central prescriptions, targets and indicators related to raising standards through the use of prescriptive national strategies and high stakes tests of pupil attainment, league tables, and procedures of external inspection (e.g., Day et al. 2007; Furlong 2008; Jones et al. 2008; Swann et al. 2010).

There is evidence that the culture of target setting still prevails, in England at least, and is of fundamental significance in shaping teachers' practice and bringing with it, as it does, the threat of too great a focus on compliance. The recently launched, and soon abandoned, Master's in Teaching and Learning can attest to that (Frankham and Hiett 2011). It remains to be seen how the Coalition Government strategy of extending to professional learning activities its mantra of 'give the money to head teachers and schools' will affect the professional learning landscape. It also remains to be seen how the newly established raft of Teaching Schools will support and lead the sector in this enterprise, now that local authorities are effectively written out of the educational support infrastructure, and over half of secondary schools (and a small but growing proportion of primary schools) are funded and managed directly by central government.

Master's Provision

Much of the master's level provision located in higher education institutions has long been concerned with workplace learning. Courses were variable in their approaches, depending on the interest and expertise of staff available to teach. Many courses employed action research and practice-based approaches and helped teachers investigate and evaluate their professional practice, and develop curriculum and subject knowledge.

Following the period when local authorities held the funding for master's degrees, the funding was then transferred to the Higher Education Funding Council for England, and higher education institutions bid for funded places which were offered competitively to teachers, who paid part-time reduced fees. In 2003, following the government's comprehensive spending review which redirected much of the central funds for continuing professional learning to schools, the funding for award bearing In-service Education and Training (INSET), including master's level provision, was reviewed. The TTA had taken over responsibility for the scheme in 1997, and since April 2000 had managed it on behalf of the DfES. The funds were distributed to INSET providers through a triennial bidding round. Bids were scrutinised against national priority areas and other quality criteria. An evaluation of the provision was commissioned by the TTA and a report produced by Soulsby and Swain (2003). The report covered the following aspects of provision: impact on improving participants' knowledge, understanding, skills and effectiveness in teaching and on improving pupils' standards; decline in registrations; distinctive features of provision; the funding system for the scheme; and options for change. The report was positive about the value and impact of the INSET Scheme:

> It is clear . . . that teachers who complete an award feel they have gained new and specific skills, knowledge and understanding from the sustained study required. For some, the gains are in the research skills needed to investigate an issue in their own school. For others, the gains come from a fresh look at the pedagogy of their subject or of a phase, such as early years education. (Soulsby and Swain 2003, p. 7)

The report also concluded that the decline in registrations was not due to the quality of the provision, but mainly to teachers' increasing workload and an increase in imposed innovations and related training. The report detailed evidence that, in recent years, much of the provision had become more accessible, more flexible, and more responsive to the needs of individual teachers and of schools, and found scope for further development along these lines. The picture was overwhelmingly positive. Grades in Ofsted inspections suggested that the great majority of courses not only had a positive impact on teachers and schools but were also strong on needs identification and in the quality of the training. It also indicated, through assessment of impact, that learning was being transformed into improved practice in the workplace, the classroom. Courses tailored for particular local authorities or schools or focused on school improvement were praised in the report, as were the many school-based projects undertaken by head teachers and teachers. Finally, comments from the report, which it would serve the proponents of workplace learning to seriously consider, include:

> The evidence suggests that the impact on schools is most productive where:
> - the headteacher takes a personal interest and takes account of the training in performance management
> - a significant number of staff are involved in longer-term CPD projects and outcomes are evaluated and disseminated
> - the provision is both intellectually stretching and focused on practice
> - assignments are flexible enough in form and content to enable teachers to engage with issues which are relevant to them and to their schools.
> (Soulsby and Swain 2003, p. 12)

The Postgraduate Professional Development (PPD) Programme

The PPD Programme was initiated in 2005. It was a model based on the development of partnerships with the main stakeholders (higher education, schools and local authorities) in order to plan, deliver and evaluate provision with a much stronger focus on providing evidence of impact and workplace learning. Partnership was at the heart of the PPD, as were: needs analysis; personalised enquiry; improvement of pupil outcomes; and critical evaluation. There were many positive outcomes as a result of the development of the PPD Programmes, as documented by large-scale longitudinal reviews conducted by the Centre for the Use of Research and Evidence in Education (CUREE 2008) and Seaborne (2010). They identified the clear development of partnerships, the power of action research and needs analysis as positive outcomes of five years of PPD (2005–2010). The report also highlighted that there was quite widespread lack of support in schools for those undertaking school-based projects, a worrying trend that could blight the development and success of any workplace learning initiatives. Collaboration was identified as a key component of workplace learning (Day 1999, p. 175; and Cordingley et al. 2005), signalling the need for teachers to work together, both inside and outside the classroom. Research points to the effectiveness of continuing professional learning that is collaborative, classroom-based, experiential and research informed (CUREE 2008; Pedder et al. 2005).

Seaborne (2010) attests to the success of the PPD Programme in his report, and cites providers as being keen to support the development of the Master's in Teaching and Learning qualification, but repeatedly having expressed concern that this should not be at the expense of the PPD Programme. He writes 'The national framework for MTL [Master's in Teaching and Learning] outlines the principles behind a new scheme that is palpably a natural evolution from the good practice in school-based PPD' (ibid., p. 21). He states that, when the personal study programme also sets objectives for how improvements in teachers' capabilities will affect the learning experiences of pupils, the impact on pupils' attitudes, engagement, behaviour and attainment can be significant. The experience of successfully achieving this 'bridge' through the PPD Programme should inform the Master's in Teaching and Learning and any workplace learning initiative developments.

As more PPD providers have become expert in tailoring programmes to address the development needs of schools, bespoke school-based PPD has increased and prospered. Recently, greater attention has been paid to matching PPD provision to teachers' performance management targets, and many providers now plan provision in accordance with the professional standards for teachers. However, there is sometimes a tension between school needs on the one hand and individual needs on the other, and providers need to be aware of this tension and seek to minimise it. PPD providers have also noted apathy and sometimes hostility from schools that see master's level study as distracting newly qualified teachers from the 'real business of getting to grips with teaching' (Seaborne 2010, p. 7). Such opposition may affect workplace learning initiatives.

Another key aspect of learning in the workplace is quality and co-ordination of the support from mentors in schools and staff from higher education or external bodies. Processes of identifying personal needs, setting and reviewing objectives, and matching study and learning experiences to evolving circumstances, call for tutors, coaches and mentors with appropriate expertise, knowledge and skills. Lessons learned from pre-service teacher education demonstrate that being an expert in one's own school or university classroom is not sufficient, as the interpersonal skills of working with adults, facilitating change and the ability to both support and challenge to improve practice are seen as keys to success (Furlong and Maynard 1995; Campbell and Kane 1998, p. 67; Hurd et al. 2007).

Seaborne (2010, p. 22) claims that since 2006 PPD providers have begun to identify some unanticipated negative features of individualised and bespoke study programmes. Several have reintroduced collective course components or group seminars because: a needs driven 'just-in-time' approach to teaching enquiry and research techniques proved inefficient and reduced capacity to discuss research with their peers; and participants based their understanding too narrowly on their experiences and circumstances of their own school, leaving them unable to evaluate objectively alternative teaching strategies and curriculum approaches.

Barriers that adversely affect teachers' participation in master's level study were identified by Seaborne (2010, p. 23). These included: time needed to undertake master's level study; access to provision; cost; support in the workplace; plus a range of personal and emotional factors. The specification set out in the national framework for Master's in Teaching and Learning recognises these barriers. It also emphasises the importance of preserving a satisfactory work/life balance for participants. However, evidence from PPD clearly shows that school-based provision can do much to overcome these barriers, but they cannot be entirely eliminated while at the same time preserving the academic integrity of master's level study.

The future funding of the PPD will not be part of the government's plan for teachers' professional learning.

Teachers' Perceptions of Continuing Professional Learning and Development

How do teachers perceive professional learning and development? Judith Warren Little (2002, p. 714) argues that one of the most significant resources for teacher professional learning is to be found in the teachers themselves and their interactions one with each other when they

> collectively question ineffective teaching routines, examine new conceptions of teaching and learning, find generative means to acknowledge and respond to difference and conflict and engage actively in supporting professional growth,

somewhat akin to the practices of effective mentoring and coaching. Teachers' perceptions of professional development and learning greatly shape their experience of learning.

In a government funded survey of teachers' perceptions of continuing professional learning, Hustler et al. (2003) identified key issues: most teachers are working with traditional notions of continuing professional development; tensions exist between personal needs, school improvement needs and national priority needs for teachers and schools; there is an association between a high valuation of continuing professional learning and the level of teacher choice and control over their learning activity; inquiry-based learning, such as that provided by the Best Practice Research Scholarships Programme, allows for bespoke continuing professional learning activity and an increase in self-determination and control of professional development; one size does not fit all; the role of the continuing professional learning leader is crucial and can have either a positive or negative effect on the management of the learning; whilst 'planned' change in connection with school improvement agendas is important, serendipity has a place in teacher development; and collaboration is important.

The survey further indicated that there is some evidence that emerging Professional Learning Communities are helping to embed collaborative and collegial practices for professional development within schools and networks; that continuing professional learning evaluation and accountability require attention; and that approaches must be balanced and flexible to cater for local and national needs.

Analysis of case study data indicated: the need for a balanced diet of professional learning as there are different agendas for different teachers; the challenges of meeting a variety of learning styles; that autonomy and responsibility go hand in hand; that ideas should be contextualised and customised—we all need props but need to beware of 'recipes'; and the power of collaboration between enthusiastic beginners and experienced practitioners. The report also found that establishing a lifelong learning culture in schools (Day 1999) was a key aspect for success. This was aided through: a 'balanced' diet of workplace and offsite learning; a balance of individual personal learning with collective school development and national priorities; keeping up the momentum and keeping motivated; and experiencing joy, creativity and ownership.

More recently, Opfer and Pedder (2010a) reported on the State of the Nation research project and identified a less than positive picture. In the summary of the research presented at the 2010 British Educational Research Association (BERA) conference, the *Times Educational Supplement* noted that 'teachers' professional development is haphazard, poorly planned and poorly assessed' (TES, 10 September, 2010).

Earley, (2010, p. 475), in his discussion of four TDA-funded projects looking at professional development, concludes that:

> many teachers think of staff development as activities to be engaged in rather than as the actual development of their knowledge and expertise, which may (or may not) result from their participation in such activities. They conceive of professional development in terms of inputs and not as the changes effected in their thinking and practice.

One way forward to counter such passive roles in professional learning is to place teachers at the centre of the stage, as action researchers and inquirers, planning and designing questions to investigate in pursuit of improvement of practice.

The Case for Practitioner Inquiry and Research

It could be argued that participation in teacher inquiry and research increases teacher engagement in reform and improvement, and results in a better quality of teacher learning.

Stenhouse's (1975, p. 144) notion of 'autonomous professional development through systematic self study' provides a logical starting point for workplace learning in teacher education in England, as he envisioned practitioners investigating their practice as a basis for professional renewal and change. He proposed professional learning communities of teacher researchers and inquirers. His basic argument for placing teachers at the heart of educational research was 'Teachers are in charge of classrooms . . . classrooms are the ideal laboratories for testing educational theory . . .' and he thought it difficult to deny that the 'teacher is surrounded by rich research opportunities' (Stenhouse 1981, p. 109). Whilst the workplace was important as a place to trial and experiment with curriculum materials, the focus in the 1970s and 1980s was primarily on teachers' centres and groups of teachers working together in a model of curriculum development and action research exemplified in the Humanities Curriculum Project (Lawton 1983; Elliott 1974, 1981). Mostly, these initiatives involved partnerships and collaborations between teachers and academics in a variety of sites: the workplace, the locality (teachers' centres or other local authority forums), and higher education institutions.

The move from curriculum development to professional development in the 1980s was influenced by a focus on the processes of teaching and learning rather than the content of the curriculum, which by the late 1980s was substantially prescribed by the government. This focus also increased the need to look at classrooms and schools as sites for professional learning and improvement. Little (1982, p. 338) discussed the power of the workplace for professional learning and development and the importance of collegial interaction, and linked these to school success.

> First, the school as a workplace proves extraordinarily powerful. Without denying differences in individuals' skills, interests, commitment, curiosity, or persistence, the prevailing pattern of interactions and interpretations in each building demonstrably creates certain possibilities and sets certain limits.

Her research findings at that time helped to shape future approaches to teacher learning, emphasising teachers engaging in frequent, continuous and increasingly concrete and precise talk about teaching, building up a shared language with which to talk about their practice. She advocated teachers planning, designing, researching, evaluating and preparing teaching materials. Her study of six schools produced an illustrative inventory of characteristic teacher interactions which described the patterned norms of interaction amongst staff. She identified 'critical practices of success and adaptability' (ibid. p. 339) which resonate greatly with Groundwater-Smith and Mockler's (2003, p. 1) tenets in their resource for learning to listen and listening to learn 20 years later. These tenets are: evidence-based practice as a strategy for school improvement and teacher professional learning; developing a community of practice using appropriate technology; building research capability in schools by engaging teachers and students; and sharing methodologies which are appropriate to practitioner inquiry as a means of transforming teacher professional learning.

Grundy (1982, p. 358) argued for the acceptance of practitioner research as a means of addressing teacher professional learning and school improvement, making the crucial link between inquiry, research and professional learning which Groundwater-Smith and Campbell (2009, p. 205) argue would 'counter overly simple solutions packaged in short courses'. They believe that authentic inquiry will require risks and mistake-making and looking backwards as well as forwards. This, they assert, requires courage, resilience and healthy dissent.

Viewing the workplace as a learning environment fits well with the notion of practitioners inquiring and researching their practice with a view to improvement. The workplace as a learning environment facilitates:

- Experiential learning;
- Theory–practice interaction;
- Opportunities for collegiality and collaboration;
- Direct links to impact on pupils and students and their learning;
- Taking a risk in a 'safe' environment';
- A community of practice.

Campbell et al. (2004) argued that inquiry and research had a central place and that teachers should research their own professional practice, development and learning in the workplace supported by and in partnership with staff in higher education on master's level courses. The relationships between practitioner research and professional knowledge and learning are becoming clearer as teachers investigate the modifications and changes they can make through learning and producing knowledge in action research initiatives in their classrooms and schools. Ken Zeichner (2003, p. 319) identified several conditions under which school-based teacher research becomes a transformative professional learning activity for teachers—and I would argue also for those academic partners who support them—as the following:

- Creating a culture of enquiry and respect for teacher knowledge;
- Encouraging learner-centred instruction;
- Teachers developing and controlling their own foci for enquiries;
- Engaging in collaborative work and study groups for intellectual challenge and stimulation.

Engaging in inquiry and research as a powerful tool for professional learning, creating knowledge and improvement of practice is attested by many (Carr and Kemmis 1986; Elliott 1991; Cochran-Smith and Lytle 1993; Gore and Zeichner 1995; and Campbell and McNamara 2009). There are many examples of small and large-scale projects that demonstrate the power of action research, for example: Elliott (1991); Hall et al. (2005); Beveridge et al. (2005); McLaughlin et al. (2006); and Taylor and Pettit (2007). However, we still have a long way to go and there are some notes of caution to be considered. Adequate funding for inquiry and research in schools must not be forgotten, and the old adage—quality costs—applies here. With regards to quality we must remind ourselves that quality is a culture not just a set of tick boxes, and that criticality is part of that culture that enables learning and change to happen. Collaboration with colleagues and partners was mentioned earlier and it is a lynchpin of high quality professional learning. There are inherent tensions in school improvement between individual, collective and national priorities which need careful consideration and negotiation. Setting the agenda for collaborative inquiry and research requires negotiation and regard for the processes of mutuality and reciprocity. Care must be taken to avoid turning genuine inquiry into a simplified implementation of school or government policy. The making public of, in perhaps more innovative and creative ways, the findings and lessons from classroom and school research would help to debate and disseminate educational practice. A major area is that of support for inquiry and research. Recently, Opfer and Pedder (2010a, p. 428), in a major project researching professional development, concluded:

> First, teachers need to be supported at school in developing more collaborative and research informed approaches to their CPD. CPD provision needs to involve teachers in more active forms of learning with a clear link to classroom teaching and learning. It also needs to emphasise continuous, long-term, sustained professional learning. Teachers need to be supported in developing practices for collaborative, classroom-based and research informed approaches to their professional development.

Finally, some of the implications that can be drawn from this chapter's review of the policy and context for workplace learning can be summarised as: first, less prescription and more acceptance of differences of opinion and of provision to suit schools' perceived needs; second, a search for balance in the repertoire of professional learning activities between the needs of the individual teacher, of the school and of national priories; and third, to embed, review and refine initiatives. Other implications include the re-conceptualisation of roles of academic partners to facilitate workplace change and to promote professional learning and high quality support for teachers and schools in their endeavours to inquire, research and improve their practice.

To conclude on a positive note, the current climate in England could be seen as another opportunity to develop, refine and renew approaches to professional learning in the workplace. We await to see if this is the case!

References

Anderson, J. R. (1982). Acquisition of cognitive skill. *Psychological Review, 89*(4), 369–406.

Beck, J. E. (1994). The new paradigm of management education: Revolution and counter-revolution. *Management Learning, 25*(2), 231–247.

Beveridge, S., Groundwater-Smith, S., Kemmis, S., & Wasson, D. (2005). Professional learning that makes a difference: Successful strategies implemented by priority action schools in New South Wales. *Journal of In-Service Education, 31*(4), 697–710.

Billet, S. R. (1996). Situated learning: Bridging sociocultural and cognitive theorising. *Learning and Instruction, 6*(3), 263–280.

Billett, S. (2006). Constituting the workplace curriculum. *Journal of Curriculum Studies, 38*(1), 31–48.

Borko, H. (2004). Professional development and teacher learning: Mapping the terrain. *Educational Researcher, 33*(8), 3–15.

Bubb, S., Earley, P., & Hempel-Jorgensen, A. (2009). *Staff development outcomes study*. London: Institute of Education.

Campbell, A., & Kane, I. (1998). *School-based teacher education: Telling tales from a fictional primary school*. London: David Fulton.

Campbell, A., & McNamara, O. (2009). Mapping the field of practitioner research, inquiry and professional learning in educational contexts: A review. In A. Campbell & S. Groundwater-Smith (Eds.), *Connecting inquiry and professional learning in education: International perspectives and practical solutions* (pp. 10–25). London: Routledge.

Campbell, A., McNamara, O., & Gilroy, P. (2004). *Practitioner research and professional development in education*. London: Paul Chapman.

Carr, W., & Kemmis, S. (1986). *Becoming critical: Education, knowledge and action research*. Deakin: Deakin University Press.

Cochran-Smith, M., & Lytle, S. (1993). *Inside/outside: Teacher research and knowledge*. New York: Teachers College Press.

Cordingley, P., et al. (CPD Review Group). (2005). The impact of collaborative CPD on classroom teaching and learning review. How do collaborative and sustained CPD and sustained but not collaborative CPD affect teaching and learning?. London: EPPI-Centre.

CUREE (Centre for the Use of Research and Evidence in Education). (2008). *Qualitative study of school level strategies for teachers' CPD*. London: General Teaching Council for England.

CUREE & University of Wolverhampton. (2010). *Postgraduate professional development programme (PDP) Quality assurance (QA) Strand Research Report Year 3*. London: TDA.

Day, C. (1999). *Developing teachers: The challenges of lifelong learning*. London: Falmer Press.

Day, C., & Hadfield, M. (2004). Learning through networks: Trust, partnerships, and the power of action research. Educational Action Research: An international journal, 12(4), 575–586.

Day, C., Sammons, P., Stobart, G. Kington., & Gu, Q. (2007). *Teachers matter: Connecting lives, work and effectiveness*. Maidenhead: Open University Press.

DFE. (2010). *The importance of teaching. The Schools White Paper*. London: Department for Education.

DfES. (2001). *Learning and teaching: A strategy for professional development*. London: Department for Education and Skills.

Earley, P. (2010). *State of the nation: A discussion of some of the project's key findings*. Paper at BERA Annual Conference, Warwick, September 2010.

Earley, P., & Porritt, V. (Eds.) (2009). *Effective practices in continuing professional development: Lessons from schools. Bedford Way series*. London: Institute of Education/TDA.

Edwards, A., & Collinson, J. (1996). *Mentoring and developing practice in primary schools: Supporting student learning in schools*. Milton Keynes: Open University Press.

Elliott, J. (1974). *Implementing the principles of inquiry/discovery teaching*. CARE publications, University of East Anglia.

Elliott, J. (1981). *Action research: Framework for self-evaluation in schools*. TIQL Working Paper No.1, Cambridge Institute of Education, mimeo.

Elliott, J. (1991). *Action research for educational change*. Buckingham: Open University Press.

Frankham, J., & Hiett, S. (2011). The Master's in teaching and learning: Expanding utilitarianism in the continuing professional development of teachers in England. *Journal of Education Policy, 26*(6), 803–818.

Furlong, J. (2008). Making teaching a 21st century profession: Tony Blair's big prize. *Oxford Review of Education, 34*(6), 727–739.

Furlong, J., & Maynard, T. (1995). *Mentoring student teachers: The growth of professional knowledge*. London: Routledge.

Furlong, J., Salisbury, J., & Coombes, L. (2003). *Best practice research scholarships: An evaluation, June 2003*. Cardiff University School of Social Sciences.

Furlong, J., McNamara, O., Campbell, A., Howson, J., & Lewis, S. (2009). Partnership, policy and politics: Initial teacher education in England under New Labour. In J. Furlong, M. Cochran-Smith & M. Brennan (Eds.), *Policy and politics in teacher education* (pp. 45–56). London: Routledge.

Gore, J., & Zeichner, K. (1995). Connecting action research to genuine teacher development. In J. Gore & K. Zeichner (Eds.), *Critical discourses in teacher development* (pp. 203–214). London: Cassell.

Groundwater-Smith, S., & Campbell, A. (2009). Joining the dots: Connecting inquiry and professional learning. In A. Campbell & S. Groundwater-Smith (Eds.), *Connecting inquiry and professional learning in education: International perspectives and practical solutions* (pp. 200–206). London: Routledge.

Groundwater-Smith, S., & Mockler, N. (2003). *Learning to listen: Listening to learn.* Sydney: Centre for Practitioner Research, University of Sydney and MLC School.

Grundy, S. (1982). Three modes of action research. *Curriculum Perspectives, 2*(3), 23–34.

Hall, E., Wall, K., Higgins, S., Stephens, L., Pooley, I., & Welham, J. (2005). Learning to learn with parents: Lessons from two research projects. *Improving Schools, 8*(2), 179–191.

Hodkinson, P., & Hodkinson, H. (2004). The significance of individuals' dispositions in workplace learning: A case study of two teachers. *Journal of Education and Work, 7*(2), 167–182.

Hurd, S., Jones, M., McNamara, O., & Craig, B. (2007). Initial teacher education as a driver for professional learning and school improvement in the primary phase. *Curriculum Journal, 18*(3), 307–326.

Hustler, D., McNamara, O., Jarvis, J., Londra, M., & Campbell, A. (2003). *Teachers' perceptions of continuing professional development.* Nottingham: DfES publications, (Research 429).

Jones, L., Pickard, A., & Stronach, I. (2008). *Primary schools: The professional environment. Interim report for the Primary Review. Cambridge: University of Cambridge.*

Lave, J., & Wenger, E. (1991). *Situated learning: Legitimate peripheral participation.* Cambridge: Cambridge University Press.

Lawton, D. (1983). Lawrence Stenhouse: His contribution to curriculum development. *British Educational Research Journal, 9*(1), 7–9.

Little, J. W. (1982). Norms of collegiality and experimentation: Workplace conditions of school success. *American Educational Research Journal, 19,* 325–340.

Little, J. W. (2002). Professional community and the problem of high school reform. *International Journal of Educational Research, 37*(6), 693–714.

Mahony, P., & Hextall, I. (2000). *Reconstructing teaching: Standards, performance and accountability.* London: Routledge/Falmer.

McCormick, R. (2010). The state of the nation in CPD: A literature review. *Curriculum Journal, 21*(4), 395–412. doi:10.1080/09585176.2010.529643.

McCormick, R., Banks, F., Morgan, B., Opfer, D., Pedder, D., Storey, A., & Wolfenden, F. (2008). Literature review report. Schools and Continuing Professional Development (CPD) in England—State of the Nation Research Project (T34718). A report commissioned by the training and development agency for schools, Cambridge/Milton Keynes: Cambridge University/Open University. www.tda.gov.uk/upload/resources/pdf/c/cpd_statenation_report_literature.pdf. Accessed 15 Jan 2010.

McIntyre, D., Hagger, H., & Wilkins, M. (1993). *Mentoring: Perspectives on school-based teacher education.* London: Kogan Page.

McLaughlin, C. (2009). Networks of researching schools: Lessons and questions from one study. In A. Campbell & S. Groundwater-Smith (Eds.), *Connecting inquiry and professional learning in education: International perspectives and practical solutions* (pp. 152–165). London: Routledge.

McLaughlin, C., Black-Hawkins, K., Brindley, S., McIntyre, D., & Tabor, K. S. (2006). *Researching schools: Stories from a schools-university partnership for educational research.* London: Routledge.

Opfer, V. D., & Pedder, D. (2010a). Access to continuous professional development by teachers in England. *Curriculum Journal, 21*(4), 453–471. doi:10.1080/09585176.2010.529680.

Opfer, V. D., & Pedder, D. (2010b). Benefits, status and effectiveness of Continuous Professional Development for teachers in England. *Curriculum Journal, 21*(4), 413–431. doi:10.1080/09585176.2010.529651.

Pedder, D., James, M., & MacBeath, J. (2005). How teachers value and practice professional learning. *Research Papers in Education, 20*(3), 209–243.

Pedder, D., Opfer, V. D., McCormick, R., & Storey, A. (2010). Schools and continuing professional development in England—State of the Nation research study: Policy context, aims and design. *Curriculum Journal, 21*(4), 365–394. doi:10.1080/09585176.2010.529637.

Puttnam, R. T., & Borko, H. (2000). What do new views of knowledge and thinking have to say about research on teacher learning? *Education Researcher, 29*(1), 4–15.

Resnick, L. (1987). Learning in school and out. *Educational Researcher, 16*(9), 13–20.

Robinson, M., Walker, M., Kinder, K., & Haines, B. (2008). Research into the role of CPD leadership in schools. Slough0: NFER.

Seaborne, P. L. (2010). *A longitudinal review of the postgraduate professional development of teachers*. London: TDA.

Soulsby, D., & Swain, D. (2003). *A report on the award bearing INSET Scheme*. London: TTA.

Stenhouse, L. (1975). *An introduction to curriculum research and development*. London: Heinemann Educational Books.

Stenhouse, L. (1981). What counts as research? *British Journal of Educational Studies*, XX1X(2), 103–114.

Swann, M., McIntyre, D., Pell, T., Hargreaves, L., & Cunningham, M. (2010). Teachers' conceptions of teacher professionalism in England in 2003 and 2006. *British Educational Research Journal, 36*(4), 549–571.

Taylor, P., & Pettit, J. (2007). Learning and teaching participation through action research: Experiences from an innovative masters programme. *Action Research, 5*, 231.

TDA. (2009). *Strategy for the professional development of the children's workforce in schools 2009–12*. London: Training and Development Agency.

TTA. (2005). *The teacher training agency's role in the future of continuing professional development: Response to the Secretary of State*. London: Teacher Training Agency.

Zeichner, K. (2003). Teacher research and professional development. *Educational Action Research, 11*(2), 301–326.

Chapter 11
Workplace Learning in Pre-service Teacher Education: An English Case Study

Olwen McNamara, Jean Murray and Marion Jones

Introduction

We noted at the beginning of Chap. 1 the almost ideological zeal apparent in the English Government's highly partisan approach to the theory-practice divide in the education of pre-service teachers. The recent intensified drive to locate teacher professional learning more centrally in the classroom was, we noted in Chap. 1, to be led by a raft of outstanding Teaching Schools (Gove 2010). Yet the central vehicle for the delivery of the Government's ambitious proposals for pre-service teacher education is not the Teaching Schools but a new and untested training route, School Direct, which at the time of writing has, in one year, been scaled up to deliver 25 % of pre-service teacher training in England.

This large-scale 'experiment' is by any standards a step change, even in the history of reform of English pre-service teacher education; but although radical it does not represent a discontinuous change. The direction of travel pursued in England by recent governments, of all political persuasions, has increasingly been towards a more extensively workplace model of pre-service teacher education. The recent acceleration in the rate of change is perhaps rendered more perplexing given that postgraduate pre-service teachers already spend two-thirds of their training in the workplace on professional placement (practicum). The logic is also baffling given the confidence reported at the time, by the government's own inspectorate of pre-service

O. McNamara (✉)
School of Education, The University of Manchester,
Manchester, UK
e-mail: olwen.mcnamara@manchester.ac.uk

J. Murray
University of East London,
London, UK
e-mail: j.m.f.murray@uel.ac.uk

M. Jones
Liverpool John Moores University,
Liverpool, UK
e-mail: M.Jones@ljmu.ac.uk

O. McNamara et al. (eds.), *Workplace Learning in Teacher Education,*   183
Professional Learning and Development in Schools and Higher Education 10,
DOI 10.1007/978-94-007-7826-9_11, © Springer Science+Business Media Dordrecht 2014

teacher education, in the quality of university-based training routes compared to school-based routes: 'There was more outstanding initial teacher education delivered by higher education-led partnerships than by school-centred initial teacher training partnerships and employment-based routes' (Ofsted 2010, p. 59). We ponder later whether there is any evidence that a further increase in the proportion of practice-based training (over and above the two-thirds currently mandated) will automatically and inevitably lead to better quality learning for pre-service teachers; whether the ideologically based policy imperatives have created a disarticulation between rhetoric and reality in relation to quality principles in allocation and provision; and, whether system failure in the training sector or the teacher supply model is in danger of being triggered by this near seismic change.

There is also to be considered the question of whether this model of policy development and implementation represents good practice in the governance of such a vital element of our public sector provision as developing a high performing school system. As noted in Chap. 1, nowhere is this more explicitly articulated than in the highly influential McKinsey Report (2007), which claims that two of the three key characteristics of high performing school systems internationally relate directly to the quality of teacher pre-service education. The third relates to high expectations, teacher knowledge and understanding, and self-awareness about beliefs and (best) practices, informed by the international evidence base relating to effective teaching and learning.

National league tables and international audit data from surveys such as those undertaken by the Organisation for Economic Co-operation and Development (OECD 2011), and based on evidence from their systematic Programme for International Student Assessment (PISA), have brought education, and specifically pupil performance, into sharp focus. In England this has meant that, over the last 30 years, pre-service teacher education has become as highly politicised as the school sector. Some ascribe the move of teacher education from relative obscurity to strategic significance to an assumption, on the part of the successive governments, that pre-service teacher education was an effective mechanism to transform teacher professionalism and steer change in the school curriculum (Furlong 2001, 2005). We will briefly rehearse now a little of the relatively recent history of pre-service teacher education in England and consider what the key drivers of system change have been.

The English Context

Pre-service teacher education in England had its origins in the poverty of the nineteenth century elementary school system, from whence pupil-teacher apprenticeship training developed. In the late 1800s specialist, and mostly, denominational colleges emerged, independent of the university system, to become the main training route for elementary school teachers. The establishment of the day-training colleges, under the auspices of universities in 1890, aimed to strengthen this elementary training system and was the first point at which teacher education moved to the university sector (Gardner 1993). As they evolved into university departments of education in the 1920s, the university based day-training colleges opted out of training elementary school teachers, preferring to focus instead on the emerging market of the elite secondary school state system and the independent school sector. This early, and temporary, divorce of the college and university traditions in teacher education meant that by the 1930s the latter was established as a secondary-focused, elite, and minority but influential, training sector in which teachers followed one-year postgraduate courses after completing university degrees. In the former 'college of education' system, primary (elementary) school teachers, most of them women, followed a two-year Teacher's Certificate. This training was reformed and extended in the latter half of the twentieth century so that all primary school teachers studied for Bachelor of Education degrees (Alexander 1984; Thomas 1990). Mandatory training was phased in and became compulsory for all primary and secondary teachers by the mid-1970s. Over the next 15 years, already fearful of the regulatory excesses of the government, colleges of education entered into institutional mergers with universities and polytechnics (which became universities in 1992). In part this was in the hope, or expectation, that increased protection would be offered by alliance with these larger independent institutions. This proved misguided. Not only was pre-service teacher education not protected from government centralising tendencies but colleges, having lost their institutional autonomy, struggled to establish their credibility within the somewhat contemptuous wider academy. This was not least because education, a field rather than a discipline, lacked a unique specialist knowledge base to underpin its values, principles and practical judgements. It grew instead to rely on the application of the 'foundation disciplines' of psychology, philosophy, history and sociology to create its practical professional knowledge base (Nixon et al. 2000; Gardener and Cunningham 1998), but as a result, some would argue, teacher education became increasingly academic and its relationship with practical teaching skills became extremely tenuous (Bell 1981).

The centralising tendencies which first emerged during the Thatcher conservative governments of the 1980s were constituted in the seminal 1988 Education Reform Act (DES 1988). Although the Act did not legislate directly in the area of pre-service teacher education, it was hugely influential, setting in motion significant and far-reaching changes to the school system—such as allowing them the option of release from local authority control and establishing local management of schools—that are still currently unfolding. The Act also importantly introduced the National Curriculum and 'Key Stages' of schooling and prepared the way for national testing by establishing objectives that children should achieve at the end of each key stage. The stage was set for the accountability and performativity culture to flourish. Over the next decade it became endemic across education, and indeed much of the public sector, growing apace during the conservative governments of the 1990s. It was further intensified when 'New Labour' took office in 1997. Professionalism, now largely determined by externally prescribed standards of conduct and performance, underwent a transformation from 'inside-out' to 'outside-in' (Stronach et al. 2002).

The last 30 years have also been a period of unremitting change for the pre-service teacher education sector in relation to the scope, pace and increasingly radical nature of the reform agenda. For pre-service teacher education, the establishment of the Council for the Accreditation of Teacher Education in 1984 was a key watershed; introducing the notion of accreditation it was the first major state intervention into pre-service teacher training. A decade later plans were announced to replace the Council with the Teacher Training Agency.[1] The move from 'Council' to 'Agency' signalled a change in the governance of teacher education, and the formal re-designation of the process from 'education' to 'training' augured a profound ideological shift (Wilkin 1999) as we shall hear later.

The Agency, as we will dub it, only had jurisdiction in England (other than for some of its teacher recruitment functions which extended to Wales). We will digress briefly to note that it was around the point of the creation of the Agency that education policy across the UK began to diverge markedly. Scotland had always maintained different educational traditions, but there was also a trend toward increasing divergence of education policy-making in Wales and Northern Ireland in the run up to the devolution (in 1999) of significant executive and legislative powers to the Welsh and Northern Irish Assemblies and the Scottish Parliament. It should also be mentioned that independent teacher regulatory bodies—'General Teaching Councils'—were created in England, Northern Ireland and Wales soon after Labour came to power in the late 1990s. They were modelled on the General Teaching Council Scotland, which was established in 1965, and, as we shall see in Chap. 12, developed to be a very powerful and well-respected professional body. The General Teaching Councils in Northern Ireland and Wales have also prospered as independent professional bodies with a remit to enhance the status of the teaching profession and promote high standards of professional conduct and practice. The General Teaching Council England was not so much admired by the workforce, and its fate we shall relate below.

Meanwhile in England, in the mid-1990s, the new Agency was becoming established; its wide-ranging remit was to include teacher recruitment, quality control/assurance and funding, and accreditation of training routes and subsequently teacher professional development. The proposals attracted much opposition (Edwards 1994). Pressing ahead with its reform agenda, the Agency survived its first turbulent years: a change of government; concerns raised in parliament about the impact of ongoing change and the rigorous and punitive inspection regime on the resilience of the pre-service teacher education sector (HoC 1999); a mounting teacher supply crisis; and a national debacle over an ill-conceived continuing professional development policy (Gilroy 1998). During New Labour's second term in the early 2000s, there was a slight plateauing in the rate of change in the pre-service teacher education sector, and efforts were focused instead upon the remodelling of the school workforce (DfES 2003) more directly (Gunter 2007). The remit of the Agency was widened in 2005 to encompass the training and development for the whole school workforce, but universities, and pre-service teacher education specifically, did not feature as a partner in the government's strategy to drive up standards

---

[1] In 2005 the Agency became known as the Training and Development Agency; from April 2012 as the Teaching Agency; and from April 2013 as the National College for Teaching and Leadership.

(DfES 2002a, 2004). Pre-service teacher education was, it seems, taking a back seat, and as Furlong (2005, p. 132) reflected, 'the last 30 years may have been uncomfortable for many of us, but at least there was an arena in which to engage [. . .] the end of the era is to be regretted'.

Five years on the apprehension generated by the emergence of a new arena in which *not to engage* was perhaps regretted even more poignantly when Michael Gove, the incoming Secretary of State for Education, announced his intention to 'reform teacher training to shift trainee teachers out of college and into the classroom' (DfE 2010). This followed the peremptory announcement, two weeks earlier, of the abolition of the General Teaching Council England, a little over ten years after it had been created. An already over-regulated profession put up little resistance to the loss of an organisation that had not won the battle for hearts and minds (Shepherd 2010). If not the outcome, then the manner of its departure sent shock waves through the teacher education sector because of the lack of due process in relation to consultation and decision-making, as did the Schools White Paper (DfE 2010). Four other pre-service teacher education-focused documents followed in close succession and made reassuring noises about the continuing role of universities in the process: 'Training our Next Generation of Teachers: improvement strategy for discussion' (DfE 2011a), and Implementation Plan (DfE 2011b); a parliamentary Education Committee Report on the Training of Teachers (HoC 2012); and a government response (DfE 2012b). The positive messages were unfortunately completely undermined when, in June 2012, a 'government source' was reported in the Daily Telegraph as saying: 'For too long left-wing training colleges have imbued teachers with useless teaching theories that don't work and actively damage children's education'. The article went on to report that ministers were 'also planning to slash the number of students on university-based courses over the next three years—half shifting to on-the-job training in schools by 2015. The worst training colleges will be shut altogether' (Patton 2012).

Drivers of Change: 1984–2013

From the preceding, albeit brief, résumé of the main landmarks on the pre-service teacher education landscape, we will identify what have been the key drivers of systemic change in the pre-service teacher education sector since the 1984 watershed referred to earlier.

First, the professional certification of teachers: this was initiated by the Council for Accreditation of Teacher Education who developed a skill-based competences assessment framework and sought to make recommendations about the content of teacher education courses, the links between subject study and the needs of schools, and academic entry requirements (Reid 1985). The incoming Agency replaced the competences, developed by its predecessor, with a set of outcome standards. The first version of the resultant Qualified Teacher Status standards, badged as a National Curriculum for Initial Teacher Training (DfEE 1998a), was 'imposed' on the sector in 1998 (Hextall and Mahony 2000). It prescribed, in unbelievable detail, standards for assessment of pre-service teachers, and also specified an exhaustive catalogue of subject knowledge requirements for all training routes and raised questions about whether beginning teachers were being trained as classroom technicians rather than autonomous professionals able to respond appropriately in complex and unpredictable situations. Since their inception the Qualified Teacher Status standards have undergone several revisions (DfES 2002b; DCFS 2007; DfE 2012a), each one thankfully less prescriptive than the previous; the latter two versions encompassing a full and coherent set of National Professional Standards for the teaching profession. Although the outcome standards had slimmed down, the pre-service teacher education curriculum content continued to increase, causing an intensification of pressure on the already limited and reducing non-practice based time available. Pre-service teachers were required to broaden their key focus on the academic curriculum to encompass outcomes such as community cohesion, safety and health; as well as developing an understanding of an extended range of professional contexts, from working with others in the classroom to working in multi-professional teams on specialist services including policing, childcare, parenting and family support.

Second, the accreditation of routes into teaching: this covered requirements for entry into training programmes and the regulation of training providers' management of partnership, recruitment and selection, and planning and delivery of training. These regulatory mechanisms have been mobilised over the years to make pre-service training more school-focused starting with the prescription of minimum periods of school-based training (DES 1984, 1989). Latterly, as school-based training developed into a full university-school partnership model, mandated regulation became more comprehensive and minimum lengths of school-based training periods increased. Accreditation has also been used to diversify training provision to include school-based routes and later the introduction of School-Centred Initial Teacher Training (DFE 1993). The new routes were also intended to widen and diversify the pool of applicants to teaching. Initially these interventions had very limited impact; in 1991 the first national survey of training provision (Modes of Teacher Education) found that 99 % of pre-service teachers still followed traditional routes offered through universities and colleges of education (Barrett et al. 1992). Even a decade later the overall percentage of teachers trained through higher education institution-led routes had not changed significantly (Furlong et al. 2000). School-based programmes were re-launched by the Agency in 1998, under the umbrella of 'Employment Based Initial Teacher Training', and the proportion of pre-service teachers (predominantly secondary) following these routes increased to around 20 % by the late 2000s. The most recently launched generic route is School Direct, and we will return to consider this in detail later.

A number of focused training routes have also been launched (DfE 2010), such as Troops to Teaching and Teach Next (for highly skilled and professional career changes). The most significant, however, has undoubtedly been Teach First, a small and elite hybrid employment-based route endorsed by the political elite of all persuasions. Modelled on 'Teach for America' it was developed for high-flying graduates willing to commit to teaching in schools facing complex and multiple disadvantage for a minimum of two years. The Teach First model was built on a quintessentially

New Labour 'third-way' politics, sponsored by high status corporate and social enterprise organisations: participants who left teaching could become ambassadors for the programme and continue to contribute to the mission in other ways. Established in London in 2002, and rolled out regionally from 2006, it trained 1,000 students in 2012/2013 (around 2.5 % of new entrants to teaching) but is set to rise to 1,500 by 2014/2015. Not currently established in the UK outside England (although plans to launch in Wales in 2013/2014 are underway), the model has expanded to numerous European and Commonwealth countries under the 'Teach for All' banner.

Third, the management of the inspection process: just as legislation was deployed to focus the content of pre-service teacher education, so inspection was mobilised to ensure that providers were 'on message'. From 1994 this role was undertaken by the recently reorganised schools' inspectorate, Ofsted (Office for Standards in Education), and the change heralded an era of 'surveillance and control' that professed greater transparency, validity and consistency of judgements across contexts and between inspectors. Lack of confidence was, however, expressed in the piloting, evaluation and rigour of the evidence base for judgements (Gilroy and Wilcox 1997) and the validity and reliability of the process (Grahamand Nabb 1999). Early rounds of inspections came thick and fast. An increasing focus on partnership became apparent, both in relation to recruitment and selection and the planning and delivery of training. Inspections were also planned to coincide with curriculum change, such as the introduction of the National (Numeracy and Literacy) Strategies in the late 1990s. Inspections are still being planned strategically to focus the sector on nationally defined goals, as evidenced by the 'Unannounced focused monitoring inspections', undertaken as part of the 2012 Initial Teacher Education Inspection Framework and in which 'Inspectors will focus on trainees' skills in teaching early reading using systematic synthetic phonics'(Ofsted 2012).

Fourth, the development of the audit and accountability culture: in line with a current UK audit trend of using National Student Survey data to rank universities' undergraduate courses, the Agency undertakes an annual survey of newly qualified teachers. The survey garners perceptions of how well prepared the newly qualified teachers feel by various aspects of their training programmes. The aggregated sector data from the survey is used to set national training priorities and strategy. The data is also used as a key evidence source in inspection and monitoring of individual training providers and is factored into national league tables for ranking providers, despite deep concerns about the survey methodology and the currency of the data (McNamara et al. 2012). The Agency's own inspection unit has also assumed a more explicit and prominent role in the policing of compliance and standards. Most particularly with regard to systematic synthetic phonics—the method of teaching early reading that has been nationally prescribed, despite a dearth of evidence that it is an effective method (Wyse and Goswami 2008). Additionally, in 2008, the Agency introduced an annual monitoring exercise which required all teacher training providers to submit a self-evaluation of each programme they delivered, identifying its strengths and weaknesses and its capacity to improve. No formal evaluation of this process has yet been commissioned, although an independent study concluded overwhelmingly that the process added hugely to workload, did not lead to better trainee outcomes and was not cost-effective (McNamara et al. 2012).

Fifth, the control of allocations and funding: providers' Ofsted quality grades are linked to allocations, along with their recruitment and employment performance and other factors such as geographic and denominational distribution. Although these principles are presented as a systematic and transparent allocations methodology, ideological drivers could be deduced from the steadily rising numbers on the employment-based Graduate Teacher Programme during the 2000s, despite a series of improving, but still less than favourable, survey inspection reports (inter alia Ofsted 2007). The Graduate Teacher Programme has now been axed in favour of the development of the new School Direct training route, and the various ramifications of this will be discussed in more detail below.

Learning in the Workplace: Adaptive or Developmental?

Let us first turn to the ideological position informing the government's recent reforms of pre-service teacher education in England: that teaching 'is a craft and it is best learnt as an apprentice, observing a master craftsman or woman'. This model, presented by Gove (2010), has much in common with that of the 'pupil-teacher' apprenticeship training used from 1846 until its reform in 1870. For apprentice pupil-teachers:

> training and education took place at their elementary schools under the supervision of the headmaster, but after the Elementary Education Act 1870 their instruction was undertaken at separate establishments called pupil-teacher centres, run by local school boards, with teaching practice at their elementary schools (www.nationalarchives.gov.uk/records/research-guides/teachers.htm Accessed 10/10/12).

In practice, secondary-level personal education was made available to all apprentice pupil-teachers and, if successful, they progressed to some limited professional education in day centres. However, there is much evidence that many young people, especially those from remote working class communities, could not access much, if any, of this provision. Hence the apprenticeship route—in all its main features including most professional education taking place in schools—was still in existence well into the twentieth century. Importantly, however, the political endorsement of total emersion in the workplace as a training model lasted only 25 years, before a more formal academic and professional education away from the workplace was understood to be needed.

In England, the first example of this training being undertaken in an academic setting was at Owens College (later to become the University of Manchester) which—in 1890 (for men) and 1892 (for women)—opened Day Training Centres (DTC).

> Trainee teachers studied standard academic subjects alongside professional subjects such as the history and philosophy of education and educational administration. DTC staff were keen that training should include a significant amount of classroom teaching. Manchester's School Board proved supportive, opening its elementary schools to students, but there was an emerging consensus among educationists that the best experience was gained at so-called "demonstration schools". These schools, usually administered directly or indirectly by the

training colleges, were specially designed for trainee teachers to allow them to engage critically with the theories they had learnt in the lecture rooms through practical experience of teaching children. This concept had proved successful in Germany and the U.S.A, but Owens College, fearful of the administrative and financial burdens of running such a school, initially proved resistant to the idea. (http://archiveshub.ac.uk/data/gb133-fed.txt)

By way of a personal anecdote, 120 years later, the University of Manchester was invited by the Department of Education to open just such a Demonstration School (now rebadged as a University Training School, see Chap. 1) and their response was exactly the same!

'Sitting by Nellie', which even in the nineteenth century did not last long as a model for teacher training, was premised on the notion of learning through apprenticeship. Lave and Wenger's (1991) brief accounts of apprenticeship learning shows that the social practice model of learning-by-doing was effective amongst midwives and tailors, but for naval quartermasters and meat cutters the apprenticeship incorporated a more formal training structure. Lave and Wenger think of apprenticeship as a form of 'legitimate peripheral participation', which:

> provides a way to speak about the relations newcomers and old-timers, and about activities, identities, artefacts and communities of knowledge and practice. It concerns a process by which newcomers become part of a community of practice. A person's intentions to learn are engaged and the meaning of learning is configured through the process of becoming a full participant in sociocultural practice. (Lave and Wenger 1991, p. 29)

The main principle of 'legitimate peripheral participation' is that learning occurs incrementally as the learner increases the extent of their participation in and with the expert's role and activities. This situated learning, perceived of as a social practices model, is focused upon the newcomer gaining access to a 'community of practice'. This is an 'adaptive' model of learning (Ellström 2001) where the learner (in this case the pre-service teacher) gradually masters or comes to replicate the behaviours of the master (in this case the school-based mentor). It is worth noting at this point that this places pre-service teachers centrally in the very location where styles of practice and standards of performance are apparently seen by government as in need of change. Of the 5,000 schools inspected in 2010/2011only 4 % of teaching in primary schools and 3 % of teaching in secondary schools was outstanding (Ofsted 2011, p. 51). Let us for the moment set aside, however, the concern that 'experts' or master craftsmen and women appear not to be in plentiful supply in the nation's schools, and consider another flaw in the argument. That is, the assumption that teaching and learning to teach is essentially a 'craft' rather than an 'intellectual' activity. Edwards and Protheroe (2003, p. 232) argue that 'The challenges facing a participatory version of teacher education are complex. Student teachers need to develop a generality of knowing which will enable them to interpret new teaching situations and see the pedagogic potential in them'. The adaptive model, however, is one that privileges performativity and practical knowledge over theoretical, pedagogical, subject and curriculum knowledge, and knowledge about learners and learning.

To reflect further upon whether the adaptive model of training is appropriate for twenty-first century pre-service teachers we need to consider the nature of the role for which they are being prepared. To do this let us return to answer the questions we first posed in Chap. 1, when framing our thinking about returning to a model of pre-service teacher education predominantly grounded in the workplace: is it the 'same' learning, the 'same' place, the 'same' work? We interrogate the concept of 'sameness' in two respects. First, is it the 'same' now as it was in the nineteenth century; and, second, is it the 'same' across the sector in the twenty-first century. We will, for the sake of brevity, not return to the first of these and the debate begun in Chap. 1 about the cyclical nature of education policy and practice and sameness and difference of work and place and even learning since the Victorian era. It is the second of these interpretations that we focus on, and that is particularly relevant to the development of our argument. Reviewing the evidence we believe that, in England at least, there are very significant differences in workplaces across the sector in all respects. The case appears to be compelling. The deregulatory forces, which started in the early 2000s with the introduction of the Specialist Schools and Academies Trust and the remodelling of the workforce under the New Labour Government (DfES 2003), became significantly more radical with the rapid expansion of the Academies Programme in 2010, when the new (Conservative/Liberal Democrat) Coalition Government assumed power. The Academies Bill, rushed through in 2010, made it possible for all publically funded schools in England to become Academies, and by September 2012 over 50 % of secondary schools, but less than 5 % of primary schools, had become or applied to become academies (DfE 2012c). Academies are funded directly by the State and, it is argued, freed from local authority control they will be empowered 'to innovate and raise standards'.[2]

Thus, as argued in Chap. 1, although there are many continuities in relation to the basic essentials of learning for pupils as well as for teachers' work, there have been some radical changes resulting from the reconfiguration of the school system which has caused fragmentation and diversification and had significant impact on the workplace learning landscape.

First, in terms of work settings, traditional school boundaries have become blurred in the new and significantly different designations of schools (Academies and Free/Technical/Studio Schools), and challenge the meaning of 'place' of employment. For example, national chains of (Academy) schools have been established and new models of school governance have emerged which link multiple schools in Alliances and Federations. Traditional understanding of what constitutes a school and the parameters of its activities have been questioned, through initiatives such as New Labour's Extended Schools Programme (2006–2011). Such schools provide a range of services and activities, beyond the school day, to meet the needs of children, their families and the wider community.

Second, in terms of working practices, Academies (and Free Schools) can set their own pay and conditions for staff which may involve varying the length of the school day and term. The re-modelling of the workforce (DfES 2003) has meant that, in all schools, traditional professional boundaries between teachers and paraprofessionals (such as teaching assistants) have been eroded (Gunter 2007). Local practices can

---

[2] See www.education.gov.uk/schools/leadership/typesofschools/academies/b00205692/whatisanacademy. Accessed 10 October 2012.

require teachers to work in cross-professional teams and engage in multi-agency work, such as with social and health care workers. Increasing numbers of hybrid educators are now working in and across school and higher education boundaries. Universities in England were invited to open University Training Schools (DfE 2010) modelled on Finnish Practice Schools, (see Chap. 16).

Third, in terms of learning, there has been a shift in location of initial and continuing professional learning from the university to the school, with an increase in interest in the learning that occurs outside structured, pre-determined curricula and a need to be prepared to teach radically different curricula and undertake ever more varied roles. In terms of the learning context there are very significant and increasing differences between schools. Academies (and Free Schools) have been permitted to disapply the National Curriculum for pupils and offer a bespoke curriculum. These schools are also permitted to employ teachers without any professional certification and this, needless to say, has significant implications for initial training and continuing professional learning. But it is important to note that such schools are still subject to the same performativity agendas around pupil learning levels and the same inspection frameworks.

We thus observe in England a rapid deregulation of school governance, the curriculum and teacher certification, and a freeing of the school system from local control and accountability. The school sector is set to become increasingly disparate and fragmented in terms of curriculum and pedagogic practices, and it is clear that there is a considerable need for both pre-service and in-service teachers to be more versatile in terms of their skill set, knowledge base and pedagogic practices.

In terms of the locus of professional learning, pre-service teacher education is, as we have noted, progressively being moved from the universities into the school sector. The same is also true of in-service education for teachers. Of the £ 25–30 million annually of government funding that has been available over the last decade for in-service teachers to draw upon for supporting professional learning (Christie et al. 2012), there now remains just a £ 2 million National Scholarship Fund. Thus, for the majority of serving teachers, professional learning is also in-house.

We therefore see a dichotomy emerging between training model and training needs: the former being 'adaptive learning' and the latter 'developmental learning' (Ellström 2001). Both pre-service and in-service teacher learning has become adaptive, focused on replicating behaviours in particular practice schools: 'the way we do it here'. Yet there is a need for teacher learning to be developmental, based on inquiry or investigative methods in order that teachers develop and extend their skill sets to meet the varied curriculum and practice needs that afford them the flexibility to move from school to school. Engeström (2004, p. 145) argues for 'a new generation of expertise around, not based on supreme and supposedly stable individual knowledge and ability, but on the capacity of working communities to cross boundaries, negotiate and improvise'. The need for new expertise identified by Engeström has been exacerbated in England by the current fragmentation and diversification of the school system.

Partnership: The Contested Space

Partnership, and specifically the university–school based partnership, has been at the core of all reform in England over the last 30 years or more. Crozier et al. (1990, p. 54) were very prophetic in 1990 when they identified it as 'the site of an ideological struggle'. We chart it through what we characterise as four distinct eras. In the late 1980s/early 1990s 'voluntary partnerships' of schools and universities had already begun to establish formal agreements: the Oxford Internship Scheme (Benton 1990) launched in 1987 was one such ground-breaking initiative. Crozier et al.'s (1990) study of pre-service education partnerships at the time identifies partnership not as locating 'the greater good for all' (ibid, p. 44), but as 'slippery and imprecise' (ibid, p. 53). They view it as a 'complex, problematic and heavily ideological phenomena . . . the site of an ideological struggle' (ibid, p. 54). Once it moved into an era of 'pre-scribed partnership' (DFE Circular 14/93, 1993a) many providers challenged what they saw as the government's simplistic depiction of the trainee developing practical skills in schools and subject knowledge in the university (inter alia, Edwards 1995). They argued that the changes had reinforced 'hierarchical relations' and the 'demarcation of practice in schools from educational theory' (Dunne et al. 1996, p. 41). Furlong et al. (2000) identified a continuum in partnership models from entirely university-led to entirely school-led. Both models, they argued, had undermined the concept of partnership. Partnership underwent another transformation in 1998 (DfEE 1998a) with the introduction of the first set of standards and raised expectations of partnership. This was exacerbated by a concurrent teacher supply crisis and ensuing rapid increase of 40 % (between 1998 and 2004) in training numbers. This brought with it very well-founded concerns about the capacity and capability of the school system to deliver good quality training, and a number of interventions were planned which 'commodified partnership' and marketed it to schools. These included a network of Training Schools (DfEE 1998b) and a National Partnership Project (2001–2005) which developed and disseminated good practice and promoted pre-service teacher education partnership.

Furlong et al. (2006, p. 33) claimed that despite substantial international interest, England and Wales still remain the only countries where pre-service education 'partnership has become institutionalised at a national level as a core principle of provision'. Six years on there have been moves to institute more formal partnership models elsewhere in the UK, in Scotland for example (see Chap. 12), but the extent of mandated regulation in relation to partnership working in England still remains wholly exceptional. Brisard et al. (2005, p. 50), in a review of partnership across the UK, suggested that the 'detachment of some forms of entry away from the university sector perhaps reflects the relatively low standing of teaching within the English culture'. This detachment, and the development of the Qualified Teacher Status standards, also caused a bifurcation between academic and professional teaching qualifications. Indeed a small but significant proportion of teachers enter the profession through non-academic (Qualified Teacher Status-only) routes; most of these would have followed employment-based routes.

The ascendancy of School Direct routes are now catapulting England into a new 'market-led partnership' model. To recap the (albeit brief) history of the reform to date is as follows: (1) in autumn 2010 the 'Importance of Teaching' (DfE 2010) White Paper announced the move of pre-service training into schools led by a raft of outstanding Teaching Schools; (2) in autumn 2011 the 'Training our Next Generation of Outstanding Teachers: implementation plan' (DfE 2011b) announced the launch of the School Direct training route, with 500 places in 2012/2013, to rise sharply in response to school market; (3) in autumn 2012 it was clear that less than 400 of the nearly 900 School Direct places, that had in the event been allocated, were filled; (4) in autumn 2012, despite the first cohort having recruited badly and having barely embarked upon their training, the places allocated to School Direct, which now included School Direct Salaried (a new employment-based version) were increased ten-fold. After slight adjustments during the recruitment cycle the position in August 2013 was that 9,500 places had been allocated to School Direct (just over one-third of these to the Salaried route[3]); representing 25 % of the total 38,900 training places[4] (DfE 2013). The uptake of School Direct in the primary sector was low at around one-third of the total and, as we will hear later, highest in the secondary shortage subjects. At the end of the recruitment cycle, as this book goes to press, the level of uptake to School Direct places looks to be around 50 %[5] which if it continues will be sufficient to trigger a supply crisis in secondary shortage subjects in coming years.

School Direct is a market-led model in which schools recruit and train pre-service teachers with a view to subsequently employing them. Schools bid to the Agency for places, having entered into a training partnership with a provider of their choice; of the 2013/2014 cohort (currently recruiting), 70 % chose to enter into a training agreement with university partners. The £ 9,000 training fee is split by agreement between individual schools and training providers. The route is riven with tensions and incongruities, including: (1) the difficulty that individual schools, or even alliances of schools, have in being able to predict with any certainty their employment needs two years in advance (one year for the recruitment and selection cycle and one for training); (2) the impracticality of policing the destination of pre-service teachers and penalising schools' failure to employ them at the end of their training; and (3) perhaps the greatest concern, however, is the lack of quality control measures or quality assurance processes built into the design of the routes. Noble-Rogers (2012), Chief Executive Officer of the Universities' Council for the Education of Teachers, speaking at a University and College Union conference, observed 'The hard won link between quality of provision and ITT [initial teacher training] allocations, as set out in the 1994 Education Act, has been largely abandoned' and he quoted the conclusion from the Parliamentary Select Committee report (HoC 2012) on teacher training:

---

[3] This reflects a very large shift from School Direct Salaried back to non-salaried as schools began to work out the economics of the funding scheme.

[4] Of the remainder 51 % (20,000) were allocated to university postgraduate routes, 6 % (2,500) to school-based postgraduate routes, 17 % (6,800) to university undergraduate routes (virtually all primary and accounting for nearly 30 % of primary numbers).

[5] Howson (2013) personal communication.

'The evidence has left us in little doubt that partnership between schools and universities is likely to provide the highest quality initial teacher education, the content of which will involve significant school experience but include theoretical and research elements as well . . . '; and 'We believe that a diminution of universities' role in teacher training could bring considerable demerits, and would caution against it . . . '. (www.ucet.ac.uk/4370, Accessed 1 December 2012)

The New Learning Landscape: Impact on Workforce Planning, University Departments, Teacher Educators and Learners

Any institutional risk analysis of such rapid and untested change in the approach to workforce planning and pre-service training and funding models would be almost bound to incur a rating of both 'high impact' and 'likely to happen'. The potential casualties include: the university teacher education sector, teacher learning, teacher supply, and ultimately pupil learning. If questioned as to what actions he had effected to mitigate this high level of risk to the supply of trained teachers, the Secretary of State for Education would undoubtedly have responded that he first took the precaution of ensuring that the majority of secondary schools were no longer required to employ trained teachers. And that although most primary schools (not having taken the academy route) were still required to employ trained teachers, the supply was unlikely to be jeopardised because of significant over subscription and because as a generalist training model it was likely to remain viable.

We will now consider in more detail the risks deriving from School Direct but also more generally from the politics that have increasingly striated the landscape that defines teacher education in England. First we look at the potential threat at a national level to the supply of trained teachers.

- The reforms have put the security of the regional/subject workforce planning models at risk. There is no mechanism to stop a heavily skewed geographic distribution occurring, since School Direct allocations have been awarded on demand and the remaining places have been distributed on the basis of quality indicators, rather than demographic considerations. This is of particular note because the average age of pre-service teachers has increased significantly over the last decade and evidence indicates that, particularly in the current economic conditions, mature pre-service teachers (with partners, houses and families) often lack the mobility to move for employment (Howson and McNamara 2012).
- Demand/allocation to the School Direct routes has been high for priority subjects such as mathematics (43 % of all training places), chemistry (44 %), and physics (50 %). This is of particular concern because the supply pool to these shortage subjects is, to a significant degree, dependent on subject knowledge enhancement courses run by universities to upskill applicants prior to training. The courses can be up to one year in length and deferring training for such a period does not align well with School Direct routes. Additionally, the viability of the enhancement

courses are threatened because of reduced demand and because many universities have now lost their own core allocations in these subjects. If not addressed, this will quickly lead to an increased level of shortage in the teacher supply to these crucial subjects.

- Finally, as reported above, recruitment and selection has so far proved a challenge; contributory factors include a late start in the first year and annual changes to the application system. To add to that, the process is immensely resource-intensive for the sector, requiring in most cases two interviews for each applicant (who may hold multiple concurrent applications). Finally, the school year does not align well with secondary phase recruitment patterns, which characteristically, continue well into June/July—when schools are winding down for the summer break.

Second, we look at the institutional level at the vulnerability of courses and whole departments.

- Increasing selectivity in research/postgraduate research funding has meant that predominantly pre-service teacher education is not undertaken in research intensive universities and, where it is, a bifurcation is often apparent between research and teaching (Gilroy and McNamara 2009). Such loss of research capacity, we shall argue later, weakens the sector's case for its unique contribution to teacher education (Murray et al. 2009).
- There has been a loss of government funding to the university sector for postgraduate professional development for teachers amounting, as noted earlier, to between £ 25 and £ 30 million a year. This weakens the sector's potential to capitalise upon a more centrally school-based partnership able to develop a more integrated workplace professional learning community (Christie et al. 2012).
- Historically the lack of professional control, resulting from the increased level of centralisation and politicisation of teacher education, has led to a vulnerability of programmes to political whim and left institutions with reduced capacity and capability to engage fully in the quasi market place. Innovation, where it is occurring, is often incoherent, reactive and not sustainable (McNamara et al. 2009).
- Many secondary programmes were unsustainable even before School Direct emerged, because of a demographic downturn in secondary pupil numbers meaning that there has, overall, been a 35 % reduction in secondary pre-service teacher allocations since 2009/10. Additionally, the cuts have been concentrated in certain subjects (e.g. Art and Design, Music, Business Studies) which are thus already very vulnerable (Christie et al. 2012).
- The new allocation methodology sees places divided into core (those allocated by the Agency directly to universities/other training providers) and School Direct. Core numbers are still allocated using quality criteria; providers deemed 'good' and 'satisfactory' (now designated 'requiring improvement') by the inspection regime are no longer guaranteed core allocations, and the core allocations of 'outstanding' providers are only secure until 2014/2015. In the 2013/2014 allocations 'good' and 'satisfactory' providers only received training places remaining after

the 'outstanding' providers and School Direct numbers had been allocated. So, for example, all 'good' and 'satisfactory' providers lost all of their core English training provision (54 % of the training places went to School Direct and the remaining 46 % to 'outstanding' providers). In terms of institutional losses of core places overall, the greatest sustained was 70 %, the next 50 % and another six were over 30 %. The six greatest loses were all sustained by research intensive universities, adding further to the concerns voiced in bullet one above (UCU 2012).

- The rapid increase in School Direct places may well undermine the capacity in the school system to support other school-based and employment-based training routes (such as Teach First) and placements for university-based postgraduate and undergraduate routes.
- The School Direct route, because of the small-scale of the enterprise (dealing often with individual pre-service teachers), is extremely resource-intensive in terms of both tutor time and to administer, for both schools and universities—especially, as noted above, for the recruitment and selection process. Additionally, the market dynamic will inevitably drive down the proportion of funding going to universities, as schools attempt to negotiate the best deal possible for themselves.
- The recently revised inspection framework (Ofsted 2012) which has increased expectations and reduced notice time (from eight weeks to 48 hours), meaning that more provision is likely to be found wanting. There are also serious risks pertaining to the unannounced focused inspections, as mentioned earlier.

Third, we look at the vulnerability of the teacher educator workforce.

- Even before the School Direct routes came on the horizon the staffing of teacher education departments was challenging because of the: heavy workload; long teaching year; extensive range of new knowledge and skills required, often including a requirement to undertake a higher degree; research and scholarly activity which was perceived to be threatening; and finally the disparity in salary expectation compared to the school sector.
- School Direct has put teacher educators in the position where they may be required to train pre-service teachers to teach subjects in which they (the tutors) have little or no expertise. Some tutors additionally, are being required to take on a significant extra workload—there being no cap on the number of School Direct places that universities can agree to train. Schools' choice of training provider will be made mindful, one can conjecture, of: cost, location, existing relationships and reputation (six universities recorded a potential increase of over 50 % in overall training numbers and two an increase of over 60 %) (UCU 2012).
- School Direct does not provide secure funding for a permanent staffing base in teacher education departments. Numbers of pre-service teachers will inevitably vary, perhaps significantly, year-on-year, and a loss of ability to plan strategically will lead to increased casualisation of the teacher education workforce.
- An increased casualisation of the staffing base will cause a loss of capacity and skill amongst the teacher educator workforce to cover the important elements of the curriculum, most particularly, the subject knowledge needed for both pre- and in-service teachers.

Fourth, we look at the quality of learning of the pre-service teacher which is in danger of being impoverished.

- There has been increased pressure on the pre-service curriculum in terms of the academic focus but also the broader pedagogic, personal and social outcomes over the last decade, as noted earlier. Additionally, for the primary curriculum, the mandated minimum school-based time was increased in the 2012 pre-service teacher training regulations (DfE 2012a) from 90 days to 120 days (bringing it into line with the requirement for secondary pre-service teachers). This leaves only 12 weeks outside the classroom in which primary pre-service teachers—who, as generalists, are required to have knowledge of up to 11 subjects—are in 'prepare and reflect mode' rather than in 'practice mode'.
- A highly questionable assumption underlies the School Direct models of teacher learning: that longer time spent in schools inevitably—and unproblematically— leads to better and more relevant learning for beginning teachers. There is no clear evidence for such an assumption and, indeed, England is on its own in Europe and in the UK in eroding the length and academic rigor of its teacher education programmes (Brisard et al. 2005), as we see illustrated elsewhere in this volume. Edwards and Protheroe (2003, p. 230) observe that 'participatory views of learning have considerable potential for understanding the learning of student teachers and developing school-based ITT. But this view should not be oversimplified into notions of learning by doing or "sitting by Nellie" '.
- As a result of new School Direct partnership arrangements, schools will take increasing responsibility for significant elements of professional and subject knowledge training, most probably with the support of online materials provided by university partners. Yet, as noted earlier, the learning experience will differ across the phases. Primary schools, in particular, because of their small staffing base and very restricted non-contact time for staff, have limited capability to support the extended learning of individual pre-service teachers. In this sense School Direct is an ineffective model for individual primary schools, both in terms of workforce planning and resourcing. This structural weakness is best addressed through a consolidating of the system into networks and training consortia, led perhaps by academy chains and Teaching Schools. This will also mitigate the isolation of individual pre-service learners who lack access to the intellectual stimulus derived from engaging with a critical community of peers and from sharing best practice.
- The disarticulation of professional (Qualified Teacher Status only) and academic qualifications (the Postgraduate Certificate of Education, targeted at master's level and encompassing Qualified Teacher Status) over a decade ago introduced a two track entry into teaching. The Qualified Teacher Status only qualification has been undertaken, almost exclusively, on employment-based routes into teaching and is arguably an intellectually impoverished option. Since their re-launch in 1999, most employment-based training routes have moved towards a more extensive training programme with an increased academic component, and have, as a

result, considerably increased their inspection quality ratings (McNamara et al. 2009). The introduction of the new School Direct routes has led to increased risk that, in the current economic climate, schools may opt for a professional-only qualification for their teachers, with the concomitant loss of any gains made in the quality of school-based training (even though, as noted earlier, school-based training still does not, according to inspection evidence, match the quality of university-led training programmes; Ofsted 2010, p. 59).

Finally we look at the quality control measures and quality assurance processes which are endangered in three respects.

- First, the suitability of the school as a training setting:[6] no restrictions have been imposed in allocating School Direct places, even schools 'requiring improvement' have been allocated training places. The outstanding Teaching School Alliances, strategic leads for pre- and in-service professional learning in the sector, accounted for only 40 % of School Direct places.
- Second, the suitability of the applicants to enter the profession: no academic qualifications/subject knowledge requirements (e.g. to have a good honours degree) have been specified.
- Third, the suitability of the training provider: no restrictions have been specified regarding the quality of training for School Direct places, and even providers that are designated 'requiring improvement' are permitted to be contracted as trainers. Additionally, there is no restriction on training providers regarding the number of School Direct trainees or provision of subject areas. Providers are not required to have a track record of training in a particular subject area, or staff with proven expertise in that area. Equally well, there is no incentive for schools to enter into training contracts with 'good' or 'outstanding' providers.

Where are We Now and Where to Next?

The past two decades of increasingly radical reform of pre-service teacher education in England have seen significant advances, most particularly in partnership practices, but there have been too many unhelpful consequences. First, the politicisation of teacher education has resulted in an increasing lack of professional control by training providers and left the beleaguered sector subject to short-termism and the vagaries of political ideology. This has resulted in instability and the vulnerability of programmes, departments and ultimately organisations, and there could be no better example of this than the School Direct initiative. Second, the intrusiveness of policy requirements, regulation and accountability has restricted professional engagement with the training process, engendered a technical rational approach to outcomes, and

---

[6] Only 57 % of schools were judged to be good or outstanding (Ofsted 2011, p. 39), compared to 94 % of pre-service teacher education provision (Ofsted 2011, p. 75).

created a culture of compliance. Albeit a culture in which the sector's infinite capacity to self-regulate is evident, as Foucault observes: 'governing people is not a way to force people to do what the governor wants; it is always a versatile equilibrium, with complementarity and conflicts between techniques which assure coercion and processes through which the self is constructed or modified by himself. (Foucault 1993, p. 204)' (McNamara et al. 2012). Third, ideologically determined reforms are often incoherent and subject to/underpinned by contrary values, principles and even regulatory forces. The latest quasi market-driven reforms, for example, have caused a disarticulation between the control (vested in schools) and accountability (vested in training providers) mechanisms in the system as well as, potentially, a significant widening of the fracture between professional-only and academic/professional accreditation. The latter is mirrored in the debate about the intellectual or craft-based nature of teacher knowledge and skills and evidenced in the latest guidance about School Direct (salaried) which indicates 'An academic award is not usually offered alongside the training but the training leads to QTS' (DfE 2013, p. 7). Fourth, despite the great advances England has made towards genuine university–school based partnerships, much activity has been reductionist and task focused, and it is unclear how much thinking has been directed towards the intellectual, philosophical and pedagogic mechanisms of partnership. There has also been a serious failure to capitalise on the significant contribution that pre-service teacher education could make to the continuing professional learning of teachers and school improvement (Hurd et al. 2007).

If the direction of travel with respect to School Direct is maintained, the shape of the training sector will undoubtedly change radically in the next few years as universities downsize provision or pull out of teacher education. The almost inevitable conclusions are that overall the changes will be associated with poorer quality provision and more impoverished pre-service teacher learning. It is the third point above, the bifurcation of professional and academic qualifications leading to the establishment of a two track entry into the profession, that perhaps presents the greatest threat to the quality of learning of the pre-service teacher; and to partnership that offers some possibility of hope.

Let us assume for the moment that the School Direct system, with all its design flaws and logistical problems, can be mended to respond flexibly and in a timely manner to school workforce demands for high quality staff and sustain a university sector with the capacity to deliver the training. Let us also assume that an immediate crisis in teacher supply will not be triggered and that, in time, the current hybrid system will develop into a full quasi market-led system with schools collaborating more effectively under the auspices of a strategic area training authority that would manage a 'pool' of newly qualified teachers—with the proviso that the government maintains responsibility for teacher workforce modelling as a whole and co-ordinates the activities of the strategic training authorities for what has become an immensely complex, differentiated and fragmented school system.

In this different, and altogether happier, landscape new possibilities will open up for universities to work innovatively with partnerships of schools, Teaching School alliances and multi-academy chains. And indeed in the adverse conditions that currently prevail, shoots of just such practice are beginning to emerge. Visse et al. (2012,

p. 281) describe a functional model developed in response to the integration of health care services in the Netherlands as a 'moral learning process' that 'deals with how people who have a stake in the subject at hand, interactively assign, re-interpret and re-negotiate responsibilities'. In this re-framing, importantly, they do 'not regard responsibility as instrumental, something that is "assigned" by an authority'. Likewise perhaps, the control and managed autonomy vested in schools by the government through School Direct, and the Teaching Schools movement, allows for a subversive re-drawing of partnership boundaries, practices and roles: a remodelling of a critical pedagogy of teacher education, one that reclaims for pre-service teachers (and teacher educators) the assigned and striated space in which partnership operates; one in which the emphasis on workplace performance is challenged and the adult learner status (of all teachers) is acknowledged and endorsed; and where pre-service teachers, in particular, are afforded the space to reflect on how experiential knowledge relates to practical theory, to maintain an 'inquiry stance', to develop their critical thinking skills, and to perhaps direct them to problematising contemporary education policy and practice and its dominant discourses.

In this model universities could inscribe more confidently their role as an active and essential partner in teacher professional learning. This would be a role which draws on the unique strengths they have to offer the collaborative enterprise, including their expertise in: (1) developing and maintaining a scholarly culture and the capacity for critical thinking; (2) providing subject and pedagogic knowledge expertise, and academic and professional qualifications for teaching and for the continuing professional learning of the teacher workforce; (3) leading public debate about education policy, and theorising about educational values, processes and practices; (4) asserting the importance that teacher educators should stand at the forefront of their disciplines as public intellectuals (Cochran-Smith 2006); and (5) engaging in and with research (and encouraging others to do so) about educational values, process and practices. Furlong et al. (2006, p. 41) argue that a key function of the university partners in the education and training of pre-service teachers is 'theorising the epistemological and pedagogical underpinnings' of the collaborative enterprise—because in the absence of those fundamental foundations the 'complexity and contestability of professional knowledge is no longer seen to be at the heart of what partnership is about; professional knowledge becomes simplified, flattened, it is essentially about contemporary practice in schools'.

References

Alexander, R. J. (1984). Innovation and continuity in the initial teacher education curriculum. In R. J. Alexander, M. Craft & J. Lynch (Eds.), *Change in teacher education: Context and provision since Robbins* (pp. 103–160). London: Holt, Rinehart and Winston.

Barrett, E., Whitty, G., Furlong, J., Galvin, C., & Barton, L. (1992). *Initial teacher education in England and wales: A topography*. London: Goldsmith's College.

Bell, A. (1981). Structure, knowledge and social relationships in teacher education.*British Journal of Sociology of Education, 2*(1), 21–32.

Benton, P. (Ed.). (1990). *The Oxford internship scheme: Integration and partnership in initial teacher education.* London: Calouste Gulbenkian Foundation.

Brisard, E., Menter, I., & Smith, I. (2005). *Models of partnership in programmes of initial teacher training: A systematic review.* Edinburgh: General Teaching Council of Scotland.

Christie, D., Donoghue, M., Kirk, G., McNamara, O., Menter, I., Moss, G., Noble-Rogers, J., Oancea, A., Rogers, C., Thomson, P., & Whitty, G. (2012). *Prospects for education research in education departments in higher education institutions in the UK.* London: BERA/UCET.

Crozier, G., Menter, I., & Pollard, A. (1990). Changing partnerships. In M. Booth, J. Furlong & M. Wilkin (Eds.), *Partnership in initial teacher training* (pp. 44–56). London: Cassells.

Cochran-Smith, M. (2006). Teacher education and the need for public intellectuals. *The New Educator, 2*(3), 181–206.

DCFS. (2007). Professional Standards for Qualified Teacher Status. http://webarchive. nationalarchives.gov.uk/20111218081624/tda.gov.uk/teacher/developing-career/professional-standards-guidance.aspx. Accessed 10 Oct 2012

DES. (1984). *Initial teacher training: Approval of courses. (Circular 3/84).* London: HMSO.

DES. (1988). Education Reform Act 1988. London: Her Majesty's Stationery Office. www.legislation.gov.uk/ukpga/1988/40/contents. Accessed 10 Oct 2012

DES. (1989). *Initial teacher training: Approval of courses. (Circular 24/89).* London: HMSO.

DFE. (1993). *School-centred Initial Teacher Training (SCITT).* London: DFE.

DfE. (2010). The importance of teaching—the schools white paper 2010. www.education.gov.uk. Accessed 10 Oct 2012.

DfE. (2011a). Training our next generation of outstanding teachers. an improvement strategy for discussion. www.education.gov.uk. Accessed 10 Oct 2012.

DfE. (2011b). Training our next generation of outstanding teachers. An implementation strategy. www.education.gov.uk. Accessed 10 Oct 2012.

DfE. (2012a). Teachers' standards www.education.gov.uk/publications/standard/SchoolsSO/Page1/ DFE-00066 2011. Accessed 10 Oct 2012.

DfE. (2012b). Education committee: First special report. Great teachers: attracting, training and retaining the best: Government response to the committee's ninth Report of Session 2010– 12—Education Committee www.publications.parliament.uk/pa/cm201213/cmselect/cmeduc/ 524/52404.htm. Accessed 10 Oct 2012.

DfE. (2012c). Huge increase in academies takes total to more than 2300 Press Release 07 September 2012. http://www.education.gov.uk/inthenews/inthenews/a00213703/huge-increase-in-academies-takes-total-to-more-than-2300. Accessed 10 Oct 2012.

DfE. (2013) Statistical first release initial teacher training allocations in England for academic year 2013/14—Final update SFR 32/2013 https://www.gov.uk/government/uploads/system/uploads/ attachment_data/file/229468/SFR_ITT_allocations_August_2013.pdf. Accessed 13 Aug.

DfEE. (1998a). *Teaching: High status, high standards. (Circular 4/98).* London: HMSO.

DfEE. (1998b). Teachers: Meeting the challenge of change. Green Paper London: HMSO.

DfES. (2002a). *Education and skills: Delivering results. A strategy to 2006.* London: DfES.

DfES. (2002b). *Qualifying to teach: Professional standards for qualified teacher status and requirements for initial teacher training. (Circular 2/02).* London: Teacher Training Agency.

DfES. (2003). *Raising standards and tackling workload: A national agreement.* London: DfES.

DfES. (2004). *Department for education and skills: Five year strategy for children and learners.* London: DfES.

Dunne, M., Lock, R., & Soares, A. (1996). Partnership in initial teacher training: After the shotgun wedding.*Educational Review, 48*(1), 41–53.

Edwards, T. (1994). The Universities Council for the education of teachers: Defending an interest or fighting a cause? Journal of Education for Teaching, 20(2), 143–152.

Edwards, A. (1995). Teacher education: Partnership in pedagogy? *Teaching and Teacher Education, 11*(6), 595–610.

Edwards, A., & Protheroe, L. (2003). Learning to see in classrooms: What are student teachers learning about teaching and learning while learning to teach in schools? *British Educational Research Journal, 29*(2), 227–242.

Ellström, P.-E. (2001). Integrating learning and work: Problems and prospects. *Human Resource Development Quarterly, 12,* 421–435.

Engeström, Y. (2004). The new generation of expertise: Seven theses. In H. Rainbird, A. Fuller & A. Munroe (Eds.), *Workplace learning in context* (pp. 145–165). London: Routledge.

Foucault, M. (1993). About the beginning of the hermeneutics of the self (transcription of two lectures in Dartmouth on Nov. 17 and 24, 1980), (ed. by) M. Blasius.*Political Theory, 21*(2), 198–227.

Furlong, J. (2001). Reforming teacher education, reforming teachers: Accountability, professionalism and competence. In R. Phillips & J. Furlong (Eds.), *Education, reform and the state: 25 years of policy, politics and practice, 118–135.* London: Routledge.

Furlong, J. (2005). New Labour and teacher education: The end of an era. *Oxford Education Review, 33*(1), 119–134.

Furlong, J., Barton, L., Miles, S., Whiting, C., & Whitty, G. (2000). *Teacher education in transition: Re-forming professionalism?* Buckingham: Open University Press.

Furlong, J., Campbell, A., Howson, J., Lewis, S., & McNamara, O. (2006). Partnership in English teacher education: Changing times, changing definitions—evidence from the Teacher Training Agency National Partnership Project. *Scottish Education Review, 37,* 32–45.

Gardner, P. (1993). The early history of school-based teacher training. In D. McIntyre, H. Hagger & M. Wilkin (Eds.), *Mentoring: Perspectives on school-based teacher education.* London: Kogan Page.

Gardener, P., & Cunningham, P. (1998). Teacher trainers and educational change in Britain, 1876–1996; 'a flawed and deficit history'? Journal of Education for Teaching, 24(3), 231–255.

Gilroy, P. (1998). New Labour and teacher education in England and Wales: The first 500 days. Journal of Education for Teaching, 24(3), 221–230.

Gilroy, P., & McNamara, O. (2009). A critical history of research assessment in the United Kingdom and its post-1992 impact on education. Journal of Education for Teaching, 35(4), 321–335.

Gilroy, P., & Wilcox, B. (1997). OfSTED, criteria and the nature of social understanding: A Wittgenstienian critique of the practice of educational judgement. British Journal of *Educational Studies, 45,* 22–38.

Gove, M. (2010). Speech to the annual conference of the National College for leadership of schools and children's services. Birmingham, 16 June. www.education.gov.uk/news/news/nationalcollege. Accessed 12 July 2012.

Graham, J., & Nabb, J. (1999). *Stakeholder satisfaction: Survey of OfSTED inspection of ITT 1994–1999. UCET Research Paper No. 1.* London: Universities Council for the Education of Teachers.

Gunter, H. (2007). Remodelling the school workforce in England: A study in tyranny. Journal for Critical Education Policy Studies, 5(1), 1–11.

Hextall, I., & Mahony, P. (2000). Consultation and the management of consent: Standards for Qualified Teacher Status. *British Educational Research Journal, 26*(3), 323–342.

HoC. (1999). The work of Ofsted: Other inspection frameworks. Select Committee on Education and Employment, report from the Education sub-committee: June 1999. www.publications.parliament.uk/pa/cm199899/cmselect/cmeduemp/62/6213.htm. Accessed 20 September 2012.

HoC. (2012). Great teachers: Attracting, training and retaining the best teachers. London: The Stationary Office Limited. www.parliament.uk/business/committees/committees-a-z/commons-select/education-committee/publications/previous-sessions/session-2010–12/. Accessed on 10 Oct 2012.

Howson, J., & McNamara, O. (2012). Teacher workforce planning: The interplay of market forces and government policies during a period of economic uncertainty. *Educational Research, 54*(2), 173–185.

Hurd, S., Jones, M., McNamara, O., & Craig, B. (2007). Initial teacher education as a driver for professional learning and school improvement in the primary phase. *The Curriculum Journal, 18*(3), 307–326.

Lave, J., & Wenger, E. (1991). *Situated learning: Legitimate peripheral participation.* Cambridge: Cambridge University Press.

McKinsey, & Company (2007). How the world's best-performing school systems come out on top. London: McKinsey. www.mckinsey.com/locations/UK_Ireland/Publications.aspx. Accessed 10 Oct 2012.

McNamara, O., Webb, R., & Brundrett, M. (2009). Primary teachers: Initial teacher education, continuing professional development and school leadership development. In R. Alexander, C. Doddington, J. Grey, L. Hargreaves & R. Kershner (Eds.), s The Cambridge Primary Review Research Surveys (pp. 649–701). London: Routledge.

McNamara, O., Jones, M., Boyd, P., Murray, J., & Qasim, S. (2012). Professionalism rules OK? Governmentality, audit, and inspection in initial teacher education. Vancouver: American Educational Research Association. April 2012.

Murray, J., Jones, M., McNamara, O., & Stanley, G. (2009). Capacity = expertise × motivation × opportunities: Factors in capacity building in teacher education in England. Journal of Education for Teaching 35(4), 391–408.

Nixon, J., Cope, P., McNally, J., Rodrigues, S., & Stephen, C. (2000). University-based teacher education: Institutional re-positioning and professional renewal. International Studies in.Sociology of Education, 10(3), 243–261.

Noble-Rogers, J. (2012). UCET worries over School Direct to be expressed at UCU conference. www.ucet.ac.uk/4370. Accessed 20 Dec 2012.

OECD. (2011). Lessons from PISA for the United States, strong performers and successful reformers in education. OECD Publishing. http://dx.doi.org/10.1787/9789264096660-en Accessed 10 Oct 2012.

Ofsted. (2007). An employment-based route into teaching 2003–06, HMI 2664. London: Ofsted.

Ofsted. (2010). The annual report of Her Majesty's Chief Inspector of Education, Children's Services and Skills 2009/10.www.official-documents.gov.uk/. Accessed 10 Oct 2012.

Ofsted. (2011). The annual report of Her Majesty's Chief Inspector of Education, Children's Services and Skills 2010/11.www.official-documents.gov.uk/. Accessed 10 Oct 2012.

Ofsted. (2012). Initial teacher education (ITE) inspection handbook www.ofsted.gov.uk/resources/120028. Accessed 12 Dec 2012.

Patton, G. (2012). Top graduates to get £ 25000 to teach in tough schools (14 June) www.telegraph.co.uk/education/educationnews/9330113/Top-graduates-to-get-25000-to-teach-in-tough-schools.html#. Accessed 10 Oct 2012.

Reid, I. (1985). Hoops, swings and roundabouts in teacher education. In C. Mills (Ed.), The impact of CATE. Report of teacher education study group. London (26 October 1985).

Shepherd, J. (2010). Gove to abolish general teaching council for England. Wednesday 2 June. www.guardian.co.uk/education/2010/jun/02/general-teaching-council-england-abolished. Accessed 10 Oct 2012.

Stronach, I., Corbin, B., McNamara, O., Stark, S., & Warne, T. (2002). Towards an uncertain politics of professionalism: Teacher and nurse identities in flux. Journal of.Educational Policy, 17(1), 109–138.

Thomas, J. (1990). Victorian beginnings. In J. Thomas (Ed.), British universities and teacher education: A century of change. London: Falmer.

UCU. (2012). University and College Union annual seminar for teacher educators, 27 November

Visse, M., Widdershoven, G., & Abma, T. (2012). Moral learning in an integrated social and healthcare service network. Health Care Analysis, 20, 281–296.

Wilkin, M. (1999). The role of higher education in initial teacher education (UCET Occasional Paper No. 12). London: UCET.

Wyse, D., & Goswami, U. (2008). Synthetic phonics and the teaching of reading. British Educational Research Journal, 34(6), 691–710.

Chapter 12
Work-based Learning in Teacher Education: A Scottish Perspective

James Conroy, Graham Donaldson and Ian Menter

Introduction

Perhaps the two most enduring debates in teacher education—especially in pre-service teacher education—concern respectively the sites of professional learning and the relationship between educational theory and the practice of teaching (Darling-Hammond and Lieberman 2012). These two debates are very closely connected and it is the interaction between them that is the central concern of this chapter. We examine how the issues have developed, been contested and are currently being reconstructed in the distinctive context of Scotland. However, before looking at this specific national case, we summarise the nature of the debates.

One strand in the history of pre-service teacher education is the question of what balance should be struck between the study of education and the experience of practising teaching in schools (Robinson 2002). This question has interacted throughout that history with shifting conceptions of the nature of teachers' work and teacher professionalism. Even from the days of 'pupil teachers', where young people would start their teaching careers apprenticed to experienced teachers, there was a recognition that their practice should be underpinned subsequently by systematic study of educational science in some form, as well as the study of school subjects as appropriate (Dent 1977; Cruickshank 1970). Many of the colleges of education that emerged across Britain during the nineteenth century included 'criticism rooms' where model lessons could be conducted, evaluated and assessed. Furthermore, many colleges

J. Conroy (✉) · G. Donaldson
University of Glasgow,
Glasgow, UK
e-mail: james.conroy@glasgow.ac.uk

G. Donaldson
e-mail: graham.donaldson@glasgow.ac.uk

I. Menter
Department of Education, University of Oxford,
Oxford, UK
e-mail: ian.menter@education.ox.ac.uk

O. McNamara et al. (eds.), *Workplace Learning in Teacher Education,*   207
Professional Learning and Development in Schools and Higher Education 10,
DOI 10.1007/978-94-007-7826-9_12, © Springer Science+Business Media Dordrecht 2014

had elementary (and subsequently primary) schools attached to them. There were differences between preparation for primary and secondary teaching, with subject knowledge being considered much more important for the latter and, indeed, the possession of a university degree being the main requirement. University departments of education only started to develop in their own right as training centres later in the twentieth century, as educational sciences themselves were developing.

As teaching started to become an all-graduate profession in the later part of the twentieth century, there was a general escalation of the contribution that educational studies made in the preparation of teachers. Indeed, by the 1980s in England there was concern that some of the training was becoming too theoretical and that teacher education lecturers were losing touch with the 'reality' of professional practice. Thus we saw the commencement of a steadily tightening grip on teacher education which, especially in England, created a significant push towards 'school-based' teacher education. There was indeed a return to an apprenticeship model of teacher education and an attack on the intellectual element of teacher preparation that had grown. It was noticeable that trends in some other parts of the world, including some which were judged to have very successful education systems, were moving in the opposite direction, albeit also with a strong emphasis on practice, but with an orientation towards clinical practice incorporating and underpinned by a commitment to enquiry and research. It is these trends that the scheme described towards the end of this chapter seeks to build upon.

The Scottish Context

The four nations of the UK have always had some distinctive elements in their approach to pre-service teacher education and to continuing professional learning. But in Scotland, reflecting differences in the wider education system, teacher education has long been very distinctive from the other three UK jurisdictions, where Wales and Northern Ireland had tended to mirror England very closely, at least until political devolution in 1998 (Hulme and Menter 2008). So when the moves towards tighter government control commenced in England, Wales and Northern Ireland from the mid-1980s onwards, there were some similar developments in Scotland, but they were not as radical or far-reaching as in those countries. Indeed, the amalgamation of colleges of education into universities in Scotland represented a consolidation of the university contribution to pre-service teacher education and a simplification of the provision (Menter et al. 2006). By the turn of the century pre-service teacher education was provided by just seven universities of which six were 'old' and just one was a 'new', post-1992 institution (Menter 2008). It is also noteworthy that Scotland was the only part of the UK where the volume of educational research expanded between the Research Assessment Exercises of 2011 and 2008 and some of this research has been closely associated with pre-service teacher education and continuing professional learning (Christie and Menter 2009).

Furthermore, there has generally been very little diversification of routes of entry into teaching, with continuing reliance in the twenty-first century on four-year un-dergraduate programmes with honours (Bachelor of Education) and one-year post graduate programmes. The study of educational theory as part of the pre-service teacher education curriculum was also reinforced by the strong influence of the General Teaching Council for Scotland (GTCS), which was established in the mid-1960s and has had a major role in overseeing the nature and quality of pre-service teacher education provision. The GTCS has always carried out careful scrutiny of teaching qualifications, both those offered within Scotland but also those achieved by teachers moving into Scotland from elsewhere. Whilst Northern Ireland and Wales do now have General Teaching Councils, the English one was only established in 2001 and has been abolished by the current coalition government. But during its brief existence, the English General Teaching Council never did have such direct control of teacher education as the Scottish General Teaching Council, with the equivalent control being the direct responsibility of two government agencies, the Teacher Training Agency (now The National College for Teaching and Leadership) and Ofsted, the inspection service (see Hulme and Menter 2008).

So, in Scotland, there was strong professional control of teacher education and there was a united commitment to a continuing leading role for universities. While more upheavals were taking place in English teacher education, therefore (Furlong et al. 2000; Gilroy 1992), there was considerable continuity and consolidation of provision in Scotland. When, in 1992, the government at Westminster imposed a requirement for a formal partnership with schools on teacher training providers in England, there was some recognition in Scotland that there might be considerable room for improvement in the support of pre-service teachers while they were undertaking their placements in schools. So, rather than imposing a national scheme on all provision, a pilot mentoring scheme was commissioned from Moray House College of Education (as it was) in association with some local authorities. While this scheme appears to have had many successful elements, including the development of school teachers as effective mentors for pre-service teachers, the attempts to roll it out across the country were unsuccessful. There was more than one explanation for this failure, ranging from union opposition to the increased workload for teachers (Smith et al. 2006), through to hostility from college-based teacher educators who felt their professional role might be undermined (McIntyre 2006).

However, following the demise of this scheme, and during the latter part of the last decade of the twentieth century, there was wider growing unrest among the teaching workforce in Scotland, mainly focusing on pay and conditions. This led to the establishment of a committee of enquiry, which became known as the McCrone Committee, after its chairman. This committee reported to the newly devolved Scottish Executive in 2000, and this led in 2001 to the agreement called 'A Teaching Profession for the 21st Century'. While the central focus was indeed on pay and conditions (and Scottish teachers got a significant pay rise, without conditions attached, in contrast to teachers in England), there were also several other matters agreed, including some recommendations about teacher education. These included a scheme for supporting the development of classroom teaching for accomplished

teachers; The Chartered Teacher Scheme (see Reeves 2009). Specifically in relation to pre-service teacher education there was to be a two-stage review. The first
stage was commissioned immediately and was carried out by Deloitte and Touche,
a consultancy firm. They reported within a matter of months and set out a helpful
overview of current provision across Scotland, and called for closer relationships
between providers and the schools with which they were working.

The second stage review was carried out by a committee appointed by the minister
for education. This took much longer to carry out its work and its report called for
yet closer relations between stakeholders and suggested that local authorities should
play a bigger part in the allocation of school placements for pre-service teacher
education. Each local authority subsequently identified a member of staff to be
the placement co-ordinator and this did lead to some improved efficiency in the
system, so that there were fewer short-term panics for providers in finding sufficient
placements. There were some attempts to make these arrangements more than simply
technical improvements, with schemes in various universities designed to enhance
the partnerships between schools and universities, but this did not have the national
scope that the developments in England had constituted.

In 2001 the University of Aberdeen won a contract from the Scottish Executive to
develop a new approach to teacher education that would have a research orientation
and a clinical dimension. The programme was called Scottish Teachers for a New Era
(STNE) and was modelled on the Teachers for a New Era scheme in the USA. STNE
was a six-year programme for beginning primary school teachers, that would take the
form of a reconstituted four-year Bachelor of Education programme, with enhanced
subject elements, followed by two years of employment-based further learning. At
the core of the programme was to be a partnership approach to the provision that
would involve schools, local authorities and the University in creating a sustained
research-based approach to professional learning. The scheme certainly appears to
have had a powerful influence on the students who went through it, and to have
led to significant developments in the school-based support for students (Livingston
2008; Livingston and Shiach 2010). But, somewhat like the mentoring pilot from
the early 1990s, the scheme did not get 'rolled out' more widely. It was beginning
to appear as though there was a deep resistance to significant change in teacher
education in Scotland. There appeared to be significant inertia within the system,
perhaps reflecting the tendency towards conservatism in the policy community that
had been identified from the 1980s onwards (Humes 2003).

The Vision in Teaching Scotland's Future

In 2009, the Scottish Government set up a fundamental review of teacher education
led by Graham Donaldson, former head of Her Majesty's Inspectorate of Education
(HMIe) in Scotland. The review was unusual in that it covered the entirety of teacher
education, from its initial stage through induction to workplace learning throughout
a career.

The need for such a review lay partly in the unfinished business of 'A Teaching Profession for the 21st Century' which, amongst other proposals, had established new expectations of teacher professional learning but which had not been fully implemented. Arguably, however, the main impetus came from the major Scottish curriculum reform, 'Curriculum for Excellence'. That comprehensive programme sought to reform school education (ages 3–18) by focusing on developing the capacities of young people in a twenty-first century context. The approach which was taken, that national guidelines should be less prescriptive and specific, placed new demands on teachers to determine not only how they should teach but also what should be taught and how it should be assessed. This approach to educational change was much less centrally directed than had hitherto been the case, and relied heavily on both the willingness and ability of teachers to play a much more active role in shaping the curriculum.

The resulting report, 'Teaching Scotland's Future' (the Donaldson Review), was published in January 2011. The Government responded quickly to its publication and accepted all 50 of its recommendations in full, in part or in principle. A National Partnership Group involving national and local government and the universities was established to determine how the recommendations could be implemented.

What view did the Donaldson Review take of the nature of the twenty-first century teacher who could respond to the expectations of 'Curriculum for Excellence'? In recent years, an increasingly strong body of evidence and opinion had reaffirmed the importance of the individual teacher to student success. However, the question of what qualities and competences would maximise that contribution remained both open and contested. Broadly, two contrasting views of the teacher were emerging internationally. On the one hand, teaching could be defined as 'craft-based' competence which could largely be acquired in classroom settings. This view has the virtues of simplicity, of a fairly short period of preparation in workplace settings, and of attractiveness to a potentially wide set of individuals who might otherwise not have seen teaching as an attractive career. A contrasting view sees teaching as a more complex process requiring strong theoretical and research underpinning, and competences which extend considerably beyond performance in the classroom. Through a comparison of the Donaldson Review and the English White Paper, 'The Importance of Teaching', Hulme and Menter (2011) explore how such different conceptions of teaching are articulated and how they have developed within two adjacent parts of the UK. These views, and related hybrids, have different implications for the ways in which teachers are recruited and for subsequent pre-service and career-long teacher education. In that context, 'Teaching Scotland's Future' argued that Scotland needed a strong teaching profession within which each teacher was equipped to realise the benefits of new governance and curriculum models. It needed teachers who could deal not only with the needs of today's young people but who also had the capacity to engage directly with the complexities of rapid changes in educational policy and practice. That view implies teachers who can shape that future rather than respond to the expectations of others, and reflects wider issues of how best to manage change and raise educational quality in careers which would span much of this century.

The 50 recommendations of the Donaldson Review covered recruitment, early preparation and career-long learning. It also called for a new and strengthened partnership between schools and universities, both in the early phase and throughout a career. Recruitment would be based on a more explicit understanding of what it means to be a teacher, encompassing high academic standards, interpersonal skills and a strong command of literacy and numeracy. The early phase of a career, covering pre-service teacher education, induction and the first few years of practice, would be an integrated and planned experience, allowing progression and development, and avoiding over-reliance on what can be achieved in the pre-service years. Thereafter, professional growth throughout a career would be both an expectation and an obligation.

Career-long workplace learning is fundamental to the recommendations of the review. It sought to promote a culture within which an individual teacher would see professional learning as integral to their job and to establish mechanisms to stimulate and sustain the resulting demand from teachers for that learning. Development during the early phase should establish habits of collegiate working and the necessary interrelationship between classroom practice, theory and research. It should also reinforce the personal responsibility of a teacher to reflect on their work and to take the initiative in seeking relevant professional development.

Arguably one of the greatest challenges within this agenda is to build appropriate workplace learning into the culture of the profession and into the life of a school and its staff. The review report states very clearly that 'Career-long teacher education... is currently too fragmented and often haphazard'. It was clear that one-off courses or events, which were the basis of much workplace learning, have, at best, only a very limited effect and rarely have a sustained impact. It was also increasingly evident that the most effective professional learning is collegiate, relevant and local. These activities were often at too low a level of academic rigour. It therefore envisaged a profession within which master's and doctoral study would ultimately be much more the norm. Achieving that goal would require flexibility in allowing recognition to be given for appropriately challenging workplace professional activity.

The review also stressed the need for injections of fresh thinking to broaden horizons and challenge complacency. It therefore recommended a move towards more school or learning community-based professional learning, complemented by the active engagement of external agencies or individuals. Workplace learning should therefore not be seen as specific, one-off training events, but should help to establish professional growth as central to teacher identity. At first sight, universities are well placed to provide that external component of local professional development. However, the role of universities has recently been increasingly focused on pre-service teacher education, research and limited postgraduate study. That role has rarely extended to an ongoing involvement with the broad mass of teachers throughout their careers. The review saw universities as being uniquely placed to provide necessary external stimulus to local development while also building more advanced study into ongoing professional development. The review, therefore, challenged universities and employers to establish partnerships which would allow this to happen.

Of course, there remains a significant challenge in persuading teachers that they should see themselves as extended professionals who take greater responsibility for their own learning. The GTCS is critical to stimulating and sustaining such a culture. In particular, the standards set by GTCS should not just define what is integral to gaining entry to the profession, but should embody the values and expectations of a professional teacher throughout a career and therefore be a reference point for workplace learning. The review therefore recommended not just a revision of existing standards but the introduction of a new set of standards called the 'Standard for Active Registration'. This new set of standards would be more flexible than those for registration, not having to meet the exacting requirements of threshold statements which could be open to legal challenge. They should convey the obligations of a teacher throughout a career to grow and develop, both in personal terms and in their understanding of the changing context for their work. GTCS was already examining ways in which professional update could be built into the profession and saw the possibilities of such an approach as being part of that process. The subsequent re-examination of standards amounted to what they called a reconceptualisation of what it means to be a teacher, and included proposals for a new 'Standard for Career-Long Learning'.

A further piece in this complicated jigsaw relates to the terms and conditions of employment of teachers. The Scottish Government set up a further review in this area, chaired by Professor Gerry McCormac, Principal of Stirling University. The report of this review, 'Advancing Professionalism in Teaching' (the McCormac Report, The Scottish Government 2011), was published in autumn 2011 and explicitly related its recommendations to 'Curriculum for Excellence' and 'Teaching Scotland's Future'. It called for greater flexibility in the teachers' contract, and reaffirmed the view of teachers as extended professionals who had an obligation to engage in professional development throughout a career. In particular, it built on the Donaldson Review's view of professional review and development within which the new GTCS standard for career-long learning should be a key reference point for regular reviews of a teacher's work.

Scotland has embarked on a very ambitious and interlocking educational reform programme encompassing new ways of thinking about the curriculum and curriculum development, and recognising that successful and sustained change can only be achieved with the full engagement of the teaching profession. The aim is to put a very different curriculum in place but also to establish a fresh dynamic within the education system, within which renewal is integral to established patterns of working and the teachers themselves becomes key agents of change.

A Clinical Model for Teacher Education in Scotland?

As the Donaldson Review was being established, the political imperatives that en-ergised it were, as we have noted, already in train in the Aberdeen University engagement with STNE. The drivers that shaped these processes were also being felt across a small teacher education system; the advantages and disadvantages of a small polity is the facility with which policy travel is embedded. The discourse of STNE was picked up elsewhere in Scotland and its implications were being worked out in, for example, the University of Glasgow, where the drive to successfully embed a School of Education inside a research intensive university was an increasingly important internal driver of change. Coupled with the collapse in funding, as a result of the precipitous decline in teacher education student numbers and the local government reluctance to hire teachers at a time of stagnating funding, this pushed the School of Education into thinking more radically about its partnerships with schools, in the hope of securing its position within and beyond the University. And, of course, Scotland continued to be influenced by England but perhaps, in these regards, rather more by some of the work coming out of North America.

In the course of the 2000s there was an increasing belief that we should be raising the intellectual aspirations of the teaching workforce, and, as the Chartered Teacher programme for experienced classroom teachers became instantiated, Glasgow University looked to re-position its Post Graduate Certificate in Education (PGCE) as a Professional Graduate Diploma in Education (PGDE) in line with international developments. As elsewhere, this entailed the creation of a master's level course, something that had been widely resisted in Scotland up to 2008. Historically, Scottish Schools of Education moved in harmony with regard to nomenclature and level of award. Such unity of provision was partly driven by an egalitarian instinct that harked back to the rhetorical power of 'the democratic intellect' (Davie 1961), and tended to preclude difference, as such difference might imply that Scotland's schools and the pupils they served were not able to access equal intellectual resources. But the immersion of teacher education in university culture precipitated a gradual but significant erasure of common bonds, and individual Schools of Education were likely to be better served by being distinctive and offering very particular forms of professional development. The University of Glasgow was the first provider in Scotland to make a decision to develop master's level PGDE awards, driven, in part, by a wish to valorise high quality and coherent ongoing professional education, where much that passed for professional development in the post-McCrone era might not stand up well to close scrutiny. The decision to establish an intellectually grounded analysis of education as a social and pedagogical practice, a move that is echoed in the Donaldson Review, fitted well with the twin challenges of responding appropriately to a university research culture and to the professional practical need for improved educational understanding and enactment. This master's level provision raised the intellectual challenges for pre-service teachers and, in doing so, raised the expectations about what would count as appropriate professional reflection and analysis. It also gave shape to the belief that teaching was not a profession shaped by the acquisition of skills, which were subsequently honed in the field, but was a profession rooted in the life of the mind, a kind of intellectual eros. After all, it was reasoned, it is perfectly possible to be highly skilled at teaching things that are untruthful or inaccurate! Indeed there are few things more injurious to a thriving democratic culture than the effective communication of bad ideas. Hence the master's level provision in Glasgow positioned itself inside the continuum of early career development so that a beginning teacher might complete their university year, followed by their probationary year in school, followed by the completion of their master's. This represented the beginnings of a coherent continuum of professional education

So it was that the second move at Glasgow then built upon this conception and sought to develop this more robust engagement between the school and university through implementing a new way of conducting school experience, which, for the sake of short-hand, we will call 'clinical practice'. As the Donaldson Review was beginning, the Scottish Government invited tenders from universities for experimental projects in teacher education. The University of Glasgow successfully bid for three projects, one of which focused on re-imagining teaching practice and the notion of professional partnership. As we have already noted, professional education in teaching has been subjected to competing claims, many of which are not grounded in any research but, rather, a function of individuals' and groups' normative attachments—'what they think *ought* to be happening' (HonerØd Hoevid and Conroy 2008). In Glasgow, student feedback had suggested that too much school practice was judged in highly individual terms and that this resulted in quite individual judgements about competence and professionalism. In other words, while the proximate cause of these developments may well have been crises about numbers and performance in international league tables, what became known as the Glasgow West Teacher Education Initiative was a very direct response to the apparent need to think very seriously about teacher education itself. Thus, in summary, this pilot sought to:

a. enhance school experience for beginning teachers, particularly the integration of theory, practice, content and pedagogy;
b. promote the professional learning and partnership of school teachers, teacher mentors and university tutors;
c. develop frameworks for common judgement;
d. use evaluation evidence to inform programme development and future policy choices.

So it was that the Glasgow pilot scheme made some significant changes to the historic pattern of 'placement' and reshaped the relationship between tutor and school. In this model, university tutors are placed full time in a learning community (i.e. a geographical cluster of schools) with the task of providing overall co-ordination and support for supervision with respect to all PGDE students immersed in the partner schools. Formal partnership agreements were negotiated with the schools in the learning community—at least one secondary school and a number of associated primary schools—who committed to work with the University to develop a bespoke programme, in collaboration with the local authority. University tutors are embedded in the day-to-day operation of the school-based programme and work closely with teacher mentors in development and assessment activities over the sustained period of placement.

It should be noted that the use of the term 'clinical' does not imply uncritical acceptance of the applicability of the 'medical model' to the professional education of teachers. We do not aim to supplant professional judgement with lessons extracted from scientific evidence of 'what works' conveyed by clinical educators in school settings; nor do we valorise practitioner knowledge above other forms of knowledge. Rather we suggest that the development of professional craft knowledge and research-based thinking can be enhanced through collaborative inquiry into authentic pedagogical problems (TLRP 2007). While the programme is still in development and ongoing evaluations are still in train, the initial belief is sustained—that all parties would benefit from a much closer engagement based on the mutuality and common bonds of a professional commitment to improve the educational achievement and welfare of pupils. While the elements of the professional obligations and relationships continue to be developed in collaboration, there are distinctive features which include the following.

The pilot programme sought to give scope for *all* parties to teacher education to benefit from a much closer collaboration with a direct conduit into the heart of the University's School of Education, and for school partners to share in the shaping of provision. On recruitment of a local authority and volunteer schools to the scheme, remits were drawn up respectively for the tutor(s), the teachers in the schools and the pre-service teachers. Initially it was anticipated that one tutor would be based in the learning community throughout the period of school placement. In the event it was decided to appoint two tutors, each working in schools on a half-time basis; one with professional expertise in primary education and the other in secondary education. At this stage we have moved beyond a pilot, as local authority partners have become increasingly interested, and there are now five learning clusters in four quite diverse local authorities. Moreover, this particular model has acted as a catalyst for further partnership, with the other major provider in the West of Scotland (The University of Strathclyde) joining Glasgow University in a working party hosted by Glasgow City to explore partnership across the professional continuum. Central to this effort has been a joint appointment between the three bodies to liaise and develop the educational infrastructure. An important aim for the group is to explore and analyse how pre-service teacher education in the workplace fits together with probation and early career development, leading into the more advanced stages of professional life. While this work is at an early stage, this partnership places an increasing onus on the universities involved to work creatively on supporting and accrediting professional reflection and growth. However, it is important in such endeavours that accreditation is not afforded to ordinary everyday professional life, that is a validation of 'the day job', but looks to encourage and recognise levels of reflection and professional prescription that make a difference to the intellectual and practical life of a school. Some of the key features of the plan developed and agreed with the school and local authority partners in November 2010 are as follows:

Learning Rounds
Central to the project has been the development of learning rounds where the university tutor, teacher mentor and two other pre-service teachers observe lessons conducted with a particular learning or organisational focus in mind. The learning rounds would subsequently form a focus for a tutorial or seminar. The pedagogic point here is fairly straightforward. Historic practice in this area has been based on a number of observations (by school mentor

and university lecturer) that focused on an assessment of performance, whereas the learning rounds defer judgement of the subject in favour of reflection on the part of the observers.

Seminar Programme
The development of an in situ seminar programme requires that all pre-service teachers across a cluster are off timetable at the same time during the course of their school experience. As we move forward, the object is to increasingly sew this together with the schools/authorities extant probationer programme. Interestingly, the seminar topics were determined in a half-day workshop which engaged partners from schools and local authorities. (This school-based seminar programme complements the seminars held at the University during the non-school-based parts of the programme, and at this stage of development it is still true that the 'master's levelness' of the course is more readily assured through the latter than the former, but the aim is to make the two elements seamless in terms of quality and level.)

Assessment
All pre-service teachers are required to demonstrate their ability to overtake national bench-mark competences, i.e. the Standard for Initial Teacher Education. However ongoing formative assessment and feedback jointly conducted by teacher and tutor will play a larger role than heretofore. There will only be one summative assessment (per placement), which will be jointly agreed by teacher and tutor, whereas in the past there was a tendency for the teachers to be providing formative assessment and for the occasional visit by a university tutor to be for the purpose of making a summative assessment. So this continuing discussion between all three parties represents a significant advance for all, most especially for the pre-service teacher, since they will receive a more consistent account of their performance and abilities than has sometimes been the case.

It is important to acknowledge in the context of work-based learning partnership, that this model excites some concerns with some university colleagues (particularly in the area of secondary provision) considering that their professional expertise is somehow diminished (Menter and Lowden 2012). Clearly a professional partnership model of work-based learning must attempt to bring together professional expertise rather than diminish it. One interesting possibility for doing so is through the creation of 'subject clusters' led by university tutors. Perhaps most importantly what this points to is the reality that, while much has been achieved, there is much still to do.

Conclusion

In this chapter we have demonstrated, by taking Scotland as a distinctive case, how closely linked are the questions about where pre-service teachers learn and the nature of their learning. These are not new questions and indeed have been worked at for many years in other contexts, not least in some of the ground-breaking school-led schemes developed in England, including the Oxford internship scheme (Benton 1990; Hagger and McIntyre 2006). But while in England the more recent move to draw schools and teachers more firmly into teacher education work has been a result of government imposition, and some would say ideological positions taken by politicians, in Scotland there has been a more consensual and deliberative set of processes at work. Indeed in England, rather than attempts to integrate theory and practice, there has been a strong political attack on theory (or research) making any significant contribution at all (see Hulme and Menter 2011). We have shown in this chapter how some earlier attempts in Scotland to enhance workplace learning for pre-service teachers were not successful, but how more recently, during the last ten or 12 years, a groundswell of professional debate and activity appears to be leading both to a concerted movement at a national level but also to quite radical initiatives at a local level. The Glasgow scheme that was described in the final section of the chapter is the subject of continuing evaluation, and while it may not meet all of the aspirations that were set out in the report from the Donaldson Review, it does show that significant change is possible and that school staff and university staff can work with greater creative synergy than has been typical in the past. These colleagues are likely to experience significant enhancement of their professional activity as lifelong learners, but the key beneficiaries are also likely to be the beginning teachers who experience these approaches, and the school students they teach, both during the training process and hopefully for many years afterwards in the teachers' subsequent careers.

References

Benton, P. (Ed.). (1990). *The Oxford internship scheme*. London: Calouste Gulbenkian Foundation.

Christie, D., & Menter, I. (2009). Research capacity building in teacher education: Scottish collaborative approaches. *Journal of Education for Teaching, 35*(4), 337–354.

Cruickshank, M. (1970). *History of the training of teachers in Scotland*. Edinburgh: The Scottish Council for Research in Education.

Darling-Hammond, L., & Lieberman, A. (2012). Teacher education around the world—what can we learn from international practice. In L. Darling-Hammond & A. Lieberman (Eds.), *Teacher education around the world—changing policies and practices* (pp. 151–169). London: Routledge.

Davie, G. (1961). *The democratic intellect: Scotland and her universities in the nineteenth century*. Edinburgh: Edinburgh University Press.

Dent, H. (1977). *The training of teachers in England and Wales 1800–1975*. London: Hodder and Stoughton.

Donaldson, G. (2011). *Teaching Scotland's future*. Edinburgh: The Scottish Government.

Furlong, J., Barton, L., Miles, S., Whiting, C., & Whitty, G. (2000). *Teacher education in transition—re-forming professionalism?* Buckingham: Open University.

Gilroy, P. (1992). The political rape of initial teacher education in England and Wales: A JET rebuttal. *Journal of Education for Teaching, 18*(1), 5–22.

Hagger, H., & McIntyre, D. (2006). *Learning teaching from teachers*. Buckingham: Open University.

HonerØd Hoevid, M., & Conroy, J. (2008). Research in teacher education. *European Educational Research Journal, 7*(4), 456–462.

Hulme, M., & Menter, I. (2008). Learning to teach in post-devolution UK: A technical or an ethical process? *Southern African Review of Education, 14*(1–2), 43–64.

Hulme, M., & Menter, I. (2011). South and North—teacher education policy in England and Scotland: A comparative textual analysis. *Scottish Educational Review, 43*(2), 70–90.

Humes, W. (2003). Policy making in Scottish education. In T. Bryce & W. Humes (Eds.), *Scottish Education* (2nd ed, pp. 74–85). Edinburgh: University Press.

Livingston, K. (2008). New directions in teacher education. In T. Bryce & W. Humes (Eds.), *Scottish Education* (3rd ed, pp. 855–863). Edinburgh: University Press.

Livingston, K., & Shiach, L. (2010). Co-constructing a new model of teacher education. In A. Campbell & S. Groundwater-Smith (Eds.), *Connecting inquiry and professional learning in education*. London: Routledge.

McIntyre, D. (2006). Opportunities for a more balanced approach to ITE: Can we learn again from research and other experience? *Scottish Educational Review, 37*, 5–19 (Special Edition)

Menter, I. (2008). Teacher education institutions. In T. Bryce & W. Humes (Eds.), *Scottish Education* (3rd ed, pp. 817–825). Edinburgh: University Press.

Menter, I., Brisard, E., & Smith, I. (2006). *Convergence or divergence? Initial teacher education in Scotland and England*. Edinburgh: Dunedin Academic Press.

Menter, I., Lowden, K., & Hall, S. (2012). *Teacher education clinical model 2012—final evaluation report*. Glasgow: University of Glasgow

Reeves, J. (2009). Inventing the chartered teacher. In S. Gewirtz, P. Mahony, I. Hextall & A. Cribb (Eds.), *Changing teacher professionalism* (pp. 106–116). London: Routledge.

Robinson, W. (2002). *Power to teach—learning through practice*. London: Routledge.

Scottish Executive Education Department (SEED). (2001). *A teaching profession for the 21st century*. Edinburgh: SEED.

Smith, I., Bisard, E., & Menter, I. (2006). Partnership in initial teacher education in Scotland 1990–2005: Unresolved tensions. *Scottish Educational Review, 37*, 20–31 (Special Edition)

Teaching and Learning Research Programme (TLRP). (2007). Principles into practice. www.tlrp.org/pub/documents/Principles%20in%20Practice%20Low%20Res.pdf

The Scottish Government. (2011). *Advancing professionalism in teaching. (The MacCormac Report)*. Edinburgh: The Scottish Government.

Chapter 13
'Learningplace' Practices and Pre-service Teacher Education in Ireland: Knowledge Generation, Partnerships and Pedagogy

Paul F. Conway, Rosaleen Murphy and Vanessa Rutherford

Introduction: Schools as 'Learningplaces'

Informed by key ideas from the learning sciences, this chapter addresses some challenges in pre-service teacher education in Ireland and identifies a number of potentially generative concepts from workplace learning research that might advance policy and practice. The focus is primarily, but not exclusively, on pre-service teacher education, given the fact that interaction between teachers at different phases of the continuum is increasingly seen as vital in the enhancement of learning for all teachers. As the title suggests, the main point of this chapter is that, more often than not, work rather than learning appears to be the leading activity (Eraut 2007) in schools during pre-service teacher education, and that reframing the school as a 'learningplace' is central to both teacher education reform and widening the scope of workplace learning research. This reframing has implications for policy and practice vis-à-vis knowledge creation, partnerships and pedagogy for all involved in teacher education.

Drawing on the work of a number of theorists/researchers in the field of the learning sciences, key themes are identified and used in the chapter to understand the dynamics, aspirations and potential directions of workplace learning, at the level of the individual, the organisations and the region in pre-service teacher education in Ireland. Four assumptions underpin this chapter. First is the assumption that schools, in the current review and reform of teacher education (Coolahan 2007; Conway et al. 2009; Hyland 2012; Sahlberg et al. 2012; Conway 2013), are being redefined as sites of workplace learning for neophyte and experienced teachers alike. Second, the premise, a corollary of the first assumption, is that opportunities to learn to teach

P. F. Conway (✉) · R. Murphy · V. Rutherford
School of Education, University College Cork, Cork, Ireland
e-mail: pconway@education.ucc.ie

R. Murphy
e-mail: murphy.r@ucc.ie

V. Rutherford
e-mail: v.rutherford@ucc.ie

O. McNamara et al. (eds.), *Workplace Learning in Teacher Education,*   221
Professional Learning and Development in Schools and Higher Education 10,
DOI 10.1007/978-94-007-7826-9_13, © Springer Science+Business Media Dordrecht 2014

are being significantly altered in the emerging new policy and practice landscape for teaching and teacher education. Third, recognising that education and schooling are practices of human improvement implies that changing cultural practices remains challenging and somewhat prone to stasis and unpredictable outcomes—whether welcome or not. Fourth, in presenting some current themes on workplace learning and teacher education from the perspective of one country, we are conscious of avoiding the pitfalls of uniqueness and universalist positions. Avoiding the uniqueness fallacy is important in that no region is so specific in its cultural dynamics as not to share important and generalisable insights for other jurisdictions. Circumventing the universalist fallacy is vital in not assuming that research insights have equal resonance and/or applicability across very different cultural contexts.

The chapter is organised in three sections: (1) introduction: the teacher education context in Ireland and three 'big ideas' from learning sciences—metaphors, resources and levels of learning; (2) challenges for learning and workplace research in initial teacher education; and (3) conclusion. The introduction provides an overview of the teacher education policy and provision context in Ireland and then identifies three 'big ideas' in workplace learning research which are used to frame the chapter, as well as the rapidly changing policy context in relation to teacher education. A set of five key challenges central to workplace learning research in teacher education then provides the main focus of the chapter. These challenges are: (1) invisibility-visibility of learners and learning; (2) solo and assisted performance; (3) reframing the knowledge-practice relationship; (4) school-university partnership: which model(s)?; and (5) advancing learning at the system level. In light of workplace learning research, 'generative concepts' from the research literature are identified that might inform future research, policy and practice.

Teacher Education: The Irish Context

The recent fast-paced changing policy context is providing a significantly different arena within which workplace learning research will be undertaken in the coming years in Ireland. Traditionally, there has been a distinction in Ireland between the prevailing model of preparation for teaching at primary level and that for second level teaching. At primary level, the concurrent model of teacher education is the most common: a three- or four-year undergraduate degree (i.e. Bachelor of Education). The consecutive model is more common as a preparation for teaching at second level: in the majority of cases this means an initial subject-based degree followed by a postgraduate teaching qualification, both university-based. School placement consists at present of a minimum of 100 hours teaching practice during the postgraduate year. (See Conway et al. 2009, pp. 270–292 and Hyland 2012 for detailed descriptions of current provision.) This distinction between primary and second level has become somewhat blurred in recent years, with the introduction of online and blended learning programmes providing recognised qualifications for both primary and secondary levels, and the existence of some qualifications for teaching technical or specialised subjects such as physical education or metalwork at second level, where the concurrent model prevails.

The changing role of the Catholic Church, which has had immeasurable and sustained power over primary teacher education in Ireland since the nineteenth century (Inglis 1998; Coolahan 2003), is a very good barometer of current social and cultural change in Irish society, with significant implications for teacher education and teachers' work. In recent years, a number of fundamental developments in Irish society contributed to a changed role for the Catholic Church in teacher education:

> It is difficult to think of any area of Irish society that has changed so dramatically in recent decades as the attitude to organised religion and Roman Catholicism in particular (Maher 2009, p. 3).

The Colleges of Education for primary teachers have traditionally been divided on denominational lines, with the majority being run under the auspices of the Roman Catholic church, and a separate training college for Church of Ireland (Protestant) teachers. In recent years, the influence of the Churches on teacher education and on education in general has greatly diminished, though still significant nevertheless. The change is due to a number of distinct factors, 'most notably the revelations of clerical sex abuse in the 1990s, increased prosperity during the Celtic Tiger years, greater mobility' (Maher 2009, p. 3), changing family structures, the 'unprecedented increase in the numbers of students from different ethnic and cultural backgrounds' (Teaching Council 2010), and the 'diversity of religious belief systems … now represented in the State' (Coolahan et al. 2012). A structural re-shaping of primary school provision is currently on the educational and political agenda in Ireland, in response to the increased demand for multi-denominational and non-denominational education (Coolahan et al. 2012; Department of Education and Skills 2012). By contrast, at post-primary level the role and impact of the religious denominations has been much less pronounced, with teacher education taking place in secular university settings. The fast-paced nature of social, cultural and economic changes in Ireland sets a context for considering how both teacher professional identity and work environments within schools are changing with the expectation that teachers will promote inclusion, adopt an inquiry stance as a focus of both schooling and their own learning, and address the myriad of changes associated with a more diverse student population in schools (Byrne et al. 2010).

Pre-service teacher education is also undergoing other major reforms at present, as some of the recommendations made by previous review bodies (Byrne 2002; Kellaghan 2002) on the content, length and format of teacher education are finally put into effect. At second level, the Postgraduate Diploma in Education was renamed the Professional Diploma in Education in 2012 and extended from the current one-year programme to a two-year one with effect from 2014, with an extended placement in schools. At the same time, the overall organisation of teacher education is under consideration. The report of an international review commissioned by the Higher Education Authority for the Department of Education and Skills (Sahlberg et al. 2012) recommended that the number of colleges providing pre-service teacher education should be reduced and the provision of courses rationalised, with a view to creating a smaller number of centres each with the critical mass necessary to support excellence in teaching and research. This will not, however, be unproblematic. The role of the

Teaching Council (established in 2006),[1] in overseeing and accrediting programmes of teacher education has become even more crucial as new pathways into teaching become available and existing programmes are revised and reformed. The focus in this chapter is on workplace learning in pre-service teacher education for second level in Ireland, specifically in the context of the existing and about-to-be-reformed Professional Diploma in Education, although there are implications also for other pre-service teacher education programmes.

Given the range of changes noted above, there are significant changes in the dynamics of workplace learning for all involved in schools and higher education institutions providing teacher education (summarised below). Central themes in the changing policy context, pertinent to the workplace learning perspective on learning to teach, are: the increasing focus on the continuum of teacher education; an emerging more collegial professional learning environment (Coolahan 2007; Teaching Council 2011); new accountabilities (Conway 2013); and the reform of institutional arrangements (i.e. centred on joint university- and school-anchored teacher education, Sahlberg et al. 2012). Significantly, in Ireland, there has not been the move to school-led teacher education as is the case in England. As Billett (2004, p. 1) has observed:

> Workplaces intentionally regulate individuals' participation; it is not ad hoc, unstructured or informal. This regulation is a product of cultural practices, social norms, workplace affiliations, cliques and demarcations. . . . Those who control the processes and divisions of labour, including interests and affiliations within the workplace regulate participation to maintain the continuity of the workplace through regulatory practices.

Consequently, opportunities for learning in the workplace as well as researching workplace learning are inevitably shaped by the sedimentation of particular policy and practice arrangements within teaching and teacher education. For example, the OECD (1991) review of schooling and teacher education in Ireland pointed to the 'legendary autonomy' of the teacher as a defining feature of the education system. In recent years, for a variety of reasons, allied with moves toward school development planning, whole-school evaluation (McNamara et al. 2009) and new accountabilities (Conway and Murphy 2013), a more collegial professionalism is being privileged by the system and the teaching profession. The Professional Code of Conduct for the teaching profession (2007 and revised in 2012), formulated by the Teaching Council, conveys this well, with its strong emphasis on the responsibility of teachers in terms of interaction with colleagues as part of wider solidarity with the profession. Furthermore, the recent past has been characterised by the emergence of new accountabilities in teacher education (Sugrue 2011; Conway and Murphy 2013). That there has been a 'rising tide' of accountability—due to the interrelated influences of the European higher education space, education legislation and professional self-regulation policies (i.e. Teaching Council)—has been evident since the late 1990s. This was punctuated by a 'perfect storm' in 2010, comprising 'bad news' regarding the performance of Irish 15-year-olds in the 2009 Programme for International Student Assessment (PISA 2009), the economic bailout and strategic leadership at a

---

[1] See www.teachingcouncil.ie.

system level (Conway and Murphy 2013). The cumulative impact of the 'rising tide' and 'perfect storm' is evident in the way in which accountability was reframed, in terms of 'to whom' and 'for what' teacher education is held accountable. (Conway and Murphy 2013). Significantly, the new accountabilities in teaching and teacher education reflect a move toward the dominant global education reform movement (Sahlberg 2007), with its emphasis on standardisation, narrow focus on literacy and numeracy, and higher stakes accountability. As Billet (2004) observed, changes in practice of this order reflect the intentional regulation of the workplace, with implications for how we both understand and study learning practices at work.

The empirical research that forms the basis for much of this chapter is drawn from the 'Learning to Teach Study' (LETS) of teacher education (Conway et al. 2011c)— a three-year programme level study of the Professional Diploma in Education, the flagship pre-service teacher education provision in post-primary teacher education. Other publications based on the LETS study to date include Conway et al. (2011a), Hall et al. (2012), Long et al. (2012) and Conway et al. (2012). LETS was funded by the national Department of Education and Science, and conducted by a team of researchers from the School of Education, University College Cork. The methods used in LETS included a series of in-depth interviews with 17 pre-service teachers over the course of a year, and a questionnaire survey of the entire 2008/2009 cohort of pre-service teachers. The over-arching research questions were concerned with how novice teachers developed curricular and cross-curricular competences during the course of the Postgraduate Diploma in Education programme. However, the over-arching socio-cultural framework used to understand and conceptualise the findings from the study meant that the research framework allowed other findings to emerge. One of these was the overwhelming importance to the pre-service teachers of their experiences in the workplace—the schools in which their teaching practice was being conducted.

'Big Ideas' from Learning Sciences

Three 'big ideas' from the learning sciences are used to frame this chapter: (1) metaphors and learning, (2) resources for learning, and (3) learning by and for individuals, organisations and regions/systems, i.e. learning metaphors, resources and levels. A socio-cultural perspective on learning informs these three themes, drawing in particular on the work of Billet (2004), Fuller and Unwin (2005), Edwards and Protheroe (2003), Eraut (2007), Sfard (1998), Tynjälä (2008), and Paavola et al. (2004). In an effort to counter overly general observations about the distinctiveness of workplace learning, Tynjälä (2008), among others, has noted that the nature of workplace learning is both different from but also similar to school learning; that learning in the workplace can be described at different levels, ranging from the individual to the network and region; that workplace learning is both informal and formal; and, finally and importantly for this chapter, that workplaces differ a lot in how they support learning (e.g. see cross-profession comparisons: Eraut 2007; Grossman et al. 2009). That workplace learning is similar to and different from school learning is important in drawing attention to how workplace and school learning, often seen as separate learning worlds, may have some important overlapping features. Much of the research on learning, including workplace learning, traditionally focused on individuals (especially cognitively informed work). More recently, important insights on learning have come from a focus on organisations, and latterly from studies on inter-organisational and systems learning. Seminal work in this latter area is being undertaken by two sets of researchers in Finland, notably the work of Hakkarainen et al. (2004) on 'communities of networked expertise'; and Engeström (1999a, 1999b, 2001) and colleagues' research on 'knotworking', that is, the 'pulsating movement of tying, untying and retying together otherwise separate threads of activity' (Tynjälä 2008, p. 136).

Metaphors for Learning

Sfard's (1998) widely influential conceptualisation of learning research comprising two metaphors—acquisition or participation—has been elaborated upon by focusing on a vital missing feature, that is, knowledge generation which, from the perspective of teacher education, is important as 'inquiry'. This is now a policy priority, with increasing recognition that teaching and teacher education ought to focus on it as a key programme and workplace design feature. Paavola et al. (2004) extended Sfard's two-metaphor framing by noting a third metaphor of knowledge creation, going beyond enculturation via participatory socialisation into existing practices. Drawing on Nonaka and Takeuchi's (1995) model of knowledge-creation, Engeström's (1999a, 1999b, 2001) model of expansive learning, and Bereiter's (1992) model of knowledge building, they note that all three 'emphasize dynamic processes for transforming prevailing knowledge and practices' (Paavola et al. 2004, p. 557) and direct our attention toward the investigation of 'mediated processes of knowledge creation that have become especially important in a knowledge society' (ibid., p. 557).

Resources for Learning: (i) The Knowledge-practice Relationship (ii) Support

The role of material, cultural and symbolic resources available for learning is a guiding assumption of a socio-cultural perspective on learning. The conceptualisation and enactment of the knowledge-practice relationship permeates professional education. In the case of teacher education, this is reflected in a long-standing focus on moving beyond rational-technical models toward more 'reflective practice' oriented models of professional education.

A second vital resource for those learning to teach is the extent to which pre-service teachers experience gradual and supported entry into full classroom responsibility. This assumption is based on research on learning as assisted performance (Vygotsky 1978; Tharp and Gallimore 1988) and on more recent teacher education studies (Moore-Johnson 2004; Mewborn and Stinson 2007). Significantly, these suggest that the 'sink or swim' model of learning to teach ultimately undermines teaching;

it provides far fewer opportunities to develop a wide repertoire of skills, and the pressure to survive consigns pre-service and beginning teachers to an over-reliance on their 'apprenticeship of observation' (Lortie 1975).

Learning by Individuals, Organisations and the System

Earlier in the introduction we noted that the work of Hakkarainen et al. (2004) on 'communities of networked expertise' and Engeström and colleagues' research (Engeström 1999a, 2001; Engeström et al. 1999) on 'knotworking' has brought a systematic approach to understanding learning at the regional or wider system level, that is, a focus that includes, but extends beyond, focusing on individual persons and organisations to encompass how multiple organisations and networks together can learn. In an era of major review and reform of teacher education in Ireland and elsewhere, understanding the dynamics of how an entire region/system learns is increasingly important. According to Tynjälä (2008, p. 559), the field has focused on the role of 'networking and other forms of social exchange for both individual learning and organisational development', captured in such concepts as 'innovative knowledge communities' (Hakkarainen et al. 2004) and 'ba', that is, a space for learning (Nonaka and Konno 1998). Attention in the formulation of these concepts has focused on the social and organisationally embedded nature of the knowledge creation process in which explicit and tacit knowledge is interwoven. In the case of Ireland, a range of significant networks focused on both the development and research dimensions of teacher education have arisen in the last decade, providing new types of support for system learning.

Eraut's Two Triangle Model (see Fig. 3.2, Chap. 3 this volume) provides a concise summary of the dimensions of change in the workplace learning environment. Using Eraut's model, we can see how teacher education is changing in Ireland, in terms of both learning and context factors. Informed by the metaphors, resources and levels of learning outlined above, in the main section of this chapter we present five challenges within workplace practice in teacher education, noting their implications for research on learning to teach. In the case of each we note a potentially generative concept from research on workplace learning (see Table 13.1). For example, in the first challenge identified, that is, the significant extent to which pre-service teachers feel compelled to become invisible as learners, this short circuiting of their experience of 'liminality'—of being what Cook-Sather (2006) terms 'betwixt and between'—has the potential to provide important insights into their experience of the field placement in schools. These generative constructs, we think, provide a way of re-framing and possibly widening perspectives on some aspects of current policy and practice in pre-service teacher education in Ireland. In the next section of this chapter, we identify five challenges, in light of existing practices, and associated generative constructs. In each case, the generative construct focuses our attention on some aspect of teacher education through which we might consider making schools more like 'learningplaces' than workplaces, in support of more powerful pre-service teacher education.

Table 13.1 Challenges, practices and generative constructs

Challenge	Existing practices	Generative construct
Invisibility-visibility as a learner	Pre-service teachers feel compelled to become invisible as learners	Liminality
Deepening engagement with pedagogy	Considerable mentoring on field placements but little access to pedagogy	Assisted performance and horizons of observation
Reframing the knowledge-practice relationship	'Knowledge-for-teaching' dominant historically... policy and practice challenging this in last decade	Inquiry cycle
Moving beyond 'host' model of school-university collaboration	'Host' model dominant with some more partnership models emerging. No tradition of nor aspiration for school-led teacher education	Professional learning cultures: novice, veteran and integrated
Advancing learning and collaboration at system level	New networks focused on teacher education review, reform and research	'Knotworking'

Challenges and Tensions

Invisibility-visibility of Learners and Learning

> There are no formal structures, arrangements or requirements in relation to teacher observation, coaching or mentoring ... While there is no tradition of teacher observation, peer coaching or mentoring in Ireland, there have been a number of pilot projects involving groups of schools and Education Centres in which different approaches to mentoring have been monitored and researched. (OECD and LDS 2007, pp. 43–44)

One of the central workplace learning dynamics in teacher education in Ireland has been the relative absence of a formal mentoring culture within pre-service teacher education. Conway et al. (2011c), in the LETS study at post-primary teacher education, documented some degree of 'hidden mentoring'. However, compared to some other professions and some teacher education programmes in other jurisdictions, the LETS findings suggested that without quality mentoring support, pre-service teachers in the study preferred to become 'invisible' as learners (Long et al. 2012). Furthermore, the quote above from the OECD and LDS (2007) review lends support to the claim that this phenomenon is quite typical across the system. As such, the LETS study characterises the pre-service teachers' appetite for isolation in terms of 'invisibility' (Conway et al. 2011c; Long et al. 2012), and noted that they are less successful at negotiating curriculum or assessment issues in schools when no one in the school takes responsibility for their learning as novice teachers. In terms of workplace learning, this finding presents the somewhat puzzling conclusion that, while pre-service teacher education field placements are intended as primarily a site for learning, the adoption of a visible learner identity was counter to the manner in which pre-service teachers were regulated by the existing cultural practices in their field placements. This is similar to Edwards and Protheroe's (2003, p. 228) findings on pre-service teacher education in England: 'unlike the West African tailor apprentices observed by Lave (Lave 1977), student teachers are given little opportunity for "peripheral participation" (Lave and Wenger 1991) in pedagogic practices'. In terms of research on workplace learning, the potential of the field placement site as a liminal space (Cook-Sather 2006) is short-circuited, with pre-service teachers cast into full responsibility roles prematurely. As McNamara et al. (2002, p. 863) noted in their pre-service teacher education study: 'we identify the transition not as a linear progression but as a complex process of extended and ambiguous "in-betweenness" that involves play, performance and ordeal'. Accepting the fact that moving from legitimate peripheral to central participation, in the classic Wengerian sense, may not be generally attainable in pre-service teacher education demands other concepts to understand and extend the various positions open to pre-service teachers within workplace settings. Importantly, liminality is, we think, useful here in portraying the 'extended and ambiguous "in-betweenness"' central to the learning to teach experience.

Deepening Engagement with Pedagogy: From Solo to Assisted Practice

In the case of the PGDE [Post Graduate Diploma in Education] students, their "horizon of observation" is significantly limited, despite the widespread access to one or more types of mentors. Even for the 40 % who did have observation opportunities, these were rare events, with one in six experiencing this once or twice, and a similar number having opportunities to talk to the observed teacher following the lesson. (Conway et al. 2010, p. 111)

Two studies, almost 20 years, apart provide food for thought in relation to the regulation of teachers' workplace learning in Irish schools and its implications for pre-service teacher education. In 1991 the OECD country review of Ireland's education system noted what the review team termed the 'legendary autonomy' of Irish teachers. In 2009, the OECD's Teaching and Learning International Survey (TALIS) (Gilleece et al. 2009) identified a distinct pattern of teacher collaboration across participating countries, including Ireland. That is, the dominant form of professional collaboration is characterised by what the TALIS study termed 'exchange and coordination' activities more frequently than by 'more complex professional collaboration'—the latter involving activities such as jointly teaching the same class, taking part in year or subject area meetings, observing another teacher's class and providing feedback, engaging in joint activities across different classes and age groups (e.g. projects), and discussing and co-ordinating homework practice across subjects (Gilleece et al. 2009, p. 84). Furthermore, the OECD and LDS (2007, p. 43) report on leadership in Irish schools noted that 'There are no formal structures, arrangements or requirements in relation to teacher observation, coaching or mentoring'. As such, when pedagogical solitude characterises the practice of teaching, and exchange and co-ordination level activities typify teachers collegial relations, there are, by implication, inadequate opportunities collectively to see, understand and develop pedagogy in the workplace for pre-service teachers. Consequently, with the heart of schooling remaining largely unobservable by peers, opportunities for professional learning are significantly fore-closed, with, we argue, significant implications for pre-service teacher education and induction.

In the LETS study, we found that, under the prevailing system, most of the pre-service teachers surveyed went straight into classroom teaching without a prior period of observation in their teaching practice school. A few schools did provide for such observation sessions, and those who experienced this spoke very favourably of the learning opportunities they experienced as a consequence. This might seem obvious; nevertheless it has not traditionally been a feature of Professional Diploma in Education placements in general up to now. Underpinning contemporary reforms in teacher education is an assumption that access to the pedagogy of accomplished teachers is a key feature of teacher education programmes. A central mechanism for this is the pre-service teachers' experience on field placements, where opportunities to observe and be observed, as well as to engage in professional conversations are assumed to be a staple aspect of learning to teach. In LETS, a contradiction emerged: the vast majority of pre-service teachers surveyed had support within their schools from mentors, but this mentoring did not include, except in a small minority of notable cases, access to observing these same teachers' pedagogical practice or to discussions on pedagogical practice. Some pre-service teachers in our study reported that there was little opportunity for professional dialogue in their schools, either among existing teachers, or between experienced teachers and novices.

The idea of assisted practice (rather than solo practice) as the basis for learning to teach is at the core of contemporary policy on teacher education, at pre-service teacher education, induction and continuing professional learning stages (Tharp and Gallimore 1988; Feiman-Nemser 2001; Mewborn and Stinson 2007). Internationally, this is evident in, for example, mentoring and coaching initiatives across the continuum (Staub and West 2003). One of the distinctive features of learning to teach is the manner in which, especially in the Irish context, opportunities for structured observation and mentoring have been significantly under-developed to date, as noted above (and in OECD and LDS 2007, p. 44, 47). Furthermore, our focus on deep-ening engagement with pedagogy as a key aim in enhancing workplace learning is informed by the socio-cultural concept 'horizon of observation', that is:

> Lines of observation and limits on observation of the activities of others have consequences for the knowledge acquisition process. . . Let us refer to the outer boundary of the portion of the task that can be seen or heard by each team member is that person's horizon of observation. (Hutchins 1993, p. 52)

The strong cultural dynamic of autonomous teaching and professional collabora-tion, focused mainly on co-ordination issues, seems to have a significant impact on pre-service teachers' horizon of observation (Conway 2007; Conway et al. 2011c, Conway et al. 2011b). We argue that the horizon of observation available to both students in pre-service teacher education and to newly qualified teachers on induc-tion is limited by current structural and cultural arrangements—notwithstanding the existing significant support available to pre-service teacher education students and newly qualified teachers in schools by mentoring in a general sense, as noted earlier.

Importantly, two constructs—Hutchins' 'horizon of observation', based on research with quartermasters learning to navigate on aircraft carriers, along with Tharp and Gallimore's Vygotskian-inspired 'assisted performance'—have significant potential in sensitising researchers and policy-makers to the moment-to-moment transactions around supporting pedagogical enculturation and knowledge creation. A number of recent studies in pre-service teacher education in Ireland are mapping the changing engagement between neophyte teachers and experienced teachers, as the whole area of mentoring in pre-service teacher education and induction has become a focus of policy (see Young 2012; Chambers et al. 2012; Kozina 2010; O'Sullivan 2013). Furthermore, the work of Leavy (Leavy 2010; Leavy et al. 2010) with final year students in a teacher education programme, using the lesson study idea developed in Japan, promotes the concept of sharing practice in order to develop teaching knowledge and skills. We address the issue of knowledge creation later in this chapter.

Reframing the Knowledge-practice Relationship

> All forms of professional education share the goal of readying students for accomplished and responsible practice in service to others. Thus, professionals in training must master both abundant theory and large bodies of knowledge; the final test of their efforts, however, will be not what they know but what they do. (Cooke et al. 2006, pp. 1340–1341)

The knowledge-practice relationship is one of the central concerns in professional education, in school teaching as well as in medicine and other professions. For example, writing on the development of medical education 100 years after the landmark Flexner report (Flexner 1910), Cooke et al. (2006) note that the assimilation of medical education into universities in the USA and Europe 100 years ago profoundly influenced the nature of what knowledge is viewed as important and the way in which students encounter this knowledge. This has led to ongoing efforts to balance the emphasis placed on scientific, cultural and humanistic knowledge, as well as professional values essential for practice. Similarly, many other professions, including teaching, social work, and psychology, have sought to foster scientific and social-scientific research-generated knowledge as the basis for professional practice and as a means to enhance their professions' status. While the link to universities of teacher education vastly expanded the knowledge base and enhanced professional status, the nature of the knowledge-practice relationship remains problematic.

In Ireland over the last decade, a re-framed understanding of that problematic relationship (Conway et al. 2008) has featured prominently as a consideration in how best to re-design teacher education, and thus has implications for how to undertake workplace learning research in that context. Furthermore, the Teaching Council's policy on the continuum of teacher education identified the reframing of the knowledge-practice relationship as an important dimension of reform. Consequently, in addressing this issue in terms of workplace learning, the framework of Cochran-Smith and Lytle (1999) on the knowledge-practice relationship is useful. It is structured around three different types of relations: (1) knowledge *for* practice, (2) knowledge *in* practice, and (3) knowledge *of* practice (see Table 13.2). In summary, the reframing of

Table 13.2 Conceptions of the knowledge-practice relationship

Knowledge for practice	Knowledge in practice	Knowledge of practice
Knowledge-base for teaching exists. Typically based on research (may include codified 'wisdom of practice').	Teacher knowledge expressed in artistry of practice, reflection, narratives.	Knowledge generation and knowledge use problematic. Generated through collaborative critical appraisal of various types of knowledge sources with marked focus on practice-based professional networks and inquiry groups.

Table summarising the distinctions made by Cochran-Smith and Lytle (1999)

this relationship has become a central theme in teacher education review and reform (Conway et al. 2009; Teaching Council 2011), as evidenced by the emphasis on rethinking assessment of teaching practice, putting knowledge integration at the core of pre-service teacher education, and developing an inquiry orientation within teacher education programmes (this latter point is addressed in more detail in the next section).

Cochran-Smith and Lytle (1999) argue that different conceptions of teacher knowledge and learning imply very different understandings of teacher education. All three conceptions encompass knowledge generation and knowledge use, but have very different understandings of these two processes at the heart of professional education and work. Critiquing the shortcomings of both knowledge *for* practice and knowledge *in* practice perspectives, they advocate an *inquiry as stance* perspective in terms of how 'inquiry produces knowledge, how inquiry relates to practice, and what teachers learn from inquiry within communities' (ibid., p 250). The knowledge *for* practice perspective assumes that teachers who know more (that is, who have a deep and flexible understanding of the knowledge base emanating from disciplines) will teach better. The knowledge *in* practice conception assumes teacher knowledge is expressed in artistry of practice, reflection and narratives, given the way in which professional knowledge is situated, social, and rooted in the uncertainty of a professional practice. This type of knowledge is acquired and enhanced through deliberate reflection on practice and inquiry into professional experiences. Improvement of practice also involves teachers making explicit the tacit knowledge and assumptions underpinning their practice, through collaborative reflection on practice with colleagues.

The knowledge *of* practice conception questions the formal-practical knowledge distinction in terms of the origin of and power associated with adherence to the distinction. This conception assumes that 'basic questions about knowledge and teaching—what it means to generate knowledge, who generates it, what counts as knowledge and to whom, and how knowledge is used and evaluated in particular contexts—are always open to discussion' (Cochran-Smith and Lytle 1999, p. 272). This conception, like the others, has implications for teachers across the continuum of teacher education, but is distinctive in its focus on the ways in which teachers' professional knowledge (not practical knowledge, as in the knowledge in practice conception) can be no less powerful than formal knowledge. As such, 'The basis of this knowledge-practice conception is that teachers across the professional life span play a central and critical role in generating knowledge of practice by making their class-rooms and schools sites for inquiry, connecting their work in schools to larger issues, and taking a critical perspective on the theory and research of others' (ibid., p. 273).

In terms of workplace learning, there are a number of important points to emphasise in relation to Cochran-Smith and Lytle's conception of knowledge *of* practice. Firstly, it does not assume that it is only teacher-generated knowledge that is essential to professional practice. It acknowledges the value and necessity of different types of knowledge for optimal professional practice (e.g. knowledge generated in other settings by researchers from different disciplinary backgrounds). Secondly, it does not assume that teacher-generated knowledge needs necessarily to adopt the same knowledge-generating strategies as those adopted by professional researchers—although it does not preclude this either. Thirdly, they argue, given their rejection of the formal-practical knowledge distinction underpinning conceptions one and two, that the knowledge *of* practice (conception three) is not merely an amalgam of conceptions one and two but represents a fundamentally different understanding of knowledge generation and use across the continuum. Based on their advocacy of this third conception, they proposed *inquiry as stance* to highlight the potential of framing the knowledge-practice relationships in a new way that provides greater recognition for locally generated school knowledge, eschews the formal-practical knowledge distinction, and has the potential to create new synergies between university- and school-based researchers in efforts to enhance teaching and learning. Importantly, in our view, Cochran-Smith and Lytle's more explicit attention to the politics of professional knowledge—something that is often neglected in cognitive framings of knowledge—has an important place in workplace learning research. In particular, the policy prioritisation given to the promotion of an inquiry stance in the initial phase of teacher education in recent teacher education reforms in Ireland, and elsewhere (see OECD's 'Teachers Matter' report 2005), highlights, we think, a potential future priority within workplace learning research in pre-service teacher education.

School of Teacher Learning Workplace: Which Model, Which Culture?

The potential role of formal and more structured school-university partnerships has become a policy focus in teacher education in Ireland in the last few years (Teaching Council 2011). In light of the relative absence of a tradition of formal mentoring and coaching in pre-service teacher education, the development of new school-university partnership practices informed by workplace learning research is significant. Two frameworks in particular we see as generative in this context: models of schools-university partnership (Maandag et al. 2007), and the types of professional learning culture in schools (Moore-Johnson 2004).

Maandag et al.'s analytical typology of school-university partnerships based on a five-country study identified possible arrangements: host, co-ordinator, partner, network and training school models (see Box 13.1).

Box 13.1

Five Models of University-school Partnerships in Pre-service Teacher Education (based on a five-country cross national study)

Model A: Workplace/Host Model

In this model, the school is the location where the pre-service teacher undertakes a placement. The tertiary institution provides all coursework. This model typically involves some coaching by supervising teachers.

Model B: Co-ordinator Model

In this model, the school has a central supervisor or liaison teacher with the tertiary institution. This model is a variation on Model A. The difference is that in this model the school takes on the task of supervising pre-service teachers by appointing an experienced colleague to co-ordinate teacher education.

Model C: Partner Model

A teacher in the school acts as a trainer of professional teachers. The school is partly responsible for the course curriculum. In addition to coaching the pre-service teacher, the school also provides some of the training itself.

Model D: Network Model

In this case, the trainer is in the school as the leader of a training team in the school. The school is only partly responsible for the course curriculum. The school has a teacher education training team consisting of one or more trainers at school, and coaches who are trained in teaching methods.

Model E: Training School Model

In this model, the entire training course is provided by the school. The tertiary institution functions as a backup or support institution, focusing on training the trainers at school and developing teaching and training methods.

Source: Maandag et al. 2007

The host model (Maandag et al. 2007) is dominant in current school-university partnership practices in relation to pre-service teacher education in Ireland. Evidence for this is suggested by a number of observations made of practice in deliberations underpinning the recent reviews of teacher education cited earlier in this chapter, and by the emerging reforms to practices which are recommending re-designing practice to focus on co-ordinator and partner models (i.e. Models B and C respectively).

However, the wide variation in the degree of support experienced by pre-service teachers in the LETS study prompts us to examine other constructs that might inform our analysis. Moore-Johnson's conceptualisation of professional learning cultures, even though based on a study of newly qualified teachers during their induction, is also informative. In particular, it primes us to consider how, even within a single school-university model, (in this case the dominant host model in current practice as evidenced in LETS), different school cultures can provide widely differing opportunities to learn to teach. In terms of cultures of professional learning in schools, we draw upon a large-scale study of induction in the USA—the 'Project on the Next

Generation of Teachers' (Moore-Johnson 2004)—which identified three school cultures vis-à-vis teacher learning that have very different implications for the types of support offered to neophyte teachers:

- **Novice-oriented professional culture**: beginner teachers support each other with little or no mentoring or opportunities to observe and share practice;
- **Experienced/veteran-oriented professional culture**: experienced/veteran teachers are supportive in a general way, yet by and large provide no mentoring, observation opportunities or feedback on classroom teaching;
- **Integrated professional culture**: learning to teach is seen as a task for all in the school. Support for newly qualified teachers is generally widespread across the school, with peer observation, feedback and a coaching culture centred around sharing professional practice and a deep focus on pedagogy.

This 'school culture' model also provides a frame for reflecting on and integrating the 'horizon of observation' construct, and its focus on micro processes of moment-to-moment transactions, within the more macro framing of school cultures.

Advancing Learning at the System Level

During the last five years the development of three projects[2] has provided a rich cross-institutional and cross-border context for discussions focused on the initial phase of teacher development, as well as other phases of the continuum. From a workplace learning perspective on inter-institutional learning, this development is a potentially informative case of learning at a system level. The first of these projects is the Standing Conference on Teacher Education, North and South (SCoTENS, e.g. Burke 2003), which was set up primarily to support teacher educators on the island of Ireland through conferences, publications, resources and discussions. The second is the Colleges of Education Research Consortium (CERC), established in 2003 as a locus of information, networking and collaboration for research and research-related activities in primary teacher education. Finally, the Ubuntu Network supports the integration of Development Education and Education for Sustainable Development into post-primary pre-service teacher education in Ireland (funded by Irish Aid, Department of Foreign Affairs). This network provides an important context for teacher educators to share practice innovations, goals and principles, and to collaborate on innovative small-scale research projects on enacting development education principles of participative action research. The purpose of highlighting these within this chapter on workplace learning is to draw attention to how teacher educators collectively are re-orientating their work to incorporate research; typically small-scale studies of their own practices, but with notable cross-institutional, and cross-border in the case of SCoTENS, collaborative dimensions to this work. Furthermore, the

---

[2] Web addresses for the three projects are as follows: SCOTENS, http://scotens.org; CERC www.cerc.ie; Ubuntu www.ubuntu.ie.

CERC project, for example, includes a programmatic longitudinal study of a cohort of teachers' lives (Morgan and O'Leary 2004; Morgan et al. 2010).

The cross-border dimension has added a valuable comparative perspective on the dynamics of pre-service teacher education in Ireland. In this context, a recent North-South/SCoTENS study of teaching practice and university-school partnership arrangements is indicative of the current issues being addressed by teacher educators (McWilliams et al. 2006). McWilliams et al. examined teacher education in Northern Ireland and Ireland in the context of an exchange programme between pre-service teachers from Northern Ireland and Ireland for a period of school-based work in each other's jurisdictions. Locating the study in recent curricular developments, partnership with schools, college requirements and cultural diversity in both jurisdictions, the study illustrated the effects of different system arrangements on pre-service teacher preparation, classroom delivery and tutor involvement in the received curriculum of pre-service teacher education. The researchers noted, for example, the highly prescribed and assessed Northern Ireland primary curriculum compared to that of 'the Republic of Ireland, which appears to offer more in terms of freedom, flexibility and independence in planning' (ibid., p. 67). They also documented different supervisory practices and responsibilities for the assessment of pre-service teachers' practice in schools. For example, they documented how college of education tutors in Ireland typically

> . . . exercise more control over student teachers' preparation and professional development for teaching, while in Northern Ireland the partnership arrangements have given more influence to schools. The paper illuminates the shift of locus of control and influence of Colleges of Education in Northern Ireland in the education of student teachers, while in Ireland [i.e. the South] Colleges of Education have retained their influence. (ibid.,p. 67)

The key lesson from this cross-border study is the undeniable importance of context and history in shaping current workplace learning practices in pre-service teacher education. Furthermore, as Tynjälä (2008) noted, the focus on networks (going beyond the individual learner and individual organisation) is one of the defining features of workplace learning perspective in recent years. However, research on this recent notable networking phenomenon in teacher education in Ireland has yet to be undertaken. Aside from the commissioned evaluation of the SCoTENS project 2003 to 2010 (Furlong et al. 2011), which identified a range of positive outcomes associated with key design features of that network, how exactly the 'knotworking' (that 'tying and untying') occurs is under-examined and might be the focus of future workplace learning research. The metaphor of the knot describes the variable, distributed and collaborative nature of complex interactions between agents and social structures within workplace settings (Engeström et al. 1999). Communication, artefacts and technologies are vital in order to navigate the volatile workplace activity system.

Conclusion: Reflections on Workplace Learning and Looking to the Future

Focusing on the need to revisit how learning can occur in schools during pre-service teacher education, we have emphasised ways in which current practice in pre-service teacher education typically short circuits learning opportunities in schools, such that schools are often not 'the learningplaces' for neophyte teachers that they might be. As such, in this chapter we have noted that current reforms provide a strong motivation, given their focus on extended and more varied placements in schools, to consider insights from workplace learning research. Drawing on the three key ideas from the learning sciences—metaphors, resources and levels of learning—we have suggested some potentially generative constructs for addressing emerging practice in pre-service teacher education, but with wider potential use across the continuum of teacher education. The direction of reform being taken in Ireland is not toward school-led teacher education, rather toward a twin-pillars model in which both schools and higher education institutions broker new ways of working. In doing so, we have noted key challenges which prompt us to consider how knowledge is created through inquiry, how pedagogical practice of experienced teachers is made more accessible to neophytes, and how schools and universities can jointly begin to reconceptualise the knowledge-practice relationship. Research on workplace learning, which we have noted in this chapter and which is also addressed throughout this book, can make important contributions to deepening and extending research and professional practice for all involved in pre-service teacher education.

Acknowledgements The 'Learning to Teach Study' (LETS) was funded by the Department of Education and Skills (DES), Ireland. Work on this chapter was supported by funding from the 'Re-imagining Initial Teacher Identity and Learning Study' (Rii-TILS) through an Advanced Collaborative Research Award (2012–2013) to the first author from the Irish Research Council: www.irchss.ie.

References

Bereiter, C. (1992). Referent-centered and problem-centered knowledge: Elements of an educational epistemology. *Interchange, 23*, 337–362.

Billett, S. (2004). Workplace participatory practices: Conceptualising workplaces as learning environments. *Journal of Workplace Learning, 16*(6), 312–324.

Burke, A. (2003). Report on second north south conference on initial teacher education. In A. Pollak (Ed.), *Challenges to teacher education north and south* (SCoTENS Annual Report 2003) (pp. 77–79). Armagh: Centre for Cross Border Studies.

Byrne, K. (2002). *Report of the Advisory Group on Post-Primary Teacher Education.* Dublin: Department of Education and Science.

Byrne, D., McGinnity, F., Smyth, E., & Darmody, M. (2010). Immigration and school composition in Ireland. *Irish Educational Studies, 29*(3), 271–288.

Chambers, F., Armour, K., Luttrell, S., Bleakley, W., Brennan, D., & Herold, F. (2012). Mentoring as a profession-building process in physical education teacher education. *Irish educational Studies, 31*(3), 354–362.

Cochran-Smith, M., & Lytle, S. L. (1999). Relationships of knowledge and practice: Teacher learning in communities. *Review of Research in Education, 24,* 249–305.

Conway, P. F. (2007). Mentors and mentoring: Individual and contextual factors. Paper presented at the European Association for Research on Learning and Instruction (EARLI), Budapest, Hungary, September.

Conway, P. F. (2013). Cultural flashpoint: The politics of teacher education reform in Ireland *The Educational Forum, 77*(1), 51–72. (M. Cochran-Smith (Ed.), Special Issue, The politics of teacher education policy: International perspectives)

Conway, P. F., & Murphy, R. (2013). A rising tide meets. a perfect storm: New accountabilities in teacher education in Ireland. *Irish Educational Studies, 32*(1), 11–36. (Special Issue. E. Kelly & A. Leavy (Eds.), Research in education related to teacher accountability).

Conway, P. F., Rath, A., & McKeon, J. (2008). Knowledge-practice relationship trends and dilemmas in reviews of primary and post-primary initial teacher education. Paper presented at American Educational Research Association, New York, April.

Conway, P. F., Murphy, R., Rath, A., & Hall, K. (2009). Learning to teach and its implications for the continuum of teacher education: a nine-country national study. Report commissioned and published online by the Teaching Council of Ireland. www.teachingcouncil.ie/_fileupload/Research/Commisioned%20Research/LearningToTeach-ConwayMurphyRathHall-2009_10344263.pdf. Accessed 21 Jan 2013.

Conway, P. F., Murphy, R., Delargey, M., Hall, K., Kitching, K., Long, F., McKeon, J., Murphy, B., O'Brien, S., & O'Sullivan, D. (2010). Learning to teach study (LETS): Developing curricular and cross curricular competences in becoming a 'good' secondary teacher. [Final Report]. Cork: School of Education, University College Cork.

Conway, P. F., Delargey, M., Murphy, R., & O'Brien, S. (2011a). Learning to teach in the context of reform-oriented mathematics. In T. Dooley & D. Corcoran (Eds.), *Proceedings of fourth national conference on research on mathematics education* (pp. 94–111). Dublin: St Patrick's College.

Conway, P. F., Murphy, R., Hall, K., & Rath, A. (2011b). Leadership and teacher education. In H. O'Sullivan & J. Burnham-West (Eds.), *Leading and managing schools* (pp. 89–110). London: Sage.

Conway, P. F., Murphy, R., Delargey, M., Hall, K., Kitching, K., Long, F., McKeon, J., Murphy, B., O'Brien, S., & O'Sullivan, D. (2011c). *Learning to teach study (LETS): Developing curricular and cross-curricular competences in becoming a 'good' secondary teacher. Executive Summary.* Cork: School of Education, UCC/ Department of Education and Science. http://cora.ucc.ie/bitstream/10468/880/1/PFC_LearningPV2011.pdf. Accessed 31 Jan 2013.

Conway, P. F., Murphy, R., Delargey, M., Hall, K., Kitching, K., Long, F., McKeon, J., Murphy, B., O'Brien, S., & O'Sullivan, D. (2012). Developing 'good' post-primary teachers and teaching in a reform era: Cultural dynamics in a programme level study of the 'Dip'. In F. Waldron, T. Dooley & J. Smith (Eds.), *Re-imagining initial teacher education (ITE): Perspectives on transformation.* Dublin: Liffey Press.

Cook-Sather, A. (2006). Newly betwixt and between: Revising liminality in the context of a teacher preparation program. *Anthropology & Education Quarterly, 37*(2), 110–127.

Cooke, M., Irby, D. M., Sullivan, W., & Ludmerer, K. M. (2006). American medical education 100 years after the Flexner report. *New England Journal of Medicine, 355*(13), 1339–1344.

Coolahan, J. (2003). Church-State relations in primary and secondary education. In J. P. Mackey & E. McDonagh (Eds.), *Religion and politics in Ireland at the turn of the millennium* (pp. 132–151). Dublin: The Columba Press.

Coolahan, J. (2007). The operational environment for future planning in teacher education: OECD and EU initiatives. In R. Dolan & J. Gleeson (Eds.), *The competences approach to teacher professional development: Current practice and future prospects*, (*SCoTENS Annual Report 2007*) (pp. 7–14). Armagh: Centre for Cross Border Studies.

Coolahan, J., Hussey, C., & Kilfeather, F. (2012). *The forum on patronage and pluralism in the primary sector: Report of the Forum's Advisory Group*. Dublin: Department of Education and Skills.

Department of Education and Skills. (2012). *Report on the pilot surveys regarding parental preferences on primary school patronage*. Dublin: Department of Education and Skills.

Edwards, A., & Protheroe, L. (2003). Learning to see in classrooms: What are student teachers learning about teaching and learning while learning to teach in schools? *British Educational Research Journal, 29*(2), 227–242.

Engeström, Y. (1999a). Innovative learning in work teams: Analyzing cycles of knowledge creation in practice. In Y. Engeström, R. Miettinen & R. L. Punamäki (Eds.), *Perspectives on activity theory* (pp. 377–404). Cambridge: Cambridge University Press.

Engeström, Y. (1999b). Activity theory and individual social transformation. In Y. Engeström, R. Miettinen & R. Punamäki (Eds.), *Perspectives on activity theory*. Cambridge, MA: Cambridge University Press.

Engeström, Y. (2001). Expansive learning at work: Toward activity theoretical reconceptualization. *Journal of Education and Work, 14*(1), 133–156.

Engeström, Y., Engeström, R., & Vähääho, T. (1999). When the center does not hold: The importance of knotworking. In S. Chaiklin, M. Hedgaard & U. J. Jensen (Eds.), *Activity theory and social practice*. Aarhus: Aarhus University Press.

Eraut, M. (2007). Learning from other people in the workplace. *Oxford Review of Education, 33*(4), 403–422.

Feiman-Nemser, S. (2001). From preparation to practice: Designing a continuum to strengthen and sustain teaching. *Teachers College Record, 103*(6), 1013–1055.

Flexner, A. (1910). *Medical education in the United States and Canada*. New York: The Carnegie Foundation for the Advancement of Teaching.

Fuller, A., & Unwin, L. (2005). Older and wiser? Workplace learning from the perspective of older employees. *International Journal of Lifelong Education, 24*(1), 21–39.

Furlong, J., Pendry, A., & Mertova, P. (2011). SCoTENS an evaluation of the first 8 years. www.scotens.org/wp-content/uploads/2011-scotens-evaluation.pdf. Accessed 21 Jan 2013.

Gilleece, L., Shiel, G., Perkins, R., & Proctor, M. (2009). *Teaching and learning international survey: National report for Ireland*. Dublin: Educational Research Centre.

Grossman, P., Compton, C., Igra, D., Ronfeldt, M., Shahan, E., & Williamson, P. (2009). Teaching practice: A cross-professional perspective. *Teachers College Record, 111*(9), 2055–2100. www.tcrecord.org/Content.asp?ContentId=15018. Accessed 11 Nov 2012.

Hakkarainen, K., Palonen, T., Paavola, S., & Lehtinen, E. (2004). *Communities of networked expertise: Professional and educational perspectives*. Amsterdam: Elsevier.

Hall, K., Conway, P. F., Murphy, R., Long, F., Kitching, K., & O'Sullivan, D. (2012). Authoring oneself and being authored as a competent teacher. *Irish Educational Studies, 31*(2), 103–117.

Hutchins, E. (1993). Learning to navigate. In S. Chaiklin & J. Lave (Eds.), *Understanding practice* (pp. 35–63). New York: Cambridge University Press.

Hyland, A. (2012). *A review of the structure of initial teacher education provision in Ireland*. Background report for the international review panel. Ireland: Higher Education Authority. www.hea.ie/files/AineHylandFinalReport.pdf. Accessed 21 Jan 2012.

Inglis, T. (1998). *Moral monopoly: The Catholic Church in modern Irish society*. Dublin: Gill and Macmillan.

Kellaghan, T. (2002). *Preparing teachers for the 21st century: Report of the working group on preservice teacher education*. Dublin: Department of Education and Science.

Kozina, E. (2010). Exploring the socialisation of newly qualified primary teachers. Unpublished doctoral thesis, Trinity College Dublin.

Lave, J. (1977). Cognitive consequences of traditional apprenticeship training in West Africa. *Anthropology and Education Quarterly, 8*(3), 177–180.

Lave, J., & Wenger, E. (1991). *Situated learning. Legitimate peripheral participation.* Cambridge: University of Cambridge Press.

Leavy, A. M. (2010). The challenge of preparing preservice teachers to teach informal inferential reasoning. *Statistics Education Research Journal, 9*(1), 46–67.

Leavy, A. M., Hourigan, M., & McMahon, A. (2010). Facilitating inquiry based learning in mathematics teacher education. In Proceedings of the Third Science and Mathematics Education Conference. Dublin City University, 16th and 17th of September, 2010.

Long, F., Hall, K., Conway, P. F., & Murphy, R. (2012). Novice teachers as invisible learners. *Teachers and Teaching: Theory and Practice, 18*(6), 619–636.

Lortie, D. (1975). *Schoolteachers: A sociological study.* Chicago: University of Chicago Press.

Maandag, D. W., Deinum, J. F., Hofman, A., & Buitink, J. (2007). Teacher education in schools: An international comparison. *European Journal of Teacher Education, 30*(2), 151–173.

Maher, E. (2009). Issues in contemporary Irish Catholicism'. *Doctrine and Life, 59*(5), 3

McNamara, O., Roberts, L., Basit, T. N., & Brown, T. (2002). Rites of passage in initial teacher training: Ritual, performance, ordeal, and numeracy skills test. *British Educational Research Journal, 28*(6), 863–878.

McNamara, G., O Hara, J., Boyle, R., & Sullivan, C. (2009). Developing a culture of evaluation in the Irish public sector. Evaluation. *International Journal of Theory, Research and Practice, 15*(1), 100–112.

McWilliams, S., Cannon, P., Farrar, M., Tubbert, B., Connolly, C., & McSorley, F. (2006). Comparison and evaluation of aspects of teacher education in Northern Ireland and the Republic of Ireland. *European Journal of Teacher Education, 29*(1), 67–79.

Mewborn, D. S., & Stinson, D. W. (2007). Learning to teach as assisted performance. *Teachers College Record, 109*(6), 1457–1487.

Moore-Johnson, S. (2004). *Finders and keepers: Helping new teachers survive and thrive in our schools.* San Francisco: Jossey Bass.

Morgan, M., & O'Leary, M. (2004). A study of factors associated with the job satisfaction of beginning teachers. *Irish Journal of Education, 35,* 73–86.

Morgan, M., Ludlow, L., Kitching, K., & O'Leary, M. (2010). What makes teachers tick? Affective incidents in the lives of teachers. *British Educational Research Journal, 36,* 191–208.

Nonaka, I., & Konno, N. (1998). The concept of 'ba': Building a foundation for knowledge creation. *California Management Review, 40*(3), 40–54.

Nonaka, I., & Takeuchi, H. (1995). *The knowledge-creating company. How Japanese companies create the dynamics of innovation.* New York: Oxford University Press.

OECD. (1991). *Reviews of national education polices for education.* Ireland. Paris: OECD.

OECD. (2005). *Teachers matter: Attracting, retaining and developing teachers.* Paris: OECD.

OECD, &L. D. S. (2007). *Improving school leadership: Country background report, Ireland.* Paris: OECD.

O'Sullivan, D. (2013). The experiences of newly qualified teachers in Irish primary schools. Unpublished manuscript, University College Cork.

Paavola, S., Lipponen, L., & Hakkarainen, K. (2004). Models of innovative knowledge communities and three metaphors of learning. *Review of Educational Research, 74*(4), 557–576.

PISA. (2009). *Results: What students know and can do: Student performance in reading, mathematics and science (Vol. 1).* Paris: OECD.

Sahlberg, P. (2007). Education policies for raising student learning: The Finnish approach. *Journal of Education Policy, 22*(2), 147–171.

Sahlberg, P., Munn, P., & Furlong, J. (2012). *Report of the international review panel on the structure of initial teacher education provision in Ireland: Review conducted on behalf of the Department of Education and Skills.* Dublin: Dept of Education and Skills.

Sfard, A. (1998). On two metaphors for learning and the dangers of choosing just one. *Educational Researcher, 27*(2), 4–13.

Staub, F., & West, L. (2003). *Content-focused coaching: Transforming mathematics lessons.* Portsmouth: Heinemann.

Sugrue, C. (2011). Between the twin towers of autonomy and accountability: Performative accountability or transformative leadership? In H. O'Sullivan & J. West-Burnham (Eds.), *Leadership and management in schools: Irish perspectives* (pp. 59–74). California: Sage.

Teaching Council. (2010). Draft policy on the continuum of teacher education. Background report: teacher education in Ireland and Internationally. www.teachingcouncil.ie/_fileupload/Teacher%20Education/policybackgroundpaper%20brf24dec2010.pdf. Accessed 20 Jan 2013.

Teaching Council. (2011). Policy on the continuum of teacher education. www.teachingcouncil.ie/_fileupload/Teacher%20Education/FINAL%20TC_Policy_Paper_SP.pdf. Accessed 20 Jan 2013.

Tharp, R. G., & Gallimore, R. (1988). *Rousing minds to life: Teaching, learning, and schooling in social context*. Cambridge: Cambridge University Press.

Tynjälä, P. (2008). Perspectives into learning at the workplace. *Educational Research Review, 3*(2), 130–154.

Vygotsky, L. S. (1978). *Mind in society: The development of higher psychological processes*. Cambridge: Harvard University Press.

Young, A. M. (2012). Defining possibilities for learning: The learning trajectories of Irish physical education cooperating teachers. Unpublished doctoral thesis, University of Limerick.

Chapter 14
Teacher Learning in the Workplace in Pre-service Teacher Education in Portugal: Potential and Limits from a Pre-service Teacher Perspective

Maria Assunção Flores

Introduction

This chapter focuses on pre-service teacher education in Portugal under the new legal framework resulting from the implementation of the Bologna process in European universities. It draws upon a broader piece of research aimed at investigating pre-service teachers' views of their learning process within pre-service teacher education, as well as their motivations for entering teaching, their sense of preparedness and their expectations for their trajectories in their future profession.

Unlike many European countries, in Portugal teacher surplus and unemployment amongst new teachers are two intertwined realities with implications for the recruitment of pre-service teachers in higher education institutions and for new teachers' job expectations. Along with these, more recently, a profound financial and economic crisis has been affecting Portuguese society at various levels (leading to salary cuts and higher taxes), including the teaching profession and pre-service teacher education, with higher rates of unemployment. Thus, the teaching profession and teacher education have been facing complex challenges over the last few years.

The goal of this chapter is twofold. It aims to describe the pre-service teacher education curriculum following the implementation of the so-called Bologna process in Portuguese universities under the legal framework published in 2007, which led to a process of restructuring pre-service teacher education programmes in Portugal. It also looks at workplace learning as a key component of pre-service teacher education curriculum from the perspective of pre-service teachers.

These issues are addressed based upon a brief review of existing literature and upon data drawn from research currently underway in which the author is involved. In the first part of the chapter, an overview of current challenges and trends in pre-service teacher education will be presented from an international perspective. There will also be a brief account of the ways in which pre-service teacher education is organised in Portugal as a result of the restructuring process following the implementation of

M. A. Flores (✉)
Institute of Education, University of Minho,
Campus de Gualtar, Braga, Portugal
e-mail: aflores@ie.uminho.pt

O. McNamara et al. (eds.), *Workplace Learning in Teacher Education,*   243
Professional Learning and Development in Schools and Higher Education 10,
DOI 10.1007/978-94-007-7826-9_14, © Springer Science+Business Media Dordrecht 2014

the Bologna process. The key components of the pre-service teacher education are discussed, and particularly the role of practicum as a key element in the curriculum. In the second part, the context of the study is presented as well as the main findings. The chapter ends with some conclusions and implications.

Challenges and Trends in Pre-service Teacher Education

Pre-service teacher education has been investigated from a variety of perspectives, including its curriculum organisation, its rationale and key components, and its impact on the education and professional learning of pre-service teachers (e. g. Darling-Hammond et al. 2010; Flores 2011). In general, researchers, policy-makers and teacher educators look at the education of teachers as one of the key elements in efforts to improve the quality of teachers, and consequently, the quality of teaching and learning in schools and classrooms.

Much has been written about the organisational features of pre-service teacher education and the role of universities and schools in the process of learning to teach. Diversity in its form and content (including different modes of government intervention) and concerns about its quality and outcomes have been major issues in the debates regarding pre-service teacher education in Europe and elsewhere (Flores 2011). Despite this, the idea that teacher education can make a difference in quality teachers and quality teaching in schools is advocated in existing literature. Zeichner and Conklin (2008) argue for the complexity of pre-service teacher education programmes and their various components, and for the need to discuss their meaning in both their content and structural characteristics.

Reporting on a review of existing research, Cochran-Smith (2005) asserts that consistent vision, strong collaborations between universities and schools, school/community fieldwork, and effective use of certain teacher education strategies are amongst the distinctive features of pre-service teacher education programmes. Similarly, Korthagen et al. (2006), based upon the analysis of three teacher education programmes in Australia, Canada and the Netherlands, identified seven principles: (i) learning about teaching involves continuously conflicting and competing demands; (ii) learning about teaching requires a view of knowledge as a subject to be created rather than as a created subject; (iii) learning about teaching requires a shift in focus from the curriculum to the learner; (iv) learning about teaching is enhanced through (pre-service) teacher research; (v) learning about teaching requires an emphasis on those learning to teach working closely with their peers; (vi) learning about teaching requires meaningful relationships between schools, universities and pre-service teachers; and (vii) learning about teaching is enhanced when the teaching and learning approaches advocated in the programme are modelled by the teacher educators. In other words, the authors stress the importance of coherence between three components: views of knowledge and learning, programme structures and practices, and quality of staff organisation in order for pre-service teacher education to make a difference.

A look at existing literature reveals that one of the critical elements in pre-service teacher education relates to the (missing) link between theory and practice (Elstad 2010), which is said to be the 'perennial problem of teacher education' (Korthagen 2010, p. 408). Korthagen explains this gap by identifying a number of reasons: the socialisation towards patterns existing in schools; the complexity of teaching itself; the learning process within teacher education; the epistemological nature of the transfer process; and the lack of attention to the affective dimension in the technical-rationality approach (ibid., p. 409). The idea that pre-service teacher education is mainly theoretical and disconnected from the real world of schools has been referred to in a number of studies (Ebby 2000; Flores 2001, 2006). In this regard, Formosinho (2009a) stresses the emphasis on the academic-oriented logic prevailing in many pre-service teacher education programmes in detriment to the professional one. The former is associated with knowledge fragmentation and with the existence of subject-related territories linked to university departments (Formosinho 2009a) which, in turn, hinders teaching co-ordination and curriculum articulation (Vieira et al. 2012). The latter recognises the specific nature of learning to teach, in which the practical and professional dimensions are of paramount importance, including workplace learning.

In general, practicum has been seen as a key element in pre-service teacher education curricula and as a place in which the theory and practice divide may be overcome. The connection between two sites of professional learning (schools and universities), the collaboration between university supervisors and co-operating teachers and pre-service teachers, and the possibility to link and to put into practice knowledge and competencies acquired at university have been identified as its major contributions (see, for instance, Flores 2000; Dawson and Norris 2000; Al-Hassan et al. 2012). Workplace learning is, therefore, perceived as the most important part of pre-service teacher education (Wilson et al. 2001; Flores 2005), but, at the same time, diversity in its form, content, duration and focus reveals the lack of consensus in its regard (Wilson et al. 2001).

Some major critical issues have been identified in learning in the workplace within pre-service teacher education. Previous research has shown the insufficient time for practicum within the curricula (Cardoso 2012), the development of practicum at the end of the programme (Cardoso and Flores, in press), and the lack of awareness and quality of supervisors' roles, including lack of feedback (Flores 2006; Cardoso 2012). As Korthagen et al. (2006, p. 1038) argue, 'the theory-practice issue seems intractable: telling new teachers what research shows about good teaching and sending them off to practice has failed to change, in any major way, what happens in our schools and universities'.

Understanding the nature, the purpose and the impact of pre-service teacher education implies the analysis of the conceptual and epistemological assumptions underpinning its models and organisational systems, but it also entails the consideration of the social, political, cultural and economic context in which it is embedded (Flores 2011). In the next section, I explore briefly the major features characterising pre-service teacher education in Portugal, with particular attention to the model adopted at the University of Minho which was put into place for the first time in 2008/2009, as a result of the new legal framework.

Pre-service Teacher Education in Portugal: Transitions Between the Old and the New Curriculum

Over the last years, pre-service teacher education in Portugal has been subject to restructuring under the so-called Bologna process. It has implied debates about the nature of teaching as a profession and the kinds of teachers that are to be trained within the context of current school curricula and challenges in the Portuguese society (Flores 2011).

The so-called Bologna process led to the publication of the Decree-Law n° 42/2005 which stipulates, amongst other features, the shift from a system based upon the transmission of knowledge to a competency-based one, and the adoption of the European Credit Transfer and Accumulation System. Portuguese higher education institutions have faced a number of changes, some of which include the organisation of a three-cycle structure (*Licenciado*, Master's and PhD), the construction of curricula based upon a credit system, student mobility and his/her centrality in his/her process of learning (see Decree-Law 42/2005, and Decree-Law 74/2006).

As far as teacher education is concerned, the Decree-Law n° 43/2007 stipulates the professional qualifications for teaching (from pre-school to secondary education). It is said that 'the political priority is the improvement of the quality of teaching' (ibid., p. 1320) which implies the clarification of the domains of qualification for the teaching profession within a broader view, making it possible for teachers to move from one cycle to the other. The same legal text clarifies the domains for teacher qualification (i. e. levels and areas in which teachers are to be trained, such as pre-school, primary school, pre and primary school, Portuguese, Maths, and so on) upon which teacher education may be organised. These need to be approved by the national agency for accreditation, through a demanding process which entails the clarification of aims and assumptions, study plans and curriculum, resources, including protocols with co-operating schools for practicum, amongst others.

Higher professional qualification (at a second cycle level, i.e., master's degree); curriculum based upon leaning outcomes in the light of teacher performance; research-based qualification; the importance of practicum (observation and collaboration in teaching situations under the supervision of a mentor/supervisor); school-university partnerships; and quality assurance of teachers' qualification and of pre-service teacher education, etc., are key assumptions of this new policy (ME 2007). In order to become a teacher, a three-year degree (*Licenciatura*) is needed, plus a master's degree in teaching (usually a two-year programme, varying from 90 to 120 credits). Table 14.1 summarises the main distinctive features of the pre-service teacher education programme before and after the implementation of the Bologna process, in regard to the so-called integrated model of training (taking as an example the model of the University of Minho for subject matter teachers). Other models did exist alongside the integrated model (as is the case of the sequential model of the classic universities), the analysis of which is beyond the scope of this chapter.

It is important to note, however, that although the integration of its different components was a distinctive feature of the integrated model, at least in theory, research

Table 14.1 Key distinctive features of pre-service teacher education before and after Bologna process

	Integrated model of training	New framework
Duration	5-year degree (*Licenciatura* in Teaching)	2-year master's degree in teaching
Structure	Four years of full-time study at university plus one year of practicum at a school	Separation between 2-year master's degree in teaching (2nd cycle) and 1st cycle in a given subject
Practicum	One year (final year of the 5-year programme)	45 credits in Year 2 of master's in teaching
Key characteristics	Educational sciences and subject matter simultaneously from the very beginning of the course	Fragmentation between subject matter and educational sciences
		Valorisation of research component and professional practice

has shown that, in practice, the gap between theory and practice was prevailing in many cases (see, for instance, Flores 2000, 2001).

As it implies a separation between training in the first cycle (three-year programme called *Licenciatura*) and second cycle (master's degree level which is now needed in order to enter the teaching profession), this new configuration represents a drawback from previous models of teacher education (i.e. the so-called integrated model— 4–5 years of training in which pre-service teachers would benefit from training in educational sciences and subject matter simultaneously from the very beginning of the course. See Flores 2006). Previously the subject area (e.g. English, Biology, Mathematics, etc.) and the pedagogical component were distributed simultaneously throughout the course. The new model, however, emphasises the subject knowledge and didactics and the professional practice occurring mainly at universities (which implies less time in schools).

Added to this is the prevalence of the academic-oriented culture (which emphasises knowledge fragmentation and individualism) in detriment to the professional culture (which attends to the specific nature of learning to teach) (Canário 2001; Formosinho 2009a). Along with this are: the nature of the academic culture (the organisation of university departments and the valorisation of research in detriment to teaching within faculty careers, and individualistic working patterns related, in many cases, with promotion), which makes curriculum articulation and the coherence of the pre-service teacher education project rather difficult; the separation between two institutional sites for learning—schools and universities (Flores 2000; Braga 2001; Estrela et al. 2002; Formosinho 2009b); and, consequently, the ways in which professional practice is understood and put into practice (the lack of articulation between discourse and practice is prevalent).

This new configuration of professional training results in a reduced time and space for practicum (which occurs only at master's level), with implications for the pedagogical activities that pre-service teachers are able to do. (In the previous model a one-year teaching practice was provided for pre-service teachers in a school, usually after four years of full-time study at university). As Moreira and Vieira (2012, p. 97) stated, 'the impact of this structural change is not yet clear; will second-cycle student teachers take teaching more seriously because they had more time to decide to become teachers, or will they take it less seriously because their training is shorter. And will they be able to integrate subject and pedagogical knowledge now that these curricular components are clearly separated?'.

The New Pre-service Teacher Education Curriculum and Workplace Learning

The curriculum of pre-service teacher education includes: (i) general educational training; (ii) specific didactics (for a given level of teaching and subject matter); (iii) professional practice; (iv) cultural, social and ethical education; (v) educational research methods; and (vi) training in the subject matter. The credits given to these different components vary according to the characteristics of the master's course, related to the level of teaching in which pre-service teachers are going to teach. It is noteworthy that the cultural, social and ethical education and the educational research methods components do not have specific credits within the pre-service teacher education curriculum; rather they are included in the credits given to general educational training and professional practice. The Decree-Law n° 43/2007 entails the valorisation of subject knowledge, and an approach to teaching based upon research and teaching practice. It also values 'educational research methodologies, taking into account the need for the performance of the teachers to be less as a mere doer or technician and more and more as a professional able to adapt to the characteristics and challenges of particular situations in the light of students' characteristics and school and social contexts' (Decree-law n° 43/2007).

Under the new framework, practicum is valued and it implies teaching under supervision. It is seen as the 'key and indispensable moment for learning' in order for pre-service teachers to apply 'knowledge, abilities, competencies and attitudes, learned in the other components' including the 'development, in real contexts, of professional practices adequate to concrete situations in classrooms, in schools and in the articulation between schools and communities' (Decree-Law n° 43/2007, p. 1321).

Practicum might have 30–45 credits within the pre-service teacher education curriculum plan, but it is up to the training institution to define it. However, the framework for organising practicum is seen in the legal texts regulating the general and specific professional performance of teachers (Decree-Law n° 240/2001 and Decree Law 241/2001) which point to four key dimensions: (i) professional, social and ethical dimension; (ii) development of teaching and learning; (iii) participation in school activities and relationship with the community; and (iv) training and professional development within a lifelong perspective (Decree-Law 240/2001).

Practicum is accompanied by a supervisor from the university and a co-operating teacher from the school in each subject matter. Within pre-service teacher education, professional practice is understood within a perspective of 'professional development of student teachers aiming at their performance as teachers-to-be and at promoting a critical and reflective stance vis-à-vis the challenges, processes and performances of the professional day-to-day practice' (Decree-Law n° 43/2007, p. 1324).

Unlike previous models of pre-service teacher education, under the current framework practicum results in a report presented in a public viva voce examination with three to five staff members including the supervisor (the other members include the co-ordinator of the pre-service teacher education programme and the examiners). The university supervisor should hold a PhD, although a given person with recognition as a specialist may also undertake the role. The co-operating teacher (the teacher who monitors and supports pre-service teachers' practicum at school), in contrast to previous models, does not participate directly in the final grading of the pre-service teacher, although the university supervisor shares ideas with him/her to collect information. As for the recruitment of co-operating teachers, their role is reinforced as they need to have at least five years of experience, and preferably specialised training in pedagogical supervision or training of trainers, or professional experience in supervision. Co-operating teachers are selected by the training institution based upon the agreement of the school administration. The Decree-Law n° 43/2007 also determines that 'higher education institutions should support teachers in the cooperating schools, particularly, cooperating teachers in their professional development' (ibid., p. 1325), fostering collaboration between universities and schools within the context of practicum (Flores 2004).

Ambiguity and diversity have been major characteristics of practicum as a key component of the pre-service teacher education curriculum. Although there is consensus in recognising the key importance of practicum in the process of learning to teach, there is less agreement with regard to its aims, the views of education and professional training underpinning it, the strategies and professional competencies to be developed, the role of the different key players, and the relation and place of practicum with regard to other components of pre-service teacher education curriculum, etc. (Flores et al. in press).

According to the formal documents existing at the University of Minho regulating the practicum, it is seen as a curricular unit (during one or two semesters, depending on the level of teaching, although for the large majority of cases it occurs in Year 2 of the programme degree, concomitantly with other curricular units) and as a key component of the Master's Degree in Teaching. It is developed under protocols with co-operating schools.

As a key component of pre-service teacher education, the practicum is developed under the national legal framework, in particular the credits it is given, the integration of the research component, and the writing up of a final report to be defended in a viva voce examination (a novelty in relation to previous models). The role of co-operating schools and universities in pre-service teacher education, and the reflective component oriented towards pre-service teacher professional development under a democratic view of education, were also elements taken into account, as well as the articulation between theory and practice, between teaching and research (Flores, Vieira and Ferreira, in press).

The goals of practicum include: to promote a critical understanding and intervention in pedagogical contexts, to deepen the development of subject matter and pedagogical competencies; to develop a research culture and collaboration in professional training; and to develop the integration of the cultural, social and ethical perspective in professional training. Three main dimensions associated with the professional profile of the teacher-to-be are identified: conceptual dimension—which relates to the theoretical framework of professional practice (subject knowledge, didactics, general educational knowledge, research and context); strategic dimension—associated with the methodological framework of professional practice (processes and techniques of analysis and development of subject knowledge and of teaching and learning, regulation and research of teaching, and understanding and transformation of intervention contexts); and axiological dimension—which deals with the values of professional practice (ethical and political values that lie behind educational action with its ethical and political implications) (Flores, Vieira and Ferreira, in press). Pre-service teachers develop a 'pedagogical project' within their practicum in a school, under the supervision of the co-operating teachers and university supervisors. Throughout Year 2, pre-service teachers attend seminars and modules that are supposed to support the development of the 'pedagogical project' in light of their needs and interests (e.g. curriculum project, learning environments, behaviour problems of pupils, etc.). Before the development of the project, pre-service teachers undertake observation of professional contexts, and in particular of the teaching of the co-operating teachers (which may last for three months).

The assessment of the practicum results from the work developed both at university and at school/in the classroom, and in particular from the development of the 'pedagogical project'. It includes participation of the pre-service teachers in supervising seminars (university and school), in classroom observation and in developing a portfolio. The portfolio serves as a basis for the final report on the practicum, which is between 20,000 and 25,000 words in length and is seen as a professional narrative of pre-service teachers' practicum.

The changes that have been introduced in the practicum component of the pre-service teacher education curriculum, after the so-called Bologna process, include important changes such as the research component, the role of co-operating teachers and schools, the existence of new ways of assessing practicum, etc. It is, therefore, important to get to know the perspective of the different stakeholders in pre-service teacher education in order to better understand its role and impact in the preparation of prospective teachers. It is within this view that the project reported in the chapter was developed.

The Study: Goals, Participants and Methods

This chapter draws upon a broader piece of research aimed at looking at the key components of pre-service teacher education at the University of Minho in order to better understand its mission and outcomes and to improve existing practices, particularly from the point of view of pre-service teachers—especially at a time when universities and schools, and particularly teacher education and teacher educators, face important challenges within current financial, economic and social crises. The overall research questions are:

1. How do pre-service teachers evaluate their pre-service teacher education programme?
2. Why have they decided to enter a teaching degree?
3. How do they rate different components of their training programme including workplace learning?
4. How and what do they learn in the workplace during pre-service teacher education?
5. What is their sense of preparedness to enter the teaching profession?
6. What are their expectations with regard to their trajectories in the teaching career?

The study reported in this chapter was carried out with pre-service teachers in the two-year Master's in Teaching programme. In this chapter, questions 3 and 4 will be dealt with. Data was collected through questionnaires and written narratives, both at the beginning and at the end of the master's degree programme. In this chapter, data arising from the narratives written at the end of the programme is analysed. The narratives included pre-service teachers' overall evaluation of the programme, their views of its key components, and their learning experience throughout the course, including suggestions for improvement. They were also asked at the end of the programme to write a letter to a prospective pre-service teacher. They were asked to talk about their experience in the programme and to give some recommendations and suggestions for future teaching candidates.

Participants in the study reported here included pre-service teachers enrolled in different two-year teaching programmes at the University of Minho (Physical Education, Portuguese and Spanish, History and Geography, Portuguese and Classical Languages, Mathematics, Biology and Geology, Philosophy, English and Spanish). Data was collected via email or delivered in person in 2011 and 2012. In total, 47 written narratives were collected. Out of the 47 participants, ten were male and 37 were female; their ages ranged from 22 to 45 years old (17.4 % were 22 years old). All of them were at the end of Year 2 of the master's degree programme. The process of qualitative data analysis was undertaken according to a vertical analysis (Miles and Huberman 1994): each of the respondents' accounts was analysed separately and there was a comparative or horizontal analysis (cross-case analysis) (Miles and Huberman 1994) to look for similarities as well as differences. In this chapter, two main dimensions are presented: (i) the most important learning experiences in pre-service teacher education; (ii) learning in the workplace: potential and limits.

Findings

The Most Important Learning Experiences in Pre-service Teacher Education

When asked about the most significant learning experiences in pre-service teacher education, pre-service teachers highlighted practicum, methodologies of teaching

Table 14.2 Most relevant
learning experiences in
pre-service teacher education

	Number of pre-service teachers who identified this issue
Practicum	20
Teaching and learning methodologies	13
Contents related to their subject matter	11
Transversal competencies	6

and learning, contents related to the subject matter they are going to teach, and other transversal competencies (see Table 14.2).

The most significant learning experiences occurred during practicum, which student teachers saw as the key component of pre-service teacher education as it made it possible for them to get in touch with real schools and classrooms. It provided them with an opportunity to "get to know what being a teacher is all about" (student (ST)3). Although they recognised the difficulties and challenges faced during practicum, especially because they had to undertake other courses at the university concurrently, pre-service teachers stressed the key features of their learning in the workplace. Issues such as dealing with students in classrooms, to get to know more about how they learn and behave and to identify their learning difficulties, were but a few examples highlighted by the participants:

> The most significant learning experiences I have done took place in my practicum when I was able to confront practice and theory. I felt that my practicum was a crucial learning experience for my future professional practice. (ST19)

> The practicum was the most important bit for me as I was given the opportunity to get to know the reality of a school and to get support and assistance in a school and this was proven to be more helpful than what I had at university. (ST26)

> During the practicum, I had the opportunity to learn a lot. But teaching was the most important one. I guess you learn from practice and you try to be a teacher in practice. Being able to share ideas with experienced teachers was also very important to me. (ST33)

Pre-service teachers valued the possibility of sharing and learning with other teachers at school, reiterating the key importance of practice and workplace learning in becoming a teacher. They also appreciated support and guidance during practicum in order to the get the most out of it, although some also claimed that there was room for improvement in this area, as will be discussed later in the chapter. These findings corroborate earlier work showing that the quality of the practicum as a learning experience depends upon the quality of the supervision, teamwork and support (Flores 2006; Flores and Day 2006).

Pre-service teachers also recognised the relevance of the components related to teaching and learning methodologies. They stressed in particular the knowledge and competencies they had developed, such as course planning, teaching strategies, learning processes, student motivation, and student behaviour, amongst others. Also of importance were content acquired within their specific subject matter modules:

> Learning how to use different methods of teaching, being able to reflect upon different aspects of the Spanish language learning, sharing experiences online with the lecturer were important to me. Also, getting to know and reflect upon student behaviour was of relevance to my training as a teacher-to-be. (ST22)

Table 14.3 Overall evaluation of practicum

	Number of pre-service teachers who identified this issue
Positive	24
Negative	2
Not positive or negative	20

> I guess specific contents related to the subject I am going to teach were relevant in terms of learning as well as teaching and learning methodologies. (ST21)

> I think that the most important component of my training related to teaching and learning strategies and mathematics, of course. Learning different methods of teaching both in theory and in practice (especially during my practicum) will make me a better teacher in order to teach students to be active citizens, interested in learning Mathematics. (ST44)

From pre-service teachers' accounts, transversal competencies also emerged, such as the use of information and communication technologies in the classroom, critical reflection and self-assessment:

> Critical reflection on the work done, not only concerning its weaknesses, but also its strengths, was an important learning experience to me. (ST5)

> I think that competencies in information and communication technologies for teaching mathematics were important. The different pedagogies and perspectives discussed in the module of Teaching and Learning Methodologies were also very important, as well as the knowledge acquired in History of Mathematics, which I enjoyed a lot. (ST23)

> The most important learning experience was the improvement of my communication competencies in the Spanish language, as well as the development of continuous and critical reflection on alternative pedagogical practices in regard to student motivation. The pragmatic exercises about oral strategies to interact with students allowed me to understand how to carry out student-centred methodologies. As a matter of fact, getting used to a given methodology for years and years without a break or without time to reflect upon it leads you as a teacher to a mechanic process which needs to be reinvented all the time! Thus, reflection was, without any doubt, the key learning experience for me in terms of personal and professional growth. (ST28)

Learning in the Workplace: Potential and Limits

Pre-service teachers also evaluated their practicum. Most of them considered that it was a positive experience (24), although 20 identified it as both a positive and negative experience (see Table 14.3). For two of them it was a negative experience.

The reasons behind the positive view of practicum had to do mainly with the support and guidance received from supervisors and with the possibility of interacting with and learning from them. Some of the participants also highlight the support from the co-operating teachers:

> The model of the practicum that has been implemented is positive as well as the role of supervisors and cooperating teachers. They made me grow a lot as a person as a professional. (ST5)

> Despite the difficulties, I guess my supervisors and my students made the different because they helped me a lot. (ST9)

> The truth is that you learn a lot in practice, mainly from the interaction with your supervisors and students. (ST31)

Further, the opportunity to get to know the real world of schools and classrooms; the possibility to interact with real students, with their challenges and difficulties; and the possibility to link theory and practice were cited as positive gains arising from learning in the workplace. These findings lend support to earlier work that has shown the advantages of practicum, such as getting to know the workplace, having first-hand experience and working directly with children, observing teachers and getting advice from them, as well as planning and giving lessons (Al-Hassan et al. 2012).

> I had the opportunity to get to know a real school and to get to know the reality of classrooms and students. I had the opportunity to link theory and practice and I realised that what you have been told at university is in general true and you should put it into practice. (ST23)

> I guess the most important bit in workplace learning was to get to know real schools and classrooms. You are able to understand what being a teacher looks like in reality. However, there was not enough time... (ST46).

> I have learned a lot and I was able to investigate and to apply strategies in order to develop the pedagogical project. However, the support and guidance at school could be better, as planning were not read nor were discussed the activities... (ST22).

As these last quotes suggest, although pre-service teachers in general had a positive view of their learning in the workplace during practicum, they also identified some issues—such as the development of the pedagogical project, the lack of time, and lack of guidance and support—as negative features.

These were also the reasons for the negative views expressed by two pre-service teachers. They claimed that they lacked adequate preparation. They also identified the gap between theory and practice and, again, the lack of support and guidance:

> I think practicum needs to be developed in a different way. You should have more support and guidance from your university supervisor. Sometimes you get very vague guidance and it doesn't help you in your learning. On the contrary, it hinders your work... (ST11)

> I think you do not have enough preparation. Theory does not apply to practice. (ST18)

The gap between theory and practice and the lack of time and support, as well as the lack of adequate conditions for practicum, were also stressed by those participants who expressed mixed feelings about whether it was a positive or negative experience. Although they recognised the research and reflective component of the practicum as positive features, they also pointed to its poor quality in terms of getting experience and having time to plan and give lessons:

> You always learn something. It allows you to reflect and to learn from it, but it isn't enough, at least, it is not enough in terms of quality. Supervisors and lecturers in general should give you more support. It seems that all they care about is marking and making you do oral presentations in classroom. Also, there is lack of organisation in the programme in terms of

articulation of its components. It seems that meetings and questionnaires on your opinion about the course are useless. On the other hand, you always learn new things that might be important especially with your colleagues. (ST21)

I think the research and reflective component of the practicum is very important and I agree with that. But I think you should have had more experience and practice in the workplace as it will be important for your future as a teacher. (ST43)

I guess in general my practicum was positive because I have learned, but it was also negative because it should be broader and including more lessons. The practicum should have more emphasis within ITE [pre-service teacher education] programme. I think it is globally poor... (ST 42)

Pre-service teachers provided some suggestions to improve the teacher education programme. These included a better articulation between the different components; the contribution of given modules for their practicum; and a better articulation of its assessment components, such as the portfolio and the final report, which, for some of them, overlapped. They also suggested more time for practicum, with a better articulation of the different modules that are supposed to support the development of the 'pedagogical project'. These findings corroborate earlier reports based on a 35-item questionnaire given to pre-service teachers, co-operating teachers, supervisors and lecturers—in 2010, 2011 and 2012—which pointed to a number of problems, such as lack of time and conditions for the development of the 'pedagogical project'; insufficient co-ordination (in general and amongst lecturers at university); lack of relevance of given modules for the analysis of pedagogical contexts and the development of professional competencies; and lack of adequate assessment methods in given modules and seminars (Vieira 2010/2011/2012).

Conclusion and Discussion

The practicum is considered to be both a crucial component and a critical element in pre-service teacher education (Flores, Vieira and Ferreira, in press), to a certain extent, because it entails different views, perspectives, and practices. However, learning in the workplace is seen as an opportunity to develop relevant knowledge and competencies for becoming and being a teacher. The structural component of practicum in pre-service teacher education has been, paradoxically, at the same time reinforced and limited under the new legal and institutional framework. On the one hand, the reflective and research components were emphasised along with the introduction of a public viva voce examination of the work done by the pre-service teachers during practicum. The development of a 'pedagogical project' and a portfolio represents an opportunity for them to develop not only subject and pedagogical related knowledge and competencies, but also the reflective and research skills, which are of crucial importance in learning to teach. One can also say that, in theory, the existence of different modules to support the development of the 'pedagogical project' may foster its potential as a learning strategy. On the other hand, however, there is less time for pre-service teachers to spend in schools, if we compare with the previous model described earlier in this chapter.

The participants in the study recognised that they had learned and developed knowledge and competencies relevant to their professional practice, but they also claimed that there was room for improvement in order to make their learning experience in pre-service teacher education, and particularly in practicum, more meaningful. In particular, they pointed to the need for a better articulation between the different components and the contribution of the different modules for their practicum, and a better articulation of its assessment components such as the portfolio and the final report, as well as more time for practicum, with a better articulation of the different modules that are supposed to support the development of the 'pedagogical project'. They also recognised the quality of supervision and the existence of support and guidance as key factors which made a difference in their process of becoming a teacher. This was not only a problem related to the practicum itself, but also had to do with the organisational and pedagogical culture within the institution (Vieira, Flores and Ferreira 2012). The separation of the different components of the practicum and the fragmentation of the pre-service teacher education curriculum, in part due to the disciplinary academic culture, have implications for the internal consistency of the programme with regard to the preparation of the pre-service teachers as far as research is concerned (Vieira et al. 2012). There is a need for 'direct and explicit attention to the place of experience in learning about teaching' (Korthagen et al. 2006, p. 1039).

The impact of the new model for pre-service teacher education remains to be seen. However, a number of conclusions may be drawn from what is known at the moment, which has implications for teacher education and teacher educators' roles. Clearly, it is crucial to work on the articulation of the key components of the pre-service teacher education curriculum and the place of practicum within it. This is far too important to be left to the pre-service teachers to make sense of it by themselves. The structural and organisational dimensions need to be made more explicit and clearer, not only in the curriculum plan but also in the work developed by teacher educators throughout the programme. In advocating a 'realistic approach, to teacher education, Korthagen (2010, p. 41) argues for a 'bottom-up process', which implies that 'it is impossible to make a clear distinction between different subjects in the teacher education programme. The realistic approach is not compatible with a programme structure showing separate modules'.

Another feature relates to the centrality of the pre-service teachers in the design and development of the teacher education programmes, in order to 'create suitable learning experiences' for them (Korthagen 2010, p. 418). As stated elsewhere (Flores 2001, p. 146), learning to teach 'is a process that goes beyond the mere application of a set of acquired techniques and skills. Not only does it imply the mastery of practical and more technical issues, but it also encompasses the construction of knowledge and meaning in an ongoing dialogue with the practice'.

This may be approached, amongst other features, through careful programme design, an elaborated view of the intended process of teacher learning, specific pedagogical approaches and investment in the quality of staff members (Korthagen et al. 2006). The recruitment of co-operating teachers, the selection of schools for practicum, and the development of a common philosophy or project of training need to be taken into account so that learning to teach becomes a meaningful experience for pre-service teachers. This implies a joint reflection about what kind of teacher is being trained and what kind of teacher is intended to be trained, and what we are going to with the model and the development of the current pre-service teacher education programme.

As a teacher educator, one of my main concerns has been the coherence between what and how I teach and the kinds of competencies and skills that I want to develop in my students. It revolves around the question: what are my students doing in my classes? What kind of learning experiences do I provide them? What is the relevance and contribution of my teaching and my work with them for their development as pre-service teachers?

Concerned with the development of pre-service teacher education in our institution, a number of teacher educators engaged in a study group, which started in March 2012, in order to investigate the training model and to discuss and disseminate training practices. In total, around 20 teacher educators volunteer to participate in this group, studying pre-service teacher education and our own practice as teacher educators.[1] Evaluating the pre-service teacher education model, and its aims, nature and impact, and understanding and developing innovative training methodologies through research are amongst the goals of the study group. The overarching aim is to develop a research culture on and in pre-service teacher education; a scholarship of teacher education aiming to better understand what we do and why we undertake given practices, as well as questioning their rationale and their implications (Flores et al. in press).

The potential of the self-study of teacher education has been recognised in the literature over the last decade, pointing to its key role in understanding and challenging teacher education programmes, processes and practices (see, for instance, Loughran 2005, 2009; Kitchen 2005; Schulte 2005). However, this is not an easy job. Changes in existing practices, especially those which imply a 'profound cultural shift in the existing views of teacher education which is often threatening to experienced educators' (Korthagen 2010, p. 419) are difficult but challenging processes as they may well require us to go beyond our 'comfort zones' as teacher educators.

The study group has been an important step in order to share and discuss different views of teacher education and to enhance a professional dialogue aimed at understanding better what we do in teacher education and why and how we can improve our programme and our practice as teacher educators. It has also been a relevant space for co-training and professional development as teacher educators, one of the issues that has been overlooked (Koster and Korthagen 2001). The findings from this study group may well add to data arising from other initiatives, an example of which is the study involving pre-service teachers described in this chapter.

The role of universities and schools in pre-service teacher education remains a critical issue which needs to be discussed, along with the understanding of the role of

---

[1] The Pedagogical Innovation Group was created in 2010 under the support of the Dean of the Institute of Education to promote reflection and professional development opportunities for staff in our institution. Amongst its initiatives is the development of the study group to reflect on teacher education in our institution.

different stakeholders, and in particular the role of learning in the workplace within the context of practicum. By and large, pre-service teacher education in Portugal has been characterised by *universitisation* which relates to the 'passage to higher education, typically to university education, of all the components of teacher education programmes for all levels of schooling' (Formosinho 2002, p. 3). Higher status and recognition of the teaching profession, higher academic status for Education Departments and Education Faculty, and the internalisation of the need for a lifelong perspective are amongst the positive features of this perspective (Formosinho 2002). However, a number of risks may be identified, namely 'the use of university autonomy to pursue individual interests and career rather than to develop the professional mission of teacher education courses (misuse of university autonomy); devaluation and/or mishandling of the professional certification process; mismatch between the experienced academic university culture and the advocated professional teaching culture' (Formosinho 2002, p. 19). This has led, to a large extent, to a process of 'academicisation' of pre-service teacher education, an example of which is the practical and professional component (in a broader sense) in many programmes which tend to be turned into a rather theoretical and disconnected component in pre-service teacher education curricula (Formosinho 2002, p. 3).

Through joint reflection and research of our own practice as teacher educators, and a deeper analysis of pre-service teacher education in terms of its philosophy and curriculum organisation in order to 'support the link between experience and theory in ways that are responsive to the expectations, needs and practices of teacher educators and student teachers' (Korthagen et al. 2006, p. 1037), it may well be possible to overcome some of the limits and difficulties encountered, and to enhance the potential of the current pre-service teacher education model.

References

Al-Hassan, O., Al-Barakat, A., & Al-Hassan, Y. (2012). Pre-service teachers' reflections during field experiences. *Journal of Education for Teaching, 38*(4), 419–434.

Braga, F. (2001). *Formação de professores e identidade profissional*. Coimbra: Quarteto Editora

Canário, R. (2001). A prática profissional na formação de professores. *Revista portuguesa de formação de professores, 1,* 25–38.

Cardoso, E. (2012). *Problemas e desafios na formação inicial de professores em Angola: Um estudo nos ISCED da Região Académica II*. Unpublished doctoral dissertation, University of Minho, Portugal.

Cardoso, E., & Flores, M. A. (in press). A formação inicial de professores em Angola: propósitos, desafios e oportunidades. In M. A. Borges & O. F. Aquino (Eds.), *A Formação inicial de professores em diferentes contextos: Políticas, práticas e perspectivas. Minas Gerais*, Brazil: EDUFU.

Cochran-Smith, M. (2005). Studying teacher education: What we know and need to know? *Journal of Teacher Education, 56*(4), 301–306.

Darling-Hammond, L., Newton, X., & Wei, R. C. (2010). Evaluating teacher education outcomes: A study of the Stanford Teacher Education Programme. *Journal of Education for Teaching, 36*(4), 369–388.

Dawson, K., & Norris, A. (2000). Pre-service teachers' experiences in a K-12/university technology-based field initiative. *Journal of Computing in Teacher Education, 17*(1), 4–12.

Decree-Law n° 240/2001, 30th August, Diário da República, I Série-A, pp. 5569–5572.

Decree Law n° 241/2001, 30th August, Diário da República, I Série-A, pp. 5572–5575.

Decree-Law n° 42/2005, 22nd February, Diário da República, I Série-A, n° 37, pp. 1494–1499.

Decree-Law n° 74/2006, 24th March, Diário da República, I Série-A, n° 60, pp. 2242–2257.

Decree-Law n° 43/2007, 22nd February, Diário da República, 1ª série, n° 38, pp. 1320–1328.

Ebby, C. B. (2000). Learning to teach mathematics differently: The interaction between coursework and fieldwork for pre-service teachers. *Journal of Mathematics Teacher Education, 3,* 69–97.

Elstad, E. (2010). University-based teacher education in the field of tension between the academic world and practical experience in school: A Norwegian perspective. *European Journal of Teacher Education, 33*(4), 361–374.

Estrela, M. T., Esteves, M., & Rodrigues, A. (2002). *Síntese da investigação sobre formação inicial de professores em Portugal (1990–2000).* Lisboa: FPCE-UL/INAFOP/IIE.

Flores, M. A. (2000). *A Indução no Ensino: Desafios e Constrangimentos.* Lisboa: ME/IIE

Flores, M. A. (2001). Person and context in becoming a new teacher. *Journal of Education for Teaching, 27*(2), 135–148.

Flores, M. A. (2004). The impact of school culture and leadership on new teachers' learning in the workplace. *International Journal of Leadership in Education, 7*(4), 297–318.

Flores, M. A. (2005). How do teachers learn in the workplace? Findings from an empirical study carried out in Portugal. *Journal of In-Service Education, 31*(3), 485–508.

Flores, M. A. (2006). Being a novice teacher in two different settings: Struggles, continuities, and discontinuities. *Teachers College Record, 108*(10), 2021–2052.

Flores, M. A. (2011). Curriculum of initial teacher education in Portugal: New contexts, old problems. *Journal of Education for Teaching, 37*(4), 461–470.

Flores, M. A., & Day, C. (2006). Contexts which shape and reshape new teachers' identities: A multi-perspective study. *Teaching and Teacher Education, 22*(2), 219–232.

Flores, M. A., Vieira, F., Ferreira, F. I. (in press). Formação inicial de professores em Portugal: problemas, desafios e o lugar da prática nos mestrados em ensino pós-Bolonha. In M. A. Borges & O. F. Aquino (Eds.), *A Formação inicial de professores em diferentes contextos: Políticas, práticas e perspectivas.* Minas Gerais: EDUFU.

Formosinho, J. (2002). Universitisation of teacher education in Portugal. In O. Gassner (Ed.) *Strategies of change in teacher education, European views.* ENTEP Conference Proceedings (pp. 105–127). Feldkirch: European Network on Teacher Education Policies.

Formosinho, J. (2009a). A academização da formação de professores. In J. Formosinho (Coord.), *Formação de Professores. Aprendizagem profissional e acção docente* (pp. 73–92). Porto: Porto Editora.

Formosinho, J. (2009b). A formação prática dos professores. Da prática docente na instituição de formação à prática pedagógica nas escolas. In J. Formosinho (Coord.), *Formação de Professores. Aprendizagem profissional e acção docente* (pp. 93–118). Porto: Porto Editora.

Kitchen, J. (2005). Looking backwards, moving forward: Understanding my narrative as a teacher educator. *Studying Teacher Education, 1*(1), 17–30.

Korthagen, F. A. J. (2010). How teacher education can make a difference. *Journal of Education for Teaching, 36*(4), 407–423.

Korthagen, F., Loughran, J., & Russell, T. (2006). Developing fundamental principles for teacher education programs and practices. *Teaching and Teacher Education, 22,* 1020–1041.

Koster, B., & Korthagen, F. (2001). Training teacher educators for the realistic approach. In F. A. J. Korthagen, J. Kessels, B. Koster, B. Lagerwerf & T. Wubbels (Eds.), *Linking practice and theory: The pedagogy of realistic teacher education* (pp. 239–253). Mahwah: Lawrence Erlbaum Associates.

Loughran, J. (2005). Researching teaching about teaching: Self-study of teacher education practices. *Studying Teacher Education, 1*(1), 5–16.

Loughran, J. (2009). A construção do conhecimento e o aprender a ensinar sobre o ensino. In M. A. Flores & A. M. Veiga Simão (Eds.), *Aprendizagem e desenvolvimento profissional de professores: contextos e perspectivas* (pp. 17–37). Mangualde: Edições Pedago.

ME, M. E. (2007). Política de Formação de Professores em Portugal. Lisboa: ME/DGRHE

Miles, M., & Huberman, M. (1994). *Qualitative data analysis*. London: Sage.

Moreira, M. A., & Vieira, F. (2012). Preservice teacher education in Portugal. The transformative power of local reform. In J. M. Paraskeva & J. Torres (Eds.), *Globalism and power. Iberian education and curriculum policies* (pp. 94–105). New York: Peter Lang.

Schulte, A. (2005). Assuming my transformation: Transforming my assumptions. *Studying Teacher Education, 1*(1), 31–42.

Vieira, F. (2010/2011/2012). Balanço Final do Estágio. Documentos produzidos no â mbito da coordenação do Estágio dos Mestrados em Ensino da Universidade do Minho (policopiados).

Vieira, F., Flores, M. A., & Ferreira, F. I. (2012). *Articulação curricular e pedagógica. Relatório interno do Grupo de Trabalho-Inovação Pedagógica*. Braga: Universidade do Minho, Instituto de Educação.

Wilson, S. M., Floden, R. E., & Ferrini-Mundy, J. (2001). Teacher preparation research: Current knowledge, gaps, and recommendations (A Research Report prepared for the U.S. Department of Education and the Office for Educational Research and Improvement by the Center for the Study of Teaching and Policy in collaboration with Michigan State University). Washington: University of Washington.

Zeichner, K., & Conklin, H. G. (2008). Teacher education programs as sites for teacher preparation. In M. Cochran-Smith, S. Feiman-Nemser, D. J. McIntyre & K. E. Demers (Eds.), *Handbook of research on teacher education* (3rd ed., pp. 269–289). New York: Routledge.

Chapter 15
Learning to Teach in Norway: A Shared Responsibility

Kari Smith and Marit Ulvik

Introduction to the Norwegian Context

The central role teachers play in promoting students' learning is well acknowledged in international research literature (Hattie 2009; Timperley et al. 2007; OECD 2005). The rich evidence, which tends to point to the teacher as the skeleton key to improved student achievements (see Teachers Matter, OECD 2005), has also generated interest amongst policy-makers in Norway. Pre-service teacher education has been recognised as the place where future teachers are prepared for the profession and this has led to comprehensive reforms. The first cohort of pre-service teachers enrolled on the new programme will teach classes 1–10 (primary and lower secondary grades) and will graduate in 2014. The reform will also affect upper secondary teacher education, and the new steering documents will be in force from autumn 2013. The main features of the new framework are a stronger emphasis on teachers' content knowledge; a more applied approach to subject pedagogy (which has been criticised by pre-service teachers for being too theoretical (Roness 2011)); and improvement to the quality of the practicum through partnerships between higher education institutions and schools (Ministry of Education and Research, Framework Plan 1–7, 5–10 2010; Framework Plan 8–13 2012). Additional steps taken to strengthen the practical component are that schools have to be accredited to become practice schools. One of the criteria for accreditation is the requirement that mentors are qualified by completing a formal course on mentoring, awarding 30 European Credit Transfer and Accumulation Systems (ECTS) points. The education is funded by the government and provided by higher education institutions.

K. Smith (✉) · M. Ulvik
Department of Education, University of Bergen,
Bergen, Norway
e-mail: kari.smith@uib.no

M. Ulvik
e-mail: marit.ulvik@uib.no

O. McNamara et al. (eds.), *Workplace Learning in Teacher Education,*   261
Professional Learning and Development in Schools and Higher Education 10,
DOI 10.1007/978-94-007-7826-9_15, © Springer Science+Business Media Dordrecht 2014

The transition from pre-service education to professional practice is also addressed, and from 2010 all newly qualified teachers in Norway are supposed to be mentored during the first year of induction (Ministry of Education and Research, White Paper 11 2008–2009). The responsibility for implementation of this government decision lies with the local authorities and head teachers. At this point in time, Norway does not yet have formal certification of qualified teacher status upon completion of the induction year.

Teacher education in Norway is increasingly perceived as a shared responsibility between higher education institutions, the practice field (schools) and policy-makers (local and central authorities).

Structure of Norwegian Teacher Education

A brief overview of the structure of Norwegian teacher education will be helpful in providing the reader with a basic understanding of the parameters within which it is located. Pre-service teacher education for primary school consists, in the main, of undergraduate programmes, and is provided by university colleges. However, there are ongoing discussions whether, similar to the Finnish model, the four-year bachelor's programme should be extended to a five-year master's level programme. There are two pathways. One is concerned with teachers intending to teach younger learners (grades 1–7), the other has a focus on middle school level (grades 5–10). The main difference lies in the demand for more ECTS points in disciplinary subjects. There has been a rapid increase in the number of programmes offered to teachers who want to continue to master's level by adding the necessary ECTS as full-time or part-time students. Secondary school teachers are mainly educated at the universities, via two routes, both of which are at master's level. One is a five-year integrated programme, at the end of which the candidate graduates with a master's degree in a subject and a teaching qualification for two subjects for lower and upper secondary school. The second route is a one-year Post Graduate Certificate in Education (PGCE) programme for candidates who already hold a master's qualification in a subject discipline. Both programmes are built around four components: subject studies, didactical studies, pedagogical studies and the practicum. There is a trend emerging which indicates a shift from a traditional, theory-laden to a more practice-related programme. Although the pedagogy has become more applied and the practical component has been extended, it is still distinctly different from the heavily school-based programme operating in England.

Teacher Education: A Shared Responsibility

As a result of the new reforms, teacher education in general has taken on a more applied and practical approach. The Norwegian reforms do not only increase the practical component of pre-service programmes in terms of time spent in schools,

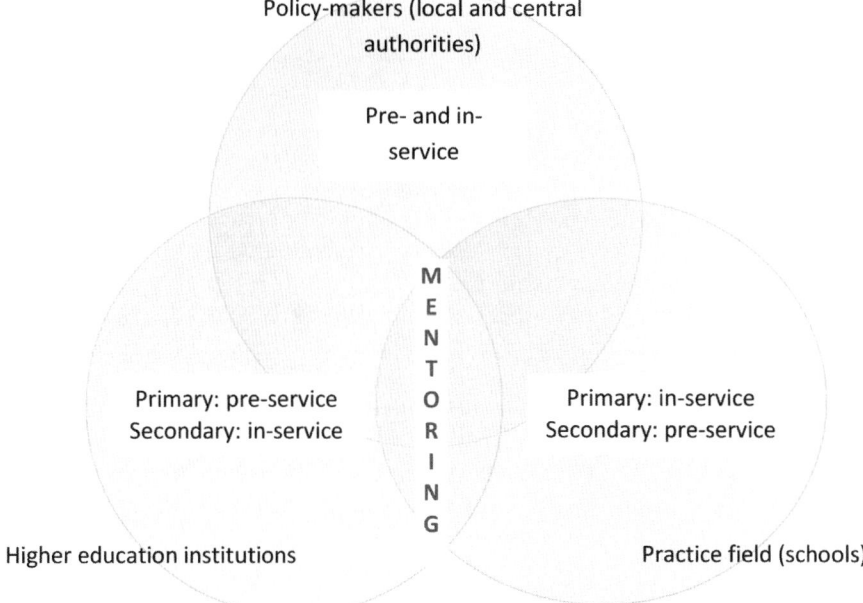

Fig. 15.1 Teacher education: a shared responsibility

they also place more responsibility on schools, which is reflected in the requirement of school accreditation and formal mentor preparation. Teacher education is
increasingly becoming a shared responsibility, as illustrated in Fig. 15.1.

A general understanding which serves as the foundation for this chapter is that
teachers' professional learning starts with enrolment on a higher education institution's pre-service teacher education programme, and continues into the induction
phase (Anthony and Kane 2008; Cameron 2007; Cochran-Smith 2001) and beyond.
In fact, we believe that teachers' professional learning continues throughout their
career. Pre-service teacher education in Norway is the responsibility mainly of the
higher education institutions. Yet, the practice field plays an important role for the
practical component of the programme. Conversely, in-service education is, to a
large extent, on-the-job learning (Eraut 1994) situated in the workplace, but it can
also involve formal courses at a higher education institution or other input from
an institution's faculty members (MacBeath 2012). Policy-makers make formal decisions about course requirements, professional standards, and not least, provide
the resources which make it possible to put decisions concerning the pre- as well
as in-service education of teachers into practice. The responsibility can therefore
be viewed as a shared responsibility along a continuum, where only the focus of
responsibility shifts between higher education institutions and the practice field.

A second understanding on which the below text is based is that mentoring is the
connecting link between the three responsible stakeholders: policy-makers, higher
education institutions and the practice field. Central authorities have made political

decisions about the role mentors play in teachers' pre-service education and during the induction year, and the qualifications they need to obtain. They also provide the resources for mentor education, which is the responsibility of higher education institutions. These offer academic courses for mentoring pre-service teachers and newly qualified teachers (in-service). Mentor education is a formal in-service programme for experienced school teachers. The educational conception underlying the programme is that mentors, like teachers, are educated in the profession to become academically empowered to make professional autonomous decisions. Therefore, in the current paper, the term mentor (teacher) education is used, in full awareness that to some international readers 'training and development' would be a more familiar term. It is the schools' responsibility to ensure they have qualified mentors among the staff and to allow teachers to obtain such qualifications by releasing them from their teaching duties. The schools also have a joint responsibility with the higher education institution for the pre-service practicum, the quality of which depends on the quality of the mentoring the pre-service teachers get. Moreover, the schools share responsibility with the local authority for providing induction support for newly qualified teachers through high quality mentor support. Thus the connecting link of the shared responsibility for teacher education in Norway is mentoring (Yandell and Turvey 2007).

Brief Overview of Mentoring in Norway

There is an increased focus on the importance of the pre-service practicum and the induction of newly qualified teachers, where mentoring has become a key strategy in teachers' professional workplace learning (Anthony and Kane 2008; Zeichner 2006; Jones 2010; Smith and Ingersoll 2004). The literature highlights the need for mentoring (Smith and Ulvik 2010), but the individuals performing this important role have received less attention. They are often experienced teachers with no formal qualification in mentoring, which raises the question whether a good teacher automatically becomes a good mentor (Bullough 2005; Jones 2010). We argue that mentors need to be prepared for their role. In this chapter the Norwegian context is used as a backdrop for generating a more general, critical discussion on current practices.

Mentor education has existed in Norway for a number of years, however, it has been small-scale and mainly related to mentoring pre-service teachers during the practicum. Therefore, most school-based mentors do not have formal mentor qualifications. Prior to the White Paper 11 (2008–2009) mentors were usually chosen because they were experienced and had the reputation of being good teachers. During recent years, however, there has been a growing understanding in Norway that high quality mentoring of pre-service and newly qualified teachers is essential in the shared effort to raise educational achievement in Norwegian schools.

Whilst the practical component of pre-service teacher education in Norway has a long history, newly qualified teachers' induction into the profession has only received scant attention (NOU 1996; Government Report 2003). Since 2010, newly qualified teachers have an entitlement to be mentored. However, policy-makers have not yet concluded that there is a need for a formal induction programme. During their first year, newly qualified teachers in Norway have no induction support nor a reduced teaching load. They are expected to shoulder the same responsibilities as their experienced colleagues from day one. As an alternative to an induction programme, voluntary mentorship was initiated through a national project in 2003 (Government Report 2003). Mentoring newly qualified teachers in Norway started as a pilot project as early as 1997. It was organised in different ways throughout the country, and was offered through the collaboration of the school or local authorities and higher education institutions. There was a regional mentor and a kind of external network, often co-ordinated by the higher education institution. Participation was voluntary and took place in addition to the full-time teaching responsibilities of mentor and mentee. Based on the success of this project, White Paper 11 (2008–2009) presented as a political goal that all newly qualified teachers will be mentored on site during the first year of teaching. An agreement was made between the Ministry of Education and Research and the Norwegian Association of Local and Regional Authorities about mentoring for newly qualified teachers in elementary and secondary schools from 2010/2011, and nursery school from the following year. It is still only an offer. There is no obligation to be mentored and there are no requirements with respect to the content. Mentoring is supposed to happen without giving mentors protected time to perform their role effectively. The mentor is still selected on the basis of his or her experience as a teacher, but does not require any formal qualifications. However, the Government has strongly supported the training and education programmes for mentors supporting newly qualified teachers by delegating funds to higher education institutions in an attempt to raise the quality of mentoring through formal mentor education. Many higher education institutions now offer a first module which is concerned with mentoring pre-service teachers, and a second module which focuses on mentoring newly qualified teachers. Although in England newly qualified teachers have been entitled to mentoring support as part of a statutory induction programme introduced in 1999 (Capel et al. 2012), this is, to our knowledge, unique in the European and international context. In many countries mentors have undergone minimal training (Anthony and Kane 2008).

The initial Norwegian project was evaluated in 2006 by SINTEF, an independent research institution (Dahl et al. 2006). Even though most participating teachers found that the project provided help and support, it was only offered to a small number of new teachers, and was less valued in upper secondary school than in lower grades and kindergarten. Furthermore, it is uncertain how the project contributed to the practice field beyond the participants' personal satisfaction, which was for the newly qualified teachers primarily an opportunity to share experiences with other newcomers. Mentoring was found to be of less benefit in relation to pupil behaviour and classroom management (Dahl et al. 2006). The evaluation report provides limited information about organisation/planning, teaching and learning strategies, content and assessment in the individual mentoring context (Lekang et al. 2009). The conclusion, therefore, was that voluntary mentorship seems to offer support on a personal level, but does not necessarily improve teaching and learning.

As previously said, mentoring pre-service teachers during the practicum is not new in teacher education, either in Norway or other countries, whereas mentoring newly qualified teachers is a concept with only two years of history in Norway. We have therefore chosen to focus our discussion on mentoring newly qualified teachers by addressing the following questions: Why is mentoring needed, and what do mentors need in order to offer high quality support?

Why do New Teachers Need Mentoring?

Mentoring newly qualified teachers is linked to the idea of induction as a unique phase in teachers' development, making the transition from being a pre-service teacher to becoming a professional classroom practitioner. The first year in teaching could be described as an important and critical stage in their professional learning, where identities undergo transformation and development (Fresko and Alhija 2009; McNally et al. 2008). During this stage, newly qualified teachers are still in the process of learning how to teach, at the same time as they are in the process of forming a professional identity (Langdon 2007). The quality of mentoring is therefore paramount.

Mentoring has been found to be a contributing factor in enhancing newly qualified teachers' workplace learning in the profession, and to be a factor motivating them to continue teaching (Rots et al. 2012). The purpose of mentoring is not only to increase new teachers' professional competence and make them committed and linked to the profession, but also to be beneficial to the professional growth of mentors and school development. Mentoring is thereby more than helping teachers to survive. It plays a central role in improving education; it is the link between the three main actors in teacher education, as illustrated by Fig. 15.1.

The Mentor's Role and Responsibility

Mentoring is difficult to define as it depends on the purpose and the context in which it occurs. It can be described as culturally scripted activities which support the newly qualified teachers to meet on-the-job challenges (Wang et al. 2008). In some countries mentoring is designed to help newly qualified teachers reach the professional standards for teachers (standard-centred), whereas in other countries the main goal of mentoring is professional learning (learning-centred) (Harrison et al. 2004). Consequently, the mentor role is subject to different interpretations, and mentoring could be described as a fluid concept.

The challenge is how to prepare mentors for such a multi-faceted role, and whose responsibility is it? These questions are rarely raised in the literature. To educate mentors we need to know more about what they need to learn to be able to address the needs of the mentees (Jones 2010).

Teaching has become increasingly complex during the last decades, due to knowledge explosion and the widening of curriculum demands (Hargreaves and Fullan

1999; MacBeath 2012). Most teachers today need to learn how to teach in new ways, and we cannot assume that the mentor always knows best. Hargreaves and Fullan recommended already in 1999 to make mentoring less hierarchical, less individualistic, more wide-ranging and more inclusive. Mentoring offers an opportunity for renewal and re-orientation of the teaching profession, and it should not be viewed only as a means to provide new teachers with practical tools whilst forgetting that mentees also need emotional support (Nias 1996; McNally et. al. 2008; Wang et al. 2008). The overall aim of mentoring is to improve teaching and learning (Jones 2010). Within this remit mentors need to find a good balance between providing novice teachers with support, and challenging 'taken-for-granted ideas' by reframing and challenging underlying theories (Wang et al. 2008) which are often deeply rooted in the mentees' experiences as students (Bruner 1999; Timperley 2010). In countries with an extensive mentor preparation programme, like in Israel and New Zealand, the problem with unsuitable mentors has become more visible (Fresko and Alhija 2009; Anthony and Kane 2008). Since there is no clear definition of the role, mentors tend to focus on support and solving problems (ibid.), which is a rather limited role. Therefore we see it as crucial to educate mentors to enhance workplace learning and not only make the teaching manageable for newly qualified teachers.

The literature points at a number of useful mentor skills to enhance the mentee's professional learning and growth. They function as a bridge between newly qualified teachers and the organisation (Löfström and Eisenschmidt 2009). This requires understanding of the contexts shaping the classrooms, and a broad understanding of schools (Achinstein 2006). To support others, mentors should be able to analyse their own work; questioning their own practices and developing their own teaching (ibid.). Moreover, what mentors know, often as tacit knowledge, should be made accessible to others (Polany 1966; Smith 2005). Mentors need to understand how adults learn, to nurture critical capacity and reflection skills (Jones 2010). Without critical thinking, there will be no development, and deprofessionalisation could be a consequence (ibid.). Professional learning is open-ended and builds on independent judgements. As a result, the mentor should inquire into reasons for actions rather than telling the new teacher how to perform (Timperley 2010). In addition, the mentors need to have mediation skills and emotional intelligence, as teaching is an emotional practice (Hargreaves and Fullan 1999).

These skills do not naturally grow out of accumulated teaching experience, which is the reason we argue that formal mentor education is needed. Mentoring in the profession is different from teaching. Furthermore, mentoring adults is different from mentoring children and young people. Lastly, to mentor a newly qualified colleague is different from mentoring a pre-service teacher—especially in a context where newly qualified teachers are not going to be assessed, as in Norway. In brief, we see mentoring newly qualified teachers as a new and complex responsibility which requires further attention.

Mentor Education

When reviewing the literature, however, we found little information and less research on the education of mentors, which raises the following questions: Can everybody become a mentor, and does experience in itself qualify one for the mentor role? Whose responsibility is it to safeguard the quality of mentoring? Hattie (2003) has shown that there is correlation between being an experienced teacher and being an expert teacher on multiple teaching-related parameters, some of which are guiding learning, monitoring and feedback, and influencing learning outcomes. The expert teacher, however, performs at a significantly higher level than what is gained through experience in itself. Similarly, we argue, experience alone will not suffice to enable mentors to provide the highest level of support and guidance. By selecting mentors only based on years of experience, there is a danger of having disillusioned and tired teachers (Gonçalves 2000) influencing pre-service teachers' and newly qualified teachers' motivation and enthusiasm for the profession. As a means to prevent this from happening, we argue that mentor education becomes a requirement for all mentors in pre- and in-service teacher education.

The approach taken in this chapter, and which we try to implement in our local context, is that the practice of mentoring is a profession within the profession, or a special expertise teachers acquire through experience and mentor education. If we look at the medical profession, there are medical doctors who specialise in cardiology, paediatrics, etc. We can also see this being relevant to the teaching profession. It is not necessarily only the case where subject specialists are concerned, but also applies to teachers who specialise in, for example, ICT or in assessment, and act as counsellors for other teachers within these fields. All schools employ newly qualified teachers at some time, and Norwegian schools that want to become accredited partner schools with a higher education institution are expected to have professionally educated mentors amongst their teachers.

The Professional Knowledge of Mentoring

When a claim is made that mentoring is to be viewed as professional practice which requires systematic education, it is necessary to briefly discuss what this education should include. What is the professional knowledge mentors need to hold?

The points listed below are by no means meant to form an exhaustive list. However, as we have gained increasing experience through our delivery of mentor education programmes and listening to what mentors have said they find important, and drawing on the literature, we believe mentors need to acquire the following knowledge and skills:

• Knowledge about the national and local educational system;
• Knowledge about work-related issues, rights and responsibilities for teachers, and about the organisation of the current school;

- Knowledge about theories of learning, specifically of adult learning, work-based learning, teachers' professional development, and of mentoring;
- Knowledge about and skills in assessment, assessment for learning, such as feedback and feed-forward, and the role feedback plays in motivation and developing self-efficacy;
- Practical mentoring skills, how to nurture reflection in others, including communication skills and co-operation skills.

The above list addresses three main types of knowledge: structural/practical, theoretical, and inter-personal knowledge and skills. Research suggests that newly qualified teachers often ask for structural and practical knowledge at the very beginning of the year (Anthony and Kane 2008; Ulvik et al. 2009). Pre-service teacher education does not always provide teachers-to-be with this kind of information, and its urgency often becomes apparent when the pre-service practicum starts or the newly qualified teachers realise they are responsible for a class on their own. This is the time when mentors can act as an important point of contact. A central component of mentors' theoretical knowledge base is learning, and more specifically, workplace learning. They need to be able to detect learning-rich situations in workplace learning and be skilled in exploiting them during meetings with the novice teacher. Mentors act as partners in a dialogue in which novice teachers attempt to construct meanings from experiences in a particular context or situation (Brodie and Irving 2007). This requires knowledge about adult learning and professional development found in, for example, the work of Gonçalves (2000, 2009), Berliner (1986, 1992), Timperley (2010), and many others. Affective sides of learning are crucial to all learners, and perhaps specifically to adult learners in the beginning of their professional career. They often lack confidence and are anxious about the level of competence at which they perform their teaching role, and consequently fear that their job and future career might be at stake. Formative assessment, especially the practice of giving feedback and feed-forward (Hattie and Timperley 2007), plays a crucial role in relation to developing the newly qualified teachers' self-efficacy as teachers and in maintaining their motivation for teaching (Skagen and Smith 2010). Thus, assessment practice needs to be built into the mentor's professional knowledge and skills base.

Theoretical knowledge can only be useful if the mentor possesses effective communication skills to engage in supportive, critical and constructive dialogues with the mentee. There is a subtle, yet important, balance to be achieved between motivating and de-motivating during the mentoring process, and the mentor needs to be able to 'read' the context and the mentee carefully to provide appropriate and constructive feedback.

Good mentoring requires knowing the *what* of mentoring, and *how* to practise the *what* in an optimal manner in a certain context with a specific mentee. This is professional practice which can only be exercised by people with relevant professional knowledge and wisdom, both of which depend on education and experience. The responsibility for providing education and experience lies with the higher education institution and the practice fields, supported by appropriate political decisions. There is a shared responsibility.

Mentoring as a Profession

We argue that mentoring is to be regarded as a profession. A profession is traditionally understood as an occupation built on scientific knowledge (Grimen 2008). The knowledge base is compound and includes both practical and scientific knowledge available to professionals when taking autonomous decisions (ibid.). Professions are also characterised by uncertainty (Grimen and Molander 2008). Without uncertainty, it is not necessary to judge or consider different possibilities, but only to act mechanically (Grimen and Molander 2008). A professional practises discretion and reasons, without knowing exactly the outcome of decisions made and actions taken (ibid.).Thus professional practice is heavily dependent on professional wisdom (Brunstad 2007). Biesta (2007) supports this when he says that professional actions are not about following recipes, but to address concrete and unique challenges. Moreover, discretion is practised within professional and ethical codes of conduct. A professional needs to give reasons for actions which can be in contradiction to what is needed when practising common sense. Therefore, the professional needs a professional language to express the reasoning.

To present an overview of the core characteristics of a profession, we have chosen Burbules and Densmore's list from 1991 which is, to a large extent, supported by MacBeath in 2012. A profession is characterised by:

- A clearly defined practical and theoretical knowledge base;
- Systematic education;
- Certification of professional practitioners;
- Professional autonomy;
- An explicit ethical code;
- Prioritising serving others over personal economic gains.

When relating these characteristics to the mentoring profession, it means that the field of mentoring needs to develop a clearly defined practical and theoretical knowledge base. This is, we believe, still in its initial stages, but the increasing research on mentoring and the current focus, politically and scientifically, on the induction phase of teachers, have made it possible to say that there is a developing professional knowledge base on mentoring. The remarkable observation, (Smith et al. 2013) though, when looking at the literature, is that those who act as mentors are not required to be familiar with the knowledge base of their profession. Our argument is that those who take on a mentoring responsibility need to be adequately prepared by completing a formal training and development programme, which should include practical as well as theoretical aspects. Certified mentors should be trusted and allowed to practise with a high degree of professional autonomy, without being subject to external limitations enforced by macro and micro politics, such as national lists of professional competencies that need to be addressed, or internal power tensions in school. Even though policy-makers share the responsibilities of teacher education and of mentoring, they need to accept that mentoring, like teaching, is highly contextualised. Good practice depends to a large extent on exploiting unexpected moments of contingency (Black and Wiliam 2009) to support the mentee's professional learning and development.

However, professional autonomy can only be granted when professional responsibility, deeply rooted in ethical aspects of professional action, is exercised. As members of a profession, mentors should develop an explicit ethical code, and our idea is that a future ethical code for mentoring ought to have an international, a national and a local component. There are elements within mentoring which relate to all mentors, independently of where mentoring is practised. In addition, there is a national system that needs to be addressed, and beyond all, there is the local context of a specific school or any other educational setting in which mentoring takes place, and which will always be unique. The explicit ethical code will guide mentors to act in the best interest of their mentees, pre-service and newly qualified teachers, which will benefit the children and young people they teach. Developing an ethical code for mentoring should be considered an additional shared challenge of the policy-makers, higher education institutions and local authorities.

Mentor Education at the University of Bergen

In light of the recent Norwegian policy decisions put into force from 2010, the Government has followed up by allocating funds to higher education institutions to develop mentor education programmes based on the above principles. The goal is that all teachers performing mentoring in Norwegian schools shall be certified mentors based on a 30 ECTSs academic programme. Most teacher education institutions are today offering academic mentor education. Although there is still a long way to go before we achieve this goal, it seems that Norway, like England and Scotland, has undertaken a more systematic approach to mentor education than many other countries.

At our university the idea of mentor education is not new. We have for several years offered free academic education (15 ECTSs), funded by the university, to our supervising teachers from the partner schools where the pre-service teachers do their practicum. We are now in the fourth year of a follow-up module (an additional 15 ECTSs) in mentoring of newly qualified teachers, for those mentors who have completed the first module. Altogether, the current mentor education is a 30 ECTSs academic programme. The entire course is a two-year programme consisting of eight one-day seminars (of eight hours) each year. The syllabus, which is under constant revision, is developed around the three main aspects of mentors' professional knowledge and skills: structural/practical, theoretical and affective, as identified above. We put much emphasis on the articulation of tacit knowledge in the first module, during which student mentors are required to reflect in writing on cases and personal experiences, using the literature to illuminate and understand mentor practice beyond a descriptive level. Peer discussions and feedback are central in the programme, as we believe that professional practitioners learn much from each other as part of continuous workplace professional learning (Anthony and Kane 2008; Poyas and Smith 2007). Discussions are often initiated by micro-mentoring activities during the sessions. The task of the module teachers is mainly to facilitate the joint learning and to introduce the participants to theoretical aspects and relevant research. In the second module, the student mentors are introduced to action research as a means to enhance systematic critical reflection of mentor practice, and which later can be used to support the newly qualified teachers' reflective practice by encouraging them to engage in action research (Helleve and Langørgen 2010). The action research project has to be written up and presented to fellow student mentors and handed in for summative assessment at the end of the course. The action research projects are assessed internally by the module tutor and by an external examiner. As in most action research processes (Ponte et al. 2004) the student mentors find action research very confusing in the beginning. However, little by little they sort it out and acknowledge the learning benefits of the process as they start developing a feeling of accomplishment. An explicit goal of the mentor education at our university is to enable mentors not only to be consumers of research on mentoring, but also producers of research. Good practitioner research is an essential part in the work of continuously developing a knowledge base on mentoring, which is a central goal in our work. With this vision in mind, our next goal is to develop a full mentor development programme at master's level.

What Have We Learned so Far?

The main themes emerging from the ongoing evaluations and research into our own practice with the university's mentor education are outlined below.

First, the most striking observation we have made is that teachers who choose to enrol on the mentor education programme are not only successful teachers, they also represent experienced teachers who are still full of enthusiasm and motivated to learn (Gonçalves 2000). They are constantly looking for new challenges and renewal. They are often critical about the way they themselves were introduced to teaching, and they want to support a new generation of teachers at the beginning of their professional career. We have not met many student mentors who are disillusioned and unhappy with their choice of profession. These teachers are, indeed, the type of teachers with whom newly qualified teachers will enjoy working.

Second, most practising teachers have difficulties in articulating tacit knowledge (Smith 2005), and they sometimes find it even more difficult to express reflections of their own practice in writing to be read by peers and course tutors. As written reflections are strongly emphasised in the programme, it takes time before the student mentors feel confident and find a language that enables them to talk about their practice. The process seems to take longer with teachers of sciences and vocational subjects.

Third, many schools do not make use of the qualified mentors by giving them mentor responsibilities, and this issue is now being examined more in depth (Helleve and Langørgen 2011). To what extent are the mentoring competences put to use in working with pre-service teachers, newly qualified teachers, and in supporting other colleagues' professional development? Very preliminary findings suggest that school leaders tend not to take advantage of the skills and competencies acquired by mentors who have completed the university's mentor development programme. It appears that the practice field is not yet sufficiently aware of the shared responsibility in relation to assisting pre-service and newly qualified teachers in their workplace learning and professional development. We realise that we have to work much more closely with the school leadership in implementing the idea of using mentors to support newly qualified teachers as well as to act as counsellors of professional development for all teachers. The steering documents are often adopted as a formality but the intention behind the policy-makers' decisions is lost. On the whole, it seems as if there is a tendency for school leaders and local authorities to pay lip service to government policy instead of seeking professionally optimal solutions. They follow the regulations and name a mentor for new teachers, however, sometimes it is the principal or the vice-principal or a teacher whose teaching hours are not filled. Our preliminary findings align with a recent report published by a teachers' union in Norway (Union of Teachers, region Hordaland 2012) and a report from New Zealand, that formalising the induction phase does not automatically guarantee a high quality experience (Anthony and Kane 2008). The new regulation that every pre-service and newly qualified teacher shall be mentored has to be closely examined in order to ensure that the good intentions behind the regulation are maintained in its implementation. Fulfilling only the formal requirements of appointing a mentor, economic solutions are sometimes chosen, and these do not meet the expectations of providing every new teacher with quality mentoring (Harsvik and Norgård 2011). The shared responsibility is not taken sufficiently seriously by all parties involved.

Conclusion

The increased awareness of the importance of having highly qualified and motivated teachers to improve children's learning, puts the quality of teacher education under the critical magnifying glass of society, and even more so of policy-makers. As a result, many countries have engaged in the discussion of how to strengthen teacher education, and in their ongoing efforts for improvement, multiple reforms have been launched. Norway is no different. The most recent reform is still in a process of implementation. It emphasises a shared responsibility for teacher education among institutions of higher education and the practice field, in light of how policy-makers perceive a shared responsibility for improving the quality of education (Fig. 15.1). Mentoring has clearly been identified as the connecting link in this partnership.

The argument put forward in this chapter is first of all that teacher education is viewed as a continuum comprising pre-service as well as in-service education, formal as well as informal learning, off-the-job as well as on-the-job learning (Eraut 1994). Moreover, recent Norwegian policy rhetoric repeatedly strengthens the role of the mentoring activity, though not sufficiently the role of the mentor and what it means to be a mentor. Therefore, the choice has been in this chapter to present our perception of mentoring and the role of the mentor, putting forward a claim that mentoring, if it is to fulfil the many expectations as presented in the steering papers, has to be viewed as a profession within a profession.

As a conclusion of this chapter we present a model for induction of new teachers in Norway.

The transition from teacher education to the teaching profession is to be understood as a phase of three years (Cochran-Smith 2001, among others), and the whole school takes on the responsibility to support the new teachers during this period. In addition, the newly qualified teacher is being mentored by a qualified mentor who, in order to perform the role effectively, will be allocated protected time.

- In the first year 20 % of the newly qualified teachers' and the mentors' employment is dedicated to mentoring. This allows for a tight support which includes time for formal and informal meetings and communication, and time to document mutual professional growth processes.
- In the second year the mentor as well as the mentee will have 10 % of their working time protected to ensure continuity in mentoring, but at the same time to develop increased independence. The form of the mentoring activity changes and it becomes, little by little, more peer mentoring. The clear roles of the new and the experienced teacher become less salient.
- In the third year, neither the newly qualified teacher, nor the mentor enjoys protected time for meetings. During the two first years it is likely that strong collegial relationships between the mentee and the mentor have developed, and these will not disappear because there is no protected time to meet (Anthony and Kane 2008). However, the relations are now more collegial and equal, based on open communication and mutual trust, which is of benefit to professional learning and growth for both.
- In addition, we suggest that separate regional networks for newly qualified teachers and mentors are established with the support of the regional school authorities, but under the responsibility of higher education institutions. Through these networks the participants can discuss mutual experiences and be professionally updated out of their own teaching situation, in a neutral context. The aim is to continuously support teachers as well as mentors making links between their practical experiences and old and new theoretical developments (Smith and Ulvik 2010).

If mentoring is to be accepted as a profession within the teaching profession, we believe that the mentor should have at least five years of teaching experience and should be a practising teacher when undertaking mentor education. The candidates ought to be recommended by the school principal with special focus on teaching competence, ethical behaviour, and a high level of interpersonal intelligence (Gardner 2006). The education of mentors should be a minimum of 30 ETCSs and their qualifications should be internally (by the course teachers) as well as externally assessed. Finally, upon completion of the mentor education programme, mentors will be expected to participate in a community of mentoring practice.

The visionary model presented here requires tight co-operation between governmental bodies, regional school authorities, the teaching profession, schools and higher education institutions. We all have a joint responsibility, to improve the quality of learning. Working in co-operation to achieve the stated goal, to improve our schools will, we believe, enforce the good intentions in the ongoing reforms. Today, shared responsibility to reach the goal is mainly explicit in the rhetoric, and there is still a long way to go before the good intentions are translated into action. Shared responsibility means that all parties jointly adopt a continuous inquisitive disposition, seeking improvement which leads to growth and development.

References

Achinstein, B. (2006). New teacher and mentor political literacy: Reading, navigating and transforming induction contexts. *Teachers and Teaching: Theory and practice, 1*(2), 123–138.

Anthony, G., & Kane, R. (2008). *Making a difference: The role of initial teacher education and induction in the preparation of secondary teachers.* Wellington: Teaching and learning Research Initiative.

Berliner, D. C. (1986). In pursuit of the expert pedagogue. *Educational Researcher, 15*(7), 5–13.

Berliner, D. C. (1992). The nature of expertise in teaching. In F. K. Oser, A. Dick, & J. Patry (Eds.), *Effective and responsible teaching* (pp. 227–248). San Francisco: Jossey Bass.

Biesta, G. (2007). Why 'what works' won't work: Evidence-based practice and the democratic deficit in educational research. *Educational Theory, 57*(1), 1–22.

Black, P., & Wiliam, D. (2009). Developing the theory of formative assessment. Educational Assessment, *Evaluation and Accountability, 21*(1), 5–31.

Brodie, P., & Irving, K. (2007). Assessment in work-based learning: Investigating a pedagogical approach to enhance student learning. *Assessment and Evaluation in Higher Education, 32*(1), 11–19.

Bruner, J. (1999). Folk pedagogies. In J. Leach & B. Moon (Eds.), *Learners and pedagogy* (pp. 4–21). London: Paul Chapman Publishing.

Brunstad, P. O. (2007). Faglig klokskap-mer enn kunnskap og ferdigheter. (Professional wisdom-more than knowledge and skills). *Pacem, 10*(2), 59–70.

Bullough, R. V. (2005). Being and becoming a mentor: School-based teacher educators and teacher educator identity. *Teaching and Teacher Education, 21,* 143–155.

Burbules, N. C., & Densmore, K. (1991). The limits of making teaching a profession. *Educational Policy, 5*(1), 44–63.

Cameron, M. (2007). *Learning to teach: A literature review on induction theory and practice.* Wellington: New Zealand Teachers Council.

Capel, S., Leask, M., & Turner, T. (2012). *Learning to teach in the secondary school: A companion to school experience.* London: Routledge.

Cochran-Smith, M. (2001). Learning to teach against the (new) grain. *Journal of Teacher Education, 52*(1), 3–4.

Dahl, T., Buland, T., Finne, H., & Havn, V. (2006). Støtte til praksisspranget for nyutdannete lærere. (Support to the leap into practicum evaluation of support for newly educated teachers). Trondheim. SINTEF (Norwegian Institute of Technology) Teknologi og samfunn. http://udir.no/upload/Rapporter/evaluering_av_nyutdannede_laerere.pdf Accessed 18 March 2009.

Eraut, M. (1994). *Developing professional knowledge and competence.* London: Routledge.

Fresko, B., & Alhija, F. N.-A. (2009).When intentions and reality clash: Inherent implementation difficulties of an induction program for new teachers. *Teaching and Teacher Education, 25*(2), 278–284.

Gardner, H. (2006). *Multiple intelligences. New Horizons.* New York: Basic Books.

Gonçalves, J. A. (2000). *Ser Professora do 1°. Ciclo. Uma Carreira em Análise*. Doctoral thesis. Lisboa: Faculty of Psychology and Educational Sciences of the University of Lisbon.

Gonçalves, J. A. (2009). Professional development and teaching career. Career phases, curriculum and supervision. Sísifo. *Educational Sciences Journal, 8*, 21–32. http://sisifo.fpce.ul.pt. Accessed 18 Aug 2010.

Government Report. (2003). Strategi for økt kompetanse i skolen (Strategy for Increased Competence in School). http://www.regjeringen.no/nb/dokumentarkiv/Regjeringen-Bondevik. Accessed 18 March 2009.

Grimen, H. (2008). Profesjon og kunnskap. (Profession and knowledge). In A. Molander & L. I. Terum (Eds.), *Profesjonsstudier* (pp. 71–87). Oslo: Universitetsforlaget.

Grimen, H., & Molander, A. (2008). Profesjon og skjønn.(Profession and discretion). In A. Molander & L. I. Terum (Eds.), *Profesjonsstudier* (pp. 179–196). Oslo: Universitetsforlaget.

Hargreaves, A., & Fullan, M. (1999). Mentoring in the new millennium. *Professional Speaking*, 19–23 Dec 1999.

Harrison, J., Dymoke, S., & Pell, T. (2004). Mentoring beginning teachers in secondary schools: An analyses of practice. *Teaching and Teacher Education, 22*, 1055–1067.

Harsvik, T., & og Norgård, J. D. (2011). The *best intentions. About introducing mentoring arrangements for newly qualified teachers*. Report from enquiry 2. Oslo: Union of Education, Norway.

Hattie, J. (2003). *Distinguishing expert teachers from novice and experienced teachers*. New Zealand: University of Auckland Publication.

Hattie, J. (2009). *Visible learning: A synthesis of over 800 meta-analyses relating to achievement*. London: Routledge.

Hattie, J., & Timperley, H. (2007). The power of feedback. *Review of Educational Research, 77*(1), 81–112.

Helleve, I., & Langørgen, K. (2010). Mentorutdanning (Mentor education). In K. Smith & M. Ulvik (Eds.), *Veiledning av nye lærere- nasjonale og internasjonale perspektiver. (Mentoring novice teachers—national and international perspectives)* (pp. 176–90). Oslo: Universitetsforlaget.

Helleve, I., & Langørgen, K. (2011). *Mentors as support for experienced teachers professional development*. Paper presented at the annual ECER conference in Berlin, 13–16 Sept, 2011.

Jones, M. (2010). The needs of mentors. In K. Smith & M. Ulvik (Eds.), *Veiledning av nye lærere. Nasjonale og internasjonale perspektiver*. (Mentoring novice teachers—national and international perspectives) (pp. 115–29). Oslo: Universitetsforlaget.

Langdon, F. J. (2007). Beginning teacher learning and professional development: An analysis of induction programmes. The degree doctor philosophiae. The University of Waikato.

Lekang. T., Olsen K. R., & Engvik G. (2009). Veiledning av nyutdannede lærere—et speil for kvalitetsutvikling i lærerutdanningen? (Mentoring newly qualified teachers- a mirror for quality development in teacher education?). Norsk nettverk—veiledning av nyutdannede lærere. (Norwegian network for mentoring novice teachers) Report, Jun 2009.

Löfström, E., & Eisenschmidt, E. (2009). Novice teachers' perspective on mentoring: The case of the Estonian induction year. *Teaching and Teacher Education, 25*(5), 681–689.

MacBeath, J. (2012). The future of the teaching profession. University of Cambridge, Department of Education, Educational International Research Institute. http://www.educ.cam.ac.uk. Accessed Aug, 2012.

McNally, J., Blake, A., Corbin, B., & Gray, P. (2008). Finding an identity and meeting a standard: Connecting the conflict in teacher induction. *Journal of Education Policy, 23*(3), 287–298.

Ministry of Education and Research. (2008–2009). White paper 11. http://www.regjeringen.no/nb/dep/kd/dok/regpubl/stmeld/2008-2009/stmeld-nr-11-2008-2009-.html. Accessed 20 Jan 2011.

Ministry of Education and Research. (2010). Framework plan, 1–7 and 5–10. http://www.regjeringen.no/nb/dep/kd/dok/rundskriv/2010/rundskriv-f-05-10-forskrifter-om-ny-grun.html?id=598615. Accessed June 2012.

Ministry of Education and Research. (2012). Proposal to framework plan, 8–13. http://www. regjeringen.no/nb/dep/kd/aktuelt/nyheter/2012/horing-om-larerutdanningene-for-trinn-8-. html?id=698322. Accessed Sept 2012.

Nias, J. (1996). Thinking about feeling: The emotions in teaching. *Cambridge Journal of Education*, *26*(3), 293–306.

NOU. (1996). Lærerutdanning. Mellom krav og virkelighet. (Teacher Education between Demands and Reality; in Norwegian). Oslo: Ministry of Education and Research.

OECD. (2005).Teacher Matters.: Attracting, developing and retaining effective teachers. OECD-report. www.oecd.org/document/52/0,3343,en_2649_201185_34991988_1_1_1_1,00.html. Accessed 18 May 2009.

Polany, M. (1966). *The tacit dimension*. New York: Doubleday.

Ponte, P., Beijard, D., & Ax, J. (2004). Don't wait till the cows come home: Action research and initial teacher education in three different countries. *Teachers and Teaching. Theory and practice*, *10*(6), 591–621.

Poyas, Y., & Smith, K. (2007). Becoming a community of practice, the blurred identity of faculty teacher educators. *Teacher Development*, *11*(3), 313–334.

Roness, D. (2011). Still motivated? The motivation for teaching during the second year in the profession, *Teaching and Teacher Education*, *27*(3), 628–638.

Rots, I., Kelchtermans, G., & Aelterman, A. (2012). Learning (not) to become a teacher: A qualitative analysis of the job entrance issue. *Teaching and Teacher Education*, *28*, 1–10.

Skagen, K., & Smith, K. (2010). Mentoren som veileder og vurderer. (Mentor as supervisor and assessor). In K. Smith & M. Ulvik (Eds.), *Veiledning av nye lærere- nasjonale og inter-nasjonale perspektiver.* (Mentoring novice teachers—national and international perspectives). Oslo: Universitetsforlaget.

Smith, K. (2005). Teacher educators' professional knowledge. How does it differ from teachers' professional knowledge? *Teaching and Teacher Education*, *21*, 177–192.

Smith, K., & Ulvik, M. (Eds.). (2010). *Veiledning av nye lærere- nasjonale og internasjonale perspektiver.* (Mentoring Novice Teachers—national and international perspectives) Oslo: Universitetsforlaget.

Smith, T. M., & Ingersoll, R. M. (2004). What are the effects on induction and mentoring on beginning teacher turnover? *American Educational Research Journal*, *41*(3), 681–714.

Smith, K., Ulvik, M., Helleve, I. (2013). *Førstereisen- Lærdom hentet fra nye læreres fortellinger.* (The First Voyage—lessons learned from novice teachers' narratives). Oslo: Gyldendal akademisk.

Timperley, H. (2010).The mentor's voice. In K. Smith & M. Ulvik (Eds.), *Veiledning av nye lærere-nasjonale og internasjonale perspektiver.* (Mentoring novice teachers- national and international perspectives) (pp. 39–48). Oslo: Universitetsforlaget.

Timperley, H., Wilson, A., Barrar, H., & Fung, I. (2007). *Teacher professional learning and development: Best evidence synthesis iteration*. Wellington: Ministry of Education.

Ulvik, M., Smith, K., Helleve, I. (2009). Novice in secondary school. The coin has two sides. *Teaching and Teacher Education*, *25*(6), 835–842.

Union of Teachers, Norway, Region Hordaland. (2012). *Rettleiing av nytilsette og nyutdannete.* (Mentoring of newly employed and newly qualified teachers). Personal communication from Head of Union.

Wang, J., Odell, S. J., Schwille, S. A. (2008). Effects of teacher induction on beginning teachers' teaching: A critical review of the literature. *Journal of Teacher Education*, *59*(2), 132–152.

Yandell, J., & Turvey, A. (2007). Standards or communities of practice? Competing models of workplace learning and development. *British Educational Research Journal*, *33*(4), 533–550.

Zeichner, K. (2006). Reflections of a university-based teacher educator on the future of college- and university-based teacher education. *Journal of Teacher Education*, *57*(3), 326–340.

Chapter 16
Teaching as a Master's Level Profession in Finland: Theoretical Reflections and Practical Solutions

Pertti Kansanen

Introduction

Teacher education in Finland does not happen in a vacuum, it is a part of social policy in the country. The current situation is based on historical and traditional developments and reflects the economic state of affairs in the Finnish society. On the international level, teacher education may seem relatively homogeneous, following the same body of research literature and referring to the same articles and handbooks (Biddle et al. 1997; Cochran-Smith and Zeichner 2005; Cochran-Smith et al. 2008). There is no doubt that the national politicians and educational policy-makers have access to relevant knowledge of the current research base for teacher education and can thus make their decisions using appropriate information. Despite that, the local teacher education programmes vary to a great extent and offer an assortment of alternatives.

The success of Finnish students in the international comparative surveys has aroused quite a lot of interest in the Finnish school system, teacher education, and teaching and studying in classrooms (e.g. Sahlberg 2011; Niemi et al. 2012). Although it is almost impossible to explain why the results of Finnish students have been so good, many speculations have been presented during recent years (e.g., Kansanen 2010). One popular assumption has been that it relates to the quality of the Finnish teacher education system and, accordingly, the high quality of its teachers. Indeed, the Finnish teacher education system has some features of an exceptional nature; one of these is that all teachers (in grades 1–12) pass a master's degree in the university and have direct access to doctoral studies, should they wish. All the programmes in different universities follow a relatively loose common national frame that is characterised with a main organising theme (Galluzo and Pankratz 1990) that we call a research-based approach.

P. Kansanen (✉)
University of Helsinki, Helsinki, Finland
e-mail: pertti.kansanen@helsinki.fi

O. McNamara et al. (eds.), *Workplace Learning in Teacher Education,*
Professional Learning and Development in Schools and Higher Education 10,
DOI 10.1007/978-94-007-7826-9_16, © Springer Science+Business Media Dordrecht 2014

In this chapter, my purpose is to describe and analyse the most important theoretical aspects that underpin the Finnish teacher education programmes and why it may be called research-based teacher education. Teacher education in primary education and secondary education differ in some important aspects. Class teachers responsible for primary education (grades 1–6) study education as their major, while subject teachers (grades 7–12) have their own subject (mathematics, history, language, etc.) as their major. That has also consequences in terms of the curricula, which emphasises the content according to the major. In the Finnish system, the primary class pre-service teachers write their master's thesis in 'education', while the secondary subject pre-service teachers write it in their 'main subject' within their own faculty (mathematics, physics, history, language, religion, etc.). In some cases it may be an education-related master's (e.g. mathematics education) but that is rare.

Basic Level of Teacher Education

It may be said, with good reason, that all possible types of programmes for teacher education have been experimented at some time, somewhere (e.g. Howey 1996). Accordingly, opinions vary about the effectiveness of different kinds of pre-service teacher education programmes. The programmes are, of course, also an economic issue and even more a political question. In addition, educational policy in some countries steers the content of teacher education more than in other countries. A well-known dilemma in teacher education is that the conception of what makes a good teacher, and also good teaching, changes over time. One resolution to this quandary is that the teacher education programme should be as general as possible so that it will be applicable in the future. Technology in education develops at a very rapid tempo, and can change school life and teaching as well as teacher education. It is impossible to know how future innovations in medical (pharmaceutical or neurological) technology and/or research into the functioning of the brain may bring about advances in knowledge of learning, and student's attention and motivation, etc., and how these innovations may develop and influence teaching, studying and learning. What is certain, however, is that we do not know what will happen in the future, nor what challenges these kinds of prospects will bring for teacher education.

One possible suggestion to solve this dilemma is to consider teacher education from two perspectives or strata (Kansanen 2004). The first deals with everyday practice with all possible standard teaching methods and activities in practice. We can call this a basic level of teacher education. For most people it is useful to go through the basic level of teacher education with all its activities and everyday experiences. An interesting question is whether the basic level is necessary for all, or is it possible to compensate with other activities. There are plenty of examples of individuals who have succeeded quite well in school as a teacher without any formal teacher education at all. In discussions, the idea of a so-called innate teacher is often presented, that is, an individual who works with children and young people naturally and easily. A common belief is also that it is possible to learn much of a teacher's work in the school. Teacher education, however, ensures that pre-service teachers have the support to develop competencies systematically and with confidence.

Teacher education on the basic level may be organised in many different ways relatively easily. In continuing professional learning for teachers it is also possible to develop these basic competencies with courses and seminars that concentrate on practical themes without deeper theorising. It is fairly probable that teacher education on this basic level is, in principle, relatively similar in different parts of the western world. There are, of course, differences regarding the content: common to them all is that the programmes are quite normative without demands for scientific depth. Research methods, for example, are not emphasised, and research is not essential in the programmes. This basic level of pre-service teacher education may be sufficient for teachers of younger pupils, and indeed maybe for teachers of older students as there is good evidence that the essential elements of the instructional process are quite similar with older students (e.g. McCourt 2005).

A common practice in constructing a teacher education programme at this basic level is to divide it into three main parts: studies in education, subject matter studies along with pedagogical content knowledge, and practice with student teaching. These areas overlap, and no strict boundaries can be drawn between them; this kind of totality can be constructed in numerous ways. In some way all teacher education programmes contain these fundamental elements; how to build a dynamic and successful curriculum founded on these elements is apparently the key to getting good teachers into the education system of the country. The programmes usually concentrate on practical skills and fundamental knowledge of the instructional process. The content requirements are so extensive that it is not difficult to fill a four-year or a five-year programme with rich content, and it is necessary to prioritise only knowledge and skills which cannot be acquired elsewhere in the teacher education curriculum. Content courses, one after another or alongside each other, however, only bring about horizontal knowledge, and this kind of knowledge has no end. New requirements are produced all the time and this is one of the reasons why there is an increasing expectation of lifelong studying throughout teachers' careers. Terhart (2000), for example, regards in-service teacher education as the third phase of teacher education in the German system.

Institutes which concentrate on this basic level of teacher education share certain characteristics. For example, teacher educators working at these institutes would not generally have research competence (Labaree 2003). For that reason it is understandable that practical aspects of the programmes are emphasised, such as developing teaching skills and building a base for further professional learning. An important question then, is how teaching practice is organised and integrated with other content in the pre-service programme. A second important question is how, from the theoretical point of view, the quality of the teacher education programme is developed further, from the basic level to a conceptually enriched curriculum. To do this, theory must come into play and a conceptual level with metacognitive aspects is therefore needed, and this will be discussed in the next section. The Finnish system has a special feature which supports both a theoretically enriched programme and its integration with practice. This is that every university with a department of teacher education has a university practice school where the pre-service teachers can become familiar with everyday school life and do teaching practice in controlled circumstances. The purpose of these schools is to participate in teacher education with professional mentors and university supervisors; experimenting and research is secondary in their role.

Conceptual Level of Teacher Education

Besides the basic level of teacher education, the other stratum that is built may be called a conceptual level of teacher education. It aims at the sustained development of a teacher's work, and it is closely connected to the basic level. It is claimed here that this conceptual level is not achieved without special attention to its requirements. Further, a certain distance from practice is needed, at the same time as teachers are working in this very practice. This means there needs to be discussion, thinking, reflection, research, and related activities (Bengtsson 1993, 1995). In addition to practice and experiences, conscious efforts are needed. The core of the idea is a kind of metacognition—discovering by looking at one's own work and decisions concerning teaching. In the literature about building a teacher education programme, this point of view is not directly seen (e.g. Howey 1996). Thinking skills, metacognition, problem-solving, decision-making, and similar topics are often mentioned, but as separate courses, not as a means to look at the totality of the programme. As an organising theme, a research-based approach is presented here.

Research-based Approach of Teacher Education

The location of teacher education in the universities is a relatively new phenomenon in Finland. Traditionally teacher education was training-based, with normative advice directing the studies.

Labaree (1997) describes the historical development of teacher education and teacher education institutes, as well as their quality and reputation in the academic world, especially in the USA. The position of teacher education, and the teaching profession itself, and the academic esteem in which they have been held has characteristically been low. This is true of the status of Teachers' Colleges in the USA (Allison 1995; Labaree 1997, 2003) and similar problems have also been identified in the Nordic countries. According to Labaree (1997, 2003) Teachers' Colleges in the USA tended to be local institutes, and their teaching staff modestly educated. The students did not belong to the best academic groups, and the curricula were practice-oriented and the studies lacked depth. The status of research on education and teacher education in particular, and the low esteem in which it is held, has also aroused international discussion in the professional journals (Kaestle 1993; Sroufe 1997). The most common expression has been that of contempt (Prange 2008). Teacher education has not, however, been lacking defenders. Gage (1994) and above all Berliner (2000, 2002, 2005) have, in a convincing way, answered the critique.

In Finnish universities teacher education currently has the same position, regulations and status as traditional academic subjects (e.g. mathematics, physics, history, languages, etc.) Research is central to the function and identity of the university. Griffiths (2004, p. 722) divides teaching in higher education according to four research orientations: (i) research-led, (ii) research-oriented, (iii) research-based, and (iv) research-informed teaching. The Finnish model of teacher education resembles the research-based orientation, with the following characteristics. First, the study programme is structured according to a systematic analysis of education. Second, all teaching is based on research; teaching and research on teaching are integrated. Third, pre-service teachers can practise argumentation, decision-making and justification when inquiring about and solving pedagogical problems. In addition, pre-service teachers learn formal research skills during their studies.

Research-based teacher education defined in this way has two facets. First, the programmes are built on evidence of research. Although the educational research base is still meagre in this respect, it is developing all the time and apparently plays a greater role in the future teachers' work (e.g. Hattie 2009; Cochran-Smith and Zeichner 2005). Second is the skill of metacognition in the role of reflection or pedagogical thinking (Schön 1983; Westbury et al. 2005; Kansanen et al. 2000; Jakku-Sihvonen and Niemi 2006, 2007). This is the means for autonomous teachers to develop their own work. When teaching is based on research, teachers teach what they study, or their teaching draws from well-articulated knowledge of current research (Toom et al. 2010).

The term 'evidence-based' seems to have various interpretations. Its roots can be traced to medicine, in which two types of evidence-based activities have been suggested: evidence-based guidelines and evidence-based individual decision-making (Eddy 2005). Similarly, we can discuss two types of research-based teacher education. Through research on teacher education we obtain results, or evidence, that can be used as guidelines for its further development. Another type of evidence-based practice concerns the daily practice of the individual teacher, the teacher's pedagogical thinking. Thus, evidence-based teaching means that teachers' activities are based on research results of, on the one hand, what we know about teaching, and on the other hand, what we know about teacher education. It should be noted that the evidence base is very modest and diffuse, and the issues with both are extensive and difficult to examine. This means that the development is slow because the evidence for building a programme for teacher education is difficult to assemble. Accordingly, in addition to research, theorising is needed.

Knowledge of research is needed in interpreting research evidence. This means that teachers should be able to read scientific literature and follow the discussion among professionals. The active part, producing new knowledge while reflecting on one's own work, presupposes studies in research methods. For that reason, the common frame of teacher education curriculum in Finland contains systematic studies of research methods and follows certain principles:

- Every study unit is connected with research and the conceptualisation of practice.
- Courses of research methods include: quantitative, qualitative and mixed methods.
- Pre-service teachers must demonstrate overall competence in research methods: all are known generally, some are known specifically.
- A master's thesis must be undertaken.
- There is an expectation that teachers should become practitioner researchers
    - consumers of research: able to understand and use research;
    - producers of research: able to conduct research.
- Teachers have direct access to doctoral studies, should they wish.

To avoid misunderstanding, it is important to emphasise that practice on the conceptual level does not mean that teachers should act like professional researchers. It is appropriate, instead, to call this kind of teacher a 'practitioner researcher' and the activities that teachers perform 'practitioner research'. This reminds us very much of action research, and a teacher's work as a practitioner researcher can, for good reason, be acknowledged as a type of action research. The difference between a professional researcher and a practitioner researcher (Richardson 1994) is an essential one. The professional researcher works in order to participate in scientific discussion and to publish in scientific journals. The practitioner researcher utilises research to develop knowledge and skills and become more effective as a teacher; the practitioner researcher accordingly investigates his/her own practice without any intention of publishing the findings (Cochran-Smith and Lytle 1990; Maaranen 2009, 2010).

Teachers' Pedagogical Thinking

In a teacher's work, the normative and the descriptive sides are combined into 'taking a stand'. When a teacher takes a stand, they choose their way; they make a decision. Teachers can look at things descriptively without taking a stand, but as soon as they act they go to the normative side. Teachers make decisions all the time; when searching for the common features in a teacher's work, decision-making has often been highlighted as the most central and important skill (Shavelson 1973; Fitzgibbons 1981; Calderhead 1984; Kleven 1991; Kansanen 1991; Penso and Shoham 2003).

Fitzgibbons (1981) emphasises that behind the teacher's decision-making process is a whole belief system. In order to be able to make decisions there must be alternatives. During the fast and fleeting instructional process, the alternatives usually do not ascend to consciousness; most of the decisions are unconscious or partly conscious. If, however, we look at the phases of pre-interaction and post-interaction, there is more time to reflect and to decide consciously. For this reason, Schön (1983) divided reflection into two categories: reflection-in-action and reflection-on-action.

Teachers' pedagogical thinking always takes place in a pedagogical context, usually in a school. This context is a bounded system and its boundaries are defined by a certain curriculum. Although the boundaries may not be strict, they do define the mental range of the teacher and the students. The criteria of the decisions are determined by the aims and goals of this curriculum. In this context, the responsibility of the teacher is to bring about the kind of learning that is defined in the curriculum. The task of the students is to study according to this curriculum and, through their own efforts, to achieve the aims and goals in the curriculum. Most of these will be learning goals, but other changes are also possible and realistic.

Most of the researchers' thinking is descriptive and systematic. The normative side is usually not included in this kind of thinking. Making pedagogical decisions can, however, never be restricted to the descriptive side; taking a stand requires normative thinking. In addition to knowledge, other parts of the personal belief system come into operation. Emotions, feelings, opinions, attitudes, and other kinds of affective factors mix with descriptive arguments. Reflection leads to decisions, the descriptive changes to the normative; in the pedagogical context, this is thinking with pedagogical arguments and justifications.

Teachers' pedagogical thinking may be analysed from many standpoints: i.e., the content with numerous details, the teaching-studying-learning process, as well as the wider contextual angle with curricular matters. All this may be interesting and informative; however, going behind these horizontal aspects is necessary for a deeper understanding of the teachers' pedagogical thinking. This means an analysis from the argumentative standpoint: how teachers justify their decisions and what kinds of reasons they give for their decisions and activities. The analysis of arguments reveals the inner motives and the overall professional skill of a teacher (cf. Fitzgibbons 1981; Paschen and Wigger 1992; Kansanen et al. 2000).

There are many ways of getting to know how teachers justify their decisions: Toulmin's analysis of arguments (1958), Hilbert Meyer's rezeptological approach[1] (1980) and Kuhn's system approach (1991). A common characteristic is that the arguments are classified. This may be done in various ways, according to the purpose of the analysis. From the point of view of conceptual teacher education it is interesting to know how teachers justify their decisions consciously or systematically. For this purpose a division into intuitive and rational may be used (cf. Kindsvatter et al. 1992). Empirical results indicate, however, that most of the arguments are mixed; they contain both intuitive and rational elements (Kansanen et al. 2000). In addition, the arguments may be viewed from different theoretical levels. Pedagogical level thinking is reminiscent of the typically three-level hierarchy (König 1975; Guhl and Ott 1985; Handal and Lauvås 1987): (i) the action level, (ii) the first thinking level or object theories, and (iii) the second thinking level or the meta-theory level. It is understandable that most of the teachers' arguments belong to the action level, some to the object theory level and quite a few to the meta-theory level (Kansanen 2001). The interesting question here is; would it be possible to raise the level of the arguments and could we build a teacher education programme with this purpose in mind? Our answer is positive and the solution is a research-based teacher education programme.

---

[1] Rezeptological approach: research on recipes and tips that the supervisors give and the pre-service teachers ask during their teaching practice.

Theory-practice Relation

Research-based thinking is seen as the connecting factor which integrates theoretical and practice-based aspects during teacher education studies. The essential elements of the programme are combined in accordance with integrative principles (Hytönen 1995; Jyrhämä 2006). The first principle is to begin teaching practice as early as possible. The second, is that the interaction between teaching practice and educational theory is emphasised throughout the entire study time. This means, in practical terms, that there should be teaching practice during every year and every study period. Every study period has its own aims and characteristics. Teaching practice in Finland is organised in special university practice schools, as well as in ordinary field schools. In the beginning, the pre-service teachers observe pupils of different ages, noting their role as group members, and their interaction in the instructional process in different classes and grades. Gradually, the content of teaching practice is extended to all aspects of a teacher's work. Teaching practice periods increase from small units to larger combinations. The special characteristics of different practice periods are taken into consideration. The requirements of primary class teachers and secondary subject teachers differ in several important ways. Primary teachers have many different curriculum areas to deal with, and the total development of each child is of special importance to them. Secondary teachers are stronger in content knowledge competence, and their students need the special attention due to their particular age group. The larger perspectives of a teacher's work, in the form of links with parents and carers are of importance. Also, the co-operation of teacher educators is essential.

Every practice period is combined with detailed theoretical studies that relate to the topic of the practice period. The following outlines how this works for pre-service class teachers.

There is an initial orientation stage, where the pre-service teachers become acquainted with the university practice school and some of its classes and pupils. At the same time the pre-service teachers attend lessons about pedagogy and teaching, knowledge of pupil personality and their capabilities, etc. At the end of the first year the pre-service teachers practise teaching in mother tongue language and drama lessons; connected with the content studies. Class teachers in the practice schools are supervising or mentoring this stage.

In the second stage, the pre-service teachers practise with subjects (mathematics, humanities subjects and arts, etc.). This goes according to the pedagogical content knowledge. This practice period is connected to the different courses of subject content knowledge and pedagogical content knowledge that the pre-service teachers are taking. The class teachers in the practice school and the supervisors at the department of teacher education have a common responsibility for the support of the pre-service teacher.

Following this, the master's practice involves at least 20 practice lessons per week, mentored by the class teachers in the practice school and the supervisors at the department of teacher education. In the theoretical studies the pre-service teachers attend courses, among others, where personal practical theories are analysed and applied in practice.

To obtain more knowledge to support their teaching practice, the pre-service teachers may read relevant texts and discuss them with each other and with the teacher educators. Pre-service teachers undertake teaching practice in university practice schools and field schools alternately. Field schools are more representative of schools in general. The university practice schools also function as ordinary schools, following the same curriculum, however, special proficiency requirements are expected of their teachers, such as advanced mentoring skills. The university practice schools play an important role in the integration of theory and practice. The teachers in these schools have a twofold task. They are representatives of the school but as teacher mentors they are experts both in teaching and mentoring. The university supervisors function as a link between teacher mentors in the school and the theoretical studies at the university (Jyrhämä and Syrjäläinen 2011).

It is important to note that research-based teacher education, along with evidence-based teaching, means that pre-service teachers practise simultaneously in teaching and researching. It can be called as twofold practising (Krokfors 2007) and its purpose is to integrate both areas into one's own teaching. On the basic level this involves undertaking research methods courses and practising the techniques; to begin with the pre-service teachers are simply absorbing without deep autonomous understanding. At the same time their own teaching is fact-based, with hardly any competencies relating to critical pedagogical evaluations. Regarding research their role may be as a consumer which means a passive approach in the sense that they can read research articles and use the knowledge in their own work. Consuming is adaptation but a deeper understanding is lacking. When the teacher education continues it is possible to adopt a more active role, teachers become productive. As practitioner researchers they can reflect on their own work, they have now a role of a producer (Young 2001).

The conceptual dimension and practising become blended as the pre-service teachers move along the level dimension (see Fig. 16.1.) In teaching the metacognitive competencies begin to take their position. Pre-service teachers learn to justify their decisions with reference to research knowledge and experiential knowledge gained by reflecting on their own practice. It is a question of producing new knowledge, new for the teachers themselves concerning their own work (Young 2001). The basic purpose is the development of a personal conception of teaching, the development of one's own pedagogical theory (Fitzgibbons 1981).

Teacher Educators in Universities and University Practice Schools

To provide research-based teacher education, all teacher educators should have a specialised knowledge of research. Further, if the department of teacher education has identical requirements to other departments then there will be high expectations of teacher educators in relation to supervising master's theses on the conceptual level, which demands a high level of scientific competence. This means that teacher educators should have a PhD. The development in this respect may be slow, which can be seen from the following example from the University of Helsinki. Teacher

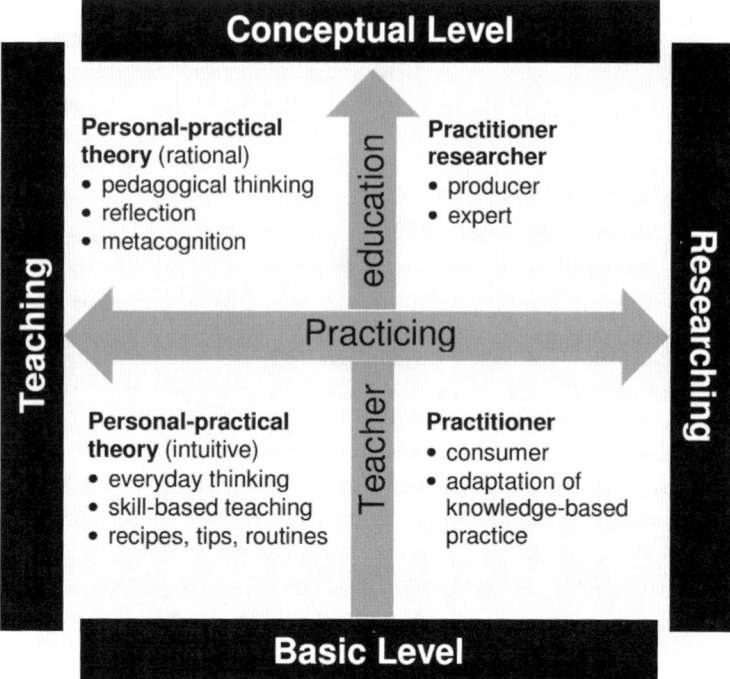

Fig. 16.1 Teacher education as twofold practicing with teaching and researching

education was reformed in 1979 with a master's examination for all teachers in the school system. This means the examination was on the same academic level for all teachers from grade 1 to 12. Along with the development of teacher education programmes, the requirements for teacher educators have also increased. Now there are three categories of university teachers: professors, university lecturers who are doctors, and doctoral students. In addition, in the university practice schools where the pre-service teachers are practising, the supervising teachers have master's qualifications themselves. Research is a responsibility for all of them in some way. Table 16.1 shows how the scientific competence of teacher educators has increased in the course of the last 30 years (Rantala et al. 2010).

In-service teacher education in Finland has achieved much attention recently and new ideas have been launched. For example, a model of peer-group mentoring has been developed to support new teachers (Heikkinen et al. 2012). It is a collaborative network between the Finnish teacher education institutions, including the vocational teacher education institutions and teacher education departments of universities. Instead of one-to-one discussions, peer-group mentoring is implemented in groups where both novice teachers and their more experienced colleagues share and reflect on their experiences, discuss problems and learn from one another and learn together. The group usually meets once a month after school hours and consists of

Table 16.1 Increase of scientific competence among teacher educators at the University of Helsinki (%)

	1979	1989	1999	2008
PhD	19	18	35	65
Licentiate[a]	*17*	*19*	*7*	*5*
MA	39	43	47	28
BA	6	8	6	2
Other	19	12	6	0
N	52	67	71	93

[a] Between master's and doctorate

4–10 teachers and their mentor. The model of peer-group mentoring apparently is one alternative to realise the third phase of teacher education as suggested by Terhart (2000).

Conclusion

Considering the totality of the Finnish teacher education programme, two special issues should be emphasised and reflected on once more. In the integration of theory and practice in professional learning in the workplace, the university practice schools play a peculiar role. Most of the teaching practice takes place in the university practice schools; these belong to the university and work in close collaboration with the department of teacher education. The curriculum of these schools follows the same curriculum as all schools in the country. The teachers in the university practice schools are master's level and they have a dual responsibility: while they are teaching their own class they function as mentors as well. Also the lecturers of pedagogy from the department of teacher education visit the university practice schools and participate in supervision together with the mentors.

The university practice schools are a safe place to become acquainted with practice and a teacher's work. The mentors are experts in supervision and work in collaboration with the department of teacher education. According to the recommendations of the Ministry of Education, about two-thirds of teaching practice should take place in the university practice schools and about one-third in the local field schools. The field school-university partnership is organised in such a way that the interaction should promote pedagogical value for both sides. Schools are invited to apply to become networking schools and teachers are asked to apply for a course on supervision. Jyrhämä and Syrjäläinen (2011) report that, at the beginning of 2009, the total number of teachers who had attended supervision courses at the University of Helsinki was about 500. In this way, the teachers in the field schools have been integrated into the teacher education curriculum. Network meetings are organised and the teachers get a small salary for the mentoring. Jyrhämä and Syrjäläinen (2011) report also some promising results about the nature and conceptions of supervision among the teachers in the field schools.

Related questions are: what are the consequences of the research-based programme in practice and in the workplace, and what is the role of a practitioner researcher in a teacher's daily work. In the first place, research-based teacher education is the main organising theme in the programme, and conceptually is an attitude or disposition that guides the studies and workplace activities after the studies. To define it in practice or operationalise it for empirical research is possible in many different ways, although difficult. The most important feature is that teachers are able to reflect on their own work, and to change and develop their own practice according to practitioner research. this should be separated from the idea of a teacher as a researcher (Cochran-Smith and Lytle 1990). A teacher as a researcher may work as a partner in a research project, participate in its work equally and also publish the results in journals, whereas a teacher as a practitioner researcher utilises the research skills in pedagogical thinking and decision-making; it is not professional research and not meant to be published. All the colleagues working with teacher education at the department of teacher education, in the university practice schools and also in field schools are familiar with the research-based theme and apply it in some way within their work.

At the moment there are no large-scale empirical research results about the consequences of the research-based programme; we must content ourselves with subjective experiences and indirect indications (e.g. Programme for International Student Assessment results). Logically, it is difficult to find a better way to justify or develop one's own work than research and pedagogical thinking based on research. Despite this, a large-scale research project dealing with the research-based teacher education programme would be most welcome.

References

Allison, C. B. (1995). *Present and past. Essays for teachers in the history of education.* New York: Peter Lang.

Bengtsson, J. (1993). Theory and practice: Two fundamental categories in the philosophy of teacher education. *Educational Review, 45*(3), 205–211.

Bengtsson, J. (1995). What is reflection? On reflection in the teaching profession and teacher education. *Teachers and Teaching, 1*(1), 23–32.

Berliner, D. (2000). A personal response to those who bash teacher education. *Journal of Teacher Education, 51*(5), 358–371.

Berliner, D. (2002). Educational research: The hardest science of all. *Educational Researcher, 31*(8), 18–20.

Berliner, D. (2005). The near impossibility of testing for teacher quality. *Journal of Teacher Education, 56*(3), 205–213.

Biddle, B. J., Good, T. L., & Goodson, I. F. (Eds.). (1997). *International handbook of teachers and teaching.* Dordrecht: Kluwer.

Calderhead, J. (1984). *Teachers' classroom decision-making.* London: Holt, Rinehart and Winston.

Cochran-Smith, M., & Lytle, S. (1990). Research on teaching and teacher research: The issues that divide. *Educational Researcher, 19*(2), 2–11.

Cochran-Smith, M., & Zeichner, K. M. (Eds.). (2005). *Studying teacher education: The report of the AERA panel on research and teacher education.* Washington, D.C.: AERA and Lawrence Erlbaum.

Cochran-Smith, M., Feiman-Nemser, S., McIntyre, D. J., & Demers, K. E. (Eds.). (2008). *Handbook of research on teacher education: Enduring issues in changing contexts (3rd ed.)*. New York: Routledge.

Eddy, D. (2005). Evidence-based medicine: A unified approach. *Health Affairs, 24,* 9–17.

Fitzgibbons, R. E. (1981). *Making educational decisions. An introduction to philosophy of education*. New York: Hartcourt Brace Jovanovich.

Gage, N. L. (1994). The scientific status of research on teaching. *Educational Theory, 44,* 371–383.

Galluzo, G. R., & Pankratz, R. S. (1990). Five attributes of a teacher education program knowledge base. *Journal of Teacher Education, 41*(4), 7–14.

Griffiths, R. (2004). Knowledge production and the research-teaching nexus: The case of the built environment disciplines. *Studies in Higher Education, 29*(6), 709–726.

Guhl, E., & Ott, E. H. (1985). *Unterrichtsmetodisches Denken und Handeln*. Darmstadt: Wissenschaftliche Buchgesellschaft.

Handal, G., & Lauvås, P. (1987). *Promoting reflective teaching. Supervision in practice*. Milton Keynes: Open University.

Hattie, J. A. C. (2009). *Visible learning: A synthesis of over 800 meta-analyses relating to achievement*. London: Routledge.

Heikkinen, H., Tynjälä, P., & Jokinen, H. (Eds.). (2012). *Peer-group mentoring for teachers' professional development*. New York, NY: Routledge.

Howey, K. (1996). Designing coherent and effective teacher education programs. In J. Sikula (Ed.), *Handbook of research on teacher education* (pp. 143–170). New York: Macmillan.

Hytönen, J. (1995). The role of school practice in teacher education. In Kansanen (Ed.), *Discussions on some educational issues VI* (pp. 77–83). Research Report 145. Department of Teacher Education, University of Helsinki (ED394958)

Jakku-Sihvonen, R., & Niemi, H. (Eds.). (2006). Research-based teacher education in Finland. *Research in Educational Sciences, 25.* Turku: Finnish Educational Research Association

Jakku-Sihvonen, R., & Niemi, H. (Eds.). (2007). *Education as a societal contributor. Reflections by Finnish educationalists*. Frankfurt a. M.: Peter Lang.

Jyrhämä, R. (2006). The function of practical studies in teacher education. In R. Jakku-Sihvonen & H. Niemi (Eds.), *Research-based teacher education in Finland—Reflections by Finnish teacher educators*. Turku: Finnish Educational Research Association

Jyrhämä, R., & Syrjäläinen, E. (2011). 'Good pal, wise dad and nagging wife'—and other views by teaching practice mentors. In A. Lauriala, R. Rajala, H. Ruokamo & O. Ylitapio-Mäntylä (Eds.), *Navigating in educational contexts. Identities and cultures in dialogue* (pp. 137–149). Rotterdam: Springer.

Kaestle, C. F. (1993). The awful reputation of education research. *Educational Reseacher, 22*(1), 26–31.

Kansanen, P. (1991). Pedagogical thinking: The basic problem of teacher education. *European Journal of Education, 26,* 251–260.

Kansanen, P. (2001). Using subjective pedagogical theories to enhance teacher education. *Unterrichtswissenschaft, 29*(3), 268–286.

Kansanen, P. (2004). The role of general education in teacher education. *Zeitschrift für Erziehungswissenschaft, 7*(2), 207–218.

Kansanen, P. (2007). Research-based teacher education. In R. Jakku-Sihvonen & H. Niemi (Eds.), *Education as a societal contributor* (pp. 131–146). Frankfurt-am-Main: Peter Lang.

Kansanen, P. (2010). HORRIBILE DICTU: The success story of the Finnish school system. In A. Liimets (Ed.), *Denkkulturen. Selbstwerdung des Menschen. Erziehungskulturen* (pp. 95–110). Frankfurt am Main: Peter Lang.

Kansanen, P., Tirri, K., Meri, M., Krokfros, L., Husu, J., & Jyrhämä, R. (2000). *Teachers' pedagogical thinking: Theoretical landscapes, practical challenges*. New York: Peter Lang.

Kindsvatter, R., Wilen, W., & Ishler, M. (1992). *Dynamics of effective teaching* (2nd ed.). New York: Longman.

Kleven, T. A. (1991). Interactive teacher decision-making—still a basic skill? *Scandinavian Journal of Educational Research, 35,* 287–294.

König, E. (1975). *Theorie der Erziehungswissenschaft. Band 1. Wissenschaftstheoretische Richtungen der Pädagogik.* München: Wilhelm Fink.

Krokfors, L. (2007). Two-fold role of reflective pedagogical practise in research-based teacher education. In R. Jakku-Sihvonen & H. Niemi (Eds.), *Education as a societal contributor* (pp. 147–159). Frankfurt-am-Main: Peter Lang.

Kuhn, D. (1991). *The skills of argument.* New York: Cambridge University Press.

Labaree, D. F. (1997). *How to succeed in school without really learning. The credentials race in American education.* New Haven: Yale University Press.

Labaree, D. F. (2003). The peculiar problems of preparing educational researchers. *Educational Researcher, 32*(4), 13–22.

Maaranen, K. (2009). Practitioner research as part of professional development in initial teacher education. *Teacher Development, 13*(3), 219–237.

Maaranen, K. (2010). Teacher students' MA Theses—A gateway to analytic thinking about teaching? A case study of Finnish primary school teachers. *Scandinavian Journal of Educational Research, 54*(5), 487–500.

McCourt, F. (2005). *Teacher man. A memoir.* London: Harper Perennial.

Meyer, H. (1980). *Leitfaden zur Unterrichtsvorbereitung.* Frankfurt am Main: Cornelsen Verlag Scriptor.

Niemi, H., Toom, A., & Kallioniemi, A. (Eds.). (2012). *The miracle of education: The principles and practices of teaching and learning in Finnish schools.* Rotterdam: Sense Publishers.

Paschen, H., & Wigger, L. (Eds.). (1992). *Pädagogisches Argumentieren.* Weinheim: Deutscher Studien Verlag.

Penso, S., & Shoham, E. (2003). Student teachers' reasoning while making pedagogical decisions. *European Journal of Teacher Education, 26*(3), 313–328.

Prange, K. (2008). Review of the book: Ricken, N. (2007). (Hrsg.). Über die Verachtung der Pädagogik. Analysen—Materialien—Perspektiven. *Zeitschrift für Pädagogik, 54* (3), 438–441.

Rantala, J., Salminen, J., & Säntti, J. (2010). Teorian ja käytännön ristiaallokossa—luokanopettajan koulutuksen akatemisoituminen ja sen heijastuminen opettajaksi opiskelevien praktisiin valmiuksiin. In A. Teoksessa, A. Kallioniemi, A. Toom, M. Ubani, & H. Linnansaari (Eds.), (toim.), *Akateeminen luokanopettajankoulutus: 30 vuotta teoriaa, käytäntöä ja maistereita* (pp. 51–76). Kasvatusalan tutkimuksia 52. Jyväskylä: Suomen kasvatustieteellinen seura

Richardson, V. (1994). Conducting research on practice. *Educational Researcher, 23*(5), 5–10.

Sahlberg, P. (2011). *Finnish lessons: What can the world learn from educational change in Finland?* New York: Teachers College Press.

Schön, D. A. (1983). *The reflective practitioner. How professionals think in action.* New York: Basic Books.

Shavelson, R. J. (1973). What is the basic teaching skill? *Journal of Teacher Education, 24,* 144–151.

Sroufe, G. E. (1997). Improving the 'awful reputation' of education research. *Educational Researcher, 26*(7), 26–28.

Terhart, E. (Eds.). (2000). *Perspektiven der Lehrerbildung in Deutschland.* Abschlussbericht der von der Kultusministerkonferenz eingesetzten Komission. Weinham und Basel: Beltz.

Toom, A., Kynäslahti, H., Krokfors, L., Jyrhämä, R., Byman, R., Stenberg, K., Maaranen, K., & Kansanen, P. (2010). The experiences of research-based approach of teacher education: Suggestions for the future policies. *European Journal of Education, 45*(2), 339–352.

Toulmin, S. (1958). *The uses of argument.* Cambridge: Cambridge University Press.

Westbury, I., Hansen, S.-E., Kansanen, P., & Björkvist, O. (2005). Teacher education for research-based practice in expanded roles: Finland's experience. *Scandinavian Journal of Educational Research, 49*(5), 475–485.

Young, L. J. (2001). Border crossing and other journeys: Re-envisioning the doctoral preparation of educational researchers. *Educational Researcher, 30*(5), 3–5.

Chapter 17
Improving Workplace Learning in Teacher Education

Jean Murray, Olwen McNamara and Marion Jones

Section 1: Workplace Learning Across Professional and Cultural Boundaries

Chapter 1 details the origins of this book in the work of the Teacher Education Research Network (TERN) (2008 to date) and the seminar series on workplace learning which TERN ran in 2011. In that chapter we outlined, as our reasons for setting up the series, that we felt workplace learning in teacher education was not well theorised or conceptualised (Rainbird et al. 2004), in part because, as Hodkinson and Hodkinson (2005) identify, there was little integration between the research on teacher learning and the workplace learning literature. Consequently, few of the powerful insights on supporting learning in the workplace, which theoretical and empirical research on professional learning in other areas had revealed to be important, were drawn down into teacher education. Further, there was little work considering how such insights might lead to alternative conceptualisations and structures of pre- and in-service teacher learning in schools and universities.

Rather, as teacher education researchers and practitioners, we found ourselves in 2010 confronted with a series of often uncritical ways of looking at teacher learning in the workplace, with scant attention paid, for example, to how 'expansive learning environments' (Fuller and Unwin 2004) might be created for adult learners within schools. This omission was, in part, the result of the numerous reforms and government interventions that have shaped teacher education programmes in England

J. Murray (✉)
University of East London, London, UK
e-mail: j.m.f.murray@uel.ac.uk

O. McNamara
School of Education, The University of Manchester, Manchester, UK
e-mail: olwen.mcnamara@manchester.ac.uk

M. Jones
Liverpool John Moores University, Liverpool, UK
e-mail: M.Jones@ljmu.ac.uk

O. McNamara et al. (eds.), *Workplace Learning in Teacher Education,*   293
Professional Learning and Development in Schools and Higher Education 10,
DOI 10.1007/978-94-007-7826-9_17, © Springer Science+Business Media Dordrecht 2014

during the past 30 years, as detailed in Chaps. 1 and 11. In pre-service teacher education, the English system continued to follow paths to more 'relevant' and practical school-based programmes, including, for higher education-based courses, an increase in the proportion of pre-service education undertaken in the workplace. As Chap. 11 details, for pre-service education this emphasis has continued apace through the School Direct scheme, despite protests from the university sector and many other stakeholders.

In terms of formal provision of continuous professional development, central, ring-fenced funding for learning outside the school workplace has been largely axed, as Chap. 7 outlines. This means that schools now make decisions on staff learning needs and how to address them, drawing on their already overstretched general budgets for resourcing. As Chaps. 6 and 10 outline, this situation has led to justifiable concerns about the loss of opportunities for innovative continuous professional learning, alongside fears of increasing 'localisation' of teacher knowledge around the imperatives of the school. Those imperatives are in turn, of course, related to national performativity agendas for school improvement. Although, as Ball (1994, p. 16) notes, policies should be seen as

> representations which are encoded in complex ways (via struggles, compromises, authoritative public interpretations and re-interpretations) and decoded in complex ways (via actors, interpretation and meanings in relation to their history, experiences, skills, resources and context).

In other words, despite their seemingly deterministic, one-size-fits-(nearly)-all prescriptions, government policies for pre- and in-service teacher learning are decoded, mediated and implemented in differing ways at local levels. Following Ball's definitions then, discourses of performativity may be seen as constructed differently within institutions, and they are shaped by and shape the perspectives of senior leaders and teachers as agents. This is a further powerful factor in defining the opportunities for workplace learning at school levels, as we discuss later in this chapter.

In a book of this diversity and richness it is impossible to reflect on all the concepts and ideas encapsulated in earlier chapters. We therefore fully acknowledge that the themes explored here are very much a personal selection by us as editors. This selection is, inevitably, influenced by our concerns about the contexts for teacher education policy and practice in England at the time of writing in 2013. These are contexts in which the school system is undergoing a period of rapid and essentially irreversible change, with increasing deregulation and a freeing of schools from local authority control and accountability. Many schools are also being expected to take more responsibility for all stages of teacher learning. Beyond our personal concerns about those changes, England is, as we noted in Chap. 1, an interesting test-bed for theorising workplace learning, because whilst the ongoing changes in pre-service teacher education are radical, they also reflect something of the direction of policy being developed in other nations. Our aims, therefore, have wider relevance for teacher education internationally, as Chaps. 12–16 on workplace learning in other national systems indicate (see also the analysis of Darling-Hammond and Lieberman (2012) which identifies commonalities across teacher education systems). Our focus in this chapter also addresses international issues in workplace learning for serving teachers, as shown by recent pan-European calls (European Commission 2010a, b) to improve the quality of teaching through continuous professional learning relevant to, and often conducted in, the workplace. The chapter's aims also have relevance for the workplace learning of other professionals, including doctors, other health workers and educational psychologists. In these professional contexts, as in teacher education, there are debates about the value attached to experiential knowledge gained in practice-based settings, and the knowledge delivered or co-constructed in a professional university-based programme.

The case studies presented in this book give multiple perspectives on workplace learning which transcend national, cultural and often professional boundaries. Workplace learning—regardless of professional domain or national context—emerges as highly complex and multi-layered, taking place within formal or informal, structured or unstructured programmes, resulting in good, bad and indifferent outcomes. Some of these may be planned but others are quite unforeseen and unintended in their forms and in their short- and long-term effects. In addition, as the preceding chapters clearly show, learning at and through work is, inevitably, influenced by the structural and socio-cultural factors inherent in the workplace and in the broader professional, socio-economic and cultural contexts in which it occurs. Many of the chapters here underline the findings of Hodkinson and Hodkinson (2004) about the complex ways in which personal dispositions and senses of agency affect how individual professionals interact within the workplace, participate in different learning territories and take advantage of the opportunities offered in very different ways. In this sense, what is learned by any professional in his/her workplace might be seen as an individual product, achieved through an individualised learning process whilst working towards individual and differentiated outcomes and differing levels of 'impact' on personal practice. Productive workplace learning might then be positioned as, at root, highly individualised and specific.

Nevertheless, from reading our case studies it is clear that—even across very different professional, cultural and national boundaries—there is considerable consensus around the key principles which inform the design and implementation of high quality workplace learning. There is also consensus about the need to mediate the inherent tensions in many arenas of public sector work between individual, school and government priorities for schooling and teacher education. The key principles include: (1) a collegiate learning culture within the workplace in which workers' achievements, contributions and learning gains are valued; (2) a culture in which a symbiotic relationship between the multiple discourses about theory and practice, teaching and learning can be facilitated; (3) participation in a well-planned, rich and flexible variety of activities focused on a balance of organisational and individual needs, both during and away from the 'day job', to allow for informal (tacit) learning to occur, in addition to any formal and planned learning; (4) the availability of time and space for quality learning opportunities and experiences to occur, and then further time to reflect upon them, secure in the knowledge that any professional boundaries encountered are not restrictive, but form part of an infrastructure for the facilitation of dialogue and the development of mutual understanding; (5) teaching colleagues undertaking roles as facilitators and supporters of learning which are appropriately challenging and focused in relation to both individual and organisational needs.

Crucially, if organisational needs, particularly those which are dictated by narrow and instrumental outcomes and targets, are not to be allowed to dominate learning territories and agendas, then many teachers particularly those at the beginning of their careers, will need support from colleagues in developing integrated ways of conceptualising and articulating their workplace learning. They may also need guidance in developing the individual agency which will allow them to articulate their specific learning needs and to seek access to relevant knowledge bases and support systems. These points have particular relevance for teachers in England, many of whom are already living different professional and learning lives within the rapidly deregulating school and teacher education systems, as we discuss in Sect. 3.

In Chap. 3, Michael Eraut's discussion of workplace learning across a number of professions identifies and underlines many of these attributes of good quality provision. In particular, the summary provided in Table 3.4 stresses organisational commitment to, and valuation of, learning in the workplace based on principles of knowledge sharing, active collaboration and a culture of openness. The leadership of senior managers is also seen as important in ensuring that these values are translated into the design and allocation of appropriate work roles and processes. Good leadership, together with the skills of learning facilitators and a supportive, open culture helps to ensure that both planned and unplanned opportunities for learning in the workplace take place.

These findings have some similarities with the work of Fuller and Unwin (2004, p. 1) that developed a spectrum of workplace learning environments around the extremes of 'expansive' or 'restrictive'. In particular, there are strong commonalities between the recommendations for creating workplace learning opportunities in parts of this book and what Fuller et al. define as an 'expansive learning environment'. In the latter there is a shared valuation of, and vision for, workplace learning, aligned to organisational goals whilst also allowing for the development of individual skills and capacities. For new and inexperienced workers, progression is supported and gradual, incorporating appropriate levels of challenge and valuing a 'multi-dimensional view of expertise'. Learning occurs through participation in 'a range of settings inside and outside the workplace', including boundary crossing into other organisations and practice settings, and time for learning and reflection away from work.

As many of the chapters in this book underline, performativity regimes within both schools and universities have profound implications for the ways in which workplace learning takes place. Such pressures 'affect the expansiveness of learning environments and impact significantly upon workers' ability to access learning' (Fuller and Unwin 2004, p. 1), shaping—and all too often—limiting the forms of teachers' pre- and in-service learning. Examples of the impact of performativity on workers' learning may be seen in these authors' model of 'restrictive learning environments', where definitions of learning and the required knowledge/skills are narrow and restricted to organisational needs, and virtually all so-called learning occurs on the job within an often intensive schedule, which allows little space for reflection. The work itself offers a limited number of positive learning opportunities and there are few chances for workers to participate in other work settings within or outside the organisation. There is little value placed on the importance of workers also being learners, meaning that novices and trainees are required to make rapid transitions to fully functioning worker status, acquiring any necessary new knowledge and skills swiftly. Here the ability for newcomers to adopt an identity as a learner and the sense of agency to access necessary support may well be limited by the structural, social and cultural boundaries inherent in this restrictive environment.

But, as we have indicated above, the effects of performativity are not uniform. Rather, these discourses and practices play out in diverse ways across different schools, with senior leaders and teachers mediating pressures, creating specific cultures and defining local territories and opportunities for workplace learning. There is clear evidence that formal and informal micro-cultures or communities of practice *within* schools—for example, subject or year teams or mutual support and friendship groups—vary again (Hodkinson and Hodkinson 2004, 2005) in terms of being or becoming positive learning territories. To add to the complexity, there is clear evidence of diversity across the ways in which individual teacher learners are able to access and benefit from the learning opportunities or affordances offered (Hodkinson and Hodkinson 2004; Billett 2001).

Drawing on the multiple perspectives offered by earlier chapters, this final chapter is structured as follows: after this introduction, Sect. 2 looks specifically at how we might improve teacher learning—across all career stages—in the workplace. Our primary focus here is the school itself which, as Chap. 1 identifies, remains the place in which most work and learning takes place for many educational professionals. We focus in this second section on the status of teachers as learners, the importance of the adult educator in workplace learning, and the need to re-conceptualise roles in supporting and guiding teacher development. In the conclusion of Sect. 2 we return to the issue of the places/spaces within and beyond the school in which workplace learning might be generated, identifying universities, the settings for cross professional practices and established and emerging technologies as spaces which offer important affordances for teacher learning. We place a particular focus at the end of the section on the potential of technologies, including simulations, for generating new modes of workplace learning for pre-service teachers. The third and final section of this chapter returns to the issue of how we might re-conceptualise workplace learning for teachers in the rapidly changing policy landscapes of schools and teacher education in England at the time of writing in 2013. After debating the merits of the theoretical lenses for workplace learning offered for consideration in Chap. 1, we highlight four case studies of good practice in workplace learning presented earlier in the book.

Section 2: Towards Reconceptualising Teacher Workplace Learning

Case studies in this book have challenged assumptions about what teacher learning is, the knowledge bases upon which it rests, and the settings in which it can occur. We have also challenged prevailing ideas that the school workplace, as the immediate practice setting, is the only place in which teacher knowledge can be developed or extended—thus marginalising other settings, such as universities, cross-professional territories, and, we would posit, increasingly the use of new technologies, including virtual spaces which allow for the simulation of practice. Most particularly we have contested strongly (in Chaps. 2 and 11) the idea that, in pre-service and induction programmes, more time spent in the practice settings necessarily equates to better quality learning for beginning teachers. Such constructions of teachers' learning as a superficial linear process of improvement, directly related to very narrow constructions of 'practice' which need to impact positively and almost immediately on pupil learning, are simplistic. This also applies to notions that knowledge is effectively acquired through transmission and apprenticeship modes of training: continuing professional development of this kind is all too often based on narrow conceptions of 'keeping up to date' or 'refreshing knowledge' to reflect national imperatives and school improvement priorities. Many of our chapters work with a very different construction of workplace learning which mirrors aspects of Engeström's (2001) theory where learning is essentially expansive, ill-defined, complex and changeable in nature.

In terms of conceptualising and improving workplace learning in teacher education, our analysis is grounded in a clear recognition of beginning and serving teachers as learners, re-defining teacher knowledge for 'clinical practice' in the workplace, and strengthening the roles of teacher peers and senior leaders in valuing, planning and supporting learning. Overall, we suggest there should be a re-focusing of what needs to be learned, by whom, when, how and for whose benefit in teachers' workplace learning.

Re-Focusing on the Status of Teachers as Learners

Earlier chapters of this book have indicated worrying erosions in the recognition of the status of both beginning and serving teachers as learners. Chapters 2 and 11 indicate, for example, the ambiguous positioning of many pre-service teachers in England, and the ways in which the high emotional and professional risks involved are not always acknowledged in the 'public arena' of the practicum experience, where there is 'no safety net for the pre-service teacher, no opportunity to be tentative, and huge risk of witnessed failure' (Chap. 2, p. 29). Conway et al.'s work, discussed in Chap. 13, is also pertinent here in its exploration of the erosion of learner status through notions of the 'invisibility-visibility' of the pre-service teacher as a learner in Irish schools.

Chapters 6 and 10 have shown that current continuing professional development policy in England has often been driven by utilitarian requirements for teacher knowledge to be relevant, up-to-date and focused on current national and local policy initiatives. Teachers and their learning have been positioned as mere cogs in an educational machine, driven relentlessly by a set of practices centred on 'raising pupil learning outcomes' often through narrow and measurable exam targets. They have been subjected to performance management and appraisal processes, which often start from a deficit model of teaching defined as performance and then proceed to define and measure the 'worth' of teachers against narrow productivity measures. Such target-driven models of continuing professional development are identified by Earley and Bubb (2004) as characterised by an ethos of hard economic utilitarianism. Here, performativity agendas at school and national levels drive provision, and continuing professional development programmes must be shown to result in positive and almost immediate 'impacts' on pupil learning to be considered of high quality. These tendencies have often developed because of neo-liberal performativty regimes and regulatory structures such as Ofsted, and have also been accelerated by budget constraints in the school sector since the economic crisis.

Ironically, despite attributing superficial valuation to teachers as agents of change and improvement, such models often erode the importance of teachers as *learners,* in their own right, and leave individual motivation and sense of agency in terms of learning and development out of the equation. In adhering to these models of teacher learning, focused mainly around the imperatives of school development, the sector has—sometimes inadvertently—'hit the target but missed the point', to adapt the words of Green (2010). We argue that such models of continuing professional development, in eroding the value of seeing teachers as learners in their own rights, overlook the power of teacher learning to achieve broader, long-term goals for achieving high quality learning for both pupils *and* their teachers. As the work of Gu and Day (2013) indicates, these limited models also fail to take into account the importance of high quality teacher learning in building and sustaining teacher resilience and motivation across the career course.

We suggest then that the English system continues to adopt these target-driven, impoverished models of continuing professional development at its long-term peril. Teachers must not become positioned solely as 'tools for school improvement', but rather need to be (re)positioned as professional learners for their own benefits as well as for those of pupils (Czerniawski 2013). We are in urgent need of a renewed focus on teachers as individual learners, building professional learning from the starting points of teacher practice and thinking in ways which make sense to individuals. Obvious starting points here are re-acknowledging that many teachers are natural autodidacts, happy—in most circumstances—to see themselves as both teachers and learners in the workplace, and fully able to demonstrate agency and take charge of their own professional learning, when allowed to do so.

As Chap. 10 identifies, a number of national initiatives have tried to pay attention to the importance of teachers' voice and ownership of continuing professional development programmes, but this focus has often been tokenistic. We therefore need to ask what continuing professional development might look like if it gave teachers *genuine* responsibility for determining the direction of at least part of their professional learning. There is certainly not a blueprint here, nor is an individual 'learning agenda' likely to remain fixed, as it would need to be negotiated and re-negotiated over time as personal, professional and institutional imperatives shifted. As Hodkinson and Hodkinson (2004) identify, such an agenda is likely to be influenced by teacher habitus and dispositions (Bourdieu 1987), as well as professional aspirations and motivations. In this sense, these agendas will be deeply personal, but this should not prevent us from considering the broad forms they may take in a profession in which personal contribution to the 'common good' is still a dominant motivation for many teachers.

For serving teachers, time and space are needed to engage in, reflect on and analyse the range of planned learning affordances and opportunities in the workplace which have 'rich learning' as a by-product (Eraut et al. 2006). Engagement in work processes should focus on the questions, issues and dilemmas which new initiatives raise for established practices, for pupil learning and for the school as a learning organisation and culture. As indicated earlier, we challenge the validity of the one-size-fits-all approach of many formal continuing professional development programmes which are focused only on achieving short-term school improvement targets; although, as previously indicated, we acknowledge the ongoing tensions in workplace learning between organisational and individual needs, tensions which are identified in some detail in Chaps. 6 and 11. The solution we advocate, however, is not a return to the wholly individualised pattern of continuing professional development engendered by the James Report of 1972 (James 1972), in which teachers attended a series of one-off events outside the school. This pick-and-mix approach to professional learning was often incoherent for both individual and school, as noted in Chap. 12. The more contemporary focus towards continuing and lifelong learning, has the potential to renew the focus on individual teachers but not to lose sight of the broader vision of improving education for the benefit of children and young people as learners. This must always be the primary focus of the school, but it also offers enhanced power to improve the learning of teachers as workers *and* learners. This renewed focus means giving teachers ownership for their own learning and placing more trust in the validity of their decision-making around its directions.

Likewise the status of pre-service teachers as learners in the workplace must be recognised and acknowledged, as emphasised in Chap. 11, and they should be empowered to adopt a position as such within a structured environment which supports participatory models of learning (Edwards and Protheroe 2003). Additionally, pre-service learners need to be sanctioned to trial a range of learning approaches and to innovate and experiment. Further, in pre-service teacher education, sometimes even more than in continuing professional development, time and space are needed to engage in, reflect on and analyse the range of learning affordances offered by the school as an organisation and a learning culture.

The Importance of the Adult Educator in Workplace Learning

Research reports (see, inter alia, Barber and Mourshed 2007; Hattie 2009) clearly identify the importance of the teacher factor in generating high quality pupil learning;

but the importance of the nature and quality of adult educators, and their impact on teacher workplace learning, is only rarely the subject of sustained debate. Many current models of teachers' workplace learning overlook the impact of educators' pedagogic and andragogic knowledge of learning outcomes and the importance of senior leaders in creating cultures which value and support staff learning. But we argue that there are limited, and limiting, roles available for those managing and supporting teacher learning, whether in pre- or in-service.

These limitations occur, in part at least, because (as Chaps. 6 and 11 show), successive governments in England have eroded the role of higher education-based teacher educators in pre-service teacher learning. The current government has even disparaged their expertise and posited that they have a negative impact on teachers as learners, which then becomes a negative impact on pupil outcomes (see Chap. 1). Changes in teacher education, together with the increased casualisation of the workforce (see Chap. 11), now mean that many teacher educators spend less time in supervising the practicum in schools. This has led over time to a changed and substantially increased role for school-based mentors. Yet mentoring as a model of support, has some serious conceptual flaws and has often led to considerable variability in the quality and diversity of workplace learning experiences offered to pre-service and early career teachers, as we will argue later in this chapter. The role of higher education provision for in-service teacher learning has also been sharply reduced, as Chaps. 6 and 10 have shown. Bespoke school-based professional learning, linked to postgraduate level qualifications, flourished in the first decade of the century. Some of these programmes undoubtedly struggled to achieve a balance between organisational and individual needs, and were over-focused on meeting targets and creating immediate 'impacts' on pupil learning. Others, however, offered strong models of collaborative and communal continuing professional learning, including school-focused, enquiry-led, practice-specific degrees . . . [which] allow for teachers and schools to meet their specific needs, supported by the university tutors' knowledge of the wider field (Chap. 6, p. 116). Overall, the decline in higher education and local authority influence, and the consolidation of a broader market for continuing professional development provision, means that teacher learning is now commonly 'delivered' in the school workplace by a wide range of 'trainers' (private companies, universities, or others operating as individual consultants). This steadily increasing diversity of provision raises justifiable questions about the quality of continuing professional development and the experience and the qualifications of trainers/educators. This is particularly so if the onus is on designing and implementing effective workplace learning affordances, which have the potential to make a long-term and coherent contribution to teacher learning, rather than being a 'short-term fix'.

A further, frequently overlooked, area of expertise is the pedagogical skills and knowledge of how adult learners are best supported in becoming professionals and developing further professional knowledge. This 'second order knowledge' (Murray 2002), which good teacher educators possess, is not synonymous with that required for teaching in schools, explaining in part why a good teacher is not necessarily a good mentor or continuing professional development co-ordinator. Most university-based teacher educators have this knowledge (Murray et al. 2011) and are able to draw on it to design effective learning environments for intending and serving teachers. Their repertoires also include research-informed knowledge of schooling and pedagogical content knowledge for subject teaching, two vital areas for improving the quality of both pupil and teacher learning. Current policy, as noted in Chap. 11, risks the loss of such highly skilled educators, and we argue strongly for their continued voice. As we discuss later, this book offers a number of important examples of university-based teacher educators working in schools, alongside teachers as workers, learners and collaborators, engaged in what is defined here as 'collaborative doing'.

As the scope for higher education-based teacher educators to engage in the workplace learning environment has diminished, so the importance of mentoring roles for supporting and 'teaching' pre-service and early career teachers has grown. This increased reliance on mentoring, as the main role in helping pre-service teachers to articulate their workplace learning, has had a particular impact on provision. In 2010 a House of Commons Select Committee report on teacher education (House of Commons 2010) raised concerns about the continued inconsistency in the quality of mentoring and thus learner experiences, despite close to 20 years of partnership legislation. This inconsistency is not just a feature of the English system. As Chaps. 13 and 15 indicate, there have been similar problems in the Irish and Norwegian pre-service teacher education systems in the past.

Research evidence shows many incidences of individual mentors providing outstanding workplace learning opportunities for pre-service or early career teachers (see, for example, Jones et al. 2009; Counsell 2013). But critiques of mentoring practices in education (see, inter alia, Colley 2003) argue that, in general, the practice often re-inscribes workplace hierarchies based around the valuation of particular forms of experience and expertise and traditional power relations. Devolving responsibility for the teacher learner to the mentor as *senior* colleague, thus equating teacher expertise with experience, for example, may limit opportunities within the organisation for other colleagues to undertake differing roles and responsibilities with the newcomer.

Many of the tensions encountered in mentoring and partnership models of workplace learning in teacher education are mirrored in other workplaces, where professional hierarchies, workload pressures or status differentials often make it difficult for learners to develop personal learning through/with the expertise of their colleagues. Chapter 4, for example, describes how in medicine education, doctors balance their clinical care and educational practice roles, often with additional responsibilities as managers and/or researchers. Individuals often vary in their degrees of success at aligning those multiple roles and responsibilities with one another, but generally teaching responsibilities are more likely to be overlooked, particularly in situations where patient care must be prioritised.

Tensions in workplace learning partnerships are further complicated, however, when there are sensitivities in the workplace about revealing the trainee's 'learner' status. In some professional workplaces it may not always be possible or easy to acknowledge this status openly. As a number of previous chapters have illustrated, for example, in pre-service teacher education it is not always straightforward for beginning teachers to accept, in full, their identities as learners without the perceived loss of credibility with pupils and fellow teachers. Recent structural changes in Employment Based Initial Teacher Training routes (EBITTs), such as the School Direct Salaried scheme, where pre-service teachers are accounted for as serving teachers on school rolls, exacerbate this problem. As Chap. 5 describes, other pressures lead some supervisors of educational psychology trainees in the workplace to obfuscate the trainee's status in order to avoid any challenge to the credibility or value of services being provided by them. Here implementing an apprentice model, in which trainees shadow qualified psychologists, is not cost neutral. Psychological services pay for trainees' services, and they in turn are expected to provide services which contribute to the overall delivery of the, often 'traded', service. And in medical education, as Chap. 4 illustrates, learner and expert identities often merge and overlap in the complex educational and clinical hierarchies of Teaching Hospitals.

Re-Conceptualising Support Roles in Teachers' Workplace Learning

Given the variability in mentoring practice in teacher education, it is hard to disagree with the views of Hargreaves and Fullan (1999) that it is time to shift narrow ways of understanding mentoring. Additionally, we need to ask if current models of mentoring are strong enough to support new teachers in developing integrated ways of conceptualising and articulating their workplace learning and generating the sense of individual agency which will allow them to identify their specific learning needs. When the territories for learning and teaching are increasingly subject to the forces of performativity and regulation, can we ensure that all mentors have the professional skills and knowledge to create the spaces where critical discussion about professional practice and policy can take place freely? As an important part of developing early workplace learning in teaching—and other professions—we suggest that traditional mentoring roles certainly need to be strengthened and re-conceptualised, if not radically revised. One way of beginning a re-conceptualisation may be through recognising and formalising the importance of mentoring as a set of *additional* practices for a selected group of teachers with official acknowledgement as adult educators, who possess additional knowledge and skills clearly recognised as different from those required for teaching pupils. The House of Commons Select Committee report on teacher education in England (2010, p. 5) adopted this approach, recommending the introduction of a 'clinical practitioner' grade for mentors as part of raising the status of their work. Developing the andragogical skills of working with adult learners as they enter the profession—or extend and develop their existing professional knowledge—would be an essential element of that mentoring. Further study in a university setting was also strongly recommended. The application of this kind of model for strengthening and extending mentoring for teacher education in Norway is discussed in more depth by Smith and Ulvik in Chap. 15. Here, mentoring is to become what the authors refer to as 'a profession within a profession' (p. 274) involving formal preparation, alongside university-based teacher educators, and the generation of new knowledge and skills for adult education, leading to the award of a nationally recognised and prestigious qualification.

An alternative approach, discussed in Chap. 12, is to broaden mentoring roles by positioning all teachers as responsible for the professional development of pre-service teachers and their colleagues/peers in various ways. In teacher education contexts in England and the Netherlands, the term 'school-based teacher educators' has already gained considerable currency (van Velzen and Volman 2009; Boyd and Tibke 2012), indicating, but usually not defining, more extensive adult learning roles for teachers, well beyond those of the traditional mentor. Famously, the Donaldson Review in Scotland (2010) also conceptualised every teacher as a teacher educator. This inclusive approach has also been adopted by the European Commission in a recent policy document on developing teacher education (European Commission 2012).

One of the underpinning rationales for this model seems to be provided by the medical profession's implementation of a series of hierarchical teaching roles and responsibilities within Teaching Hospitals. Yet, as deployed within medical education, the Teaching Hospitals model has some serious limitations and these educators are often deeply conflicted, as Chap. 4 outlines. This is in part because, as outlined in Chap. 1, patient care, is clearly the core business of the hospital, yet medical education for all career stages is vital for sustaining an effective and efficient workforce. As noted above, the resulting tensions between clinical practice and teaching or educational practice is one that individual doctors manage to a lesser or greater degree, along with all their other roles. The traditional 'see one, do one, teach one' model of medical education has now been extended and formalised (encompassing assessment, training portfolios, feedback and appraisal) but educating other doctors remains, amidst all the competing pressures, the poor relation. Second, individuals are multiply positioned in their identifications within the learning landscape. Chapter 4 shows one young doctor, Sarah, crumpling under the weight of a system in which she was positioned as both teacher and learner. Operating at levels between 'conscious incompetence' and 'conscious competence' she is required to train junior doctors in procedures at which she herself is only just clinically proficient (in text book cases); and, of course, patients, like school pupils, cannot always be relied upon to respond as expected. Furthermore, Sarah is part of a close-knit working team that has to respond swiftly and cohesively in emergencies; to some of these team members Sarah is an assessor and mentor, by others she is assessed and supervised. No external and impartial moderator is available here. These examples—and many others like them from medical education—indicate that the model of Teaching Hospitals is not a straightforward one for schools, as learning organisations, to try to emulate. In particular, the expectations that all teachers become teacher educators in such schools may be fraught with tensions, not least around hierarchies and the resulting power relations within institutions.

As stepping stones in the development of mentoring in teacher education, we suggest that it would certainly be beneficial to extend the kinds of roles which teachers play in the workplace learning of pre-service teachers as well as their colleagues.

This could include experimenting with established models/ideals of mentoring, as usually conducted by a senior colleague and involving an in-depth process of one-to-one, face-to-face meetings. In the original iteration of the TERN (see Chap. 1 for further details), we experimented with a one-to-many mentoring model to promote the professional learning of the participating teacher educators. Eraut's work, outlined in Chap. 3 of this book, indicates a different and wider model of distributed mentoring in which teams of workers allocate responsibility for the learning of newcomers to the person with the most appropriate types of expertise. This work also suggests the potential of 'mentoring' from colleagues closer to the learner in terms of levels of experience. Here, empathy and awareness with the learner may be increased through the more recent professional memories and support offered by a relatively inexperienced colleague. It is also important to consider how the contributions of novice teachers to their own and others' workplace learning could be acknowledged and deployed more fully to the value of individuals and schools. Current conceptualisations of these contributions tend to offer a limited focus on the value of 'new blood' or 'bringing in new ideas' to the organisation.

As Chap. 7 amply indicates, there is also considerable evidence that coaching—envisaged here as, at its best, an extended form of professional dialogue, clearly focused on the development and empowerment of the person being coached (the coachee)—offers important, additional roles for teachers to adopt (CUREE 2005; Lofthouse et al. 2010). Coaching is, of course, open to the same challenges as mentoring around power relations within school hierarchies and the effects of performativity pressures. Again, like mentoring, it is an inter-personal process, so learning will only be effective if characterised by transparency, openness, honesty and trust between the coach and learner or coachee. In order to define the long-term benefits of coaching as a mode of workplace learning, it would seem important to investigate further how teachers behave when placed in coaching roles, the degrees of expertise they bring to the process, their interactions with their fellow teachers as learners, and the learning benefits accrued to both coach and coachee. The use of collaborative peer enquiry and coaching methods in the Welsh Master's in Educational Practice (Salisbury and Morris 2012) and in the surviving remnants of the Master's in Teaching and Learning programme in England (see Chap. 1) are important vehicles for further research, to clarify if and how coaching might develop the specific learning of teachers in the first years of their career.

Those working in schools as teacher educators of any type would benefit from more autonomous roles in organising, implementing and evaluating the quality of the professional learning they provide in and beyond the workplace. To do this in ways which ensure that teacher learning is coherent and effective over the long term, those educators need opportunities to develop advanced skills for working with adult learners. They also need to trust their colleagues' judgements and senses of agency in defining and fulfilling many of their own learning needs, as well as contributing to the achievement of organisational agendas. As in Teaching Hospitals, this may well mean educators acknowledging and living with the different dimensions of the organisation and the tensions between individual and organisational priorities. In particular, it may mean living with the professionally, intellectually and emotionally complex dimensions of teaching teachers as both facilitating pupil learning *and* teaching for adult workplace learning, not least that this dual model of teaching may sometimes involve making difficult decisions about which set of learners is prioritised, when and why.

(Re)generating The Diversity of Spaces for Workplace Learning

In this sub-section we challenge prevailing ideas that the school, as the main workplace for teachers, is the *only* setting in which knowledge relevant for the diverse practices involved in workplace learning can be developed or extended. Other settings for workplace learning, we argue, include universities, cross-professional territories and spaces created by new technologies, particularly virtual spaces which allow for the exchange, development, debate and simulation of practice.

Of these, the university is the most obvious and well-discussed setting within which teacher workplace learning can be developed and extended. The provision of research-informed models of teacher education has long been seen as one of the most powerful contributions which universities and other types of higher education institutions—with their cultures of research, critical enquiry and debate—make to the education of teachers (Dent 1977; Furlong and Smith 1996; UCET 2013). In such contexts, not only do pre-service teachers acquire broad knowledge about education and research-informed practice, but they also establish foundational identities as enquiring and researching teachers to develop further into their careers. The enduring power and importance of this model for teacher education is clearly demonstrated in Chap. 16, where Kansanen analyses the rich research-led provision which underpins learning in the university and the school workplace for all pre-service teachers in Finland. In continuing professional learning, the value of universities working with schools to provide research-informed models of practice, where teachers are clearly positioned as active researchers, is evident—as Chaps. 6, 7 and 10 articulate.

In workplace learning for teachers, as for other professionals, there are, of course, debates about how to integrate declarative (codified) knowledge and standards-led/competency-based education into coherent programmes of professional learning, with clear, ultimate relevance to the workplace. More generally, the relationship that exists between experiential knowledge, gained in practice-based settings, and that delivered or co-constructed in a professional university-based programme, is often positioned as problematic. As we have indicated above, this may be because there is dissonance between the learning contexts and the distinct competencies and knowledge bases required by the practitioners operating within them. As seen in Chap. 3, Eraut—in a study conducted for the English National Board for Nursing and Midwifery Education—found that most nurses failed to receive learning that connected their formal work with their practical work; and only some of their teachers understood the linking of declarative knowledge with professional practice to be their responsibility. Even those that did understand their roles in this respect had insufficient opportunity to pursue this objective, since curricula provided little teaching time in the workplace.

As indicated earlier, the analysis of medical training in Chap. 4 provides a contemporary case study of this. Based for centuries on the acquisition of declarative or codified knowledge, the competency discourse has heralded a significant shift in how the medical profession frames the knowledge it values by extending the assessment of medical students' abilities to possessing, evidencing and enacting functional knowledge, skills and dispositions. Along with the shift to performance assessment of demonstrable behaviours, which remain safely codifiable, has been the illusionary expectation that such assessment can measure professionalism and the softer medical skills involved, and ergo can distinguish good from less good doctors.

Accounts of beginning and experienced teachers engaging in research underline the value of higher education as a context in which research-informed teacher knowledge, with clear relevance to the workplace, can be developed. But Grossman et al.'s work on 'pedagogies of enactment' (2009) in the USA provides an alternative perspective on the direct contributions of higher education to the actual skills involved in *practice*. Grossman and colleagues indicate how formal programmes within the university can also provide 'safe', low-risk settings in which novice professionals can acquire and practise a wide range of professional and pedagogical skills. In some ways this research may be seen as a high profile and well-articulated version of the kind of practice-orientated workplace learning within university seminar rooms which many teacher educators have been doing, largely uncelebrated, with pre-service teachers for many years. Nevertheless Grossman's work and that of other colleagues (see Ball et al. 2009) is to be highly commended for drawing (re)new(ed) attention to the opportunities to challenge established views of the components of practice and the settings where they can be effectively learned.

For many teachers in England, the legacies of the 'Every Child Matters' agenda and the subsequent Children's Act (2004) mean that working as a teacher now includes crossing occupational domains and collaborating with other professionals, such as health, social workers and the police, to ensure pupils' academic achievement and physical and emotional wellbeing. This work generates cross professional learning in practice settings very different from those of the school and in collaboration with colleagues from other professional traditions. Workplace learning in such settings often involves teachers navigating their way through landscapes of competing multi-professional discourses and knowledge bases.

Although none of the chapters in this book directly addresses the use of new technologies in teachers' workplace learning, it is important to acknowledge that this is already a very important factor in contemporary learning. The use of new technologies has already changed many aspects of teachers' workplace learning, over and beyond the opportunities that Chap. 1 identified for access to knowledge and enhanced opportunities for professional networking. Increasing amounts of continuing professional learning are now mediated by or delivered directly by technology, enabling access to learning for previously excluded or marginalised groups (Walsh et al. 2013). Technology is also changing the pedagogical processes by which well-known modes of teacher learning, including action research programmes and school learning 'sets' or groups, are implemented and disseminated (Dana et al. 2013; Salisbury and Morris 2012). But the forms and effectiveness of such provision in promoting teacher learning at differing career stages are decidedly under-researched areas. The value placed upon technological modes of workplace learning by serving teachers and teacher educators, and their potential relevance to school and classroom professional learning, are also often ambiguous and in need of further investigation.

In pre-service, many aspects of teacher education are also now mediated through technology, including the ubiquitous use of e-learning environments and repositories such as Blackboard and Moodle by universities and other providers. But many current technologies offer little more than 'a (virtual) environment where existing teaching spaces and practices are simply reproduced' (Littleton and Bayne 2008, p. 27), including the relaying of information to essentially passive recipients. This lack of development in technologies is not helped by the tendency for much of pre-service teacher education to adhere to long-established, often experiential and individualised learning modes, still centred on pre-service teachers' actual presence in either school classrooms or university seminar rooms. Some use of more developmental and experimental virtual learning spaces is slowly evolving. Work by Hramiak (2010, 2011) and Wheeler and Wheeler (2009), for example, indicate how the use of blogs and wikis can certainly enhance pre-service teachers' learning.

Simulations in which beginning teachers can safely practise their pedagogical skills and teaching knowledge are also becoming more prevalent. Wright and Murray (2008), for example, describe the implementation of Virtual Schools, with a key principle here being to situate pre-service teacher learning within simulated schools to create safe workplace learning opportunities. Such simulations have considerable learning potential because they allow novices space to practise teacher skills and develop new knowledge, without being constrained by individual performance fears and the 'situatedness' of a practicum in a real classroom. But, in general, teacher education lags behind other professional fields in its use of such simulations. In legal education, for example, the SIMulated Professional Learning Environment (SIMPLE) project (Maharg et al. 2008) uses a virtual learning environment to create a virtual town in which law students engage in authentic simulations of the professional work and transactions which legal practice involves. The virtual learning environment here enables them 'to practise the collegiality, networking and values-centred community building between professions' (Maharg et al. 2008, p. 1). In nurse education and other health training, simulated practice learning has become a popular pedagogic approach (Moule 2010) used alongside clinical skills developed in practice settings. In radiology, for example, trainees use Virtual Environments for Radiotherapy Treatments (VERT) to practise their skills in diagnosing and treating patients. In all such learning environments, the stress is on the potential of simulations to enable learners to develop skills and knowledge in an authentic, rich but safe setting, removed from, but with clear applicability to, the practice setting itself.

For teacher education it seems particularly important that new teachers entering the profession understand the potential of new technologies to contribute to both their own learning and that of their future pupils. In order to achieve those things, it seems logical to suggest that pre-service teachers should encounter high quality and positive models of how technologies can develop and enhance both individual and communal knowledge. The development and implementation of more and better modes of e-learning, including virtual spaces and simulations, for workplace learning in pre-service teacher education is one clear possibility here. We would suggest that—for the future—there is considerable potential to locate more of teachers' pre- and in-service workplace learning within the affordances offered by new technologies. Further advantages are that these models of learning work across time-space boundaries, thus enhancing professional networking and the sharing of more diverse practices. But it will clearly be important to ensure that the design of technological learning environments provides authentic learning which takes place alongside, not instead of, the professional knowledge and skills developed and enhanced in the reality of schools as learning organisations. Questions to guide that future development include: What forms of technology facilitate authentic, 'deep' and long-lasting professional learning? Which technologies enable in-depth reflection by practitioners? What 'off-line' pedagogical structures and methods best support learning with and through new technologies? To what extent do teachers feel that they 'own' professional learning mediated through technology? How might the use of new technologies bridge time, space and distance to support continuing professional learning for diverse and/or marginalised groups of teachers? And how are the perceived benefits of technology for teachers' learning perceived by organisations, educational leaders and teacher educators and, of course, by teachers themselves? How can we continue to emphasise the importance of communication, interaction and dialogue in continuing professional learning? How can we create opportunities for e-infrastructures to be developed to support ideals of knowledge sharing and building across teaching communities (Leask and Younie 2013)?

Section 3: Reconceptualised Models of Teacher Workplace Learning

As we have indicated earlier in this chapter, the school system in England is currently undergoing a period of fast and essentially irreversible change, with the rapid expansion of the academies programme, the deregulation of the curriculum and teacher certification and a freeing of the school governance system from local control and accountability. Schools are now required to undertake far more responsibility for all stages of teacher learning, including taking on new roles in pre-service provision. It is also apparent that, not only will more learning be located in the workplace, but far more of that learning will be shaped to have direct relevance for it. In pre-service, as Chap. 11 identifies, the viability of the School Direct model and its impact on higher education programmes is still playing out. And it remains to be seen whether the emerging Teaching School system can fulfil its ambitious remit to provide the majority of professional learning for serving teachers. But undoubtedly these policy shifts offer some new and exciting opportunities and spaces for schools to develop and implement their own models of professional development and workplace learning. How then can we conceptualise and understand workplace learning in this rapidly changing policy landscape with its multiplicity of diverging discourses, practices and theories about teaching and learning? What do robust models of workplace learning which meet the many and complex challenges of learning and being a teacher learner in this context look like?

In Chap. 1 we drew on the ideas of Deleuze and Guattari (2004, p. 419) as a starting point for re-conceptualising workplace learning in this kind of rapidly changing and deregulating/re-regulating educational context. To recap, in Deleuse and Guattari's work the concepts of the worker as 'nomad' and the 'nomadic spaces' and 'state space' are defined, with the former space seen as smooth, unbounded and uncontrolled, whilst the latter is 'striated', coded and regulated by the state to meet its multiple and often conflicting imperatives. The current fluidity of the workplace learning landscape in England may then be conceptualised as one in which striated and smooth space exist side-by-side but, driven by current reforms, striated space is increasingly being made smooth and then re-striated. This flux is possible because the regulation of state space may be reversed by teachers operating as nomads who have the potential to disrupt or subvert the striated space (ibid., p. 426), effectively de- and re-territorialising it as a smooth space which they then take over and work within. The research of Kalmbach Phillips (2002) and St Pierre (1997) warns against over-optimism about the professional autonomy which such re-territorialising may bring but also stresses its important possibilities for achieving enhanced criticality about teaching. In such workplace spaces newly re-made as smooth, individual teachers may be able to reclaim control of their personal learning trajectories by privileging their understanding of their personal development needs, knowledge and aspirations over those articulated and regulated for them by the state and the school. Without codified and stable constructions of knowledge and identity, as Engeström (2004) suggests, what is needed is a new type of expansive learning or 'knotworking' in which working across and between different communities and territories in the workplace is vital. Drawing on these conceptualisations, we argue that further research is needed into how these processes of de- and re-territorialisation of teacher learning spaces are taking place in our rapidly evolving policy landscape, alongside an identification of the affordances for more new and more effective workplace learning which they may offer.

In Chap. 1 we also suggested the theoretical idea of 'third space' which offers a powerful way of conceptualising the diverse and fragmented epistemological landscape of workplace learning in teacher education. Originating in hybridity theory (Bhabha 1994), third space has been used by a considerable number of analysts in teacher education including Zeichner (2010) to break away from some of the traditional binaries which haunt teacher education. Zeichner (ibid, p. 94), for example, sees third space as 'a lens to discuss various kinds of boundary crossings between higher education and schools involved in teacher education'. This type of theorising leads to the idea that what is needed is a kind of 'neutral' or third space where teachers and those learning to teach are able to engage in critical inquiry about their own and colleagues' professional practice, in relation to the social, cultural and political contexts within which it is embedded. This may also be conceptualised as a space within which high quality learning takes place and there are important and multiple roles for higher education-based teacher educators and teaching colleagues, as mentors, coaches and co-facilitators of learning. As Childs et al. in Chap. 2 outline, the vision is that this multi-layered type of 'collaborative doing' provides spaces for the multiple perspectives and discourses of pre- and in-service teachers, students, teacher educators and academic researchers.

Drawing on aspects of these theoretical frames for illumination, we now highlight and discuss four earlier examples from this book of how workplace learning might be developed within and across the smooth and striated spaces of pre- and in-service teacher education, drawing on the expertise of adult educators from both schools and universities to create rich and collaborative learning spaces and to work away from traditional binaries. All four examples also attempt to provide alternative and integrated ways of encouraging teacher learners to form and enact their identities as learners in the workplace and to articulate their specific learning needs, including enhanced knowledge and skills and relevant support systems.

In Chap. 2 Childs et al. argue that learning affordances of pre-service teachers arise in the dialectic relationship between the learner and the practices of the lean-ing context. Starting from this position, their ambition is to establish an Education Deanery—based around the 'multi-layered system of distributed expertise' indicated above—and based upon a university-school partnership built around research, contin-uing professional learning and pre-service teacher education. Activities include, for example, establishing action research learning sets led by teachers, with the teacher educator or university tutor as supporter and 'critical friend', and aimed at outcomes such as developing pupil learning strategies and capacity for self-regulation and self-assessment. The multi-layering of the system provides a structure which both endorses teacher agency and promotes continuing professional learning in the work-place. This in turn, enhances the experiences of the pre-service teachers on practicum in the school.

A second example is given in Chap. 12, where Conroy et al. describe a pilot scheme in Glasgow which made some significant changes to school experience and reshaped partnership relationships by locating a university tutor in a cluster of schools—conceived as a learning community—to co-ordinate and support work with pre-service teachers. This model, dubbed 'research-informed clinical practice' by the authors, aims to enhance school experience, particularly the integration of theory, practice and pedagogy, and to promote professional learning in the partner-ship. To this latter end, three types of enrichment activities were planned: learning rounds, in which the university tutor, teacher mentors and pre-service teachers ob-served lessons and reflected upon them together; school-based seminar programmes, which complemented university-based seminars and were open to all schools and stakeholders in the cluster (including local authorities); and enhanced formative assessment and feedback to the pre-service teacher, conducted jointly by teacher mentor and university-based tutor as part of an ongoing tripartite discussion.

Chapters 8 and 9 discuss two examples of teacher professional learning in math-ematics education; in both examples the participants were working in a kind of hybridised research-practice which may be conceptualised as third space. The first account from Barnes and Solomon in Chap. 8 describes an innovative programme delivered as part of the national Mathematics Specialist Teacher project, which aimed to train teachers as 'maths champions' to be 'agents of change' in their schools. The programme focuses on engaging in and with research, and used tools such as professional dialogue, critical reflection on experience/research literature and practitioner inquiry. Barnes and Solomon give an account of two participants on the programme: Bernie, a devotee of guided discovery learning, and Liz, who prefers more didactic methods. Bernie, unsurprisingly, finds the programme endorses her pedagogic approach, but the same approach to teacher learning within the programme also gives Liz confidence to take more risks in her teaching and to develop a more flexible approach to teaching and learning. The authors conclude that the critical self-reflective approach has honed the 'noticing' skills of participants working in a third space in their hybridised teacher and researcher roles.

Williams et al. in Chap. 9 give an account of lesson study, now popular worldwide particularly in mathematics education but originating from Japan. Lesson study involves teacher collaborative inquiry into planning, teaching and analysing lessons with a view to developing pedagogic practice and both subject and pedagogical content knowledge. Risk-taking is a prerequisite for such experimental inquiry, and hence locating it in safe, smooth and unstriated space is imperative. Such a culture and practice has been quite alien in England where, as indicated, for most of the last two decades the structure of the curriculum and teacher professional development requirements have often been top-down and prescribed, making accountability, compliance and performativity endemic. Williams et al. give an account of one group of primary school teachers who overcame their initial apprehension of the lesson study method and grew to greatly value the new and safe spaces for learning they had created and controlled, and the opportunity to share their experiences with the staff as a whole. A second example of lesson study is one in which secondary pre-service teachers collaborate with their university-based tutors and experienced teachers from their practicum schools. For the pre-service teachers the risks involved here pose an even greater threat than for their teacher colleagues, as the approach positions them as potentially challenging established practice in the school, and requires them to use innovative pedagogic approaches. These are demanding to execute and, if they go wrong, could reflect badly upon the pre-service teachers' progress and ultimately on their practicum grades. The authors conclude, however, that the participating teachers greatly value working collaboratively with experienced colleagues and being empowered to experiment, in a relatively safe learning territory.

In human resource terms, all four case studies represent high cost and high quality examples of school-university collaborations in teacher education, as some of the authors acknowledge. A further consideration is that these case studies indicate complex tensions, ambiguities and role conflicts for the adult educators involved to navigate. These indications are reinforced by accounts from teacher educators in both England and the USA engaging in similar models of workplace learning (see, for example, Boyd and Tibke 2012; Martin et al. 2011; Klein et al. 2012). Such accounts suggest that the work of adult educators in the workplace is demanding, involving high levels of knowledge, pedagogical or andragogical skills and interpersonal abilities to navigate complex learning terrains and mediate those multiple spaces for pre- and in-service teachers. Certainly, in future, all those undertaking workplace learning with teachers need to be willing to engage with the heterogeneity of learner voices they will encounter. These adult educators also need to be resilient enough to deal with 'pedagogies of discomfort' (Boler 1999) around working with professional learners, including uncertainty, ambiguity and risk-taking. The ideal would, of course, be that such collaborative spaces provide a way of crossing different learning territories and should be available for all teachers, particularly those whose voices are sometimes marginalised. And we would suggest that only by providing spaces for the multiple perspectives and discourses of pre- and in-service teachers in workplace learning, can teacher educators of all types make valid, long-term and coherent contributions to school and teacher education systems that promote equality and social justice for all.

There is, of course, the risk that, particularly in times of economic austerity, participation in high quality workplace learning becomes and might remain the privilege of only a few adult educators and their teacher learners. But, as Campbell identifies in Chap. 10, high quality provision for teacher learning *is* often costly, at least in the short term. Whilst the core business of the education system, and specifically the school, is clearly pupil learning, we would reiterate one of our key points from Chap. 1 that if we do not value and invest in the development of new skills and knowledge which re-validate and re-motivate experienced staff and if we do not take due care to educate our new teachers through well-designed and integrated modes of learning in and beyond the workplace, then ultimately we will not sustain an effective and expert teacher workforce. In particular, once the economy recovers, we may be facing serious issues around the retention of exactly the kind of agentic and knowledgeable teacher learners and adult educators we will need to strengthen the school system for the coming decades of the twenty-first century.

References

Ball, S. (1994). *Education Reform: A critical and post-structural approach*. Buckingham: Open University Press.

Ball, D., Sleep, L., Boerst, T., Bass, H. (2009). Combining the development of practice and the practice of development in teacher education. *Elementary School Journal, 109*, 458–476.

Barber, M., & Mourshed, M. (2007). *How the world's best-performing school systems come out on top. (The McKinsey Report)*. New York: McKinsey & Company.

Bhabha, H. (1994). The third space. In J. Rutherford (Ed.), *Identity, community, culture and difference* (pp. 207–221). London: Lawrence and Wishart.

Billett, S. (2001). *Learning in the workplace: Strategies for effective practice*. Sydney: Allen & Unwin.

Boler, M. (1999). *Feeling power: Emotions and education*. London: Routledge.

Bourdieu, P. (1987). What makes a social class? *Berkeley Journal of Sociology, 32*, 32–45.

Boyd, P., & Tibke, J. (2012). Being a school-based teacher educator: Developing pedagogy and identity in facilitating work-based higher education in a professional field. *Practitioner Research in Higher Education, 6*(2), 41–57.

Colley, H. (2003). *Mentoring for social inclusion: A critical approach to nurturing mentor relationships*. London: Routledge.

Counsell, C. (2013). 'The other person in the room': A hermeneutic-phenomenological inquiry into mentors' experience of using academic and professional literature with trainee history teachers. In M. Evans (Ed.), *Teacher education and pedagogy: Theory, policy and practice* (pp. 134–182). Cambridge: Cambridge University Press.

CUREE. (2005). Mentoring and Coaching National Framework. London: DFES. http://webarchive. nationalarchives.gov.uk/20110809101133/nsonline.org.uk/node/132345. Accessed 11 Dec 2012

Czerniawski, G. (2013). Professional development for professional learners: Teachers' experiences in Norway, Germany and England. *Journal of Education for Teaching, 39*(4), 383–399.

Dana, N., Dawson, K., Wolkenhauer, R., Krell, D. (2013). Pushing the envelope on what is known about professional development. *Professional Development in Education, 39*(2), 240–259

Darling-Hammond, L., & Lieberman, A. (2012). *Teacher education around the world: Changing policies and practices.* New York: Routledge.

Dent, H. (1977). *The training of teachers in England and Wales 1800–1975.* London: Hodder and Stoughton.

Earley, P., & Bubb, S. (2004). *Leading and managing continuing professional development: Developing teachers, developing schools.* London: Sage/Paul Chapman.

Edwards, A., & Protheroe, L. (2003). Learning to see in classrooms: What are student teachers learning about teaching and learning while learning to teach in schools? *British Educational Research Journal, 29*(2), 227–242.

Engeström, Y. (2001). Expansive learning at work: Towards activity theory reconceptualisation. *Journal of Education and Work, 14*(1), 133–156.

Eraut, M., Maillardet, F., Miller, C., & Steadman, S. (2006). Early career learning at work: Project LiNEA. England: ESRC TLRP Project Report L139251073

European Commission. (2010a). Improving teacher quality: The EU agenda—lifelong learning: Policies and programme. Brussels, April 2010, EAC.B.2. D (2010) PSH

European Commission. (2010b). Thematic report on teachers' professional development: Europe in international comparison. Luxembourg: Office for Official Publications of the European Communities. http://ec.europa.eu/education/school-education/doc1962_en.htm

European, Commission. (2012). *Supporting the teaching professions for better learning outcomes: Commission staff working document.* Strasbourg: European Commission.

Fuller, A., & Unwin, L. (2004). Expansive learning environment integrating organizational and personal development. In H. Rainbird, A. Fuller & A. Munroe (Eds), *Workplace learning in context* (pp. 126–144). London: Routledge.

Furlong, J., & Smith, R. (Eds.). (1996). *The role of higher education in initial teacher training.* London: Kogan Page.

Green, J. (2010). *Education, professionalism and the quest for accountability.* London: Routledge.

Grossman, P., Compton, C., Igra, D., Ronfeldt, M., Shahan, E., & Williamson, P. (2009). Teaching practice: A cross-professional perspective. *Teachers College Record, 111*(9), 2055–2100.

Gu, Q., & Day, C. (2013). Challenges to teacher resilience: Conditions count. *British Educational Research Journal, 39*(1), 22–44.

Hargreaves, A., & Fullan, M. (1999). Mentoring in the new millennium. *Professional Speaking,* 19–23 Dec 1999.

Hattie, J. (2009). *Visible learning: A synthesis of over 800 meta-analyses relating to achievement.* New York: Routledge.

Hodkinson, H., & Hodkinson, P. (2004). Rethinking the concept of community of practice in relation to schoolteachers. *International Journal of Training and Development, 8*(1), 21–31.

Hodkinson, H., & Hodkinson, P. (2005). Improving schoolteachers' workplace learning. *Research Papers in Education, 20*(2), 109–131.

The House of Commons Children, Schools and Families Committee. (2010). *The training of teachers: Fourth report of session 2009–2010* (Vol. 1). London: HCSO.

Hramiak, A. (2010). Online learning community development with teachers as a means of enhancing initial teacher training. *Technology Pedagogy and Education, 19*(1), 47–62.

Hramiak, A. J. (2011). Using blogs to develop reflective practice. *Learning and Teaching Update,* 40 (Dec 2010/Jan 2011)

James, L. (1972). *The James report: Teacher education and training (1972).* London: Her Majesty's Stationery Office.

Jones, M., Campbell, A., McNamara, O., & Stanley, G. (2009). Developing professional learning communities through ITE mentoring. *CPD Update, 116,* 6–9.

Klein, E., Taylor, M., & Onore, C. (2012). Finding a third space in teacher education: Creating an urban teacher residency. *Teaching Education, 24*(1), 27–57.

Leask, M., & Younie, S. (2013). National models for continuing professional development: The challenges of twenty first century knowledge management. *Professional Development in Education, 39*(2), 273–287

Littleton, F., & Bayne, S. (2008). Virtual worlds in education. Higher Education Academy ESCalate News 2008. Bristol: HEA. Issue10. pp. 26–8

Lofthouse, R., Leat, D., & Towler, C. (2010). Coaching for teaching and learning; a practical guide for schools. Reading: CfBT. http://www.cfbt.com/evidenceforeducation/pdf/5414_CfT_FINAL(Web).pdf. Accessed 2 March 2013

Maharg, P., McKellar, P., Hughes, M., & Walker, S. (2008). SIMPLE: Innovative learning across the professionals. http://www.ukcle.ac.uk/projects/past-projects/tle. Accessed 3 April 2013

Martin, S., Snow, J., & Torrez, C. (2011). Navigating the terrain of third space: Tensions with/in relationships in school-university partnerships. *Journal of Teacher Education, 62*(3), 299–310.

Moule, P. (2010). Simulation in nurse education: Past, present and future. *Nurse Education Today, 31*(7), 645–656.

Murray, J. (2002). Between the chalkface and the ivory towers? A study of the professionalism of teacher educators working on primary initial teacher education courses in the English education system. *Collected Original Resources in Education (CORE), 26*(3), 1–503.

Murray, J., Czerniawski, G., & Barber, P. (2011). Teacher Educators' identities and work in England at the beginning of the second decade of the twenty-first century. *Journal of Education for Teaching, 37*(3), 261–277.

Rainbird, H., Fuller, A., & Unwin, L. (Eds). (2004). *Workplace learning in context.* London: Routledge.

Salisbury, J., & Morris, K. (2012). Beyond the border: Perspectives on teacher education in Wales. Paper presented at the UCET Annual Conference, November, 2012

The, S. G. (2011). Teaching Scotland's Future: Report of a review of teacher education in Scotland (the Donaldson Review). Edinburgh: Scottish Government. http://www.scotland.gov.uk/Publications/2011/01/13092132/15. Accessed 15 Jan 2012

UCET (The University Council for the Education of Teachers). (2013). *The value of university-school partnerships in teacher education.* London: UCET. Accessed 26 Feb 2013.

Van Velzen, C., & Volman, M. (2009). The activities of a school-based teacher educator: A theoretical and empirical exploration. *European Journal of Teacher Education, 32*(4), 345–367.

Walsh, C., Power, T., Khatoon, M., Biswas, S., Paul, A., Sarkar, B., & Griffiths, M. (2013). The 'trainer in your pocket': Mobile phones within a teacher continuing professional development program in Bangladesh. *Professional Development in Education, 39*(2), 186–200.

Wheeler, S., & Wheeler, D. (2009). Using Wikis to promote quality learning in teacher education. *Learning, Media and Technology, 34*(1), 1–10.

Wright, K., & Murray, J. (2008). *Student participation blended learning environments: Problem based learning and professional knowledge in teacher education. Paper presented at the BERA conference, Heriot Watt University.* Edinburgh: 3rd – 6th September 2008.

Zeichner, K. (2010). Rethinking the connections between campus courses and field experiences in college- and university-based teacher education. *Journal of Teacher Education, 61*(2), 89–99.

Printed by Printforce, the Netherlands